INTRODUCTION

EDUCATIONAL RADICALISM

This volume is an attempt to refl⟨ ⟩ reform that flourished in the period but which found themselves under in⟨...⟩ the New Right, becoming the target for sustained attempts ⟨...⟩ marginalisation by the Thatcher administration in the 1980s. The radical initiatives which our contributors evaluate – ranging from longstanding attempts at providing genuine comprehensive schooling to the more recent movements for antiracist and antisexist schooling and peace education – were, of course, part of a larger political and intellectual ferment that, amongst other things, also involved rereadings of the history of education from the variety of radical perspectives which inspired the practical initiatives then in formation. The intertwining of historical re-visioning with contemporary projects for educational transformation is reflected in this collection, which is equally concerned with interrogating the way histories of education and traditions of radicalism have been constructed in recent decades. The volume thus traverses and connects past and present, acknowledging the complex coexistence and overlapping of the historical and the contemporary in projects of radical reform.

The present post-Thatcherite period is likely to be crucial for the fate of education for some considerable time to come and thus appropriate for the kind of collective project that the volume represents. This is a period defined by at least three overlapping, overdetermining elements.

In the first place, we are continuing to live with the effects of Labour's retreat in the 1970s, which occurred in the face of a fiscal crisis of the state, impending recession and attacks from the right which rehearsed a litany of charges: falling standards; lack of attention to the needs of the 'economy'; and, increasingly, supposed 'political indoctrination' by teachers and LEAs who were beginning to insert antiracism and antisexism and other agendas into the curriculum. The narrative of Labour's retreat is chronicled, with different emphases, by Clyde Chitty and Caroline Benn. Both underline Labour's continuing loss of vision and confidence. There appear to be few prospects of finding in Labour genuine alternatives to the present Conservative agenda, which of course forms the second crucial defining element of the present moment in education. The Thatcherite and New Right assault attempted in every sphere to dismantle whatever gains were made by post-1944 social democratic reform and to insert a distinctive right-wing radical agenda: greater selectivity and inequality; the marginalisation of local education authorities; the undermining of teachers' rights and professional autonomy; particular forms of parental 'choice', consumerism, privatisation and competition through opting out and Local Management of Schools; and a crude return to the 'basics' via the National Curriculum and testing.

However, we are writing at an interesting transitional moment for both the Conservatives and Labour. The abrupt departure of Thatcher has begun the construction of a softer, more caring, 'social market' image for Conservative policy, which may have ramifications in the educational field, especially given the obstacles into which Thatcherite reforms have run on a number of fronts – the failure of the City Technology College programme, the relatively few schools choosing to opt out, and rebuffs on testing and the implementation of a wholesale traditional curriculum and pedagogy. Ironically, this is happening at a time when Labour appears to have taken over some part of the Conservative education agenda, particularly noticeable in the commitment to a National Curriculum and testing. And it may well be that a combination of Local Management of Schools and a more centralised funding arrangement, whereby educational expenditure is removed from local authority control, will become part of Labour's policy.

Just at the time in the 1970s when Labour had begun to go into retreat, the third key defining feature of our period had begun to establish a strong presence. There had been something of an explosion of more fundamental, innovative and transformatory educational practice, politics and theory, including, *inter alia*, revolutionary and libertarian teachers' organizations like *Rank and File* and the groups around *Libertarian Teacher* (subsequently *Libertarian Education*); the Radical Students' Alliance; a considerable interest in the libertarian ideas of Holt and Illich; the Free School movement; the impact on educational thinking of the more general renaissance of Marxist and radical theory and analysis in the social sciences and humanities as reflected in an interest in Gramsci, Althusser and Bourdieu, and in the influence of texts like Bowles and Gintis's *Schooling in Capitalist*

RETHINKING RADICAL EDUCATION

Rethinking Radical Education

Essays in Honour of Brian Simon

edited by
Ali Rattansi and David Reeder

LAWRENCE & WISHART
LONDON

Lawrence & Wishart Ltd
144a Old South Lambeth Road
London SW8 1XX

ISBN 0 85315 717 0

First published 1992

© Lawrence & Wishart, 1992

Each essay © the author, 1992

Photoset in North Wales by
Derek Doyle and Associates, Mold, Clwyd
Printed and bound in Great Britain by
Billing & Sons, Worcester

CONTENTS

5

America[1] and the Open University course text on *Schooling and Capitalism*[2]; the emergence of feminist and antiracist interventions; and the impact of other new social movements in the form of developments around world and peace studies and environmental education.

It is arguable that any genuine oppositional post-Thatcherite agenda will have to find its key items from this third set of developments. Nigel Wright, in his admirable and informative survey, *Assessing Radical Education*, has already provided an assessment of the successes and failures of groups such as Rank and File, and the Free School Movement.[3] In drawing up a balance sheet he points to the establishment and continuing survival of initiatives around feminism, antiracism, peace education, world studies, and so on, as a testament to the current vibrancy of radicalism in education and to the continuing legacy of the radicalism of the past two decades. But these latter interventions receive scant attention in his book. They provide, however, the key focus for this collection. What have been their achievements? To what extent can we continue to accept their underlying theoretical, pedagogical, curricular and political assumptions? How should we regard the often fundamental rethinking of the history of education that they have provoked? These questions are central to the essays in this collection. The authors have themselves been deeply involved in the formulation, promotion and implementation of the educational alternatives that were beginning to get a foothold in the educational system just as the Conservative administration took office in 1979. Having struggled for over a decade to establish their projects and having fought against Conservative attempts at marginalisation, the writers here are uniquely qualified as distinguished practitioners, researchers and activists to provide a rigorous, critical assessment of some of the main forms of recent 'radical education', place them in a broader historical context and to reflect on their real strengths and achievements as well as their limitations.

Some of our contributors are associated with education groups that already in the late 1970s were engaging in the kind of fundamental evaluation which this volume is intended to carry forward. As early as 1977, for example, Geoff Whitty, in conjunction with Michael Young, edited a set of readings on the possibilities of radical education which clearly expressed dissatisfaction not merely with Fabian social democratic thinking but also with the intellectual and political limitations of radical socialist thinking about education.[4] In *Society, State and Schooling*, the editors argued in particular that the determinism and positivism of much radical and socialist theorising of the time was limiting the possibilities for both envisaging and realising alternatives that would adequately recognise the importance of the cultural content of education. Moreover, they underlined the dilemmas confronting teachers as change agents of educational and social transformation and emphasised the importance of understanding the possibilities as well as the limits to change shaped by the historical context of schooling.

Another major attempt to articulate theory and history in the evaluation of social democratic educational policies was the widely discussed collection produced by the Education Group of the Centre for Contemporary Cultural Studies at Birmingham, although inevitably the historical, theoretical and political perspectives of *Unpopular Education*, published in 1981, provoked controversy and critique.[5] In *Education Limited*, their latest publication, the Birmingham Group remind us again of the importance of history, and how the Old Left as well as the New Right have been shaped by histories and structures to which their theories give little credence.[6] While the main concern of *Education Limited* is an evaluation of the ideological assumptions of the New Right, there is also an attempt to reflect on the possibility of developing genuine alternatives. In this context one of their arguments, which is developed much further in the emphasis of this volume, concerns the genesis of contemporary critical and reconstructive educational theories and practices. These have been connected, they point out, with the politics of gender and race, with the new social movements of the 1960s to the 1980s, and with changing class formations and experiences. At a more popular level, they argue that increasing cultural diversity and fusion have created the possibility of new orientations, although they acknowledge that sections of the political left, as well as the liberal educational mainstream, have failed to recognise the significance of these tendencies. The implication, like that of our own volume, is that 'neither socialist nor labourite traditions are adequate, without major social transformation, to found social and educational alternatives.'

Given the title of our own collection and the previous political and academic interventions of our contributors, something must be said at this stage about the term 'radical'. We have deliberately avoided setting out a formal definition and indeed will continue to resist the temptation to provide an itemisation of elements which might uniformly underwrite the 'radical' credentials of the educational movements discussed in this volume. For the simple point is that there is no essence to radicalism in education which can be excavated by historical research and secured by theoretical specification. To put it differently, there is in our view no single radical tradition in education, a theme which underlies Richard Johnson's essay. In any particular historical period there are likely to be relatively established educational orthodoxies contested by movements of opposition, which may thereby claim the mantle of radicalism for their attempts to unsettle the status quo. In this sense there is obviously a radicalism of the right as well as of the left, a point which hardly needs labouring at a time when there has been a sustained New Right attack on what its representatives have regarded as socialist and libertarian orthodoxies in education. Thus the discussion of recent right-wing radicalism in education has a place in this volume. There are, moreover, varieties of radicalism *within* the left and the right, and each of these bear a complex relation to what might be regarded as 'liberal' and 'libertarian' tendencies, such that the placing of particular educational theories, practices and movements within a left – right 'radical' – 'conservative' spectrum is by no means a straightforward matter, and further complicated by alignments with or against various feminisms and antiracisms.

'Child-centred' progressivism is a case in point, discussed here by Kevin Brehony in an account which chronicles the left's long-standing ambivalence to it, attracted by the libertarian and democratic aspects of its pedagogy, especially in the absence of any developed socialist pedgagogy, but repelled by its perceived individualism. On the socialist and feminist left, as Brehony points out, 'progressivism' is often condemned as merely 'liberal' or as having basically conservative, that is, socially reproductive consequences. However, Nigel Wright's *Assessing Radical Education*, for example, regards various forms of child-centredness as central to 'radicalism' in education. This is not merely a concern of importance to primary education, of course, since a feature of the 1970s and 1980s was the extent to which 'progressive' ideas and strategies of various kinds permeated educational thinking in secondary education, and especially in relation to post-16 educational policies. The question of how far this thinking is based on assumptions that are incompatible with comprehensive principles has been taxing many left educational analysts' as the symposium compiled by Anthony C. Green and Stephen J. Ball, *Progress and Inequality in Comprehensive Education* makes clear.[7] In *Education Limited* too, there is a salutary analysis of the way that progressive ideas underpinning the so called 'new vocationalism' have been appropriated by the industrial trainers in a ghettoised system of vocational education and training. Yet there can be no doubt that some educationalists and teachers involved with 16-plus education, including many with left sympathies, welcome the new progressivism as having a constructive role to play in the transformation of the education of the 16-plus age group as a whole.

The point of course is that child- or learner- centredness can be given 'left' or 'right' inflections and may be combined in various ways with antisexist and antiracist practices. In other words educational theories and practices such as child-centredness have a certain degree of indeterminacy which makes a discussion of whether they are *really* radical besides the point. Similar arguments can be mounted around notions such as 'community' and 'modernisation' in education, both of which have been given a variety of educational and political inflections. The potency of particular concepts of community and their articulation with projects based around class, is discussed here by Sallie Westwood in the context of the struggles to develop radical forms of adult education. Much of this anaylsis is pertinent also to understanding why the rhetoric of the 'community school' in secondary education reveals a continuing tension between those who emphasise the role of these schools as agents of social harmony and those who regard them as catalysts of cultural change.

The essays in our collection are written from within a broadly defined contemporary left radicalism and the volume itself should be seen as *constitutive* of left radicalism in education in the post-Thatcher, but alas not post-Conservative, era. In which case, some of the contours of future left radicalism in education are clearly visible and in some respects are markedly different from both the Labour agenda of the 1960s and the revolutionary and libertarian radicalism of the 1970s. Most especially, forms of feminism and antiracism have to be seen as fundamental elements, together with educational interventions around the environment, global inequalities and issues of peace and war. Another difference is the recognition of the dangers of sectarianism, which disfigured left educational politics in the recent past: the socialist, feminist, antiracist left has begun to understand the significance of instituting an effective pluralism, creating spaces for a variety of voices to be heard. Thirdly, there is growing recognition of the need to overcome the old polarities in thinking about the transformation of the educational curriculum, as for example, the old historically based and socially divisive dichotomy between the vocational and the academic. If in some areas of educational endeavour reconstructive policies turn on the ambition and efficacy of whole school curriculum approaches, in other areas, and especially in post-16 education, they turn also on the possibility of rethinking the relationship between education and employment in the context of new patterns of courses and a new system of qualifications. Hence the case for a British 'Baccalaureat' for post school education, recently put forward as a step in reducing the influence of the labour market and overcoming an academic/vocational divide that is an historical product of a divided system.[8]

The ideas of class power and class disadvantage which dominated the left radical agenda and Labourist post-war reforms have to re-enter this arena, but on different terms. They cannot have the hegemonic role of a previous era, although paradoxically – and counterproductively – they have often disappeared from the interventions of liberal versions of feminism and multiculturalist projects around questions of 'race' and ethnicity. Some of the dangers of this neglect of class are clearly evident in the resentments and anxieties generated for white working-class communities by the introduction of forms of multicultural and antiracist education which appear to give special preference to the concerns of minority communities while ignoring the continuing disadvantages and exclusions of white working-class life. Such anxieties have been politicised by New Right figures such as Ray Honeyford within nationalist and racial frameworks which widen the divisions between white communities and the ethnic minorities. The events of Burnage High School in Manchester and the subsequent report of the inquiry underline that a crucial task for the 1990s is the creation of policies and campaigns which can produce new alliances reconnecting the continuing divisions and subordinations of class power in education with the newer concerns around gender, racism and ethnicity. Moreover, as the essay on antiracist education here emphasises, more fundamental rethinking on a variety of other issues is also necessary if the outdated polarity between multiculturalism and antiracist education is to be overcome in the 1990s. The need for intellectual reassessment and changes in strategy are also emphasised in Rosemary Deem's essay on feminist interventions and in Geoff Whitty's analysis of the integrated humanities and world studies curricular movements. In similar vein Sallie Westwood, drawing upon elements of what has come to be called the 'New Times' project, calls for a rethinking of conventional forms of radicalism in adult education.

However, the kind of educational and political rethinking and campaigning required for the present period is going to have to come to terms with the new intellectual and political uncertainty expressed in many of the contributions to this volume. That is, it cannot rely on the confident Enlightenment rationalism which has consistently underwritten a certain naive optimism on the left about the possibilities for large scale structural reform and ideological transformation, often expressed in the belief that 'if only enough resources are made available' or 'if only there is a real political will for change' then everything is possible. The swamp of difficulties against which the Thatcherite programme of radical reform had to struggle is enough in itself to give cause for scepticism about glib panaceas and voluntarist fantasies; and this is further reinforced by the limited achievements over the past decade of the sorts of radical projects discussed in this collection. Hence our suggestion of a 'crisis' – no doubt an overworked term – in forms of radical education, which although deriving from many sources, is also connected with a distinctly post-modern distrust of the simplistic grand narratives and scenarios for change which have so often underwritten earlier radical manifestos.[9] There is a certain ambivalence in the volume between a continuing attachment to the view that more resources and greater political commitment from, say, another Labour government would make a substantial difference, and a sense that a much more fundamental rethinking is now necessary – about what kinds of educational reforms are required, how these might be brought about, how we conceive of the processes and mechanisms of change in educational institutions, how we win popular support for projected reforms and how those affected (teachers, pupils, parents and others) can be more effectively involved in shaping the agenda and participating in the processes of transformation.

In reflecting on these issues in relation to particular educational interventions the essays bring into sharper focus larger questions about the difference that formal educational institutions can and cannot make to social transformation. It is clear that none of our contributors hold the view that education is merely reproductive in the sense that it simply 'reflects' economic and cultural divisions 'outside' education; rather, they regard educational processes and outcomes as *productive* of the relations that constitute social differentiations. However, they also expose the continuing weaknesses and uncertainties in our understanding of how educational institutions work in the formation of gendered, racialised and other subjectivities.

Inevitably, more questions of this kind are raised rather than answered here. Yet the volume also reveals the extent to which we have moved away from the simplifications of the Marxist political economists and revisionist historians of the 1960s and 1970s, discussed here critically by Ian Davey, which represented educational processes as relatively simple outcomes of economic developments and strategies of elite control. It is symptomatic of this shift in intellectual outlook, as well as of trends in recent social history, that Ian Davey should argue a case for analysing changes in the 19th century history of popular education from the perspective of changes in patriarchal relationships. This reflects too the impact of feminist interventions in rewriting histories of education; and the influence of such interventions in the rejection of the older simplifications is spelled out by June Purvis in an essay which nevertheless looks forward also to the development of modes of analysis that take into account the complex inter-relationships between class and gender.

Few of our contributors have ventured to set out concrete agendas for radical reform. They have attempted rather to engage in a probing, reflective, open-ended exercise, one more relevant to the transitional nature of the times, when older certainties have given way, and we are in a moment when it seems more appropriate to be taking stock, and asking awkward, uncomfortable questions about the fate of earlier interventions and the lessons to be drawn from historical outcomes, intended and unintended. The volume thus contributes to a necessary task of re-evaluation and reformulation as we enter a new era.

THE RADICALISM OF BRIAN SIMON

This volume has also been conceived as a tribute to the immense educational contribution of Brian Simon over more than forty years. This continues, although he retired from the School of Education at the University of Leicester as Professor of Education in 1980. As former colleagues, we wanted to produce a volume that would mark the distinctiveness of his work. In particular we intended to generate a collection that would reflect the inter-relations forged between his researches on the history of education and his interventions in post-war educational debate in support of left radical causes. We would also like to take the opportunity of including Brian's wife, Joan Simon in this tribute: she has shared his educational and political interests throughout as well as being a significant educational historian in her own right.

Brian Simon's commitment to educational reform stems from, and uniquely characterises, a radical political outlook formed at an early stage in his life. One influence on the making of this outlook was a period of schooling in South Germany before the second World War which brought him into direct contact with Fascism. His home background in Manchester, as a member of a politically active family, must also have contributed to stimulating his political interests, and even now in conversation one is frequently reminded, from his personal references to well known public figures, of the political milieu in which he was brought up. Both his parents seem to have been sympathetic to the radical tendencies in his thought. Lady Simon in particular, a member of the Labour Party since 1935, had a longstanding and enthusiastic interest in educational reform, and took a prominent part in the move to comprehensive education in Manchester towards the end of her distinguished career.

With this background it is not difficult to understand why Brian Simon became involved in student politics when he went to Cambridge in 1933. The students of the 1930s formed one of the most overtly political generations there has ever been; and Brian Simon has himself written about the movement towards politics and the left amongst the students of that decade. His own radical political inclinations led to membership of the Communist Party in 1935, a political commitment that was maintained throughout his educational career and included a period on the executive of the Party (1957-72). Even in student days, however, he had become specifically interested in educational reform, and as secretary of the Cambridge University Education Society played a part in a movement then underway to modernise the curricula and teaching methods of the University. Through this Society he met leading educators of that time, some of them representatives of the progressive movement, such as Dora Russell, Maria Montessori and A.S. Neill, who came to Cambridge as speakers. On moving to the Institute of Education at London in 1937 for postgraduate training, he continued in student work, much of it educationally orientated, spending 1939-40 as President of the National Union of Students. During this time he was working on a book intended to represent the increasingly critical official NUS view of the Universities, but the war intervened and the book was eventually published under his own name as *A Student's View of the Universities* (1943). It was also in 1939 that he first met Joan Potter, whom he later married, at an international students conference in Paris. This was the beginning of a long professional as well as personal relationship.

It was perhaps the experience of teaching in Salford and Manchester, after war service in the army, which most shaped Brian Simon's educational beliefs. The most important aspect of this experience was his sense of outrage about the workings of the tripartite system and a realisation that psychometry and psychological testing had contributed to maintaining the ideology of this system. When the opportunity of moving to the Education Department at Leicester University arose, he found it attractive because it had acquired a reputation as a progressive department under J.W. Tibble and was not dominated by psychometry. At Leicester he began campaigning for comprehensive education, in a pro-grammar school atmosphere, working with a colleague, Robin Pedley, the best known of the early protagonists and publicists of the comprehensive school. These two were virtually alone amongst university teachers at the time in promoting this cause.

There is not space here to engage in a full evaluation of Brian Simon's history as an educational activist; but it is pertinent to be reminded of his longstanding efforts to challenge a divisive and inegalitarian system of education. In the 1950s he wrote several books which challenged intelligence testing and streaming, made the case for the comprehensive school and discussed the curriculum and organisation of comprehensive secondary education. His support for comprehensivation entailed a far reaching transformation of the contemporary secondary school. In particular he argued strongly for the abolition (and modification) of streaming in the early years of secondary education. This was crucial to his conception of the comprehensive school as a 'common school'. In 1958 he combined with Robin Pedley and a local teacher, Jack Walton, in setting up the educational journal, *Forum*, with the two-fold aim of campaigning for the abolition of streaming in the primary school and encouraging the transition to comprehensive secondary education. As well as articles from heads of schools, the journal specifically set out to publish articles by practising teachers on their classroom experiences. The journal also benefited from the reports of Joan Simon, who brought her previous experience as an educational journalist on the *Times Educational Supplement* to bear. When the comprehensive schools movement finally began to erode the old grammar-secondary modern divide, Brian Simon contributed two influential books. The first of these, *The Evolution of the Comprehensive School* was an historical introduction for students, written with David Rubinstein and published in 1969 in the Student Library series on education of which Simon was an editor. The second book, *Half Way There* was published in 1970; it was a full-length evaluative survey undertaken with Caroline Benn, a leading member of the Comprehensive Schools

Committee set up in 1965 as a pressure group to monitor developments and press for fundamental change in secondary education.

Forum is still in existence and published its hundredth number in September 1991. It has formed an important part of Simon's educational life: much time and effort went into co-editing the journal and, as its scope and ambition expanded, it afforded opportunities for commenting on a range of educational issues. His contributions to educational debate also included public lectures and essays for many educational volumes – on the study of education as well as on contemporary matters. In 1985 a selection was published in a volume significantly entitled *Does Education Matter?* These essays illustrate that felicity of expression which has characterised all Brian Simon's writings, and which enables him to convey easily a complex range of ideas whether these take the form of scholarly reflections, deeply held convictions, or are shaped into devastating critiques. The critical edge to this writing was noticeably sharpened in the 1980s by his perception of the need to resist the impact of Thatcherism on progressive educational advance and Simon ended the decade by taking the lead in powerfully exposing the reactionary agenda of the Baker Education Act in a highly successful book, *Bending the Rules: The Baker 'Reform' of Education*.

This activist role has been linked with and shaped by fundamental interests in history and theory. The development of Marxist analysis in relation to educational theory and practice has been the most important of these, as illustrated in a series of contributions to this theme in *Marxism Today* in the 1970s. Long before then, however, the Simons had become attracted to the learning theories of Russian psychologists, especially L.S. Vygotski and A.R. Luria, initially in reaction to the dominance of psychometry in Britain, and subsequently because these theories seemed to provide an effective alternative to Piagetian conceptions of child development which were in vogue in the 1960s, and to provide a basis for a more effective pedagogy in the primary school. The Simons sought to make this work better known in Britain. As early as 1957 Brian Simon published a book on psychology in the Soviet Union, followed by an edited volume of essays (with Joan Simon), *Educational Psychology in the USSR* (1963), while Joan Simon had independently translated and edited a seminal book by A.R. Luria and F. Ia. Yudovich, *Speech and the Development of Mental Processes in the Child* (1959).

This longstanding interest in educational psychology (to which

Simon had contributed in other publications) was linked to a developing concern with the pedagogical trends affecting primary education, although by the beginning of the 1970s this had a more practical focus as he initiated research to discover what was happening in the primary schools following the general abandonment of streaming which took place with great rapidity in the late 1960s and early 1970s. With his research assistant Deanne Boydell, he carried out no less than three SSRC funded research projects in the period from 1970 to 1975, all of them focussing on analysis of observational study of the primary school classroom. This was the beginning of the ORACLE project based at the School of Education in Leicester, which developed further into a programme of large scale research from 1975 to 1980, in collaboration with Maurice Galton and the support of a team of School of Education staff. ORACLE was the first large scale observational study of the primary school classroom to be carried through in this country. It produced five books, with Simon as collaborator in three of them – of which *Inside the Primary Classroom* (1980, with Maurice Galton and Paul Croll) was the first and most important.

What really marks Simon out from other Marxist-inspired British educationalists however is that he has combined this work in psychology and educational research with an enduring commitment to history as a key to understanding in education. From the outset he chose to work in this traditional field rather than the (then) newly burgeoning fields of political economy and sociology. His Marxism propelled him to seek a better understanding of the past, and he was supported in this endeavour initially by James Klugmann who made available a private library containing rich material on the Labour and Co-operative movements of the early 19th century which helped him to work out the pattern for the first historical volume. The most important inspirational influence, however, seems to have been Fred Clarke's volume on *Education and Social Change* (1940) whose socio-historical perspective greatly impressed both Brian and Joan Simon and initiated ideas about the need for a new approach to the history of education. Brian Simon has also taken on such duties as Chairman of the History of Education Society of Great Britain (as well as a term as President of the British Education Research Association) and President of the International Standing Conference on History of Education.

There is an obvious relationship between his historical studies and his Marxist intellectual outlook. His earliest major studies were influential in offering a radical perspective on the social context of educational change in the 19th century, and one which took account of the effect of class relations on educational provision: *The Two Nations and the Educational Structure, 1780-1870* (1960) and *Education and the Labour Movement, 1870-1920* (1965); whilst other more particular studies, notably his work on the history of the mental testing movement (included in *Education, Intelligence and Psychology* (1971), were regarded as contributing to that scepticism towards educational prescriptions which he saw as being an important aspect of teacher education. Several of the contributors to this volume pay tribute to the pioneering nature of his contribution in these areas. Moreover he was concerned with both popular movements in education and in the educational outlook of the middle and upper classes. For example, he wrote accounts of the emergence of a differentiated system of secondary schools, and the importance of the formation of an ideology of the public schools. An account of his interpretation of these developments was provided later in a volume of essays on comparative educational history that he helped to edit, which sought to explore the nature of structural change in education and social reproduction in France, Germany and Britain 1870-1920 (*The Rise of the Modern Educational System* (edited with Detlef K. Müller and Fritz Ringer, 1987).

Simon's account of educational change has aroused controversy and debate over particular issues, but the analysis overall has attained wide currency among historians of education and among historians generally. One reason for its influence undoubtedly stems from his emphasis on the relatively autonomous nature and effectiveness of educational change. In *The Rise of the Modern Educational System*, for instance, he explicitly repudiates deterministic social reproduction models of educational development, pointing out that the assumption of a linear relationship between economic and educational change vulgarises Marxism. Instead, in common with many contemporary Marxists, he adopts Gramsci's concept of hegemony and the importance of civil society as a site of wide-ranging political contestation. This in turn points to the need to focus on the idea of education as part of civil society, and therefore on terrain in which political forces with different objectives engage in battle.

This approach fits in with Simon's overall emphasis on how the working class, or representatives of the working class, were an educational force in their own right. It is evident of course in his determination to recover and evaluate the role of various labour movements in education from the Chartists to the ILP. But these movements were themselves seen in the context of a longer time span of a popular modernising tradition in English education beginning with the English Reformation. In that last respect Brian Simon connects with tendencies in the work of Joan Simon, whose major book, *Education and Society in Tudor England* (1966), develops the revisionist notion that the Reformation was not disruptive to English schooling and that the state at this time played an important part in modernising education through its influence on the reconstitution of schools – a thesis that has been accepted by all the leading Tudor historians. Brian Simon's historical narrative registers a broad progressive movement of educational advance contributed from many sources, a movement that suffers set backs and detours from time to time, but continually recreates itself in new forms.[10] Some of his writings pay special attention to the intellectual progenitors of this movement, and to those socialist writers whom he represented as originating and carrying forward a radical tradition which links educational reform to social advance. In this sense his work sits squarely within the tradition of Enlightenment rationalism which is today the subject of lively debate.

This sense of the continuing momentum of educational advance is maintained also in his twentieth century historical studies, although in a subdued form in *The Politics of Educational Reform 1920-1940* (1974), where the emphasis is on why conditions during this period were so unfavourable to any major educational advance in state schooling, although he shows how the potential for change did exist. He argues that this was not just a matter of economic and financial restraints, but of the ascendency of what he calls countervailing movements, as represented by the persistence of conservative bureaucratic traditions and the continuing ideological distrust of mass public education, underpinned by a fear of the power of education on the part of establishment groups. From this point of view the consensus that formed around the Education Act of 1944 was a kind of holding operation. It was not until the later 1950s and 1960s that in a period of educational ferment new progressive movements re-emerged, a rich panorama which he describes in the latest and most substantial addition to the sequence of historical studies, *Education and the Social Order, 1940-1990* (1991).

It is worth emphasising that in these accounts he has endeavoured to link educational advance not only with labour movements in a formal sense, but, beyond these, with what he represents as expressions of grass roots opinion. Thus he has paid attention to such matters as the extent of popular support for labour educational movements, as in his treatment of Chartism, and given prominence to those groups and institutions, in the 1920s especially, who were concerned to argue for and sought to implement genuinely working-class forms of adult education. Moreover, in tracing the history of institutional structures in post elementary schooling, he highlights those educational innovations which derived from what he regarded as creative grass-roots movements from within the centres of urban culture in the provincial cities of the later 19th century. Similarly in tracing out the history of comprehensive reorganisation in his latest study he emphasises what he calls the 'break-out' of the period 1963-65, with reorganisation impelled forward by an upsurge of popular opinion. The point is worth making because of the tendency in Simon's large scale narrative histories to focus on labour leaders rather than to give expression to working class voices as such. His historical trajectory was set before the recent surge of enthusiasm for history from below, although the latter has itself derived in part from the writings of Marxist and radical historians, some of them Simon's contemporaries and, at various points, his political allies. Indeed, he has been supportive of the history workshop movement and has encouraged studies that explore the experience of schooling in working-class life, as the titles published in his series on the Social History of Education testify, shortlived though this venture unfortunately was. Brian Simon would not necessarily associate himself with all the new radical initiatives in the field of education – in particular he would wish to continue to place more emphasis on class than on other differentiations such as gender or race – but his democratic spirit means that he is welcoming to new theories and supportive of new activists.

It is the transformational potential of education in people's lives that matters to Brian Simon. Thus he has contrived to avoid a paternalistic, over-centralised view of education – he is critical of the post-war record of Labour from that point of view; yet he has retained a belief in the possibility of educational progress through publicly financed schooling – provided it is subject to democratic influences. Hence the stress on the importance of local control and provision and the antagonism that he shows to centralist tendencies. It is of prime importance that the momentum of educational change should be maintained through an alliance between the labour movement, progressive local authorities and teachers around positive left programmes. But in common with several contributors to this volume, he has been critical of the failure of the left to tackle theoretical or ideological issues affecting both the content and process of education itself. As regards the content of education he has favoured a broad 'humanist' approach, but without repudiating vocationalism, looking instead for a conception of education that overcomes the old polarities (as had been attempted with the Marxist conception of polytechnical education). He has also been concerned about opening up access to knowledge, science and culture without falling into a sterile academicism; and with making a common curriculum available to all whilst transforming its content in line with popular interests, history and aspirations. In regard to process, he is no libertarian, although he has embraced those aspects of progressivism in tune with his own emphasis on the importance of self-activity in learning; respect for the autonomy of the learner is another of his guiding principles, but is combined with a belief in the importance of a structured coherent learning theory and an approach to schooling that encourages positive social attitudes.

Autonomy is a key concept in Brian Simon's educational vision – the autonomy of a student who is able to function effectively in society, but can also use abilities to change that society according to developing aspirations. And whilst he has not written specifically about some of the more recent movements of educational reform discussed in this volume, they undoubtedly figure on his educational agenda. The following set of essays attempt to carry forward a discussion to which Brian Simon has contributed much, and they attempt to do so in the positive but questioning spirit that has sustained his own radical outlook.

NOTES

1 S. Bowles and H. Gintis, *Schooling in Capitalist America: Educational Reform and the Contradictions of Economic Life*, Routledge and Kegan Paul, London 1976.

2 *Schooling and Capitalism*, Open University text.

3 N. Wright, *Assessing Radical Education: A Critical Review of the Radical Movement in English Schooling, 1960-1980*, Open University Press, Milton Keynes 1989.

4 M. Young and G. Whitty, *Society, State and Schooling: Readings on the Possibilities for Radical Education*, Falmer Press, Lewes 1977.

5 Education Group, Centre for Contemporary Cultural Studies, *Unpopular Education*, Hutchinson, London 1981; for critique and discussion of this book, see, for example, A. Rattansi, 'State Education and the State of Education: Social Democratic Reform in Crisis', *Critical Social Policy*, Vol

2, No 4, 1982, and H. Silver, *Education as History: Interpreting Nineteenth- and Twentieth-Century Education*, Methuen, London 1983.

6 Education Group, Centre of Contemporary Cultural Studies, *Education Limited*, University of Birmingham, 1991.

7 A. Green and S. Ball, *Progress and Inequality in Comprehensive Education*, Routledge, London 1988.

8 D. Finegold, *A British 'Baccalaureat': Ending the Division Between Education and Training*, Institute of Public Policy Research, Education and Training Paper no 1, 1990.

9 On this question, see R. Boyne and A. Rattansi (eds), *Postmodernism and Society*, Macmillan, London 1990.

10 Simon's Enlightenment rationalism and progressivism do not of course command uniform assent, especially in the present period; *cf* J. Donald, 'Dewey-eyed Optimism: The Possibility of Democratic Education', *New Left Review* No 193, June/July 1993.

PART I

THE CRISIS OF RADICAL EDUCATION

FROM GREAT DEBATE TO GREAT REFORM ACT: THE POST-WAR CONSENSUS OVERTURNED, 1976-88

CLYDE CHITTY

INTRODUCTION

Contrary to the view commonly fostered by journalists and the media, the political, social and economic principles, often referred to as Thatcherism, did not begin their operational life with the return of a Conservative government in May 1979. For two good reasons, which might at first appear to be mutually contradictory, there is no real justification for regarding the year 1979 as a watershed in the post-war history of Britain. As far as economic and fiscal policy is concerned, it can be argued that the Thatcherite approach was clearly evident in the policies of the preceding Labour administration (1976-79). And with regard to a number of key social areas, and, in particular, strategies affecting education and the health service, the case can be made that it was not until 1987 that the Thatcher Government felt strong enough to pursue its policies to their logical limit. This paper will seek to discuss both these premises, with particular emphasis on the development of radical new approaches to the organisation of the education system. It will be argued that although the Callaghan administration of 1976-79 sought to construct a new educational consensus, based on the greater accountability of teachers and the more direct subordination of secondary schooling to the needs of industry, it was the Education Reform Act of 1988 which marked the effective abandonment of the system established in 1944. An attempt will also be made to show how far Labour has adopted the Conservative agenda in a bid to 'modernise' its policies for the 1990s.

THE ECONOMIC CRISIS OF 1973-75 AND THE RUSKIN SPEECH

Both the Labour Government of 1974-79 and the Conservative administrations which followed were conscious of pursuing their objectives in the shadow of the economic crisis of 1973-75. Aware of the humiliating surrender of the Callaghan Government to international financial pressures, a significant section of the early Thatcher cabinets was determined to restore 'sound' money and squeeze inflationary expectations out of the economy, even at the risk of creating very high levels of unemployment.

The major world recession that erupted in 1973-74 actually came at a time when things seemed to be going quite well for the 1970-74 Conservative Government of Edward Heath. The Government had shown that it was quite prepared to risk inflation in order to boost growth. Yet its counter-inflation measures were proving remarkably successful in their initial stages, and looked like moderating the upward movement of prices and pay until such time as rising investment, profitability and output could contain them. At the same time, the British economy was suddenly expanding as fast as its rivals: its rate of growth in 1973 was 5 per cent which equalled Germany's. Yet by the end of the year, government policy and credibility were in ruins. As Andrew Gamble has pointed out, the whole strategy of the Heath government was destroyed by the oil crisis and consequent world recession of 1973-74. The old priorities of the social democratic consensus could be maintained no longer and a new political terrain, with new political possibilities, was emerging.[1]

Other commentators agree on this point, for example David Marquand, a Labour Member of Parliament from 1966 to 1977, and Tony Benn, Secretary of State first for Industry (1974-75) and then Energy (1975-79) in the Wilson and Callaghan Governments.

David Marquand argues that from the mid-1940s until the mid-1970s, most of Britain's political class shared a tacit governing philosophy which can be called 'Keynesian social democracy'. It did not cover the whole spectrum of political opinion; nor did it prevent vigorous party conflict. The two main parties often differed fiercely about specific details of policy; on a deeper level, their conceptions of political authority and social justice differed even more. But they differed within a structure of generally-accepted values and assumptions. Both front benches in the House of Commons were determined to banish the hardships of the inter-war years, and to make sure that the conflicts which those hardships had caused did not return. They accepted a three-fold commitment to full employment, to the Welfare State and to the coexistence of large public and private sectors in the economy – in short, to the settlement which had brought the conflicts of the 1930s to an end. According to David Marquand, this post-war consensus disintegrated largely because the Keynesian social democrats could not cope with the economic shocks and adjustment problems of the mid-1970s.[2] In response to this, the Conservative leadership turned towards a new version of the classical market liberalism of the 19th century; the Labour leadership stuck to the tacit 'revisionism' of the 1950s and 1960s, but large sections of the rank and file turned towards a more 'fundamentalist' socialism.

Tony Benn has also written on the 'welfare capitalist consensus', which began life in the mid-1940s, and finally came to an end in the mid-1970s when the OPEC oil crisis finally exposed all the underlying weaknesses of the economic system and capitalism seemed incapable of revival. He argues that at the end of its thirty-one-year life span, it was clear that the 'welfare consensus' had neither revitalised British industry nor had retained public support with the electorate, which successively defeated Wilson, Heath and Callaghan, who had all tried to make it work.[3]

As far as education was concerned, the economic recession served to challenge the liberal and expansionist beliefs of the 1960s. The policy-makers of that decade had seen a direct and indisputable correlation between educational reform and economic prosperity: a skilled and educated workforce would facilitate economic growth which would, in turn, constitute a firm basis for continuing educational expansion. It all seemed so beguilingly simple – a project of modernisation depending upon an increase in the opportunities available to working-class youngsters, so that the human resources they embodied could be swept up in the expected new waves of economic growth. Yet it would be wrong to give the impression that the optimism of the 1960s was, in fact, based on minute and precise calculations of the cosy relationship between educational expansion and economic well-being. Indeed, it seems clear that those calculations were never produced at all; that 'manpower' needs were never translated with any clarity into educational objectives. For the reformers of the Sixties it was enough that the economic arguments appeared the more appealing and more significant objective of enhancing social justice. As Ken Jones has recently emphasised, it was a vague belief in such concepts as 'social justice' and 'a more equal society' that helped to keep the Wilson Government's superficially imposing 'edifice of policy' in being. He argues that 'cold figuring', with its implied assignment of students to particular occupational slots in an unequal division of labour, did not become central to educational planning because of the active presence of other commitments and ideals and a concern for social justice. The failure to convert principles into a closely defined programme for reform explains many of the subsequent problems of the comprehensive school. Jones is critical of this vague liberal commitment to 'equal opportunity', which underpinned much of the thinking of the educational establishment, but which lacked rigorous conceptualisation, or practical programmes.[4]

The disillusionment that set in after the 1973 oil crisis embraced a number of human enterprises and was to have profound political consequences. It can, in fact, be argued that there were two major complementary trends influencing political developments in Britain in the 1970s, or, to be more precise, between 1973 and 1979. On the one hand, right-wing elements within the Conservative Party and groups beyond it were working to destroy first Edward Heath, then the Labour governments of Harold Wilson and James Callaghan, in order to prepare the way for the arrival of a right-wing Thatcher government dedicated to the moral regeneration of Britain. At the same time, the leadership of the Labour Party was steadily losing its nerve and seeking to stem the tide of Conservative advance by the adoption of right-wing rhetoric and policies. One of the great advantages enjoyed by the first Thatcher administration after 1979 was that it could pursue its economic and social policies in a political climate where traditional Keynesian strategies had already been abandoned by Labour in favour of a broad monetarist approach.

Stuart Maclure, editor of *The Times Educational Supplement* in the period 1969-89, remembers the 1970s as a particularly dismal and demoralising decade, commenting that 'the 1970s must on any view be among the worst 10-years this century ... It was a time when politicians and senior civil servants were defeatist; when one 'problem' after another was identified as too difficult to tackle'.[5]

In the area of education, a decision was taken by the Callaghan administration to abandon the Labour Party's admittedly half-hearted commitment to the cause of progressive reform. According to this analysis, the famous speech that the Prime Minister delivered at Ruskin College, Oxford in October 1976, intended to launch a so-called Great Debate in education, can be seen as a thinly-disguised attempt to wrest the populist mantle from the Conservatives and break the axis of agreement on comprehensive school goals and values that had existed between educational opinion and Labour politics.

In the months before October, leading industrialists and Conservative critics had been arguing with increasing vehemence that the major weakness of the education system was its remoteness from – indeed hostility to – the world of work. Callaghan argued in his speech that schools had generally over-emphasised their social role, at the expense of the economic:

> The goals of our education, from nursery school through to adult education, are clear enough. They are to equip children to the best of their ability for a lively, constructive place in society and also to fit them to do a job of work. Not one or the other; but both. For many years, the accent was simply on fitting a so-called inferior group of children with just enough learning to earn their living in the factory. Labour has attacked that attitude consistently, during sixty or seventy years and throughout my childhood. There is now widespread recognition of the need to cater for a child's personality, to let it flower in the fullest possible way. The balance was wrong in the past. We have a responsibility now to see that we do not get it wrong in the other direction. There is no virtue in producing socially well-adjusted members of society who are unemployed because they do not have the skills.[6]

What the Ruskin Speech was really trying to create was a new educational consensus built around more central control of the curriculum, greater teacher accountability and the more direct subordination of secondary education to the perceived needs of the economy. At a time of economic stringency, parents and politicians had a right to expect adequate returns for the money that education consumed:

> There has been a massive injection of resources into education, mainly to meet increased numbers and partly to raise standards. But in present circumstances, there can be little expectation of further increased resources being made available, at any rate for the time being. I fear that those whose only answer to our problems is to call for more money will be disappointed. But that surely cannot be the end of the matter. There is a challenge to us all in these days and a challenge in education is to examine its priorities and to secure as high efficiency as

possible by the skilful use of the £6 billion of existing resources.

According to Bernard (now Lord) Donoughue, the then Head of the Downing Street Policy Unit and a prime instigator of the Great Debate, the basic principle of the Ruskin Speech was 'improving the quality as opposed to the quantity of education at a time when resources were constrained'.[7]

It was at this point in the mid-1970s that Labour clearly parted company with progressive educational opinion. Far from being anxious to defend and build upon the comprehensive record of the preceding twenty years, the Callaghan Government seemed prepared to listen with sympathy to the system's right-wing critics. There was a tacit assumption in the Ruskin Speech that many comprehensive school teachers had simply abandoned the quest for higher standards and had thereby forfeited society's respect.

This impression was reinforced in the 1977 DES Green Paper *Education in Schools: A Consultative Document* which described the political climate which had prompted the Prime Minister's intervention:

> The speech was made against a background of strongly critical comment in the Press and elsewhere on education and educational standards. Children's standards of performance in their school work were said to have declined. The curriculum, it was argued, paid too little attention to the basic skills of reading, writing and arithmetic, and was overloaded with fringe subjects. Teachers lacked adequate professional skills, and did not know how to discipline children or to instil in them concern for hard work or good manners. Underlying all this was the feeling that the educational system was out of touch with the fundamental need for Britain to survive economically in a highly competitive world through the efficiency of its industry and commerce.[8]

Admittedly, the Green Paper went on to refute some of these allegations, but others, it declared, were perfectly justified:

> There is a wide gap between the world of education and the world of work. Boys and girls are not sufficiently aware of the importance of industry to our society, and they are not taught much about it. In some schools, the curriculum has been overloaded, so that the basic skills of literacy and numeracy, the building blocks of education, have been

neglected . . . Much has been achieved; but there is legitimate ground for criticism and concern. Education, like any other public service, is answerable to the society which it serves and which pays for it, so these criticisms must be given a fair hearing . . . It is vital to Britain's economic recovery and standard of living that the performance of manufacturing industry is improved and that the whole range of Government policies, including education, contribute as much as possible to improving industrial performance and thereby increasing the national wealth.[9]

Yet this attempt by the 1976-79 Labour Government to create a new consensus – which was reinforced to some extent by the publication of *Better Schools* by Sir Keith Joseph's DES in 1985 – was to be an essentially short-lived affair. It came at a time when increasingly powerful elements on the Right were developing a far more radical strategy of their own for the reorganisation of the state system. The promotion of the entrepreneurial ideal would continue to play an important part in this new strategy but it would be accompanied by a much higher degree of targeting and selection and a clear idea of the appropriate level of education and training for each sector of society.

THE RIGHT COUNTER-OFFENSIVE

The grand hegemonic enterprise known as Thatcherism had its origins in the early 1970s when a number of leading Conservatives began to grow disillusioned with the increasingly corporatist and collectivist nature of the Heath government's social and economic programme. 1972 is now looked back upon as the year of betrayal, the time when the Heath Cabinet recklessly abandoned the principles on which the 1970 election had been fought and won. Rolls-Royce aero-engines' division had already been rescued by nationalisation in early 1971 and not long afterwards Upper Clyde Shipbuilders had had its subsidies restored after being threatened with closure. 1972 saw the passing of an Industry Act which created sweeping new interventionist powers for the Department of Trade and Industry and the introduction of the statutory control of wages and prices. As Hugo Young has pointed out in his recent biography of Margaret Thatcher, this 'U-turn' was to exert a powerful influence on the future direction of modern Conservatism.

> (It) . . . took on the status of a demon, and its perpetrator was still regarded many years later as the devil incarnate . . . During the

Thatcher years, avoiding a repetition of this particular Heath disaster became a key determinant of policy, even to the extent of rendering any policy option unacceptable which Heath had ever been associated with.[10]

In an important speech to the Oxford Union in December 1975, Sir Keith Joseph argued that the Conservative Party had become obsessed with occupying the middle ground of politics. Possessing no coherent philosophical position of its own, the Party had been forced to make humiliating concessions to the left-dominated consensus. The effect of this continuing adjustment by Conservative politicians in the cynical pursuit of votes was what Sir Keith termed 'the left-wing ratchet'.[11] For too long, intellectuals of the Right had allowed the Left to draw up the agenda. As a result, the ideological battle was being lost by default, with disastrous consequences for the moral well-being of the nation. At a time of crisis, it was imperative for the Right to go on to the offensive and dominate the intellectual battlefield.

In education, the counter-offensive had already begun with the publication of three Black Papers in 1969-70. By 1971 these had sold a total of 80,000 copies, becoming the first effective critique of the post-war 'welfare consensus'. Yet it could be argued that the programme of these first three editions was a strictly limited one. It was a question of upholding standards in education alongside traditional moral and cultural values by maintaining grammar schools, direct grant and independent schools as an essential part of the education structure. The inability of comprehensive schools and of comprehensive-school teachers to defend the standards of the previous system amounted to a weakening of authority and an erosion of society's cultural heritage. The early Black Paper contributors were concerned with putting the clock back: to the days of formal teaching methods in primary schools, of academic standards and firm discipline associated with a grammar-school education and of well-motivated, hard-working and essentially conservative university students. The articles they produced were devoid of radical, forward-looking policy proposals; theirs was the voice of the past.

By the time the fourth Black Paper was published in 1975, it had been decided that it was not enough simply to *react* to the proposals put forward by the Left. This was made clear in the editorial introduction which took the form of a 'Letter to MPs and Parents':

It is time . . . that we in the Black Papers not only criticized, but suggested what should be done. Let us look at each section of education and make positive suggestions which the educational administration and the politicians could apply.[12]

It was in 1975 that the Conservative politician Rhodes Boyson became co-editor, alongside Brian Cox. Under his co-editorship, a second generation of contributors appeared – Caroline Cox, Edward Norman, Stuart Sexton – who were to become increasingly involved with the right-wing of Conservative policy-making. As Ken Jones has argued, 'there was a marked re-allocation of blame for the crisis and re-identification of the forces and programmes that could resolve it'.[13]

A clear example of the more dynamic nature of the new thinking could be found in the changing attitude towards privatisation. In the second Black Paper published six years earlier, it had simply been argued that 'in our view, the need for the times is to extend the possibility of private education to more and more people by making loans and grants available to those who qualify for entrance but cannot afford fees'.[14] In 1975, the editors were urging the introduction of the educational voucher in at least two trial areas; and the Paper included a special essay by Dr Boyson on 'The developing case for the educational voucher'. Support for the voucher was then reiterated in the editorial introduction to *Black Paper 1977* which again took the form of a 'Letter to Members of Parliament':

> The possibilities for parental choice of secondary (and primary) schools should be improved via the introduction of the educational voucher or some other method. Schools that few wish to attend should be closed and their staff dispersed.[15]

The new emphasis was on choice and competition and parental control of schools. A new policy synthesis was developed linking a return to the standards of the past with a new central role for parents in determining the organisational structures of the future. From being on the defensive at the end of the 1960s, the Right had prepared itself to move on to the offensive with the floating of radical ideas for the reorganisation of the education service. In fact, it could be argued that by 1975, the thinking of the Old Right had given way to that of the New; the politics of *reaction* had been replaced by the politics of *reconstruction*. It was in the mid-1970s that the Right first began to challenge the whole culture of the system.

A number of events were of significance in the Right's campaign to reverse the left-wing ratchet. In 1974 the Centre for Policy Studies (CPS) was founded by Sir Keith Joseph and Margaret Thatcher with Alfred Sherman installed as the first Director. Although it had to begin with an ostensibly harmless academic role – looking at the differences between European, Japanese and American economics was its supposed purpose – it soon emerged as a hard-edged right-wing rival to the Conservative Party's own Research Department. Then in 1975 Rhodes Boyson published *The Crisis in Education* which made the pioneering claim that if schools were to be made more accountable, there must be 'either a nationally enforced curriculum or parental choice or a combination of both'.[16] Yet reversing the *ideological* ratchet was only a part – albeit an important part – of the Right's tactics. Of crucial significance in translating value statements into policies which could be sold to the electorate was the election of Margaret Thatcher as Leader of the Conservative Party in February 1975. As Salter and Tapper have pointed out, the replacement of Heath by Margaret Thatcher in 1975 was of critical importance to the Right's ability to translate ideas into party policy. It gave a vital new impetus to the reversal of the policy ratchet within the Conservative Party.[17]

Mrs Thatcher was certainly anxious to distance herself from the Heath inheritance. In accepting unreservedly the interpretations of that experience made by its right-wing critics, she can feel only shame that as Education Secretary from 1970-74 she was obliged to implement policies with which she profoundly disagreed. During that period, more schools became comprehensive than either before or since.[18] Plans made under the previous Labour government, by both Conservative and Labour councils, were in the process of being implemented, and many others were waiting to be approved. In her first thirty-two months in office, Mrs Thatcher received 2,765 schemes for consideration, and actually rejected fewer than 5 per cent of them. It is the case, therefore, that, for all her strong prejudices against comprehensive schools, she was quite unable to overturn the prevailing orthodoxy that reorganisation was almost inevitable. It is often said that a lingering resentment over this helps to account for her long-standing contempt for independent local authorities, DES officials, members of Her Majesty's Inspectorate and the educational 'establishment' as a whole. And she has herself given credence to this view with a number of recollections to the effect that she had been up against entrenched conventional wisdom which prevented her from saving the grammar schools. In 1983 she told one interviewer:

There was a great battle on. It was part of this equalization rage at the time, that you mustn't select by ability. After all, I had come up by selection by ability. I had to fight it. I had a terrible time.[19]

And in May 1987, she confided to the editor of *The Daily Mail*:

The universal comprehensive thing started with Tony Crosland's Circular (in 1965) and all education authorities were asked to submit plans in which schools were to go totally comprehensive. When I was Minister for Education in the Heath Government . . . this great rollercoaster of an idea was moving, and I found it difficult, if not impossible, to stop.[20]

In Mrs Thatcher's view, the education correspondents of the time must also accept some of the blame. In an interview with the Press Association news agency at the beginning of May 1989, the then Prime Minister said that she had never forgotten a lunch with a group of education correspondents in early 1970. Many of them had 'ridiculed' everything she believed in, and she added:

They had swallowed, hook, line and sinker compulsory comprehensive education. But they and I have lived to know that they were wrong.[21]

THE RIGHT IN POWER

Despite the optimism and forward-planning of the preceding five years, the arrival of a new Thatcher administration in 1979 did not bring the educational reforms hoped for by right-wing pressure groups. For at least the first seven years of its existence, the new Government was prepared to operate largely within the terms of the educational consensus constructed by the Labour leadership of 1976. Education was accorded comparatively little space in the 1979 and 1983 Conservative election manifestos and on each occasion the programme outlined was modest and unexceptional. One of the aims of the 1980 Education Act was to give parents a far greater measure of choice among state schools than ever before, but local authorities were left with the right to frustrate a parent's choice 'if the provision of efficient education or the efficient use of resources is prejudiced'. As late as 1985, as far as the curriculum was concerned, the DES document *Better Schools* was denying any role for the Government in the determination of content:

> It would not in the view of the Government be right for the Secretaries of State's policy for the range and pattern of the 5-16 curriculum to amount to the determination of national syllabuses for that period . . . The Government does not propose to introduce legislation affecting the powers of the Secretaries of State in relation to the curriculum.[22]

Above all, the Government failed to promote the cause of the education voucher and appeared to accept that a 'market' in compulsory education was something of a logical impossibility.

Having been Education Secretary for five years (1981-86), Sir Keith (now Lord) Joseph himself admitted in an interview published in *The Independent* in November 1987 that the Government had not done enough to challenge the culture of the system:

> What we haven't done, but still need to do, are in the obvious areas of education and health . . . In my view, there's a lot still to be done to give people more choice in education . . . and to change the dependency-creating aspects of the social security arrangements.[23]

Sir Keith's view of the limited nature of Conservative achievement in education, and of the consequent need for more positive and dynamic policies, had been foreshadowed by the Prime Minister in a number of frank and revealing statements made on the eve of the 1987 election. For example, in her May 1987 interview with the editor of *The Daily Mail* she declared:

> We are going much further with education than we ever thought of doing before. When we've spent all that money per pupil, and with more teachers, there is still so much wrong, so we are going to do something determined about it . . . There is going to be a revolution in the running of the schools.[24]

This 'revolution' would embrace: a reduction in the powers of the local education authorities, a reversal of 'this universal comprehensive thing' and 'the breaking-up of the giant comprehensives'. And a month later, asked by a caller to a pre-election radio and television programme in the BBC series *Election Call* what she regretted she had not yet achieved during eight years of Conservative government, Mrs Thatcher replied:

> In some ways, I wish we had begun to tackle education earlier. We

have been content to continue the policies of our predecessors. But now we have much worse left-wing Labour authorities than we have ever had before – so something simply has to be done.[25]

After eight years of Conservative education policy, the effective break with past traditions and accepted procedures came in 1987/88. The culture of the education system – its hegemonic ideas and organising principles – was challenged and transformed. Yet it is worth asking why it had taken so long to overturn the consensus established by James Callaghan and Shirley Williams in the late 1970s.

One answer might be that it was not until the mid-1980s that a host of right-wing pressure groups suddenly came up with new and exciting ideas for dismantling the state education system and overturning the constitutional settlement devised in 1944. Yet this would probably be too simple an explanation. While acknowledging the rapidity and creativeness of New Right thinking between the elections of 1983 and 1987, it is still true that many of these ideas were available to an enterprising government – albeit in embryonic form – as early as 1979. More important, perhaps, was the fact that Mrs Thatcher did not preside over a cabinet of like-minded extremists at the beginning of her period in office. And, curiously, one of her closest political and ideological allies, Sir Keith Joseph, was more reluctant to embrace far Right strategies for reorganising the education system than might have been anticipated. Then again, it can be argued that it was not until 1987-88 that the Thatcher government actually felt strong enough to press ahead with the next stage of its programme: the transformation of the so-called 'dependency culture'. By that time, a series of adversaries – the Argentinian Government, the miners, local councils, the GLC – had been confronted and defeated. Moderate members of the Cabinet had been consigned to the backbenches; the threat from the Social Democrats had passed away and the Labour Party still appeared to lack credibility. In a speech to a meeting of Conservatives in the City of London at the beginning of June 1988, Sir Geoffrey Howe, the then Foreign Secretary, could look forward with enthusiasm to the major task ahead:

> The new frontier of Conservatism – or, rather, the later stage in that rolling frontier – is about reforming those parts of the state sector which privatization has so far left largely untouched: those activities in society such as health and education which together consume a third of our national income but where market opportunities are still hardly

known.[26]

It was also clear to Conservatives that social programmes could be swiftly converted into political gains, a point emphasised by the Prime Minister in a speech to the backbench 1922 Committee a few weeks after her triumph in the 1987 election:

> Just as we gained great political support in the last election from people who had acquired their own homes and shares, so we shall secure still further our political base in 1991-92 by giving people a real say in education and housing.[27]

THE 1988 EDUCATION ACT

The appointment of Kenneth Baker as Education Secretary in May 1986 was greeted by many as a sign that the DES would now be subject to moderating influences. This impression was reinforced when in his first weeks in office, he dismissed Stuart Sexton, one of Sir Keith's more market-orientated advisers. Yet it soon became clear that Kenneth Baker's main task was to implement the programme mapped out for him by the then Prime Minister and her more doctrinaire supporters. Described by Peter Wilby, education correspondent of *The Independent*, as 'the supreme pragmatist',[28] he appeared to care little whether or not the ideas he now found himself supporting fitted into a coherent political and philosophical framework. Most of the time they didn't.

It is not easy to be dogmatic about the precise origins of all the ideas which eventually became part of the 1988 Education Act,[29] but they can all be found, at least in a revised form, in one or other of the following right-wing publications: *The Omega File* of the Adam Smith Institute, published as a whole in 1985 but completed in the period 1983-84; *The Riddle of the Voucher*, published by the Institute of Economic Affairs in February 1986; *Whose Schools? A Radical Manifesto*, published by the Hillgate Group in December 1986; and the Stuart Sexton pamphlet *Our Schools – A Radical Policy*, published in March 1987.

The central purpose of the 1988 Act is that power should be gathered to the centre and, at the same time, devolved on to schools and parents, both processes being at the expense of the local education authorities. With the increased responsibilities to be shouldered by individual schools go the demands made by greater public accountability. It will no longer be possible for local authorities to protect schools from the effects of parental dissatisfaction with standards and performance, even where it can be shown that the disquiet is unjustified. A combination of parental choice, open enrolment and *per capita* funding ensures that unpopular schools will be allowed to wither away and die.

According to Nick Stuart, Deputy Secretary at the DES and the man chiefly responsible for drafting the 1988 Act, 'accountability is regarded by the Government as the lynchpin of its education reforms'. In his view, the legislation is essentially about three things: the provision of an improved basic curriculum for schools; increasing parental choice and influence; and the better management of institutions. 'All of those things are linked together by notions of accountability. The best curriculum in the world is not going to work where there is inefficient and ineffective management of schools which then fail to be responsive to the needs of parents'.[30]

What, in fact, the Act achieves is the abandonment of a 'national system, locally administered'. What we will now have instead is a network of separate, semi-autonomous institutions maintained either by local authorities or the DES. The local authorites' analysis of need has been replaced by market concepts of demand, and resources are to be distributed according to the new principle of consumer choice. The notion of a publicly planned and provided education service has been effectively challenged in order that education should ultimately become a commodity to be purchased and consumed.

All this clearly owes much to a belief that market mechanisms are inherently superior to all other means of organising human societies. Along with this conviction goes the view that education is essentially a private concern rather than something appropriate for government responsibility. According to Oliver Letwin, formerly special adviser to Sir Keith Joseph at the DES and then an influential member of the Downing Street Policy Unit, the Conservative administrations of Margaret Thatcher will merit a whole chapter in history on account of their outstanding contribution to the global revolution wrought by privatisation. And this has not been limited to the selling off of state assets. In Letwin's view:

> Once privatization is complete, the role of ministers in running everything will never be restored ... Britain is moving back into a position where people in government do not think it is their business to run anything. Four hundred years from now, people will still be

talking about Mrs. Thatcher. And it will be because of that profound shift in the way governments thinks.[31]

A less starry-eyed assessment of the current scene affords little cause for optimism. After ten years of Thatcherism and nearly two years of Majorism, the inconsistencies and failures are manifest in every area of social and economic policy. Britain's relative failure in manufacturing has not been due to some anti-industrial spirit or the failure of schools to equip their pupils with the skills needed in working life. Rather the fault lies with the Government's own narrow vision of an enterprising culture. Liberalising markets has done nothing to promote technical change and industrial investment. As Paul Hirst has argued, it has simply encouraged speculators and entrepreneurs to concentrate on those markets where 'all you need is short-term market and financial information – markets in national currencies, commodities, equities and property.[32]

Similarly, there is no indication that the infusion of market values will do anything to raise the standard of education in this country. The free market philosophy underpinning the Education Reform Act has everything to do with competition and privatisation and very little to do with a genuine extension of educational opportunities. According to Stewart Ranson for example:

> The market is formally neutral but substantively interested. Individuals come together in competitive exchange to acquire possession of scarce goods and services. Within the market place all are free and equal, only differentiated by their capacity to calculate their self-interest. Yet, of course, the market masks its social bias. It elides, but reproduces, the inequalities which consumers bring to the marketplace. Under the guise of neutrality, the institution of the market actively confirms and reinforces the pre-existing social order of wealth and privilege. The market is a crude mechanism of social selection. It can provide a more effective social engineering than anything we have previously witnessed in the post-war period.[33]

Yet despite its inbuilt injustices, the Conservative Government's market philosophy would appear to have carried all before it at the end of the 1980s. How, then, are we to account for the comparative ease with which the post-war consensus has been overthrown? What proportion of blame lies with the main opposition party? Are the values which underpinned the education system in the 1950s and 1960s simply out of place in the last decade of the twentieth century?

THE LABOUR RESPONSE TO THE NEW RIGHT INITIATIVE

For classical Labourism, the all-important concept in the post-war years was that of equal opportunity: the attempt to give working-class pupils a better chance of securing the high-status jobs previously monopolised by the middle classes. It was a matter of providing a different set of individuals for a division of labour that itself remained constant. It was also an extension of an earlier more parochial concept of equal opportunity which simply held that in each school, all pupils should have equal access to all the opportunities on offer. What many genuinely believed in the heady days of the 1964-70 Labour government was that capitalist society could be reformed without major surgery and that the new comprehensive system would be a step on the road towards achieving greater equality – greater equality in the sense of levering up a significant number of working-class youngsters to take advantage of the expansion of 'white-collar' layers of the workforce.

This was, in fact, making impossible demands of the education system and, as we have seen, the futility of it all became obvious when the expansionist mood of the 1960s gave way to the demoralisation and cutbacks of the 1970s. It was Labour's inability after 1974 to defend state education in terms which were relevant to the lives of the mass of people that paved the way for the Thatcherite project of the 1980s.

Those responsible for drafting Labour's education policy today continue to talk about 'equal opportunity' and 'equal worth', but much of their programme for the 1990s reads like a damage limitation exercise fought on the New Right's terms. A future Labour administration will, we are told, phase out the Conservatives' Assisted Places Scheme and bring grant maintained schools and the new City Technology Colleges within local authority control. Clearly this is all part of a laudable attempt to reconstruct the state education system; and the 1989 Policy Review document *Meet the Challenge, Make the Change* holds out the promise that Labour will re-establish a partnership with LEAs whereby 'they share responsibility with the Secretary of State and with parents, teachers and governors for developing and delivering the educational entitlements outlined in the document'.[34] All very encouraging, but little more than a return to the *status quo ante bellum.*

On matters relating to the National Curriculum and Assessment, the position is far less clear. Labour education spokesperson Jack Straw generally avoids the subject; and a piece by Mr Straw's policy adviser, Dr Richard Margrave, which purported to outline Labour education policy and was published in *Education* in March 1990 also made no reference to the National Curriculum.[35] On other occasions, Mr Straw has been content to argue that Labour thought of it all first – for example, the Labour Party discussion document *Children First* stated that 'a working party of the NEC Science and Education Sub-Committee recommended in 1973 that there should be a national core curriculum and regular diagnostic testing'.[36] According to the 1989 Policy Review document, Labour will make a clear distinction between the Curriculum's 'core' and 'foundation' subjects: all schools will be required to make 'similar provision' in respect of the core subjects English, maths and science, while the range of foundation subjects will 'not be prescriptive'. With reference to assessment and testing, Labour will 'build on the success of the GCSE and draw from a "mixed economy" of continual assessment including project work, written exams and diagnostic tests'.[37] These rather vague statements seem to indicate that Labour would largely retain the National Curriculum.

As far as comprehensive education is concerned, Labour's commitment was half-hearted and tentative at the end of the 1970s; and there is still a worrying ambiguity in its pronouncements at the beginning of the 1990s. Education Secretary Shirley Williams believed firmly in the principle of parental choice, and this meant that within the state system, there should be a variety of provision with no concession to the concept of 'neighbourhood' or 'community' schools. Choice and diversity would be the new watchwords for the comprehensive school. Within any given area, the number of schools to choose from would ensure the availability of courses to suit all tastes and requirements. And this point is developed in the 1989 Policy Review document:

> We want to see schools develop their own distinctive character within the comprehensive principle. Schools should be encouraged to develop new and existing strengths, whether in science, music, drama, the arts or sport.[38]

Yet this appears to come perilously close to the concept of comprehensive schools now being promoted by Donald Naismith in Wandsworth – where headteachers in the Borough have been moved to take the unprecedented step of declaring a vote of no confidence in their Chief Education Officer.

After over a decade in opposition, Labour still seems to be wedded to the view that Thatcherism was actually some sort of aberration – a temporary halt to the onward march of progress. Where changes are advocated, they often take the form of concessions to Thatcherite market principles or the right-wing obsession with 'standards' and accountability. As Richard Johnson has pointed out, this has serious consequences for the development of new ideas, new possibilities:

> It encourages short-term, or tactical, responses. It invites defence of 'the education service' more or less as it is – or was. It discourages the search for an alternative – a long-term or structural alternative that is as radical or far-reaching as the New Right 'solutions'. It is not enough to assert the value of pre-Thatcher public education, or to move on to Thatcherite ground, finding some socialist virtue in the market. We need a *post-Thatcher* version.[39]

The absence of an approved alternative agenda for the 1990s is all the more surprising since the left is not without major Think Tanks of its own. The educational journal *Forum*, founded in 1958, the Campaign for Comprehensive Education (now known as RICE: the Right to a Comprehensive Education), the Socialist Educational Association and, more recently, the Institute of Public Policy Research (IPPR) and the Hillcole Group have all put forward alternatives both to the educational agenda of the New Right and official Labour Party policy. At the same time, a number of key individuals have published pamphlets and articles suggesting viable strategies for a future Labour government. Some examples of these initiatives are: Caroline Benn has devised a practical solution for dealing with the problem of the private sector which would involve co-operation between private and state schools in a renewed public system;[40] Ken Jones has argued for a curriculum that acknowledges the culture which pupils bring with them to the school and is not concerned merely to transmit the versions of the national culture promoted by the dominant class in society;[41] and Andy Green has advocated the adoption of an integrated and comprehensive system of post-compulsory education and training along Swedish lines – rather than the employer-led West German model favoured by the Policy Review document.[42] These attempts to move the debate ahead continue, and would be able to exert a greater influence on the development of opposition policy if left-wing pressure groups had the same access to the relevant party machines as do their counterparts on the Right.

EDUCATION AS SOCIAL ENGINEERING

What seems obvious from a study of the history of education in this country over the last hundred years is that capitalist governments generally – whether of the Right or of the so-called Left – dislike the idea of extending educational opportunity beyond certain clearly-defined limits. Indeed, the process of education itself is often viewed with a fair degree of suspicion and apprehension. As long ago as 1958, in his book *The Affluent Society*, Professor J.K. Galbraith observed that:

> Education is a double-edged sword for the affluent society. It is essential, given the technical and scientific requirements of modern industry. But by widening tastes and also inducing more independent critical attitudes, it undermines the want-creating power which is indispensable to the modern economy. The effect is enhanced as education enables people to see how they are managed in the interest of the mechanism that is assumed to serve them. The ultimate consequence is that the values of the affluent society, its preoccupation with production as a test of performance in particular, are undermined by the education that is required in those that serve it.[43]

Brian Simon has argued that the transition to comprehensive education in the 1960s was seen to be 'necessary', in some senses at least, 'for the maintenance and smooth functioning of the existing social order'.[44] It was widely believed, particularly among reformist elements in the Labour Party, that the new system would both reduce the wastage of the human abilities so urgently required as a result of technological change and economic advance and ensure an amelioration of social class differences through the pupils' experience of 'social mixing' in a common school environment. Yet by the end of the 1960s, there were fears that educational change would bring with it social unrest and a discontented workforce. More recently, Stewart Ranson has exposed the thinking of the DES on the dangers arising from over-education in a contracting labour market. In a paper first published in 1984, more than one DES official is shown to be quite open about the need to restrict the educational opportunities available in our schools for the sake of social harmony:

There has to be selection because we are beginning to create aspirations which increasingly society cannot match. In some ways, this points to the success of education in contrast to the public mythology which has been created. When young people drop off the education production line and cannot find work at all, or work which meets their abilities or expectations, then we are only creating frustration with perhaps disturbing social consequences. We have to select: to ration the educational opportunities to meet the job opportunities so that society can cope with the output of education.

and according to another of the country's policy-makers:

We are in a period of considerable social change. There may be social unrest, but we can cope with the Toxteths. But if we have a highly educated and idle population, we may possibly anticipate more serious social conflict. People must be educated once more to know their place.[45]

The New Right view of education, and of the harm that can be done by providing too much of it, is perhaps simply the latest variation in a long-running theme. It is given confident expression by Roger Scruton in a passage in *The Meaning of Conservatism* where he ridicules the concept of equality of opportunity:

Such a thing seems to be neither possible nor desirable. For what opportunity does an unintelligent child have to partake of the advantages conferred by an institution which demands intelligence? His case is no different from that of a plain girl competing with a pretty girl for a position as model. The attempt to provide equality of opportunity, unless it is to involve massive compulsory surgery of an unthinkable kind, is simply a confused stumble in the dark ... It is simply not possible to provide universal education. Nor, indeed, is it desirable. For the appetite for learning points people only in a certain direction; it siphons them away from those places where they might have been contented. There are many occupations, from the operation of a signal-box to the management of a bank, which require great natural intelligence, and yet which may not appeal to someone who has been flattered by the gift of education. It is important for a society that it contain as many 'walks of life' as the satisfaction of its members may require, and that it accord to each of those stations its own dignity and recompense.[46]

Civil servants believe that the need for explicit social engineering is a good argument for fully centralised power and control to be exercised by the DES. The supporters of the New Right also want children to be educated once more to 'know their place' in the social hierarchy, but they believe that this can easily be achieved through the free and unfettered operation of market forces. What they all fear are the unpredictable consequences of a truly effective programme of mass education.

CONCLUSIONS

'We live in a Looking-Glass world now, where ideas which twenty years ago would have seemed eccentric and discredited are eagerly enshrined by law'.[47] So speaks a recently-retired headteacher surveying the educational scene in the summer of 1989. The post-war consensus has been overthrown and with it any real regard for the professionalism and independence of teachers. But does this mean that the new orthodoxy cannot be challenged? As far as curriculum and assessment are concerned, it may be possible for teachers to modify the Government's proposals at the points of implementation. But, as Wendy Ball and Barry Troyna point out, there are difficulties with this course of action:

> Given the powers of the Secretary of State, this will, of necessity, follow an incremental and piecemeal pattern of change, doing little to undermine the overall direction of the proposals. Moreover, the Act will discourage 'bottom-up' educational innovation through setting limits to what is possible. It will also operate indirectly in constraining initiatives by influencing what people believe to be possible.[48]

Overwhelmed by the sheer volume of new regulations and circulars – by what might be referred to as 'innovation overload' – many teachers will be brainwashed into disciplining themselves: hardly a propitious climate for transforming or domesticating government legislation. In the circumstances, it seems reasonable to argue that teachers can no longer afford to operate in isolation from broader political and social movements. An alliance between theorists of education and sociologists of the curriculum, teachers, and the wider movements is necessary to make their project part of a broader programme of political reconstruction on the Left. As Geoff Whitty points out, this will involve abandoning old conceptions of professionalism and developing new ways of working with the 'popular constituencies' – the labour movement, the women's movement and black movements. There is a need to relate to the broader concerns of those groups, which the selective tradition in education has never begun to serve.[49]

With all its admitted imperfections, it is still only state education that can serve the interests of those traditionally excluded from wealth and power. As Phil Cohen has pointed out, even if 'state schooling has never been popular amongst sizeable sections of the working class . . . it does not follow that it is not a potential site for constructing a popular educational practice'.[50]

Lord Joseph is doubtless happy to reflect that 'the left-wing ratchet' has been reversed, and that for at least the last ten years, the battlefield for ideas has been held and dominated by the right. It is now time for the left to mount a truly effective counter-offensive of its own, recognising both the triumphs and the shortcomings of the state system that caters for the vast majority of the nation's children.

NOTES

I would like to thank Andy Green for his critical comments on an earlier draft of this paper.

1. A. Gamble, *Britain in Decline: Economic Policy, Political Strategy and the British State*, Macmillan, London 1985, p 124.
2. D. Marquand, *The Unprincipled Society: New Demands and Old Politics*, Jonathan Cape, London 1988, p 3.
3. T. Benn, 'British Politics, 1945-1987' in P. Hennessy and A. Seldon (eds), *Ruling Performance: British Governments from Attlee to Thatcher*, Oxford 1987, Blackwell, pp 303-4.
4. K. Jones, *Right Turn: The Conservative Revolution in Education*, Hutchinson Radius, London 1989, p 10.
5. S. Maclure, 'Opting out', *The Times Educational Supplement*, 9.6.1989.
6. The full text of the Ruskin College Speech is reprinted under the title 'Towards a national debate' in *Education*, 22 October 1976, pp 332-3.
7. B. Donoughue, *Prime Minister: The Conduct of Policy under Harold Wilson and James Callaghan*, Jonathan Cape, London 1987, p 111.
8. DES, *Education in Schools; A Consultative Document* (Cmnd 6869) (Green Paper), HMSO, 1977, p 2.
9. *Ibid*, pp 2, 6.
10. H. Young, *One of Us: A Biography of Margaret Thatcher*, Macmillan, London 1989, p 75.
11. K. Joseph, *Stranded on the Middle Ground? Reflections on*

Circumstances and Policies, Centre for Policy Studies, London 1976, p 21.

12. C.B. Cox and R. Boyson (eds), *Black Paper 1975: The Fight for Education*, Dent, p 3.

13. K. Jones, *op cit*, p 42.

14. C.B. Cox, and A.E. Dyson (eds), *Black Paper Two: The Crisis in Education*, Critical Quarterly Society, London 1969, p 14.

15. C.B. Cox and R. Boyson (eds), *Black Paper 1977*, Maurice Temple Smith, London, p 9.

16. R. Boyson, *The Crisis in Education*, The Woburn Press, London 1975, p 141.

17. B. Salter and E.R. Tapper, 'The Politics of reversing the Ratchet in Secondary Education 1969-86', *Journal of Educational Administration and History*, Vol. 20, No. 2, July 1988, pp 61-2.

18. The number of comprehensive schools more than doubled in the period of the Heath government and by 1974 catered for more than 50 per cent of secondary school pupils.

19. Quoted in H. Young, *op cit*, p 68.

20. *The Daily Mail*, 13.5.1987.

21. Quoted in *The Independent*, 4.5.1989.

22. DES, *Better Schools* (Cmnd 9469), HMSO 1985, pp 11-12.

23. *The Independent*, 13.11.1987.

24. *The Daily Mail*, 13.5.1987.

25. The remarks were made in the BBC programme *Election Call*, broadcast 10.6.1987, and reported in *The Guardian*, 11.6.1987.

26. Quoted in *The Independent*, 7.6.1988.

27. Quoted in *The Independent*, 17.7.1987.

28. P. Wilby, 'Close up: Kenneth Baker', *Marxism Today*, April 1987, p 56.

29. A penetrating analysis of the evolution of these ideas is to be found in Clive Griggs's 1989 paper 'The New Right and English Secondary Education' in R. Lowe (ed), *The Changing Secondary School*, Falmer Press, pp 99-128.

30. The interview with Nick Stuart is part of a LEAP video on Accountability. LEAP (Local Education Authorities Project) is an in-service training programme that has been developed by a consortium of LEAs to help prepare teachers to cope with the changes brought about by the 1988 Education Act.

31. Quoted by C. Hughes, 'Privatizer on Parade: A Profile of Oliver Letwin' in *The Independent*, 6.6.1988.

32. P. Hirst, 'After Henry', *New Statesman and Society*, 21.7.1989.

33. S. Ranson, 'From 1944 to 1988: Education, Citizenship and Democracy', *Local Government Studies*, Vol. 14, No. 1, January/February 1988, p 15.

34. *Meet the Challenge, Make the Change: A New Agenda for Britain*, Labour Party, London 1989, p 46.

35. R. Margrave, 'How to heal education', *Education*, 30.3.1990. p 317.

36. *Children First: Labour's Policy for Raising Standards in Schools*, Labour Party, London 1989, p 37.

37. *Meet the Challenge, Make the Change*, p 48.
38. Ibid, p 48.
39. R. Johnson, 'Thatcherism and English Education: breaking the mould, or confirming the pattern?', *History of Education*, Vol 18, No 2, 1989, p 92.
40. C. Benn, 'The Public Price of Private Education and Privatization', *Forum*, Vol. 32, No. 3, 1990, pp 68-73.
41. K. Jones, *op cit*, p 189.
42. A. Green, 'Education and Training: a Study in Neglect', *Forum*, Vol. 32, No. 3, 1990, pp 78-81.
43. J.K. Galbraith, *The Affluent Society*, Penguin Harmondsworth 1958, pp 228-9.
44. B. Simon, 'Problems in Contemporary Educational Theory: a Marxist Approach', *Journal of Philosophy of Education*, Vol. 12. 1978, p 30.
45. S. Ranson, 'Towards a Tertiary Tripartism: New Codes of Social Control and the 17-plus' in P. Broadfoot (ed), *Selection, Certification and Control: Social Issues in Educational Assessment*, Falmer Press, Lewes 1984, p 241.
46. R. Scruton, *The Meaning of Conservatism*, Penguin, Harmondsworth, 1980 p 157.
47. G. Haigh, 'Intimations of Mortality', *The Times Educational Supplement*, 4.8.1989.
48. W. Ball, and B. Troyna, 'The Dawn of a New Era? The Education Reform Act, "Race" and LEAs', *Educational Management and Administration*, No. 17, 1989, p 30.
49. G. Whitty, *Sociology and School Knowledge: Curriculum Theory, Research and Politics*, Methuen, London 1985, p 179.
50. P. Cohen, 'Against the New Vocationalism' in I. Bates, *et al, Schooling for the Dole? The New Vocationalism*, Macmillan, London 1984, p 161.

CHANGING THE SUBJECT? RACISM, CULTURE AND EDUCATION

ALI RATTANSI

INTRODUCTION

The multiculturalist and antiracist initiatives in education that emerged in the 1980s set themselves extraordinarily difficult tasks. In challenging the structural and cultural marginalisation of Britain's black minority communities, they also began to shift the terms around which British national identities had sedimented over the years of colonial domination and imperial grandeur and before.[1] This was an absolutely necessary intervention. This article is written with some knowledge, experience and appreciation of the commitment, the personal costs and the professional risks involved for those engaged in the struggle to reform school curricula, teacher education and other spheres and practices. Nor do I wish to sell their achievements short. New cultural and political spaces have been opened up, and hegemonic racial identities and structures have been loosened.

Despite these real successes, however, my sense is that now is a time to take stock and to reflect on the theoretical, pedagogic and political foundations of multiculturalism and antiracism. This is a period of transition. Significant changes are under way in the economic, political and cultural formation of black British communities. Older certainties about the nature and direction of black struggles no longer hold. In education, the liberal optimism of the 1985 Swann Report has not only been punctured by the policies of Conservative governments and by the ideological counter-offensive of the New Right. From within the movement, as it were, the publication of the Macdonald Report on the tragic events at Burnage High School has been widely interpreted as signalling the failure of the antiracist project in education.

If antiracism is to be effective in education, it is therefore necessary to take a hard and perhaps painful look at the terms under which we have operated so far. We need to understand the extent to which oppositional practices have, wittingly or unwittingly, shared the assumptions of the dominant state-led strategies that have also attempted to respond to the black presence in British education and society. And it is necessary to assess the nature and significance of the polarisation between 'multiculturalism' and 'antiracism' in this field, especially given the Left's construction of antiracism as representing the more genuinely 'radical' intervention in this field.

The article begins by setting out Swann's terms of reference and contrasts its 'liberal' optimism with the Macdonald inquiry's condemnation of antiracist policies at Burnage High School. It then sketches in how it was that 'race' came to be constructed as a significant educational issue at all. It interrogates earlier state, academic and earlier public responses to the black presence in education and documents their continuing influence and weaknesses in a critique of the debate around the question of black 'under-achievement' in education. This is followed by a brief and selective representation of the forms of racism identified within the educational system. A sympathetic but rigorous critique of some of the assumptions underlying both multiculturalist and antiracist interventions is then erected, demonstrating some of the unacknowledged weaknesses they share. The article concludes that what is now required is not only a consolidation but also a rethinking of educational interventions if issues of racism, ethnicity and cultural difference are to be adequately addressed in the 1990s and beyond.

FROM SWANN TO BURNAGE

1985 saw the publication of *Education For All*, the 800 page Swann Report on 'The Education of Children from Ethnic Minority Groups'. Set up in 1979 under the chairmanship of Anthony Rampton, its original brief was primarily concerned with the causes of ethnic minority, and especially 'West Indian', 'under-achievement'. Amidst a series of controversial resignations and the replacement of Rampton by Lord Swann, the inquiry broadened its scope to consider the creation of an education system appropriate to a multi-ethnic society.[2] Broadly speaking, Swann provided a 'liberal', semi-official legitimation for tackling issues of racism (or, more accurately, 'prejudice') and what it coyly referred to as 'cultural pluralism' in *all* schools, including the so-called all-white schools which hitherto had maintained the stance of 'No Problem (i.e. blacks) Here'. By advocating a non-prejudiced, pluralist 'education for *all*', Swann, however obliquely and weakly, had begun to problematise *whiteness* and the deeply embedded racism of the national culture. It had begun to chip away at the common sense attribution of 'race' problems simply to a black presence.

Despite the then Education Secretary Keith Joseph's almost instant equivocations, the recommendations of the Report did give some legitimacy and impetus to local education authorities (LEAs) and schools already tentatively and sometimes vigorously pursuing one or other variety of multicultural or antiracist policy. Although its naivety and many internal contradictions and evasions were easily exposed by its critics, it is arguable that Swann put multiculturalism and at least weak versions of antiracism on the national educational agenda.[3] This multiculturalist and antiracist lobbies could regard as a partial vindication. The expectation that the Afro-Caribbean and Asian minorities would simply blend into a homogeneous British or even English stew, perhaps adding some harmless spice, was revealed as not only hopelessly unrealistic but symptomatic of a form of racism which regarded 'Britishness' and 'Westernness' as the only touchstones of cultural value. In the aftermath of the urban uprisings of 1980-81 and Scarman's subsequent call for a speedy response from the educational system, Swann attempted to construct a 'liberal' consensus in a very troubled area.[4]

Four years later came the Macdonald Report, *Murder in the Playground*, stemming from an inquiry into the murder of 13-year-old Amhed Iqbal Ullah by a white boy in the playground of Burnage High School in South Manchester. The committee of inquiry, composed of individuals with impressive antiracist credentials – Ian Macdonald, Gus John, Reena Bhavnani, Lily Khan – delivered a strong and, for some, an astonishing condemnation of the antiracist policies apparently vigorously pursued at the school, castigating them as doctrinaire, divisive, ineffectual and counterproductive.

The policies of Dr Gough (the headteacher) and his colleagues were not actually 'blamed' for the fatality. But this is exactly what large sections of the media – especially given Manchester City Council's refusal to publish the full report for fear of litigation – took to be the real meaning of the report. The day after the conclusions had been leaked, *The Daily Telegraph* had no doubts: 'Antiracist policy led to killing', it claimed. Peter Wilby in the *Independent* concluded that antiracist education had been 'a disaster'.[5] In the years between Swann and Burnage the media had in any case had a field day. There was the row over Ray Honeyford's diatribes against what he regarded as the nightmare of multiculturalism imposed on well-intentioned schools by a combination of the race relations industry and 'volatile', 'half-educated' Asian and Afro-Caribbean parents';[6] the refusal of a group of Dewsbury parents to send their children to a predominantly British Asian school; and moral panics around 'loony left councils' which had supposedly banned black dustbin liners, insisted on renaming black coffee 'coffee without milk' and had banned 'Ba-Ba Black Sheep' from the classroom – scares which turned out to rest on complete fabrications.[7] Meanwhile, in a series of moves capped by the Education Reform Act and the proposals for a national (or, as some were quick to point out, 'nationalist') curriculum, the Conservative government had effectively challenged and undermined the fragile liberal consensus Swann had tried to erect in the mid-1980s.

But how did 'race' come to occupy a place in post-war British education in the first place and what were its terms of entry?

'RACE', ETHNICITY AND CULTURE IN BRITISH EDUCATIONAL POLICY

Recent research has disrupted the conventional narrative which represented the period between the end of the Second World War and the passing of the first Immigration Act in 1962 as an era of *laissez-faire*, with restrictions on black immigration supposedly only being reluctantly considered and implemented in the wake of campaigning by small right-wing elements in parliament and a groundswell of racism in the constituencies, especially in the Midlands. In fact, there was considerable debate in official circles during the time of both the Labour administration of 1945-51 and the subsequent Conservative administration about the consequences of black immigration on the 'racial character' of the British, and several covert and sometimes illegal administrative measures were put into operation to discourage black immigration.[8] The inhibitions against introducing full-scale controls against black immigration are likely to have stemmed from their possible impact on Britain's role as head of the Commonwealth and Colonies and concern over the national and international legality of controls based on colour.[9] When controls were increasingly applied through successive Immigration Acts, these were always accompanied by official disavowals that black immigrants were the real target, a form of political rhetoric Reeves has dubbed 'discursive deracialisation' (what, more appropriately should be called *discursive* deracialisation).[10]

By the 1960s the new British Afro-Caribbean and Asian communities had become well aware of the racism embedded in the national culture and institutionalised in the practices of many public and private agencies. They daily encountered 'colour bars' in employment, housing and pubs. Their children had begun to face racial abuse on the streets and in the schools. Documents recently released by Birmingham LEA also reveal the degree of teacher and local authority hostility to the growing black presence in the schools, and the caricatures that had begun to circulate around the lifestyles and 'racial character' of 'Asiatics' and 'West Indians'. Racism, patently, was a problem that required urgent attention. Official policies geared towards the black presence did, indeed, begin to emerge from the DES and some LEAs, often under prompting from agitated schools and headteachers who refused to admit more black pupils.[11]

The policies did not develop on the terrain of racism, however, but under the sign of 'culture'. Just as in a previous era an official 'gentling of the masses' by way of induction into a culture of 'civilisation' had accompanied the educational and political entry of the working classes into citizenship within the nation, so now assimilation into an imagined British national culture and 'way of life' became the preoccupation of the educational establishment.[12] The issue of 'language' symbolised and condensed the anxiety provoked by the black presence and became the preferred site for an educational response. Soon after the first Immigration Act, the DES produced its first major intervention, revealingly entitled *English for Immigrants*.[13] Although the primary target for the policy of 'Anglicisation' was the Asian communities, schools appeared to be equally concerned with what they regarded as the 'plantation English' of Afro-Caribbean pupils.[14] Teaching English, being a metaphor for a policy of enforced cultural assimilation, dovetailed with the view expressed by a large proportion of heads and teachers that 'immigrant' cultures – the desire to hold on to which was seen as evidence of a 'ghetto mentality' – were an educational hindrance requiring vigilant exclusion from the culture of the school.[15] In this spirit, Section 11 of the 1966 Local Government Act offered financial assistance for those authorities finding themselves with substantial proportions of Commonwealth migrant communities 'whose language and customs differ from those of the community'.

The assimilationist thrust was – and still is – through and through 'essentialist'. Like all essentialisms it assumes an obvious, definable, homogeneous essence (British culture) into which the hapless migrant might be inducted, given a suitable dose of English and an undiluted diet of the official school curriculum. The simultaneous cultural, racial and educational panic and white 'backlash', moreover, led to a policy of dispersal of black students by bussing, initiated in Southall and gaining DES support and subsequent endorsement by the Labour Education Secretary, Anthony Crossland. Racism and its accompanying cultural essentialism thus received further official backing, although, eventually, protests from black parents, educational critiques, administrative problems and an emergent ideology of cultural pluralism undermined the practice of bussing.[16]

Something of a shift in official perspectives was signalled by Home Secretary Roy Jenkins's famous demand in 1966 that the ideology of assimilation be replaced by an ethic of 'equal opportunity accompanied by cultural diversity'. Here was an admission that it was not so much an issue of transforming alien black cultures, but a problem of cultures and practices of white racism leading to unequal opportunities. This racialisation of the debate was further propelled onto local and national agendas by campaigning black parents and teachers. Afro-Caribbean parents, in particular, had consistently attempted to bring the fate of their children in British schools to public attention, the frustration of Redbridge's black parents, for example, forcing them to initiate an inquiry which was published as *Cause for Concern* (1978).[17] Meanwhile, Bernard Coard's *How the West Indian Child is made Educationally Sub-Normal in the British School System*, published in 1971, had already given concrete expression to many black parents' justified fears that their children were being systematically mis-classified as educationally sub-normal and relegated to a 'special' education which effectively excluded them from any possibility of acquiring decent qualifications.[18]

By the end of the 1970s, then, the question of 'under-achievement' was firmly on the agenda.

CLASS, GENDER AND CULTURE IN THE BLACK 'UNDER-ACHIEVEMENT' DEBATE

Remember that what became the Swann Inquiry started life under the chairmanship of Anthony Rampton as an investigation into the causes of 'West Indian' 'under-achievement' and, in a curious and even paradoxical discourse of exclusion and inclusion, entitled its interim report, published in 1981, *West Indian Children in Our Schools!* Meanwhile disturbing evidence had begun to accumulate about the relatively poor performance of children of Afro-Caribbean and Asian origin in schools. This fragmentary evidence could not strictly speaking be regarded as cumulative, being based on a variety of measures and deriving from children with varying degrees of residence in Britain, to mention just two complicating factors.[20]

More pertinent here is the curious manner in which categories of class, 'race', gender, ethnicity and culture intersected or were excluded in the debates surrounding the performance of pupils of Afro-Caribbean and Asian origin. Cultural and ethnic essentialism, of one variety or another, disfigured much of the debate. In its survey of six LEAs the Rampton Report primarily divided its sample into 'Asian', 'West Indian' and 'Other' school leavers, concluding that while 'Asians' and 'Others' performed equally well at O level and CSE, 'West Indian' school leavers performed significantly worse. On the complex differences of social class, gender and ethnicity, Rampton was conspicuously silent. The emerging evidence suggested that, once social class differences were taken into account the performance of 'Asian', 'West Indian' and 'Other' students was more nearly comparable (although not necessarily identical);[21] that it was likely that British Afro-Caribbean girls, for a variety of reasons, were more successful at school level than Afro-Caribbean boys;[22] and that pupils of Bangladeshi origin were performing particularly badly,[23] although even in this last case not enough connections were made with the intersection between racism and class – poverty, unemployment, poor housing and racial harassment and violence – in the lives of the community and its children.[24]

Although it was mindful of such factors as teacher racism and recognised that 'West Indian' parents expressed considerable interest in their children's education, the Rampton Report succumbed to other cultural essentialisms which replicated the cultural presuppositions of earlier debates about working-class families and educational 'under-achievement'. It reproduced American anxieties around cultures of deprivation and the supposed pathologies of 'the black family', stressing the relatively large proportion of 'West Indian' mothers who undertook paid employment outside the home, the incidence of one-parent families, and the supposed ignorance of 'West Indian' parents about the need to help their children academically at home.[25] Although not to anything like the same extent as in an earlier period in the United States, quietly and firmly the British black family was becoming the site of official anxieties. This was no doubt reinforced by a growing concern over disaffection and alienation amongst black youth, culminating in the 'moral panic' that erupted after the urban uprisings of 1980-81: Lord Scarman, in constructing his view of the Brixton 'disorders' expressed anxieties about the black family in almost identical terms to those of Rampton.[27]

By the time the Swann Report came to be written, some progress had been made in the debate about 'under-achievement'. Swann displayed a much firmer grasp of the significance of socio-economic circumstances in explaining the fate of students of Afro-Caribbean origin in the educational system and had begun to notice that the achievement of students of Bangladeshi origin should also give cause for concern. But the terms of the Report's discussion remained ultimately trapped within the ethnic and cultural essentialism inherited from Rampton. This emerges clearly in its tortuous attempt to grapple with what it still regarded as a fundamental difference between 'Asian' and 'West Indian' patterns of educational performance. 'West Indian' 'under-achievement' was attributed to a combination of poor socio-economic circumstances, which were exacerbated by racism, and to racism within the educational system. Given the awareness that not all 'Asians' were middle class and/or immune to racism within the educational system, however, how could the apparently better 'Asian' educational performance be understood?

In the final analysis, the Swann Report not only put aside what it had already acknowledged about the relatively poor performance of students of Bangladeshi origin, but ignored evidence that students of Mirpuri Pakistani origin were also underperforming, while students of East African Asian origin seemed to be achieving exceptionally well. Social class and rural-urban contrasts, and different relations with British colonial states and educational systems, are very likely to be involved as causal influences here, and Swann could well have commissioned research to explore some of the underlying issues. Instead, despite its disavowals and qualifications the Report slid into the trap of singling out 'Asian' culture and especially its main bearer, 'the Asian family', to explain the contrast with 'West Indians'. Asians 'kept their heads down', a strategy supposedly more likely to succeed in a 'hostile' (read: 'racist') environment – a view perhaps based on a selective construction of Jewish history in Britain? – in contrast to the 'West Indian' tendency to engage in protest (against racism). The 'tightly knit' Asian community, symbolised by the 'tightly knit' Asian family was said to be more likely to create a supportive educational environment.[28] The Swann Report thus failed to break with the cultural and ethnic essentialism which had hegemonised debate in this area and which, as we shall see, continues to mark both the 'multiculturalist' and 'antiracist' discourses and programmes of educational reform.

In the period since Swann the collection of official statistics on educational achievements has displayed a slightly greater sense of sensitivity and discrimination. The Inner London Education Authority, before its abolition, had begun to classify its students as being of 'African, African Asian, Arab, Bangladeshi, Caribbean, ESWI (English, Scottish, Welsh and Irish), Greek, Indian, Pakistani, SE Asian, Turkish and Other' origin.[29] Some attempt was made to provide even finer discriminations, Gujerati-speaking pupils being singled out as 'performing better than average', for example.[30] There was even some attention to gender: the ILEA report pointed out that for every ethnic group in its area the mean performance of girls was better than that of boys.[31] But no 'sub-ethnicities' were considered, nor was there any indication of differences in performance on particular subjects. An insight into the way the official terrain is constructed can be gained by noting the exclusion of other categories, which might have yielded different 'problems': 'Muslims', 'Jews', 'Catholics', 'Protestants', etc. Crucially, social class was again a significant absence. If ethnic monitoring recommendations are anything to go by, both in schools and elsewhere, 'official' information on the fate of pupils from the minorities will continue to suffer from this lacuna. Particular cultural and ethnic essentialisms, in other words, look set to structure public debate in the future despite attempts by activists and researchers to press for more sociologically informed discussion. And this will assist the fragmentation around the imagined absoluteness of ethnic differences upon which both the New Right and the 'cultural nationalists' from the ethnic minorities have been premising their demands for cultural separatism in education.[32]

Discussions around the educational achievements of British Afro-Caribbean and Asian girls are also significant in what they reveal about the contradictions and reductionisms of both public and academic debate in the whole area of racism, culture and education. Take, first, one of the major contradictions.[33] The 'tightly knit' Asian culture and its cultural agent, the 'tightly knit' Asian family, are regarded in the Swann Report and elsewhere as a key influence in producing high educational achievements. But this same culture and family system is held responsible for the widespread pathology supposedly afflicting 'Asian' girls and thus also their education: the malaise of being 'caught between two cultures', an 'identity crisis', a form of individual splitting between two essentialised cultural forms, 'Asian' and 'British/Western'. Avtar Brah and Rehana Minhas, amongst others, have challenged the cultural racism and the insensitivity to the vibrancy of Asian female cultures embedded in this type of representation.[34] Brah's own research has revealed that the larger proportion of Asian girls continue to have strong and supportive relationships with parents and that the degree of 'inter-generational conflict' is not necessarily higher than among white families.

Lest it be thought that the form of cultural essentialism being challenged here appears only in 'lay' public debate, consider this astonishing but revealing passage from Professor John Rex, a leading figure in British race relations research. Contrasting the 'altruistic solidarity' of Asian culture with the Western 'middle class' culture of 'individualism' and 'competition', Rex concludes: 'Thus, being a good Indian and being a successful middle class student at the same time are by no means easy goals to attain. There is bound to be breakdown'.[35] What is meant by class and ethnic reductionism and essentialism is illustrated here by Rex's assumption of deterministic and invariable cultural patterns producing inevitable individual responses. (Cashmore and Troyna, the editors of the volume in which Rex's paper appeared, were widely criticised for their collapse into a cultural essentialism which accused 'black youth' of being 'arrogant, rumbustious and contemptuous' and having 'a certain fascination for violence'.)[36]

'The Asian woman' is subject to contradictory and ambivalent stereotypification. This figure acts variously as the symbol and chief bearer of the admirably strong, tightly knit family and culture, as the oppressed subject of 'traditional' Asian patriarchal practices, as a 'problem' because of her failure to learn the language and customs which might allow a smoother integration of her community and children into 'the British way of life', and full of sexual charm and allure produced by a demure seductiveness replete with the promise of a mysterious Oriental eroticism. Afro-Caribbean girls and women, on the other hand, are often represented as crushed under the weight of a 'triple oppression' of class, gender and racism. This common-sense image implies a linear model which sees these burdens as cumulative or 'additive' in operation and effect, although also overlain with images of the strong black woman, the single mother, holding the family together in the face of irresponsible black males, whether they be husbands or disruptive youth.

Most research has thoroughly problematised these conceptions. It is not merely that the incidence of single parent black families has been exaggerated,[37] but that class, gender and racism intersect in highly complex and contradictory ways in the lives of black women.[38] The notion of cumulatively disadvantaging oppressions, leading to inevitable failure, is belied by the educational responses of British

Afro-Caribbean girls. What research and evidence there is appears to suggest that at school level at least their educational achievements are higher than those of Afro-Caribbean boys, and that they exhibit a greater tenacity in the pursuit of educational qualifications than white girls. Many working-class British Afro-Caribbean girls, it appears, have been adopting a clever and effective strategy which combines resistance and accommodation, instrumentalism and commitment. They work hard at school without giving the appearance of being 'swots', thus pre-empting derision from their peers. They resist school procedures and rules but not to the point of risking outright confrontation with teachers. And they aspire to interesting and well-paid work but without any illusions about the degree of racial discrimination and sexual segregation in employment. There is, in other words, no simple 'culture of failure' or 'culture of resistance', but rather a complex set of strategies set generally within the context of strong attachments to families and black cultural identities.[39] Similar complexities need to be acknowledged in the case of British Asian girls.[40]

So far, I have sketched in some of the contours of early educational debates and policy in the field of racism, culture and education and explored the way in which the problem of cultural and ethnic essentialism, in particular, has structured and indeed disfigured public debates and the production of relevant 'knowledge'. This is how the ground was unwittingly prepared for New Right and other interventions based on rigid, absolutist conceptions of cultural and ethnic difference. The issues of social class and racism, as I have argued, have been significant casualties of the discursive formations and apparatuses of knowledge and power which defined the emergence of the black presence as an object of public discussion and policy.[41]

RACISM AND SCHOOLING

One of the fundamental charges levelled by antiracists against the culturalist assumptions underpinning much public and academic debate, especially in the field of education, is that the specificity and significance of racist ideologies and structures have received inadequate attention. Whenever the issue of racism is put on the agenda, they suggest, it is transmuted into questions of 'prejudice' and 'attitudes', thus leaving a wide range of discriminatory practices and structures unchallenged. This charge is well-aimed. As we shall see later in this essay, however, there is a definite, and what at first sight may appear to be surprising, degree of isomorphism between the two perspectives. Before I make that case, it is first necessary to set out, albeit briefly, some of the documented forms of exclusion and violence that are targeted by practices designed to challenge racism in schools.

Racial abuse and violence The sheer prevalence, intensity and normality of abuse, harassment and violence directed by white students against British Asian and Afro-Caribbean students as part of the informal, 'popular' culture of schools is horrifying. Accounts abound of the distress, trauma and injury involved. The acts range from verbal abuse – continual taunts of 'Paki', 'Nigger', 'Blacky', 'Chocolate Face', 'Black Bastard' – to vicious physical attacks by both boys and girls in corridors, on playing fields and at bus stops; hospitalisation for broken bones, stitches and broken noses is not uncommon. The extent of the problem compelled the Commission for Racial Equality to entitle its 1988 survey of racial harassment, *Learning in Terror*, giving added weight to other accounts.[42] The historical and contemporary experiences of Jewish children attest to the continuing significance of Britain's other racisms and, in the context of another phase of rising anti-semitism, clearly need greater attention.[43]

In the wake of Burnage the risk of fatality can hardly be denied. To some degree, the racial abuse and violence in schools mirrors that meted out to black minorities in British cities more generally (the anti-semitic parallels must again be recalled). In the absence of adequate police action, this is producing a growing number of self-defence and monitoring groups amongst black minorities.[44]

The culture of teacher racism A frequent complaint of black students is that their reports of racial abuse and violence are habitually ignored or their racial elements denied by white teachers. This is only one form taken by teacher collusion with racialised processes. There are a host of others, again amply documented. Black students, for example, are not infrequently humiliated with 'jokes'. Common 'witticisms' range from the threat to send a student back to the 'chocolate factory' to be 'remade' to remarks about 'jungle-like behaviour': 'Go back to the trees'; 'Stop laughing like monkeys'.[45] Many black teachers hardly fare better at the hands of their white colleagues, often finding themselves the butt of racist jokes, remarks and hostility and isolation in the staff room. Here is part of an account of the experiences of an extremely well qualified woman teacher of Afro-Caribbean origin:

In school she has had to contend with discussions about 'Pakis' in the staff room. One teacher said he would like to send all blacks back on the banana boat, and another told her that he was unable to sit by her because she was black.[46]

The Burnage Report gives a further sense of the routine culture of teacher racism:

> A teacher who showed an interest in Asian culture was asked by a colleague, 'why don't you wear Indian dress?' and was greeted by a mock Indian prayer movement every time she passed this colleague in the corridor.
>
> A Section 11 teacher who was wearing a hair slide was asked if it was a West Indian hair slide she was wearing. She replied: 'no, it's just a hair slide', and was told 'why don't you take the bone out and wear it through your nose?'
>
> The wearing of pig badges by a large group of staff, many of whom were members of middle management, after the Deputy Head, Peter Moors, had suggested that pork was less suitable than turkey for the school for the school's Christmas dinner, since it prevented Muslim boys from taking part. Pork scratching packets were pinned to his notice board and he was and still is referred to as 'Porky'.[47]

Selection and allocation procedures Schools are pre-eminently institutional sites for selection and de-selection, for the allocation of students to different levels in status hierarchies of subjects in the curriculum and public examinations, with the subsequent outcomes being of some significance in determining further educational chances and career opportunities. The various forms of allocative discrimination which operate against black students have been the subject of several investigations. Again, a few instances must suffice to show how the culture of racism and institutional processes which provide discretionary allocative power to teachers, tend to intermesh and work against many black students. Cecile Wright's research for the 1986 Eggleston Report, *Education for Some* is one of the most compelling documentations of the process at work.[48] It reveals a systematic tendency for able black students to be allocated to sets and streams and entered for examinations below their capacities, and exposes the significance of racist discourses in legitimating these practices.[49] The obverse of this process is the tendency to channel Afro-Caribbean students, especially, into sports or music on account of supposedly innate physical capacities and 'a natural sense of rhythm'.[50] Careers advice given to both Afro-Caribbean and Asian students is frequently based on conceptions of their supposedly 'unrealistic' and over-ambitious aspirations. Attempts are made to route them into low-level manual work regardless of ability or level of motivation for further education, and discrimination in entry to training-schemes acts as a further block to employment and careers.[51] One symptomatic phenomenon was revealed in my own research in Leicester for an Open University television programme, when I found that many teachers of English were unwilling to come to terms with the interest and creative potential of Asian students in English language, literature and drama. These exclusionary effects of a culture of 'Englishness' embedded in the discourses and practices of English teaching appear rather ironic in view of the significance for the growth of English literary studies of the colonial attempt to 'Anglicise' Indians.[52]

School subjects and the production of racialised subjectivities The sedimentation of caricatured images of 'natives' – African, Asian and Arab – and selective and often imagined representations of their histories and cultures, reinforced in comics, adventure stories and films, has long been a powerful presence in the official curriculum of British schools, and continues to be an important mechanism of exclusion, stereotypification and marginalisation, reinforced by representations in the mass media.[53]

Institutional procedures Black minorities have frequently been casualties of rules and procedures which may not have been intended to discriminate against them but which in effect do so, and there is considerable resistance when the hitherto taken-for-granted procedures are brought into question. Rules about appropriate modes of dress, whether concerning school uniforms or clothing for PE and sports, have been one such arena. Some schools refuse to allow Sikh boys to wear turbans, or girls to cover their legs. These constitute a form of indirect discrimination which in the case of turbans was fought successfully by a Sikh family under the terms of the 1976 Race Relation Act.[54] Other instances include the lack of availability of vegetarian food or halal meat, the failure to communicate school messages to parents in languages other than English, and the absence of policies on racial abuse or equal opportunities. Mention must also be made of the marginalisation of many black teaching staff because of their employment in 'community language' teams or as Section 11 teachers.[55]

'MULTICULTURALISM' AND 'ANTIRACISM': A BINARY OPPOSITION?

It is often asserted that the 1980s saw a polarisation between two fundamentally opposed educational movements, multiculturalism and antiracism. These were based on different understandings of racism which apparently led to radically divergent programmes of educational reform. In part the debate has been presented as an opposition between a broadly 'liberal' programme – multiculturalism – and antiracism which claimed for itself the mantle of left radicalism.[56] It is certainly the case that there have been debates, often acrimonious ones, between self-styled 'multiculturalists' and 'antiracists'. These have been played out in public arenas such as the conferences of NAME – which, symptomatically, changed its name in 1985 from the National Association for Multiracial Education to the National Anti-Racist Movement in Education – and in various journals and books.

It is less clear to what extent and in what ways this broad division has actually manifested itself in the classroom and in internal school debates and policies, and in local authority policies. In many institutions complex and varying combinations of the two have been put into practice, and there are in any case many differences and contradictions *within* the two movements.[57] Any individual teacher, Local Authority official or parent thus may find that her or his position on various issues cannot be neatly pigeon-holed into one or other of 'multiculturalism' and 'antiracism' as represented here. This does not necessarily diminish the relevance of my critique, for it not only addresses two influential systematisations but also encompasses many of the central elements from which variants of the two positions have been constructed. This applies especially to the fundamental question of the nature of racism and its operations and effects at three inter-related levels: the individual subject or agent who articulates and practices racism; institutional processes of discrimination; and texts such as school books. The significance of this critique is also reinforced by my argument that, despite some differences of approach, at a deeper level there are fundamental similarities in conceptualisation and prescription between multiculturalism and antiracism which are in my view flawed. Although both movements have made important contributions, my judgement is that their frameworks and policies *share* significant and disabling weaknesses.

I cannot emphasise too strongly that I cannot here attempt to provide a detailed exposition or erect a comprehensive critique of multiculturalist and antiracist assumptions and practices. The discussion that follows is necessarily selective, highlighting *some* key issues, but inevitably neglecting others, for example around the vexed question of cultural relativism and the problems surrounding the marginalisation of 'race' policies at the institutional level, which might be treated in a text of quite different scope.

Multiculturalism, as expressed in the Swann Report or in the writings of Jeffcoate, James, Lynch and Parekh, is based on the premise that the key issue facing schools is how to create 'tolerance' for black minorities and their cultures in a white nation now characterised by 'cultural diversity' or 'cultural pluralism'. Intolerance is conceptualised basically as a matter of 'attitudes', and is said to be constituted by 'prejudice'. The basic educational prescription is the sympathetic teaching of 'other cultures' in order to dispel the ignorance which is seen to be at the root of prejudice and intolerance. The overall social and political project is the creation of a harmonious, democratic, cultural pluralism, a healthy cultural diversity. There are internal differences amongst the multiculturalists, of course, and under relentless criticism from antiracists most multiculturalists have acknowledged the significance of tackling institutionalised racist practices in schools.[58] Nevertheless, these are the key principles held by those who see themselves more as multiculturalists, and continue explicitly to take a critical distance from antiracism.[59]

The antiracists have pointed out that in privileging 'prejudice' and 'attitudes' the multiculturalists have neglected racism as embedded in structures and institutions. As we shall see, however, the case against the discourse of 'prejudice' is deeper, more complex and more damaging.

THE CASE AGAINST 'PREJUDICE'

Prejudice, as conceptualised both in the educational literature around multiculturalism and in more specialised psychological discourses, is defined as hostile or negative attitudes based on ignorance and faulty or incomplete knowledge. It is characterised by a tendency to 'stereotype', that is, a tendency to assign identical characteristics to whole groups regardless of individual variations.[60] Thus, multicultural handbooks and official reports such as Rampton and Swann warn against common teacher stereotypes of Afro-Caribbean ('disruptive', 'lazy') and Asian ('industrious', 'passive', 'over-ambitious') students and which are also documented in academic research on teachers' attitudes.[61] As we have seen multiculturalist accounts emphasise the way in which stereotypes may be affecting classroom encounters (the Swann report, pp 45-56, reproduces a piece of research on this by Peter Green): they are also critical of the channelling of Afro-Caribbean students into sports; and the allocation of Afro-Caribbean and Asian students to streams, sets, examinations and career paths which grossly underestimate their abilities and potential.

One major difficulty about these notions of prejudice and stereotype concerns the all too common assumption that individuals hold prejudiced views consistently and express them and act in accordance with them in a systematic and uncontradictory manner. This therefore tends to essentialise 'the prejudiced individual' – the prejudiced teacher or student – who becomes the target for depathologising pedagogic therapies. There is, however, mounting evidence to suggest a more complex picture than this. For one thing, many people who might be labelled racially 'prejudiced' on the basis of attitude surveys or expressive behaviour in particular contexts turn out to be more ambivalent and contradictory in their discourses and practices. Thus Billig and Cochrane report that during their research a white girl who in discussions with them had expressed strongly racist views, was seen walking out of school arm in arm with an Asian girl.[62] Even more dramatically, Darren Coulbourn, the white boy from Burnage High School who murdered Ahmed Iqbal Ullah and triumphantly proclaimed 'I've killed a Paki', was also known to have collaborated with an Asian boy in burning down the art block and 'used to get into trouble' at school (as the Burnage report puts it) in the company of an Afro-Caribbean boy. Darren Coulbourn's 'attitudes on race are not clear cut', the report concludes.[63] In Philip Cohen's research in 1989, individual white working-class youth in south London expressed more or less sympathetic views on blacks depending on the context and topic of conversation.[64] Talking to the researcher about South Africa, they voiced sympathy for the plight of black South Africans. Talking to their mates about British blacks, they tended to complain about becoming second class citizens in their own country. Although it appears to be the same principle that promotes sympathy for South African blacks in *their* country, this confirms rather than vitiates, the point that the form and meaning of racist discourses depends on and varies in context and enables a range of verbal and practical interactions and positions. (Cohen also refers, for instance, to white youth who supported overtly racist immigration policies but dissociated themselves from the National Front; see also the research on white youth reported in Coffield et al.[65])

Billig's 1978 research on adult National Front members revealed a complexity of 'attitudes' and practices which belies what is, ironically enough, a *social scientific* stereotype of the strongly prejudiced individual who operates with a rigid 'set' or framework of categories.[66] A notable illustration of this complexity even among 'hard core' racists was the NF trade union official who pointed out that he had been elected by both black and white workmates, despite his well known NF affiliation, because he fought equally hard for blacks and whites; he claimed a liking for blacks and maintained that he played football and drank with them, although politically he supported repatriation. In the United States, Wellman has shown how anti-discrimination legislation in the sphere of employment can be supported by people who reject them in the field of housing, this being part of a much wider pattern of contradictions in white attitudes.[67] Investigation in New Zealand have pointed up the complexity and variability of white orientations towards the entitlements of Maoris within the policy.[68]

The complexities of discourses around 'race' are in part constituted by, and expressed in, the circulation of contradictory stereotypes. This is graphically illustrated by Jenkins's investigation of white managers' varying conceptions of the capacities of Asian and Afro-Caribbean workers.[69] Some regarded Asians as lazy in comparison with Afro-Caribbeans, while other managers reversed the categorisations. More generally, 'Asians' in Britain have been regarded both as scroungers *and* also so industrious that they are taking over jobs and businesses, as both 'thrifty' *and* 'flashy'. Afro-Caribbeans are seen as both 'lazy' and as extraordinarily successful in activities requiring considerable physical exertion and mental discipline such as sports and athletics. Stereotypes, moreover, are subject to historical change and geographical variation or salience. There is, too, the question of ambivalence, signified in part by the existence of contradictory stereotypes. 'Asians' or 'Pakis' may be resented or hated, but there is admiration for their supposed 'industriousness', 'ambitiousness', 'enterprise', 'family values', 'respect and care for their elderly', 'respect for authority', and so on, particularly evident in New Right discourses but also in popular culture. Afro-Caribbeans may be reviled as 'niggers', but their musical forms and stylistic innovations exercise considerable fascination, attraction and influence in popular culture.[70] Some of the most common forms of ambivalence of course are expressed in disavowals such as 'Some of my best friends are . . .', or 'you (some) are all right, it's the rest . . .'.

A further complication is the fascination with both Asian and African sexualities. This builds up another series of ambivalences into racialised encounters such as racial harassment and violence, which are not simply between 'black' and 'white', but between white and black men, white men and black women, and so on.[71] Both working-class and middle-class masculinities are involved, with defences of the neighbourhood against racialised 'others' which Cohen refers to as the 'nationalism of the neighbourhood',[72] the proving of masculinity by beating up 'Pakis',[73] the sexual harassment of black women and, an aspect that deserves much greater research, in the middle-class and professional institutional context, the complex intertwining between masculinity, class and racism in the exclusion of blacks from employment or promotion by white male managers.

Racialised discourses are always articulated in context: in an English or history class; inside a school corridor, in a dinner queue or in the playground; at work or on the streets; in one neighbourhood or another. These different sites can yield complex and shifting alliances and points of tension.[74] The ambivalences generated for many white youth by the attractions of Afro-Caribbean, Afro-American and African musical forms, and their admiration for some aggressive forms of Afro-Caribbean masculinity, have resulted in alliances in particular schools and neighbourhoods between white and Afro-Caribbean youth against Asian youth, while in some schools where black-white conflicts remain submerged the dominant form of racist insult occurs between different ethnic minority groups, for instance Asian and Afro-Caribbean or Cypriot and Vietnamese.[75] An appreciation of contradiction, ambivalence and context combined with a sensitivity to the variability of discourses amongst teachers and their practices, puts into question simplistic models of the process whereby (uncontradictory) teacher stereotypes of black pupils are supposedly translated into discriminatory practices that lead to unequal outcomes. Recent research paints a more complex picture of contradictory teacher 'attitudes' varying within and between schools and provoking a range of responses from black male and female students.[76] This point is also being registered in relation to sexism in schools,[77] and has provoked a more general rethinking of educational processes in which poststructuralist theorising is beginning to exercise a belated but, in my view, welcome influence.[78]

The Burnage Report is the first document of its kind of attempt to deal with some of these complexities. It points, *inter alia*, to the ambivalence of Darren Coulbourn's racism, and the significance of the masculine cult of violence that had a strong presence in the all-boys school. It also emphasises how the generalised context of racism in the school was relevant to their conclusion that the murder of Ahmed Iqbal Ullah was a 'racial' murder.

All this is a far cry from the simplifications of the multicultural discourse of 'prejudice' and the prejudiced subject or individual. But this is not the end of the story. Conceptions of prejudice, and associated multiculturalisms in education, are premised on the view that prejudice is primarily caused by ignorance, in this case of black cultures. The educational prescription is therefore a curricular dose of knowledge about those 'other cultures', taught in a variety of sometimes imaginative ways. The problem with this is not merely that there has been very little serious thinking within multiculturalism about how 'cultural understanding' actually occurs, about its forms, mechanisms and limits. What, after all, does it mean to *understand* any culture, including one's own, whatever what might be in ethnic, class, or any other terms? The more subversive possibility is that the discourse of prejudice contains an element that threatens the foundations of multiculturalism from within. That is, there is a contradiction between the *rationalism* of the multiculturalist project, which recommends a reduction of prejudice by teaching a combination of facts and cultural empathy, and the insistence, also within the discourse of prejudice, that prejudice involves a strong element of *irrationalism*.[79]

Prejudice, we are told by psychologists, is not easily reduced, for the prejudiced person is relatively resistant to contrary evidence, and 'a deeply prejudiced person' Aronson writes, 'is virtually immune to information'.[80] Psychological and psychoanalytic accounts have drawn upon such conceptions as 'the authoritarian personality', 'projection', and 'scapegoating', in order to explicate the forms and levels of irrationality involved.[81] I cannot discuss these theorisations here. The point I wish to register is that despite some efforts to discuss and incorporate 'affective' or emotional elements in teaching about 'other cultures', multiculturalism has generally failed to confront what is involved in one of the elements central to its own discourse on prejudice: the 'irrationality' of the 'prejudiced'. Lynch is a good example of the multiculturalist caught unawares, or at least only dimly aware, in this dilemma.[82] He recommends educational strategies which involve 'affective' elements, but he bases his entire educational and political strategy on the premise of democratic rationalism in the context of cultural pluralism. By leaving the nature of 'irrationalities' and other resistances unelaborated, he effectively sweeps them under the carpet. He prescribes a multiculturalism that lacks the intellectual and strategic tools it needs.

A further question mark over the practices of multiculturalism concerns the actual 'effects' of teaching about 'other cultures'. Little evidence, sceptics argue, has been adduced to support the claim that such teaching has a significant impact in reducing prejudice. The 'culture contact' hypothesis as investigated by psychologists has produced poor results;[83] what evidence there is often exists only in the anecdotal form of teacher accounts or in multicultural handbooks.[84] However, the whole question of the effects of teaching around 'race', whether in multiculturalist or other form, requires recasting in the light of the more complex understanding of racism and racist subjectivities being proposed here. If subjects are contradictorily and ambivalently positioned in discourses and if racist practices are significantly affected by social context, research into the 'effects' of teaching about 'race' cannot operate with the linear and essentialist models used by most conventional psychology and sociology. Far more subtle, long-term ethnographic research has to be undertaken to establish how subjects negotiate such teaching and now subjectivities are recomposed in different contexts. In the absence of such research, Troyna's confident rejection of multiculturalist strategies cannot be sustained, although of course the antiracist argument that teaching about 'other cultures' does not necessarily give an understanding of the racism of one's own remains intact.

RACISM AND THE ANTIRACISTS

Antiracists have rightly pointed to the limited nature of multiculturalism's focus on 'prejudice' and 'attitudes', and its strategy of prejudice reduction by teaching about 'other cultures'. Racism, the antiracists argue, must be challenged head on. That requires a dismantling of institutionalised *practices* of racism, whether in education or in employment, housing, immigration policy, and so on, as well as a direct confrontation with racist ideologies, for example in the school curriculum.[85] On closer examination, however, their conception of racism, both at the level of ideology and structures, also suffers from oversimplification, often of a very similar kind.

At the level of racism as a set of ideologies, for example, none of the antiracist analyses cited above displays an awareness of contradictions, inconsistencies and ambivalences of the kind I have sketched earlier. In this sense, their conception of racist ideologies and racist subjects of individuals is no more sophisticated than that of the multiculturalists. A notable absence is an understanding of the complex intertwining of racism with sexuality (not the same point as the increasingly common reference to the 'triple oppression' of the black woman). It is now quite clear that the complexities of white racism (which is the focus here) cannot be grasped without an exploration of the anxieties and ambivalences generated by especially male but also female sexual anxieties and desires. From the earliest encounters between Europeans and Others right to the present, these manifest themselves in an endless series of speculations, projections, fantasies and crimes in relation to 'African' and 'Oriental' women and men.[86] This interaction between sexuality and racism is an important source of the 'irrationalities' and resistances encountered by a rational 'facts and empathy' approach, whether of an antiracist or multicultural variety, and poses highly complex problems for any project of 'deracialisation'.

There are no easy answers here. Even the prescription of a joint approach to issues of sexism and racism does little more than scratch the surface of a very much deeper problem.[87] Educational and pedagogical strategies developed by feminists more conscious of the need to dig deeper into psychic processes in tackling sexual identities and subjectivities[88] require more serious attention within antiracism, and have found a sympathetic counterpart in Phillip Cohen's cultural studies approach to antiracism.[89]

In antiracism as much as in multiculturalism, the absence of any serious engagement with issues around sexuality in the 'irrationality' of popular racism is symptomatic of a rationalist understanding of pedagogies and educational processes. In the case of antiracism, this is further underpinned by an overly rationalist conception of state and dominant class racism. I begin by examining the antiracist's notion of racism as a form of irrationalism.

The mode by which the discourse of *prejudice* consigns racism to a form of irrationalism is, at bottom, by way of a *pathologisation* of the individual subject. Racism is interpreted as a form of displacement and objectification deriving from unhealthy neuroses and personality traits. In antiracist analyses the irrationality of popular or working class racism is conceptualised primarily as a form of 'false consciousness'. There are several variants of the argument, differing at least in part around the degree of class reductionism and the amount of reflectiveness or reflexivity allowed to the working-class racist subject. In the crudest analyses, working-class racism is interpreted as composed of a set of falsehoods perpetrated by one, or a combination, of the following agencies: capital, the ruling class, the mass media, and the state. These are conceptualised as unified, non-contradictory, omniscient 'actors', united by the common objective of dividing the working class along racial lines so as to facilitate the economic exploitation of both sections of the class. The state is viewed as an instrument of capital and state policies such as immigration and race relations legislation are seen as the outcome of deliberate, thus 'rational', manipulation by agents of capital and the capitalist state. The working-class racist, in this construction, is reduced to a 'cultural dope', to borrow a phrase from the ethnomethodological critique of conventional sociology's 'oversocialised' conception of the subject. That is, he or she is viewed as a passive and helpless victim of ruling-class, media and state propaganda. Reformist black activists are also seen as cultural dopes and/or traitors to 'class and community', 'bought off' by the race relations industry of the Commission for Racial Equality, Community Relations Councils, local authority 'race' posts, community and welfare projects, or 'multiculturalism'. All these have been supposedly cynically instituted by the state-capital complex.

Some of the highly influential writings of A. Sivanandan, director of the Institute of Race Relations and editor of the journal *Race and Class* fall squarely within this tradition.[90] These operate within a crude Marxism which became the object of considerable internal criticism within Marxism,[91] but which appears to have failed to shift the class reductionism and instrumentalism associated with his project. Other Left antiracists, like Madan Sarup, are more aware in *principle* of the pitfalls of such class reductionism, and attempt to disavow it. In practice, however, they often fall back on a similar analysis.[92] (It is worth adding that *multiculturalists* are prone to another essentialism with regard to the state, often seeing it as a neutral and uncontradictory vehicle for educational and other reforms – see Troyna's critique of the Swann Report).[93] Although it is not possible to rehearse here the many deficiencies of the antiracist brand of class reductionism, some of the difficulties are signalled by my description of 'instrumentalism' and the patronising 'cultural dope' stereotype of the white working-class racist. It is also worth emphasising the links between a view of racist subjects and ideologies which neglects contradictions and ambivalences and the conception of racism as, simply, a form of 'false consciousness'. Note, too, that nothing is said within such analyses about forms of 'middle-class racism' – the discussion pivots around a simple polarisation between a 'ruling' and 'working' class.

Not all antiracists, however, whether in education or elsewhere, appear to subscribe to such a simplified version of the racism-as-false-consciousness argument. Others (e.g. Hatcher and Shalice[94]) have drawn upon Phizacklea and Miles's North London research which, although in the final analysis conceiving of racism as a form of 'false consciousness', nevertheless gives a more active, reasoning or reflexive role to the working-class racist subject. Phizacklea and Miles argue that white racism in the particular inner-city context that they researched operated not simply in the form of cultural stereotypes but as part of the process whereby white residents and workers attempted to make sense of public housing shortages, reduction in employment opportunities, and other aspects of urban decline.[95] These features for many whites were primarily associated with the arrival of black settlers, who were thus 'blamed' for the problems. This gave rise to the resentment and hostility which Phizacklea and Miles regard as a characteristic form of modern, inner-city, working-class white racism, although they have been mindful that the findings may only apply to particular sections of the class and in particular areas. Thus racist discourses and practices are seen as emerging in specific forms. More generally, they are seen to flourish in situations of acute competition for scarce resources such as employment and housing and they are exacerbated by the insecurities of rising inflation.

Phizacklea and Miles show some sensitivity to the contradictory nature of working-class consciousness and emphasise that in a number of workers high levels of class consciousness nevertheless coexisted with considerable hostility towards local blacks. They stress the often fragmented and 'piece-meal' character of the racial hostility expressed by some white people in their survey: some of them blamed black settlers for housing shortages but not for the loss of employment opportunities, for example. Nevertheless, the forms of racism revealed here are seen as a form of false consciousness based on the 'attempt to understand and explain *immediate daily experience*, while the real reasons for both the socio-economic decline and New Commonwealth immigration are to be found in much more abstract and long-standing social and economic processes which cannot be grasped in terms of daily experience'.[96]

Note the important educational and pedagogic conclusion Phizacklea and Miles draw from their research: the significance of 'immediate daily experience' in producing and reproducing inner-city working-class racism, in conjunction with the backdrop of a widespread nationalist culture of racism in British society, means that those who express racist hostility 'are very resistant to modification as a result of argument from outsiders'.[97] Phizacklea and Miles warn of the limits of any strategy premised on the assumption (made in the 1970s by the TUC and the Labour Party) that 'the way to eliminate working class racism was to provide counter-arguments to common racist beliefs', to 'push' out of workers' heads an 'ideological baggage' primarily produced by the dominant class and replace it by 'the truth'.

This research has been expounded at some length here to demonstrate that despite some limitations it is informed by a relatively subtle and complex analysis. Antiracist educators have read it in a simplistic manner, however, much to the detriment of their pedagogic project. Hatcher and Shallice, for instance, having cited Phizacklea and Miles's research, conclude, contrary to the researchers, that in education the key task must be the provision of superior explanations for unemployment, for example, which would also involve discussions of issues of class politics. They stress the significance of a *cognitive* emphasis, and link this to an older labour movement project for the provision of 'really useful knowledge'.[98] Moreover, while Phizacklea and Miles believe that changes in the material circumstances of the working class can provide only a 'partial solution' to the problem of racist ideologies, the political project of the transformation of capitalism and working-class conditions advocated by Hatcher and Shallice (and other left antiracists in education) squeezes out of consideration the rather important caveat entered by Phizacklea and Miles about the prospects for change in racist ideologies as a result of changes in the material 'base'.

Phizacklea and Miles's own research can be faulted on a variety of grounds. There is little detailed exploration of the contradictions, and none of the ambivalences that might characterise the racism of their subjects.[99] The analysis is also considerably weakened by the empiricism of their notion of 'direct, immediate experience', which writes out the significance of the complex interpretive *frameworks* through which events, processes and 'facts' are *constructed*. 'Experience', that is, is *produced*, rather than simply *registered*. The implicit recognition of this in their work is obscured by the distinction they make between 'direct experience' and more 'abstract' 'underlying' causes which cannot be grasped at the level of immediate experience. Moreover, resistances other than those posed by 'immediate experience' are ignored; for instance, possible sexual anxieties provoked by moral panics, common enough in the 1970s and early 1980, around black 'muggers' and 'rapists'.

The implication I wish to draw out here is that, like the multiculturalists, antiracists in education have failed to confront the limitations of a rationalist approach. Again, as in the case of the discourse of prejudice underpinning the multiculturalist project, the limitations are signalled in the underlying theorisation and analysis. In the case of antiracism the *rationalism* of the educational project rests on a particular conception of the *irrationalism* of the racist subject, often conceptualised as a collective, class subject. In the context of schooling one significant issue that is paradoxically neglected is the 'rationality' of the working-class students' resistance to antiracist curricula and classroom discussions in so far as this resistance is bound up with a more generalised opposition to the degrees of surveillance, discipline, authoritarianism and class domination involved in conventional forms of schooling. (The same point can be made against multiculturalist understandings of prejudice).[100] Like the multiculturalist project of reducing prejudice by teaching about other cultures, the antiracist project of providing superior explanations for unemployment, housing shortages, and so forth, has so far, and for similar reasons, produced only patchy evidence of success. The point is not simply to abandon this type of teaching but to acknowledge and analyse its limitations in the light of a more complex understanding of the nature of racism and to develop forms of educational engagement more likely to open up racist subjectivities and 'common sense' to alternative discourses. More democratic and collaborative pedagogies, as proposed by Troyna and Carrington and exemplified by some of the projects they have developed, are a step in the right direction.[101] They are still weakened, however, by the absence of a more complex understanding of the contradictions, ambivalences and resistances of the popular cultures of racism amongst white youth.[102] Indeed Troyna and Carrington have themselves expressed doubts about the efficacy of such initiatives.[103]

One index of the theoretical and educational congruences between multiculturalism and antiracism is the underlying similarity between multiculturalist attempts to combat racial prejudice by the provision of 'positive images' and the antiracist injunction to present black histories primarily as narratives of resistance and struggle against racism.[104] The aims are laudable, given the often grotesque caricatures of African, Asian and Arab histories and cultures, the neglect of the destructive, exploitative effects of colonialism and imperialism in school texts and in popular cultural forms such as comics, adventure stories, adult fiction and the cinema, and the absence of any serious treatment of forms of resistance to imperial rule.[105] Nevertheless there are difficulties here which must be confronted if both multicultural and antiracist attempts at the development of alternative curricula and popular cultural forms are to avoid oversimplification and naivety.

There is, first, the unacknowledged disingenuity involved in replacing one lot of selective images with another set of partial representations. Amongst other things, this opens up the multiculturalists and antiracists to the same charge of 'propaganda' and indoctrination that they level at the textbooks, authors and teachers they are attempting to challenge. It also allows the New Right and sections of the media to connect the purging of 'negative images' from textbooks with other authoritarian or top-down antiracist policies by LEAs and schools and to represent the whole exercise as a left Labour-antiracist 'totalitarian' conspiracy. On this issue, the 'traditionalists', the multiculturalists and antiracists occupy the same epistemological terrain. They all share in the misleading assumption that it is possible to produce a singular, uncontestable, objective and accurate representation of the reality external to the literary, photographic or any other text. They thus ignore or obscure a different more democratic objective: that is, the search for mechanisms for giving voice to a range of representations, and for encouraging a critical dialogue and interrogation of all intellectual and political frameworks. Black artists, photographers, film-makers and cultural critics have been in the forefront of demands and attempts to break the bounds of an aesthetic of 'positive images'. They reject the reduction of the diversity of black histories, experiences and cultures down to a simple response to racism, not least because this inhibits the productive exploration of the economic, cultural and sexual differentiations within black communities; for example, 'positive images' tend to privilege middle-class, heterosexual, familial respectability. This reduction also blocks the creativity of black artistic imagination and practices of representation. Look, for example, at the photography of David A. Bailey, the films of Sankofa, the Black Audio Films Collective and Hanif Kureshi, the essays of Paul Gilroy and Kobena Mercer, the paintings of Sonia Boyce.[106] This work explores questions of racism, ethnicity, nationality and sexual difference in ways which have problematised conventional assumptions and opened up a crucial debate about the diversity and complexity of black British identities and voices. The *educational* implication is not that the contestation of caricatures of black histories and cultures in school texts should cease, but that it should not be premised on the stifling aesthetic of the 'positive image'.

Although given their underlying premise of 'cultural pluralism', multiculturalists tend to be more sympathetic to giving voice to a plurality of positions, their project is vitiated by the tendency to cling to epistemological assumptions more congruent with the discourse of 'positive images'. A decisive break with 'realist' conceptions of the curriculum is long overdue and is a precondition for genuinely pluralist forms of radicalisation of the curriculum.[107] Troyna and Carrington's dissatisfaction with simplistic assumptions about the antiracist effects of 'culture contact' and white students' 'direct experience' of black realities, as well as their growing awareness of the limits of rationalist pedagogies, points to a need on their part to break with 'realist' assumptions about the curriculum which appear to continue to underpin their antiracist projects.[108]

Both multicultural and antiracist critiques ignore the actual literary and pedagogic devices involved in the construction of subject positions for the child/reader in school texts. They neglect *how* texts construct meanings as opposed to *what* they supposedly mean. As a consequence, the complexity of the processes by which texts which form part of particular school disciplines – for example, history or geography – have effects on the 'subjects' of schools, the students, is also neglected. Too often, all the protagonist's make simplistic assumptions about the ease with which subjectivities are produced by racist or antiracist texts.[109]

Finally, with regard to the antiracists' understanding of racism, something must briefly be said about the commonly used conception of 'institutionalised racism'. Originating in the Black Power Movement's struggles in the US, the concept now generally signifies all the myriad, taken for granted, ways in which routine institutional procedures, whatever their original purposes, end up discriminating against and disadvantaging black and other ethnic minorities. Examples of some of the forms of institutional racism involved in the educational system have been provided earlier in this article. There has been, however, a tendency to use the concept in a reductive manner to infer racist processes as the only or primary cause of all the unequal outcomes and exclusions which black students experience.[110] The significance of the class and gender inequalities which are intertwined with the racism that black students encounter is thus underplayed.

This weakens the analysis and suggests inappropriate and possibly divisive policies which ignore discriminations and disadvantages common to white and black students, or which impinge in varying ways upon boys and girls. The hostages to fortune delivered by simplistic usages of 'institutional racism' can be seen in Antony Flew's New Right critique.[11]

AN ALTERNATIVE FRAMEWORK

Having criticised the limits of the antiracist account of racism, this is an appropriate point at which to explicate my own conception of racism and to indicate why I think it is more persuasive.[112] In my view the concept of *racism*, which should be distinguished from the notion of *racial discrimination*, should be restricted to discourses which group human populations into 'races' on the basis of some biological signifier – for example, 'stock' – with each 'race' being regarded as having essential characteristics or a certain essential character (as in the phrase 'the British character', or in attributions to 'races' of 'laziness', 'rebelliousness', or 'industriousness') and where inferiorisation of some 'races' may or may not be present. Such views may be held with an admixture of others, in varying combinations of elements. They may shade off into what might more appropriately be called *ethnocentrism*, where ethnic groups are defined primarily in cultural terms and are regarded as having essential traits. Although overt inferiorisation may not be present, there is a tendency to view cultures from within the categories and frameworks of one ethnic group. *Nationalism* may thus be regarded as one form of ethnocentrism, in which cultural groups and their essential characteristics are defined by 'nationality' and the cultural attributes of one or more nations may be regarded as inherently superior or inferior. Nationalism may also contain *racial* elements in so far as particular nations may be regarded as deriving from specific racial stocks; and biologically defined communities may be regarded as the prime source of cultural characteristics.

This type of analytical framework posits a spectrum of views ranging from 'strong' versions of racism to 'weak' versions of ethnocentrism. It has a number of advantages. It recognises that most discourses, and especially individuals, are likely to express a complex combination of 'strong' and 'weak' racism and ethnocentrism (and nationalism), and that these may change in emphasis in different historical, institutional and interpersonal contexts. It has a theoretical structure which allows for the possibility of a variety of 'racisms', depending upon how various elements of 'race', 'ethnicity' and 'nationality' are combined, how they are articulated with other differentiations such as gender and class, and how they are related to theories in the natural and social sciences and notions in popular culture and 'common sense'. Also, by restricting itself to the realm of discourse, the definition leaves open the relationship between particular discourses, specific practices of discrimination and particular unequal or discriminatory outcomes (although bearing in mind that discourses themselves involve acts or practices of expression). *It clearly implies that racism and ethnocentrism are not necessarily confined to white groups.* And it should be added that some degree of ethnocentrism is likely to be endemic because all discourses and individuals necessarily have to use a language and categories. All enunciations have to be produced within particular discourses, and these are always liable to contain particular ethnicities and thus likely to position individuals in specific ethnic locations, often in taken for granted and deeply unconscious ways when considered in relation to individual subjectivity.

Moreover, in keeping with my earlier remarks, I would argue that racialised and ethnic discourses and encounters have a tendency to be contradictory and ambivalent in character. These internal complexities are contextually produced and differentially deployed in particular situations and institutional locations. Also, however, racialised and ethnic discourses and encounters are inevitably suffused with elements of sexual and class difference and therefore fractured and criss-crossed around a number of axes and identities.

The contradictoriness and ambivalence of racist discourses and interactions are produced by a complex combination of social and psychic structures and forces. For one thing, the sheer range and historical variation of the sites where encounters between 'white' and the 'other' have taken place and the immense variety of specialised and popular discourses that have operated in these encounters have by now put into circulation a multitude of selective 'images'. These operate as discursive resources to be drawn upon and articulated in different combinations in particular contexts, thus constantly opening up the possibility of tension, inconsistency and contradiction within and between sites. Sociologically, politically and educationally speaking, difficult but vital questions arise as to how and why particular images, labels, categories, anxieties, forms of rhetoric and practices come to be mobilised around specific sections of a population. How, for example, do various forms of racism, ethnocentrism and nationalism interact with discourses of gender, sexuality, class and generation to produce different stereotypes and practices in official policy programmes and popular culture around 'the Asian woman' or 'black youth'?

In explorations of the texture of racist discourses in recent years, the 'inner city' has been a prime site for investigation. Although the research into the complexities of urban power relations and conflicts over resources has produced important insights into the operation of complex rhetorics and categories of racialisation,[113] there has been a relative neglect of the general institutional and discursive form of the liberal-democratic, capitalist nation-state and its effects in the production of contradictory discourses around 'race'. That is, racist, ethnocentric and nationalist ideas, which attempt to create strict symbolic and institutional barriers between collectivities, have also to coexist and continually articulate with a variety of discourses and practices around meritocracy, equal opportunities and citizenship rights. This creates a multiplicity of axes for the production of possibly conflicting subject positions and potential practices and interactions.

Nevertheless, it is unlikely that the contradictions and ambivalences of stereotypes in general, and racist discourses in particular, can be fully understood without some conception of the operations of the unconscious and the dynamics of the 'psychic reality'. This therefore involves a difficult journey through psychoanalytic theories and categories. This is not the place to explain and justify different psychoanalytic accounts of the dynamics of identification, disavowal and ambivalence which characterise racist discourses. One way of viewing the significance of psychoanalytic theories is to conceptualise the unconscious as productive of 'irrationalities' and resistances which simultaneously organise and subvert the operations of conscious subjectivity,[114] hence their relevance for transforming the rationalism which underlies the pedagogies of both multiculturalist and antiracist educational practices. But their significance also needs to be grasped with respect to the operations of splitting, desire, fantasy, pleasure and paranoia which are deeply implicated in racist discourses, and which may inherently produce dualities and ambivalences in racialised encounters between selves and others. The pyschoanalytic-historical investigations of Gilman and Bhabha[115] provide contrasting routes into this terrain while the theoretical, historical and educational work of Philip Cohen, already referred to, constitutes the most significant intervention around antiracist education informed by both psychoanalytic and sociological understanding.

Having set out a critique of multicultural and antiracist conceptions of racism and elements of an alternative theorisation, it is time to turn to notions of 'culture' in multiculturalism and antiracism.

THE QUESTION OF CULTURE

Earlier in this article I have argued that the initial debates and policies which emerged in the wake of the growing black presence were characterised by various forms of cultural and ethnic essentialism or reductionism and that this trend still persists, for example in the way ethnic monitoring and other official knowledges are produced. Latter day multiculturalisms, to turn our attention back to them, have by no means overcome the weaknesses of earlier discourses and policy interventions despite the greater attention given to notions of cultural pluralism and diversity.[116] Several key problems can be identified. First, in occupying the terrain of 'prejudice', there continues – as in so many forms of antiracism – to be a fairly simplistic notion of how racism is culturally reproduced, or 'transmitted' as the preferred term has it. 'Prejudice acquisition' is ascribed to a process of acculturation or socialisation from family, peer groups, school curricula, the media, and so on.[117] Contradictory discourses and practices within and between these 'agencies of socialisation' are given little serious attention. Secondly, although the diverse bases of cultural differentiation – ethnicity, class, gender, region – are acknowledged, the primary emphasis in multiculturalist analysis is on ethnicity, such that economic and sexual differentiations within the minority communities, for example, continue to be ignored.[118]

However, thirdly, the focus on ethnicity as part of the discourse of cultural pluralism and diversity pays scant attention to the highly complex, contextually variable and economically and politically influenced drawing and redrawing of boundaries that takes place in encounters within the minority communities and in relation to white groups. There is little exploration of the sorts of processes and events reported in research in Manchester, and London,[119] for example, which documents the shifting forms of boundary maintenance, division and alliance that emerge in relation to local politics. To put it differently, sociologically speaking there can be no simple additive model of British cultural diversity as composed of a series of ethnic groups, as posited in the discourse of multiculturalism. This implies, in turn, that the foundations of the whole project of teaching about 'other cultures' need to be rethought. The shape and character of ethnic cultural formations is too complex to be reduced to formulas around festivals, religions, world-views and lifestyles. These fail to grapple with the shifting and kaleidoscopic nature of ethnic differentiations and identities and their relation to internal divisions of class and gender. Moreover, as I have remarked earlier, thinking around the question of what it means to 'understand' cultures has hardly begun in multiculturalism, although there is a wealth of material and debate in cultural studies, social anthropology and philosophy upon which to draw.[120] Definitions of culture are either not provided at all or conflate distinct conceptions such as symbolisation, ethnicity and lifestyle.[121]

One consequence of these lacunae in multiculturalist discourse has been a failure to confront issues of cultural *difference*. These are being obscured by what I have called the additive model of cultural diversity. The Rushdie scandal has exposed the weaknesses of any benign multiculturalism premised on the assumption of easy harmony and pluralism. The problem of epistemological and cultural relativism looms large here. Only recently has there been some serious debate within multiculturalism about the issues involved, although with very little guidance on how teachers are to approach and facilitate discussion around the inevitable questions which arise regarding the evaluation of different cultural representations, knowledges and practices.[122] And the debate is apt to collapse into a gross oversimplification of 'other' cultures, for example with regard to the differing positions and politics of girls and women in Muslim cultures.[123]

It might be thought that, given their aversion to the whole terrain of 'culture', antiracists are generally immune to the kinds of criticisms set out above. This is only partly true. Whereas multiculturalism often collapses analysis and prescription into some form of *ethnic* essentialism, in antiracism cultural essentialism emerges, ironically enough, partly out of the *denial* of ethnicity. Antiracists have tended to reify the notion of 'community', and, by focusing for understandable reasons on unitary conceptions of 'The Black Struggle', to marginalise issues of ethnic, class and gender differences in the black communities.[124] Partly influenced by the Black Power Movement in the US, the category 'black' became from the late 1960s an important focus, especially amongst left antiracists, for mobilising the growing communities of Afro-Caribbean and Asian descent. 'Black', here, denotes not simply an often successful political alliance against racism. It operates as a profoundly cultural category, an attempted representation of particular experiences and a particular construction of unity around those experiences.

The category had a profound influence on antiracist activists and intellectuals of British Afro-Caribbean, African and Asian descent, and it can still serve as a powerful descriptive and political signifier. But the cultural essentialism at its core has begun to disintegrate. In the first place, there has been what one might call an ethnic 'backlash' from British Asian and Afro-Caribbean communities. Some groups within both have protested at the homogenisation of different histories, cultures, 'needs', aspirations and trajectories of migration and settlement, implied in the use of the singular category. Secondly, it has become increasingly clear that the category can marginalise the racialisation of other British minorities. Turkish and Greek Cypriots, for example, Jewish people and the Irish, have been unable to find a voice within a political and cultural space marked out as 'black'. The category, in other words, functioned both to include and exclude: in so doing it tended not to engage with the *variety* of British racisms. It is true, of course, that the category never intended to deny the existence of other racisms, nor was it conceived as an all-encompassing identity that would make ethnicity invisible or irrelevant. Here its hegemony has been challenged by a third cultural and political thrust. A range of 'black' groups have begun to explore, construct and express identities and experiences not exhausted by the experience of and struggle against racism, or the polarisation between 'social democratic' and 'revolutionary' strategic positions. In this sense the growing dissolution of the category is also part of the collapse of older certainties and polarities of the British left and the emergence of concerns around *socialist* pluralism.[125] We now have in play what Stuart Hall in a seminal essay has dubbed the 'new ethnicities'. These are evident in the projects of a wide variety of film-makers, artists, novelists, poets and photographers, some of whom I have already referred to. In films such as *My Beautiful Laundrette, Passion of Remembrance*, and *Sammy and Rosie Get Laid*, or in the paintings of Sonia Boyce and others which formed part of *The Other Story* exhibition at the Hayward Gallery in 1989, complex intersections of sexuality, ethnicity and class are imaginatively constructed through representations which break decisively with the framework of positive and negative images.

There is emerging a new cultural politics of difference which overlays the older ethnic differences whose divisive effects antiracists have always, rightly, warned against. Neither the multiculturalist nor the antiracist movement in education has yet engaged with these 'new ethnicities'. Nor have they attempted to develop with students their potential for creative explorations of the shifting contours of black and white British cultural and political identities. The issues thrown up by these works are hardly remote from the lives of students. Many of them are engaging in their own complex negotiations and renegotiations around language and music, for example, borrowing elements from 'white', Afro-Caribbean and Asian forms and creating new syncretic versions.[127]

For these developments to be taken seriously, the multiculturalists will have to abandon their additive models of cultural pluralism and their continuing obsession with the 'old ethnicities'. Antiracists, on the other hand, will have to move beyond their reductive conceptions of culture and their fear of cultural difference as simply a source of division and weakness in the struggle against racism. They need to acknowledge the political significance of questions of national culture and ethnic identity, and to grasp how these intersect with questions of 'race' and racism. They will also have to work through the consequences of other British racisms, especially towards Jewish people and the Irish, and the realignment of older Western-Islamic polarities in the context of the Rushdie scandal.

Political and cultural questions of 'representation' were always implicit in the older conception of 'the black struggle'. Now they have to be reassessed in a context where older socialist and antiracist certainties no longer hold. We need to move beyond both multiculturalism and antiracism.

Conclusions

I have not provided a manifesto for this next phase in this article. I have merely tried to unravel what I take to be *some* of the main underlying oversimplifications which have informed educational practices in the field of 'race' and education, whether state-led or self-consciously oppositionist. *This does not imply, and should not be taken to mean, that everything being practised as multicultural and/or antiracist education in schools is worthless.* Much of that work should be defended against its attempted marginalisation by the Education Reform Act, the New Right and others. But we do ourselves no service if we neglect to ask fundamental, difficult questions about our understanding of some of the key issues, processes and terms involved; if we ignore contradictions in our underlying discourses; if we fail to grapple with the limitations of our assumptions about pedagogy and how subjects and subjectivities are formed; and if we fail to notice how economic, political and cultural differentiations are undermining older fixities around the ethnic, class and political identities of the minority communities. This was surely the lesson of the Macdonald Inquiry's critique of antiracist education at Burnage High School, and this is what I have tried to indicate through my critical interrogations of the theoretical and pedagogical foundations of multiculturalism and anti-racism – especially in relation to the multi-faceted nature of racism and the complexities of its intersection with gender and class.[128]

There is a need for the development of educational practices which will build on but move beyond existing multicultural and antiracist initiatives, by taking acount of contradiction and ambivalence in the operation of racism; these practices must avoid cultural and ethnic essentialisms and reductionism, grapple with the limitations of rationalist pedagogies (and rationalist assumptions about the translation of formal policies into practices) and engage with the 'new ethnicities' and other differentiations. This is going to be a long and difficult task. Difficult, in my view, but absolutely essential.

NOTES

I am indebted to Maud Blair, Peter Braham, Phil Cohen and James Donald for their comments on an earlier version of this essay.

1. I have generally used 'black' to signify British communities of Afro-Caribbean, African and Asian descent. Whether the category should continue to be used in this way is a question posed in a later section of this article.
2. An insider account of the politicking around the Rampton and Swann phases can be found in B. Parekh, 'Britain and the Social Logic of Pluralism', in B. Parekh (ed), 'The Hermeneutics of the Swann Report', in G. Verma (ed), *Education For All: A Landmark in Pluralism*, Falmer Press, Brighton 1989.
3. For example, T. Chivers (ed), *Race and Culture in Education*, NFER-Nelson, Windsor 1987.
4. Rt Hon Lord Scarman, *The Brixton Disorders, 10-12 April 1981*, HMSO, London 1981; *Scarman Report*, Penguin, Harmondsworth 1982.
5. Cited in Macdonald, Bhavnani, Khan and John, *Murder in the Play-ground*, Longsight Press, London 1989.
6. R. Honeyford, 'Multi-ethnic Intolerance', *Salisbury Review*, 4, 1983; 'Education and Race – An Alternative View, *Salisbury Review*, 6, 1984.
7. Media Research Group, *Media Coverage of London Councils*, Goldsmith's College, University of London, 1987.
8. Carter, Harris and Joshi, *The 1951-55 Conservative Government and Racialisation of Black Immigration*, Centre for Research in Ethnic Relations, University of Warwick, 1987.
9. J. Solomos, *Race and Racism in Contemporary Britain*, Macmillan, London 1989.

10. F. Reeves, *British Racial Discourse*, Cambridge University Press, 1983.
11. I. Grosvenor, 'Racialisation and the State', unpublished 1991.
12. S. Hall, *Education and the Crisis of the Urban School, Urban Education*, Block 1, Open University, Milton Keynes, 1974; C. Jones and K. Kimberley, 'Educational Responses to Racism' in J. Tierney (ed), *Race, Migration and Schooling*, Holt, Rhinehart and Winston, London 1981.
13. Department of Education and Science (DES), *English for Immigrants*, DES, London 1963.
14. Grosvenor, *op cit.*
15. E. Brittan, 'Multiracial Education 2: Teacher Opinion on Aspects of School Life', *Educational Research*, Vol 18, Nos 2, 3, 1976, pp 96-107, 182-92.
16. D. Kirp, *Doing Good by Doing Little*, University of California Press, London 1979, pp 69-103.
17. Redbridge Community Relations Council, *Cause for Concern: West Indian Pupils in Redbridge*, Redbridge CRC and Black Parents' Progressive Association, 1978.
18. B. Coard, *How the West Indian Child is Made Educationally Subnormal in the British School System*, New Beacon Books, London 1971.
19. For a useful review, see S. Tomlinson, *Ethnic Minorities in British Schools*, Heinemann, London 1983, pp 27-59.
20. For a more detailed discussion of the evidence, see B. Troyna, 'Fact or Artefact? The "Educational Underachievement" of Black Pupils', *British Journal of Sociology of Education*, Vol 5, No 2, 1984, and A. Rattansi, *'Race', Education and Inequality*, Unit 24, *Exploring Educational Issues* (E208), Open University, Milton Keynes 1989.
21. F. Reeves and M. Chevannes, 'The Underachievement of Rampton', *Multiracial Education*, Vol 12, No 1, 1981; Roberts, Duggan and Noble, 'Young, Black and Out of Work', in B. Troyna and D. Smith (eds), *Racism, School and the Labour Market*, National Youth Bureau, Leicester 1983.
22. G. Driver, *Beyond Underachievement*, Commission for Racial Equality, London 1977; M. Fuller, 'Young, Female and Black', in E. Cashmore and B. Troyna (eds), *Black Youth in Crisis*, Allen and Unwin, London 1982; M. Fuller, 'Qualified Criticism, Critical Qualifications', in L. Barton and S. Walker (eds), *Race, Class and Education*, Croom Helm, Beckenham 1983.
23. House of Commons, Home Affairs Select Committee, *Bangladeshis in Britain*, HMSO, London 1986.
24. Commission for Racial Equality, *Brick Lane and Beyond: an Inquiry into Racial Strife and Violence in Tower Hamlets,* CRE, London 1979; *Racial Harassment on Local Authority Housing Estates*, CRE, London 1981; and P. Gordon, *Racial Violence and Harassment*, Runnymede Research Report, London 1990.
25. The Rampton Report, *West Indian Children in Our Schools*, HMSO, London 1981, pp 15ff, 43.
26. On 'race' and moral panics, see Hall, Critcher, Jefferson, and Roberts,

Policing the Crisis, Macmillan, London 1978, pp 16-7.

27. Scarman, *op cit*, pp 24-5.

28. The Swann Report, *Education for All*, HMSO, London 1985.

29. ILEA, *Ethnic Background and Examination Results 1985 and 1986*, ILEA, London 1987.

30. *Ibid*, p 15.

31. *Ibid*, p 19.

32. *Cf*. P. Gilroy, *There Ain't No Black in the Union Jack*, Hutchinson, London 1987, and 'The End of Antiracism', in J. Donald and A. Rattansi (eds), *'Race', Culture, Difference*, Sage, London 1992.

33. 'Contradiction' here and elsewhere in the text is not *necessarily* being used in the strict philosophical sense of a logical contradiction. *Cf*. D. Goldberg, 'Racism and Irrationality: the need for a new critique', *Philosophy of the Social Sciences*, Vol 20, No 3, 1990.

34. A. Brah and R. Minhas, 'Structural Racism or Cultural Difference? Schooling for Asian Girls' in G. Weiner (ed), *Just a Bunch of Girls*, Open University Press, Milton Keynes 1986.

35. J. Rex, 'West Indian and Asian Youth', in Cashmore and Troyna, *op cit*, p 61.

36. Cashmore and Troyna, 'Black Youth in Crisis', in Cashmore and Troyna, *op cit*, pp 18, 33.

37. A. Phoenix, 'The Afro-Caribbean Myth', *New Society*, 4.3.1988.

38. See, for instance, F. Anthias and N. Yuval-Davis, 'Contextualising Feminism – Gender, Ethnic and Class Divisions', *Feminist Review*, No 15, 1982; A. Phizacklea (ed), *One Way Ticket: Migration and Female Labour*, Routledge and Kegan Paul, London 1983; S. Westwood, *All Day, Every Day: Factory and Family in the Making of Women's Lives*, Pluto Press, London 1985; S. Westwood and P. Bhachu (eds), *Enterprising Women: Ethnicity, Economy and Gender Relations*, Routledge, London, 1988; C. Ramazanoglu, *Feminism and the Contradictions of Oppression*, Routledge, London 1989.

39. See for instance, M. Fuller, 'Young, Female and Black' in Cashmore and Troyna, *op cit*; J. Rex, *op cit*; K. Riley, 'Black Girls Speak for Themselves', in G. Weiner, *op cit*; M. Mac an Ghail, *Young, Gifted and Black*, Open University Press, Milton Keynes, 1988.

40. Fuller, *op cit*; Brah and Minhas, *op cit*; Mac an Ghail, *op cit*.

41. The general conceptualisation here is adapted from Foucault, articulating his earlier work on discourses and discursive formations in *The Archaeology of Knowledge* to his later investigations into the operations of power and knowledge in *Discipline and Punish*, *Power/Knowledge* and elsewhere. For the influence of Foucault in the fields of 'race', and education, see *inter alia*, D. Goldberg, 'The social formation of racist discourse' in D. Goldberg (ed), *Anatomy of Racism*, University of Minneapolis Press 1990; S Ball (ed), *Foucault and Education: Disciplines and Knowledge*, Routledge, London 1990.

42. Commission for Racial Equality, *Learning in Terror*, CRE, London 1988; for other accounts see, E. Kelly and T. Cohn, *Racism in Schools: New Research Evidence*, Trentham Books, Stoke on Trent 1988; Akhtar and Stronach, ' "They call me blacky": a story of everyday racism in primary schools', *Times Educational Supplement*, 19.9.1986; and *Swann Report, op cit*, pp 31-5.

43. E. Pilkington, 'Dilemma of the Gauntlet of Hate', *Education Guardian*, 18.12.1990.

44. P. Gordon, *op cit*.

45. See, for instance, Wright's chapter in J. Eggleston, D. Dunn, M. Anjali, and C. Wright, *Education for Some*, Trentham Books, Stoke on Trent 1986; and Macdonald *et al, op cit*, pp 140-2.

46. *Guardian*, 5.4.1988, reprinted in Rattansi, 1989, *op cit*.

47. Macdonald *et al, op cit*, pp 140-1.

48. Eggleston *et al, op cit*.

49. See also C. Wright, 'Black Students – White Teachers', in B. Troyna, *Racial Inequality in Education*, Allen and Unwin, London 1987.

50. B. Carrington, 'Sport as a Side-Track' in Barton and Walker, *op cit*, Croom Helm, Beckenham 1983.

51. J. Wrench, 'The Unfinished Bridge: YTS and Black Youth', in Troyna 1987, *op cit*; and 'New Vocationalism, Old Racism and the Careers Service', in P. Braham, A. Rattansi and R. Skellington (eds), *Racism and Antiracism: Inequalities, Opportunities and Policies*, Sage, London 1992.

52. A. Rattansi, *Black Girls in Search of Learning*, Television 13, *Exploring Educational Issues* (E208), Open University, Milton Keynes 1989; and G. Viswanathan, 'The Beginnings of English Literary Study in India,' *Oxford Literary Review*, vol 9, 1987.

53. On exclusion, stereotypification and marginalisation, see D. Mackenzie, *Propaganda and Empire*, Manchester University Press, 1984, and D. Mackenzie (ed), *Imperialism and Popular Culture*, Manchester University Press, 1986; G Klein, *Reading Into Racism*, Routledge and Kegan Paul, London 1985; J. Ahier, *Industry, Children and the Nation: An Analysis of National Identity in School Textbooks*, Falmer Press, Brighton 1988; on mass media representation see Hartmann and Husband, *Racism and the Mass Media*, Davis-Poynter, London 1974; S. Hall, 'The Whites of their Eyes: Racist Ideologies and the Media', in G. Bridges and R. Brunt (eds), *Silver Linings*, Lawrence and Wishart, London 1981; G. Murdock, 'Reporting the Riots', in J. Benyon (ed), *Scarman and After*, Pergamon, Oxford 1984.

54. A. Dorn, 'Education and the Race Relations Act', in M. Arnot (ed), *Race and Gender: Equal Opportunities Policies in Education*, Pergamon, Oxford 1985.

55. See the accounts of black teachers at Burnage in Macdonald *et al, op cit*, pp 215-44.

56. See, for instance, P. Dodgson and D. Stewart, 'Multiculturalism or

Anti-Racist Teaching: A Question of Alternatives', *Multiracial Teaching*, Vol 9, No 3, 1981; C. Mullard, *Antiracist Education: The Three O's*, National Association for Multiracial Education, London 1984; B. Troyna, 'Beyond Multiculturalism: towards the enactment of anti-racist education in policy, provision and pedagogy', *Oxford Review of Education*, Vol 13, No 3, 1987; D. Gill and E. Singh, 'Multicultural versus Anti-Racist Science', in D. Gill and L. Levidow (eds), *Anti-Racist Science Teaching*, Free Association Books, London 1987.

57. See, for example, A. Bonnet, 'Anti-racism as a Radical Educational Ideology in London and Tyneside', *Oxford Review of Education*, vol 16, 1990.

58. J. Lynch, *Multicultural Education*, Routledge and Kegan Paul, 1986.

59. Cf J. Lynch, 'Cultural Pluralism, Structural Pluralism and the United Kingdom', in B. Parekh (ed), *Britain: A Plural Society*, Commission for Racial Equality, London 1990.

60. See, for instance, J. Twitchin and C. Demuth, *Multi-cultural Education: Views from the classroom*, BBC, 2nd ed., London 1985, p 170; and E. Aronson, *The Social Animal*, W.H. Freeman, 3rd ed., San Francisco 1980.

61. E. Brittan, *op cit*.

62. M. Billig and R. Cochrane, 'I'm not National Front, but . . .', *New Society*, 68, 1984.

63. Macdonald *et al*, *op cit*, p 8.

64. P. Cohen, 'The Cultural Geography of Adolescent Racism', Centre for Multicultural Education, University of London Institute of Education, 1989.

65. F. Coffield, C. Borrill and S. Marshall, *Growing Up at the Margins*, Open University, Milton Keynes 1986.

66. M. Billig, *Fascists: A Social Psychological View of the National Front*, Harcourt, Brace, Jovanovitch, London 1978.

67. D. Wellman, *Portraits of White Racism*, Cambridge University Press, London 1977.

68. J. Wetherell and M. Potter, 'Discourse Analysis and the Identification of Interpretative Repertoires', in C. Antaki (ed), *Analysing Everyday Explanation*, Sage, London 1988.

69. R. Jenkins, *Racism and Recruitment*, Cambridge University Press, Cambridge 1986; and 'Black Workers in the Labour Market', in Braham *et al*, *op cit*.

70. S. Jones, *Black Culture, White Youth*, Macmillan, London 1986.

71. S. Westwood, 'Racism, Black Masculinity and the Politics of Space', in J. Hearn and D. Morgan (eds), *Men, Masculinities and Social Theory*, Unwin Hyman, London 1990.

72. P. Cohen, *Racism and Popular Culture*, Centre for Multicultural Education, University of London Institute of Education, 1987.

73. P. Willis, *Learning to Labour*, Saxon House, Farnborough 1978.

74. See P. Nanton and M. Fitzgerald, 'Race Policies in Local Government:

Boundaries or Thresholds?', in W. Ball and J. Solomos (eds), *Race and Local Politics*, Macmillan, London 1990.

75. Cohen 1987, *op cit*.

76. See Mac an Ghail, 'Coming of Age in 1980s England: Reconceptualising Black Students' Schooling Experience', *British Journal of Sociology of Education*, Vol 10, No 3, 1989 and P. Foster, *Policy and Practice in Multicultural and Anti-Racist Education*, Routledge, London 1990.

77. A.M. Wolpe, *Within School Walls: The Role of Sexuality, Discipline and the Curriculum*, Routledge, London 1989.

78. See Jones and Moore, 'The Curriculum and the Subject: Construction and Constraint'; V. Walkerdine, *Schoolgirl Fictions*, Verso, London 1991.

79. 'Rationality' and 'irrationality' can function within discussions of 'race' in quite different ways (see Goldberg, 'Racism and irrationality: the need for a new critique', *Philosophy of the Social Sciences*, Vol 20, No 3, 1990). In the present essay 'irrationality' is being used primarily, as in the psychological and educational literature under discussion, to *open up* the area of 'resistances' to discourses which challenge an individual's rhetorics with regard to 'race'. However, as will become apparent later, I give the concept post-structuralist and psychoanalytic inflections by insisting upon the inherently contradictory nature of identities, thus problematizing any easy division between rationality and irrationality either at the level of individuals or discourses. Goldberg accomplishes a parallel task, deploying the conceptual apparatus of analytical philosophy. It is likely that future theoretical work will have to break from the problematic of the rational/ irrational divide within which the present discussion has been circumscribed by the need to challenge conventional theories of prejudice and racism and by the allusion to a particular understanding of psychoanalysis. The critique of rationalism implied in this essay intersects with the postmodernist reassessment of the Enlightenment project; cf. R. Boyne and A. Rattansi (eds), *Postmodernism and Society*, Macmillan, London 1990.

80. Aronson, *op cit*, p 201.

81. See Adorno, Frenkel-Brunswick, Levinson and Sanford, *The Authoritarian Personality*, Harper, New York, 1950; C. Bagley and G. Verma, *Racial Prejudice, the Individual and Society*, Saxon House, Farnborough 1979; and Aronson, *op cit*.

82. J. Lynch, 1986, *op cit*, and 1987, *op cit*.

83. B. Troyna, 1987, *op cit*.

84. C. Burgess, 'Tackling Racism and Sexism in the Primary Classroom' in D. Gill, B. Mayor and M. Blair (eds), *Racism and Education: Structures and Strategies*, Sage, London 1992; J Nixon, *A Teacher's Guide to Multicultural Education*, Blackwell, Oxford 1985.

85. See, for instance, Institute of Race Relations, *The Roots of Racism*, IRR, London 1982; R. Hatcher and J. Shallice, 'The Politics of Anti-Racist Education', *Multiracial Education*, Vol 12, No 1, 1983. Mullard, *op cit*; A.

Sivanandan, 'RAT and the Degradation of Black Struggle', *Race and Class*, Vol 26, No 4, 1985; Sarup, *op cit*; Troyna, 1987, *op cit*; Gill and Singh, *op cit*.

86. S. Gilman, *Difference and Pathology: Stereotypes of Sexuality, Race and Madness*, Cornell University Press, Ithaca 1985, and 'Black Bodies, White Bodies: Towards an Iconography of Female Sexuality in late 19th Art, Medicine and Literature', in Donald and Rattansi, *op cit*; P. Cohen, 'The Perversions of Inheritance: Studies in the Making of Multi-racist Britain', in P. Cohen and H. Bains (eds), *Multi-Racist Britain*, Macmillan, London, 1988; A. Rattansi, *The Question of Racism*, Course introduction, *'Race', Education and British Society*, Open University, Milton Keynes 1992.

87. For example, A. Brah and R. Deem, 'Towards Anti-sexist and Anti-Racist Schooling', *Critical Social Policy*, Vol 6, No 1, 1986.

88. For example, Walkerdine, *op cit*.

89. P. Cohen, 1987, *op cit*, 1988, *op cit*, and *The Making of the Indian Cowgirl Warrior*, Centre for Multicultural Education, University of London Institute of Education, 1989; and 'It's Racism What Dunnit', in Donald and Rattansi, *op cit*.

90. A. Sivanandan, *Race, Class and the State*, IRR, London 1974; 1985, *op cit*.

91. See for example, J. Gabriel and G. Ben-Tovim, 'Marxism and the Concept of Racism', *Economy and Society*, Vol 7, No 2, 1978; Hall, 'Race, Articulation and Societies Structured in Dominance,' in Unesco, *Sociological Theories: Race and Colonialism*, Unesco, Paris 1980.

92. Sarup, *op. cit.* pp 40, 95-8.

93. Troyna, 1987, *op cit*.

94. Hatcher and Shallice, *op cit*.

95. Phizacklea and Miles, 'Working-class Racist Beliefs in the Inner City', in R. Miles and A. Phizacklea (eds), *Racism and Political Action in Britain*, Routledge and Kegan Paul, London 1979; and *Labour and Racism*, Routledge and Kegan Paul, London 1980.

96. Phizacklea and Miles, 1979, *op cit*, p 118.

97. *Ibid*, p 120.

98. Hatcher and Shallice, *op cit*, pp 8-10; *cf*, Troyna, 1987, *op cit*, p 316 for a similarly misleading rendering of Billig and Cochrane' research.

99. For a contrasting discussion, see Cohen, 1988, *op cit*.

100. Such resistances are themselves coded and recoded around 'race', class and gender, with shifting alliances between black and white girls and boys depending upon the nature of the antiracist (or antisexist) initiative and the 'race' and sex of the teacher; *cf*, Cohen 1987, *op cit*.

101. B. Troyna and B. Carrington, *Education, Racism and Reform*, Routledge, London 1990.

102. Troyna's co-author, Carrington, has recently proposed that antiracist work be based on Festinger's conception of the *inability* of individuals to tolerate ambiguity and contradiction (Carrington and Short, 'Policy or Presentation': The Psychology of Anti-Racism Education, *New Community*, 1989). This is very different, almost the opposite of the conception

of contradictions and ambivalence proposed in this article. For a critique of Festinger from a perspective much closer to mine see Billig, *Ideology and Social Psychology*, Blackwell, Oxford 1982; see also J. Wetherell and M. Potter, *Discourse and Social Psychology*, Sage, London 1987; J. Henriques, W. Holloway, C. Urwin, C. Venn and V. Walkerdine, *Changing the Subject*, Methuen, London 1986; and the writings of Wallman, Hall and Bhabha referred to in the text.

103. Troyna and Carrington, *op cit*, pp 114-9.

104. R. Jeffcoate, *Positive Image*, Writers and Readers, London 1979; Hatcher and Shallice, *op cit*, p 10.

105. Mackenzie, 1984, *op cit* and 1986, *op cit*; G. Klein, *Reading into Racism*, Routledge, London 1985.

106. D.A. Bailey, 'Re-Thinking Black Representations', *Ten-8*, No 31, 1988; K. Mercer (ed), *Black Film/British Cinema*, Institute of Contemporary Arts, London 1988; P. Gilroy, *There Ain't No Black in the Union Jack*, Hutchinson, London 1987, and 'The End of Antiracism', in Donald and Rattansi, *op cit*; R. Araeen, *The Other Story: Afro-Asian Artists in Post-War Britain*, Hayward Gallery, London 1989.

107. M. Alvarado and B. Ferguson, 'The Curriculum, Media Studies and Discursivity', *Screen*, Vol 24, No 3, 1983; P. Wexler, *Social Analysis of Education: After the New Sociology*, Routledge and Kegan Paul, London 1987.

108. Troyna and Carrington, *op cit*.

109. See, for a contrary analysis, Ahier, *op cit*.

110. B. Troyna and J. Williams, *Racism, Education and the State*, Croom Helm, Beckenham 1986; see also D. Mason, 'After Scarman: a Note on the Concept of "Institutional racism" ', *New Community*, Vol 10, No 1, 1982.

111. A. Flew, *Education, Race and Revolution*, Centre for Policy Studies, London 1984.

112. Cf Rattansi, 1992, *op cit*.

113. D. Wellman, *op cit*.

114. I. Craib, *Psychoanalysis and Social Theory*, Harvester Wheatsheaf, Hemel Hempstead 1989.

115. Gilman 1985, *op cit* and 1992 *op cit*; Bhabha, 'The Other Question', *Screen*, Vol 24, 1983; and 'Of Mimicry and Man: the Ambivalence of Colonial Discourse', in J. Donald and S. Hall (eds), *Politics and Ideology*, Open University Press, Milton Keynes 1986.

116. Cf Parekh (ed), *Britain: A Plural Society*, Commission for Racial Equality, London 1989.

117. J. Lynch, *Prejudice Reduction and the Schools*, Cassell, London 1987.

118. Lynch, *op cit*, 1986; B. Parekh, 'The concept of multicultural education' in Modgil, Verma, Mallick and Modgil (eds), *Multicultural Education: The Interminable Debate*, Falmer Press, Lewes 1986, and 'Britain and the social logic of pluralism' in Parekh, 1989 *op cit*; G. Verma, 'Pluralism: Some Theoretical and Practical Considerations', in B. Parekh, 1989, *op cit*.

119. R. Ward, 'Where Race Didn't Divide: Some Reflections on Slum Clearance in Moss Side', in R. Miles and A. Phizacklea (eds), *Racism and Political Action in Britain*, Routledge and Kegan Paul, London 1979; and S. Wallman, 'Ethnicity and the Boundary Process in Context', in J. Rex and D. Mason (eds), *Theories of Race and Ethnic Relations*, Cambridge University Press, London 1979.

120. C. Geertz, *The Interpretation of Cultures*, Basic Books, New York 1973, and *Local Knowledge*, Basic Books, New York 1983; J. Clifford and C. Marcus (eds), *Writing Culture: The Poetics and Politics of Ethnography*, University of California Press, Berkeley 1986.

121. See the contributions of Lynch and Verma to Parekh, 1989, op cit.

122. See the special issues of the *Journal of Moral Education*, 1986.

123. Troyna and Carrington, *op cit*, 1987.

124. For a much more sophisticated analysis of ethnicity and community politics, see J. Eade, *The Politics of the Community: The Bangladeshi Community in East London*, Avebury/Gower, Aldershot 1989.

125. M. Rustin, *For a Pluralist Socialism*, Verso, London 1985; J. Keane, *Democracy and Civil Society*, Verso, London 1988.

126. S. Hall, 'The New Ethnicities' in Mercer (ed), *Black Film/British Cinema*, ICA, London 1988, and 'The New Ethnicities' in Donald and Rattansi (eds), *'Race', Culture, Difference*, Sage, London 1992.

127. Jones, 1988, *op cit*; R. Hewitt, *White Talk – Black Talk: inter-racial friendship and communication among adolescents*, Cambridge University Press, 1986; Gilroy, 1987, *op cit*.

128. See also P. Cohen and A. Rattansi, *Rethinking Racism and Antiracism*, Runnymede Trust, London 1992.

Lessons from Radical Curriculum Initiatives: Integrated Humanities and World Studies

Geoff Whitty

It is nowadays commonplace to remark that one of the limitations of the comprehensive secondary school movement in England was its concentration on organisational matters rather than on the nature of the curriculum and pedagogy that was to go on in the reorganised schools. In other words, it had no clearly articulated concept of a comprehensive school curriculum. Whereas forms of progressive primary school practice, for all their weaknesses, became associated in many people's minds with that of the sector as a whole, no such distinctive ideology could be discerned developing in the newly emergent secondary comprehensive schools. Instead, reorganised secondary schools in the 1960s usually brought together remnants of the grammar, technical and secondary school traditions, with the grammar school tradition dominant in most cases. Only a very few schools, often those starting from scratch on greenfield sites, attempted to develop entirely new curricular models on the basis of their appropriateness to the comprehensive school mission.[1] In the context of the present volume, it is interesting to note that many of those involved in such efforts were associated with *Forum* (with which Brian Simon was centrally involved) and that there was something of a concentration of innovative schools in Leicestershire.

In view of the concerns of the comprehensive school movement with the maximisation of working-class talent, as well as with the realisation of social justice, it now seems strange that relatively little attention was paid to curricular issues, particularly amongst the labour movement as a whole. Raymond Williams' notion of the English school curriculum as a compromise between the old humanists, the industrial trainers and the public educators might have led one to expect that the success of the comprehensive school movement would provide the ideal context in which to realise a public educators' model of the curriculum at the expense of those of the old humanists and the industrial trainers. Indeed, sociological critiques of the old humanist curriculum as elitist and based upon a class-biased selection from culture, and of the industrial trainers' curriculum as narrowly instrumental and designed to produce uncritical factory fodder, were becoming fashionable within educational circles at the very time when comprehensive reorganisation was at its peak.

It could not, of course, be expected that the cultural forces that had denied parity of esteem to secondary modern and technical school curricula under the tripartite system would suddenly be transformed by comprehensive reorganisation. This was especially the case for as long as we were only 'half-way there' and comprehensive schools were being judged almost entirely in terms of their capacity to do as well as, or better than, the grammar schools on the latter's own terms.[2] The lack of a distinctive new approach across the system as a whole was also partly the result of the commitment of many of the groups constituting the public education lobby to allowing professional educators to make decisions in the 'secret garden' of the school curriculum. Despite its sponsorship of some important national curriculum development projects, the Schools' Council was constitutionally ill-suited to the advocacy of a particular curriculum model. For example, the legitimate concern of the teacher trade unions to defend their members' individual professional autonomy made it difficult for them to develop and mobilise around a specific alternative to contest both the culturally embedded assumptions of the old humanist model or the sporadic efforts by the industry lobby to challenge the hegemony of the grammar school curriculum.[3] This was particularly evident during the Great Debate of the mid-1970s when the left found itself in disarray after Callaghan's invasion of the 'secret garden', apparently on behalf of the industrial trainers.

There was already disarray amongst left educationists who might, in other circumstances, have been actively involved in developing alternative curriculum models in conjunction with the broader labour movement. A debate about the extent to which knowledge was socially constructed had developed in the early 1970s out of the new sociology of education's apparent advocacy of cultural relativism.[4] Materialist critiques of the subjective idealism of their theoretical position, and a political concern that working-class pupils might be denied access to high status knowledge and/or powerful ideas by the suggestion that all forms of knowledge were of equal value,[5] made it appear that many on the traditional left supported the adoption of a very conventional grammar school curriculum in comprehensive schools. Yet, as Williams had argued in *The Long Revolution*, first published in 1961, 'it is difficult to feel that the present grammar-school curriculum . . . is of such a kind that the problem is merely one of distributing it more widely.'[6]

Part of the problem, as I have argued elsewhere, lies in the polarity that has developed between academic and prevocational conceptions of the curriculum.[7] Academic subjects are seen to embody rigour, while a concern with relevance has tended to be restricted to those pupils perceived as unable to cope with the high-status curriculum. Yet, if young people are to engage critically with the world outside the school, the curriculum for all pupils needs to combine rigour with relevance. One solution has been seen in various forms of integrated curricula which break down the barriers both between traditional school subjects and between school and the world outside. In that context, it is often easier for ideas to be both meaningful to a wide range of pupils and critical in their purchase on social reality.[8] Denis Warwick suggests that the work of the new sociologists of education was explicitly intended to provide theoretical support for the growing 'movement for a progressive curriculum based in the concept of integration'.[9] Yet, in retrospect, it was perhaps that very connection with the new sociology of education that led to suspicion of new curriculum models by people on the left who one would not have expected to find defending traditional models of practice.

There were though, as David Halpin points out, some attempts to think the problems through further.[10] Denis Lawton tried to steer a middle path and translate it into a broad 'common culture' curriculum model for comprehensive schools, which was implemented by Maurice Holt at Sheredes School in Hertfordshire.[11] Holt himself went on to advocate a common curriculum for the comprehensive school.[12] David Hargreaves saw the curriculum issue as part of the 'challenge for the comprehensive school' and this presumably informed his later work at the Inner London Education Authority.[13] Yet, for the most part, the advocacy and implementation of new curriculum models was left to individual enthusiasts. They were neither developed in collaboration with, nor enthusiastically adopted by, the labour movement or any of its associated political parties. Indeed, the latter have sometimes seemed more attracted to the old humanist and industrial trainer models of the curriculum than to the 'progressive' alternatives proposed by professional educationists. Furthermore, the divorce of progressive initiatives from the experience of the 'popular constituencies' has subsequently been seen as one of the reasons why Thatcherism was able to attack them so successfully.[14]

For all these reasons, and no doubt many more, there has been a lack of collective thinking about an appropriate curriculum for comprehensive secondary schools. However, some of these same factors, particularly the degree of professional autonomy maintained within the system prior to the introduction of the National Curriculum, can also be seen to have permitted the development of innovative curricula in particular schools, subjects and localities. Similarly, some teachers were able to adapt the old humanist and industrial trainer models in strikingly creative ways or to exploit the tensions between them. Some of these innovations were regarded, either by their advocates or critics – or indeed both – as radical initiatives linked to the political aspirations of the left. It is to a consideration of the nature of some of these initiatives that we now turn, before considering their legacy and their implications for a future strategy. The two initiatives that I will explore here – integrated humanities and peace education/world studies – can both be considered as professional 'movements' and, although heavily influenced by individual enthusiasts, they grew well beyond innovations in isolated school classrooms. They have both been seen by some of their advocates as being radical, not only in the sense of challenging prevailing conceptions of the school curriculum but also for their potential contribution to the creation of a more just society. They have also both been condemned by the New Right as examples of a pervasive left-wing bias within state education.[15]

It is, however, important to stress from the outset that neither of these initiative is synonomous with what is sometimes called 'radical education'. Nevertheless, they are both contexts within which work informed by what might broadly be termed leftist ideals has been able to flourish. This is partly because, being less hidebound by tradition than conventional curricular subjects, both their content and their pedagogic form has tended to be more 'negotiable'. This does not mean that they were simply colonised by socialist educators, but they were fields in which contestation of the terrain brought significant changes into some schools, even if to a lesser extent than their enthusiasts and their critics have sometimes suggested. In *Developments in Social Studies Teaching* and in *Sociology and School Knowledge*, I discussed the radical potential of developments in social and political education in the 1970s and early 1980s.[16] While recognising the liberal origins of both the integrated humanities and the political literacy movement, I argued that they provided opportunities for an approach to education that combined rigour and relevance and thus provided the sort of meaningful and critical education that the left should be striving for. I also suggested that their radical potential was inhibited by their isolation from the political movements of the left and the lack of interest those movements appeared to show in them.

In this chapter, I want to consider the subsequent fate of integrated humanities and more recent approaches to political education. Reflecting upon political education in the mid-1980s, Lister concluded somewhat optimistically that political literacy education had gained legitimation and that over half our schools were offering their students 'some kind of direct political education'.[17] However, he now saw the dynamic for political education coming from what he called 'the new movements'. These included peace education, human rights education and environmental education of the ecological variety, while world studies sought to embrace them all.

INTEGRATED HUMANITIES

In discussing integrated humanities, I shall limit consideration to the way in which a movement whose influence had hitherto been largely confined to the low-status parts of the curriculum sought to take advantage of broader changes in education to enhance its own position. In doing so, I will draw largely upon the experience of the attempt to establish a Mode 1 syllabus in integrated humanities in the Southern Examining Group, one of the five examining consortia established in the early 1980s to plan for the common system of examinations at 16-plus, which eventually became the General Certificate of Secondary Education (GCSE). I shall point to the limitations of a strategy that sought to avoid confronting the question of what counts as legitimate knowledge by emphasising curriculum form at the expense of content and by leaving decisions about content almost entirely in the hands of teachers.

I have suggested elsewhere that, by the late 1970s, the movement that had led to a growth of teacher-designed Mode 3 syllabuses in integrated humanities in the late 1960s and early 1970s had gone into decline.[18] Although individual enthusiasts persuaded the Southern Examining Group to consider the need for a broadly based integrated humanities course, as well as single subject humanities courses, within the new 16-plus examination, there was little broader enthusiasm for the idea. Indeed, when the panel established to consider the matter first advocated the inclusion of humanities as an examination subject in the Group's offerings at sixteen plus, there was considerable scepticism on the part of members of the Group's senior (and subject-dominated) committees about both the necessity and the desirability of making such provision. There was also criticism of some of the more radical features of the panel's proposals, particularly the lack of prescribed syllabus content and the absence of a terminal examination. At that stage, it appeared that the old humanists, as represented by the traditions of the GCE boards and the universities, were still firmly in control of the new system, even if now working within a state-imposed framework.

However, by the time the panel resubmitted its proposals in the mid-1980s, incorporating a number of concessions to the traditionalists, the situation appeared to have changed. There was a growing enthusiasm for integrated humanities as part of the solution to an 'over-crowded' curriculum. Part of the explanation lay, of course, in falling rolls, with the ensuing difficulties they presented for schools trying to maintain a full range of curriculum subjects, especially where option choices were involved. However, alongside pressures for curriculum contraction, there were also pressures for curriculum expansion, especially as government and the public placed new demands on schools. Although teachers of most individual subjects were adept at arguing that their own subjects were ideally placed to meet all such demands,[19] others argued that they could be met far more coherently within core humanities provision. In this situation, enthusiasts were able to argue that the advantage of humanities providing that core was that it could treat these issues in a systematic rather than an ad hoc manner and that it could combine a concern with social relevance with a commitment to academic rigour. Thus, for example, it could respond positively to demands that education should pay more attention to the world of work by encouraging pupils to explore actively the world outside school, but it would do so using the tools of critical analysis. For teachers on the left, this was certainly preferable to the sort of low-status citizenship or social education course that merely inducted pupils uncritically into the labour market.

Thus, when the final proposals of the panel (by then reconstituted as a subject working party) were accepted in June 1986, it had been able to take advantage of a climate that had substantially changed. There was a general recognition in the Group that it needed an integrated humanities syllabus, if it was to meet the needs of schools in 1990s. Furthermore, the working party was positively encouraged towards the end of its deliberations to reinstate some of the more radical elements of the proposal (such as 100 per cent school-based assessment within a Mode 1 syllabus) to give schools that very flexibility which, in the early days, had been seen not only as unnecessary, but even as positively dangerous.

This was a quite fascinating development in view of the extent to which the universities and GCE boards had imposed conventional models of syllabus development and assessment on the GCSE Groups in the early days of their existence. Here though was that reopening of the issues that *Sociology and School Knowledge* had predicted would take place once ministers and the industrial lobby recognised the extent to which the academic model of education had yet again prevailed, despite attempts in the Great Debate and its aftermath to enhance the status of prevocational approaches to education.[20] In the meantime, we had seen both the emergence of the Technical and Vocational Education Initiative (TVEI) and Sir Keith Joseph's Sheffield speech[21] and these appeared to have had a discernible effect on the climate of opinion within the Southern Examining Group. Significantly, it was TVEI schools and co-ordinators who were particularly vocal in urging the Group to accept its working party's proposals on integrated humanities. Although their motives for wanting more flexible curriculum structures or more emphasis on experiential learning were by no means identical to those of the working party, it was clear that the old humanists were no longer an absolute bar to the sorts of innovations the working party was seeking. This is not to say that the industrial trainers were in control either, but that some of the tensions between the original GCSE settlement and the rise of the 'new vocationalism'[22] were already in evidence. The educational manifestations of this new vocationalism, such as TVEI, often reflected what Ball has called a 'vocational progressivism' which supports approaches to curriculum, assessment and pedagogy closer to those of integrated humanities than those of the traditional grammar school curriculum.[23]

When support for integrated humanities from this quarter combined with other proposals pointing in similar directions, such as those for modularised curricula contained in the Hargreaves Report, it appeared for a time that a serious challenge to conventional curricular arrangements could at last be mounted.[24] A long-standing advocate of integrated humanities, Doug Holly, acknowledged at that time that those who tried to foster a radical version of integrated humanities in such circumstances might be accused of 'opportunism'.[25] He, however, preferred the term 'pragmatism', the difference being that, while opportunism made use of circumstances to advance selfish ends, pragmatism reacted to circumstances by turning them to the general advantage, This, he argued was the 'positive reaction of principled realists'.

The proposal which was accepted by the Southern Examining Group was one of three which were made available to candidates in the early years of GCSE. The other two were developed by the Midlands Examining Group and the Northern Examination Association. The schemes differed in a number of respects but also had common features. The Southern Examining Group's syllabus embraced particularly broad aims including

> an understanding of human societies . . . and the range of personal futures in a world of rapid technological and cultural change; an awareness of the meaning and diversity of human values . . . and preparation for responsible participation in a multi-cultural society; social, economic and political literacy . . . at individual, community, national and global levels; and active and collaborative involvement in the learning process.

The syllabus was largely skills-based, these skills covering understanding, enquiry, analysis and evaluation, and communication. Pupils were required to develop these skills via the study of five themes for single certification or ten for double certification. Examples of possible themes, rather than prescribed content, were listed in the syllabus, as follows:

Community and Environment	People and Work
Urbanisation	Recreation and Conservation
Peace and Conflict	Beliefs and Values
Environmental Management	World Interdependence
The Impact of Technology	Race and Culture
Human Rights	Unity and Division

Teachers were free to propose quite different alternatives, though the syllabus required them to demonstrate how they intended to structure their proposed subject matter in terms of certain *key concepts* and *key contexts*. These were as follows:

Required Contextual Levels	*Required Conceptual Areas*
Individual	Power and Distribution

Community and Local Environment	Ideas and Ideologies
National	Spatial Interaction
Global and International	Continuity and Change

There was therefore some degree of prescription in that, for example, the combination of required concepts and contexts in this particular syllabus made it likely that pupils would have to confront global issues far more consistently and coherently than in most conventional combinations of single-subject options. Furthermore, if the working party's hope that integrated humanities would become core provision for all pupils were actually to be realised, the application of knowledge to social issues would be far more likely to be a feature of the curriculum for pupils of all abilities than it ever has been in the past.

However, the fact that the syllabus was a framework, which allowed considerable room for the negotiation of content, proved to be as much a weakness as a strength. While the structure enabled both radical educators and TVEI-enthusiasts to use it to mount innovative courses, the content of these varied considerably and there was no agreed programme of study around which they could unite. Even before the National Curriculum was to make this a major issue, integrated humanities (including the Southern Examining Group's syllabus) had been attacked as being both intellectually vacuous and politically biased by members of the New Right. The first charge presumably arose from its lack of specified content and the second from the particular content that some teachers chose to teach within the overall framework. Furthermore the emphasis on practical skills and training for life was seen as part of a 'progressive egalitarian ideology' posing a severe threat to 'real education'. Those members of the New Right whom Ball has termed the 'cultural restorationists' were particularly alarmed by what was seen as a coming together of radical education and vocational progressivism.[26] As North put it, in a passage which implied that the changes were already far more widespread than was, in fact, the case:

> Much of what was of value in the old system will be lost forever – the commitment to excellence; the recognition of the value of properly acquired factual knowledge; the view of knowledge as a cumulative process . . .; the respect for knowledge whose 'relevance' cannot easily be perceived; and an appreciation of the time-honoured values and principles of tolerance and self-respect enshrined within our national culture.[27]

A less than enthusiastic HMI report on integrated and modular humanities syllabuses, including the one discussed earlier, raised serious questions about their academic rigour and their value in relation to more conventional courses in the humanities subjects.[28] Although based upon a very small sample of early schemes mostly geared towards less academically able pupils, it has combined with concerns about the knowledge requirements of the National Curriculum to stem the growth in the subject that was beginning to get under way. The Southern Examining Group is currently developing an alternative scheme of Combined Humanities, with much less scope for issue-based work. Integrated humanities would have needed some exceptionally strong professional and political allies to withstand this backlash, especially as TVEI also appeared to be under threat at this time. Although an Integrated Humanities Association had been formed, it did not articulate a particularly coherent defence of its position, partly because it was having to defend so many different approaches within its overall umbrella. On the issue of programmes of study, it was initially marginalised by the widespread assumption that a curriculum planned on the basis of traditional school subjects would end up being taught in that way. Even when cross-curricular themes came to be taken more seriously, and curriculum overload had created official indecision about the status of history and geography as single subjects in Key Stage 4, the IHA seemed unable to assert itself as a key player in the deliberations.

WORLD STUDIES AND PEACE EDUCATION

World studies and peace education have confronted the issue of what counts as legitimate knowledge rather more directly than have the advocates of integrated humanities. At first sight, it is not easy to see why this should be the case, especially as, far from being conceived as an examination subject, peace studies and world studies have been presented as a dimension across the curriculum with an emphasis as much on method as on content.[29] However, Lister's 'new movements' of peace education, human rights education and environmental education of the ecological variety, and world studies, while each having some of its own peculiar characteristics, shared a lot of common concerns, as well as some common membership.[30] To this extent, they could perhaps offer a clearer curriculum position than the multifarious proponents of integrated humanities ever did.

Hicks, who could certainly claim membership of most of the groups identified by Lister, has also pointed to the common features of many recent curriculum initiatives. Writing specifically of peace education, Hicks tells us that it is 'child-centred (valuing the person) and reconstructionist (valuing positive peace)' and that it offers both a radical critique of much current educational practice but also clear indicators of how to change that practice.[31] He also points out that 'if one is teaching *for* peace and not merely *about* peace, a close relationship needs to exist between ends and means, content and form'. However, he tells us that peace education 'is only one of a range of initiatives, many of which go back to the early 1970s, all of which aim to help students deal in different ways with ethical dilemmas in a fast-changing world'. His own list of associated developments includes 'world studies, development education, political education, antiracist and anti-sexist education, environmental education, and personal and social education'. Such a list was certainly liable to lead to 'guilt by association' in the eyes of the New Right critics of 'loony left' teachers and LEAs. Although each initiative embodied a particular set of concerns, there is no doubt that there was often considerable overlap both in content and methodology. Indeed, sometimes different labels were used to describe much the same activity. Resource books for world studies, global education, peace education and environmental education often contained the same extracts, quotations and exercises. And, as Hicks himself put it, 'in the final event the terminology used by teachers and schools may well express local or LEA preferences.'[32]

The extent of overlap is obvious from Hicks' characterisation of the knowledge, skills and attitudes encouraged by peace education:

Skills	Attitudes	Knowledge
Critical thinking	Self-respect	Conflict
Cooperation	Respect for others	Peace
Empathy	Ecological concern	War
Assertiveness	Open-mindedness	Nuclear issues
Conflict resolution	Vision	Justice
Political literacy	Commitment to justice	Power
		Gender
		Race
		Environment
		Future

This list, of course, also has considerable overlap with the characterisation of integrated humanities offered earlier, but there has been relatively little liaison between the two curriculum 'movements'.

While neither movement is entirely phase-specific, in practice much of the recent activity of the integrated humanities lobby has focused on GCSE courses, while world studies has probably had its greatest impact amongst teachers of primary and lower secondary school pupils. There is little common membership at national level, although a few individual LEA advisers, notably John Simpson in Brent, have been actively involved in both movements.

The world and peace studies movement has been rather more prepared than the integrated humanities lobby to enter into a public debate about what counts as knowledge in the curriculum and what criteria should be used for selecting it. This has perhaps given a sharper edge to the criticisms made of it from both right and left. Even so, it would be misleading to suggest that complete homogeneity of approach is evident within the peace education and world studies movement. Indeed, Harber extends to peace education an earlier analysis of political education that suggests that one can find 'conservative', 'liberal' and 'radical' variants of peace education,[33] as well as the view coming from the New Right that none of these activities can be regarded as part of genuine 'education'.[34] Harber himself argues that both the 'conservative' approach, which emphasises the military status quo and importance of 'deterrence'[35] and the 'radical' approach, which is committed to change[36] are aimed at socialisation rather than education. For him, the only genuine educational approach is the 'liberal' one, which involves 'putting *all* information before pupils *in order that they can make their own decisions and come to their own conclusions*'.[37] Presumably, though, Hicks' claim that peace education is 'teaching *for* peace and not merely *about* peace'[38] puts it clearly into Harber's 'radical' and thus non-educational mode.

However, while it seems to make a clear distinction between educational and non-educational approaches, Harber's typology is of only limited value. It seems to accept the view of Cox and Scruton that there is a form of education that avoids bias in its selection of knowledge and its pedagogy. In 'radical' modes of peace education and world studies, there is an openly articulated relationship between ends and means, content and form, but that is not to say that such a relationship is non-existent where it is not clearly articulated. The critiques of 'radical' modes of world studies and peace studies from the Conservative right[39] place them firmly in the tradition of the 'liberal educational establishment' which is seen as having undermined traditional educational and social values. It is attacked as 'radical' by its very nature in that it is 'not merely . . . often taught in a biased and irresponsible way, but that it could be taught in no other way'.[40] Yet, both Aspin[41] and White[42] have demonstrated that, whatever the empirical case may be, the charge that peace studies (or world studies) is biased by its very nature does not hold up to philosophical scrutiny. But Cox and Scruton's own position is anyway only partially a defence of knowledge for its own sake, since they also see schools as engaged in teaching 'good manners' and there is thus clearly a normative component to their own approach. The suspicion remains that the New Right's defence of the traditional curriculum derives from a recognition that, perhaps to an even greater degree than Harber's explicitly conservative model, it serves to defend the status quo. As Aspin puts it, Scruton and Cox's criteria of 'irrelevance, remoteness and abstractness as sole determinants of academic respectability ... suggest covert prescription rather than any extensive investigation of what 'true education' ... might consist in, or indeed whether there could ever be such a thing'.[43]

It can be argued then that the notion that the traditional curriculum is 'educational', and that of the various 'new movements' non-educational, is of dubious value. One effect of Margaret Thatcher's interventions in the subsequent debate about history in the national curriculum has been to make explicit the extent to which the selection of knowledge in traditional subjects has normative connotations. The new movements have articulated an alternative approach to education which recognises such inter-relationships, and arguably one that combines rigour and relevance in a more fully worked out coherent way than was evident in the integrated humanities movement. At a professional level, they have had some success in organising around it.

However, the issue is further complicated when we look at critiques of peace education and world studies from the political left. Hatcher, for example, takes Hicks to task for an analysis of the global structure that 'doesn't once mention capitalism, a remarkable omission for an account of imperialism'.[44] He quotes Berry as offering a critique of another of Hick's publications on the grounds that it fails 'to get any clear guidelines for the study of the "structures and institutions of society" which ... largely dictate the minority experience'.[45] The fear of being 'tainted with Marxism' seems to produce an approach which does not even recognise it as a significant mode of analysis. Hatcher also points out that world studies courses make little reference to socialist futures, identifying 'a better future with "ecological" rather than socialist imperatives' – though this is not true of Huckle's work, for example.[46] Nevertheless, Hatcher is broadly correct to claim that world studies 'largely defines its field of enquiry within the bounds of capitalism, and its alternatives as reforms within it' and that peace studies fails to recognise that there might be a difference between the violence of the oppressor and the violence of the oppressed fighting against their oppression.

None of this is to argue for an alternative through Marxist indoctrination, but it is to point out how nervousness about broaching particular solutions to world problems, expecially in the fact of attacks from the right and the provisions of the 1986 Education (No 2) Act, may itself produce an unacknowledged (and often unconscious) bias in the selection of knowledge. Indeed, there is a sense in which omission can be considered a form of 'indirect indoctrination'.[47] Hatcher points out that 'the leaders of the World Studies movement seem generally unaware of the question of the structural limits to what is possible in schools, in spite of the considerable number of recent books and articles, mainly by socialist writers, on education under capitalism which discuss this point'. They also have an undeveloped conception of the sort of political action that is likely to contribute to significant changes in the nature of education. In that sense, Hatcher, although a Marxist in his political orientation, might even seem to be advocating Harber's 'liberal' model of education, in that he seems to be suggesting a wider range of information should be made available to pupils so that they can make up their own minds. On this reading, even movements that are 'radical' in terms of Harber's typology need to be reminded, as Aspin reminds Cox, Scruton and Sir Keith Joseph, that:

> it is not self-evident that the only or even the best form of government involves parliamentary forms nor that there are no occasions when some concerns might take precedence over the rule of law . . . Part of the preparation of future citizens in a democracy might involve encouraging them to consider whether some societies might not be better off with other forms of political arrangement than those found in advanced Western democracies; or for going against law, custom and precedent in pursuit of goals widely thought to conduce to the public good.[48]

Yet it is clear that all curricula involve a selection from knowledge and this means that it will always be possible to identify important issues that have been omitted. This is part of the appeal of the various approaches to the selection of knowledge that involve an emphasis on procedural values designed to guard against, and heighten awareness of, systematic biases in the selection of knowledge. This concept actually unites the political education movement, the new movements and the integrated humanities movement in conception if not always in execution. Although it does not, in my view, entirely remove the need to consider what might be appropriate substantive content for a contemporary curriculum, commitment to such procedural values may well be the most feasible way of keeping the notion of a socialist future on the agenda in a hostile ideological climate. Yet there has been little attempt to bring the different groups together to develop this approach further or to persuade the labour movement of its importance.

A handbook produced by the Schools Council World Studies 8-13 Project, contained 'a cautionary tale' by Robin Richardson, the original project director, who is amongst the more politically sophisticated members of the world studies lobby.[49] Using the metaphor of 'elephant education', he pointed to the danger of political education, development education, multicultural education, peace education, anti-sexist education, and social and personal education, all going their separate ways:

> They applied separately for money from charitable trusts and from central and social government; set up working parties, standing conferences, associations, networks; forumulated aims and objectives, and devised syllabuses and schemes of work; sent deputations to examination boards; made bids for the attention and commitment of influential teachers, lobbied and jockeyed for time and space in each individual school.
>
> They failed however, completely to achieve any of the values that they wished to promote; and failed also to avert any of the threats to which they wished to respond. They failed even to live out the short span of their own lives with integrity and love.[50]

Hatcher would presumably want to say that this was inevitable. He points to the fact that much of the political impetus for world studies, and some of the main financial sponsorship it has received, derived from a concern to protect the existing global order through developing support for limited changes which would prevent a major confrontation.[51] However, the origins of a movement do not determine its nature in a straightforward manner. For instance, one of the few texts that does clearly see a connection between ecological solutions and socialist politics was sponsored by the World Wildlife

Fund, whose Establishment credentials can hardly be faulted.[52] Nevertheless, developing links across a wider range of political opinion can help such movements, and indeed individual teachers who are even more exposed, to resist the often subtle pressures to restrict teaching to a narrow range of currently acceptable perspectives. What is equally important, though, is that the labour movement should develop a clearer view of the curriculum model it espouses, so that its views can be taken more fully into account.

THE NATIONAL CURRICULUM AND BEYOND

For the moment, however, the curriculum agenda has been set by quite different influences, as a result of Kenneth Baker's decision to legislate for a National Curriculum.[53] The initial proposals looked suspiciously like the traditional subject-based curriculum of the old humanists which has so often been blamed for the decline in Britain's industrial fortunes. Certainly many commentators associated with TVEI reacted with horror at the proposals. Jamieson and Watts suggested that the traditionally-oriented Hillgate Group, which includes Cox and Scruton, were clearly winning the 'battle for the high policy ground' rather than Lord Young and the advocates of an enterprise culture.[55] More recently, after the publication of the first programmes of study, the CBI expressed the fear that, in practice, the National Curriculum might emphasise narrow academic knowledge at the expense of transferable skills.[56] The obvious impact on the proposals of the neo-conservative strand of New Right thinking did not augur well for the initiatives discussed in this paper, particularly as the 'modernizing' forces within the Conservative Party, with whom Baker had hitherto been associated and upon whose influence the integrated humanities movement sought to trade, appeared once again to have lost some of their earlier influence.[57]

As Anne Sofer of the Social and Liberal Democrats put it at a conference on global education just as the Education Reform Act was about to pass into law, the 'draconian control' now to be exercised over the curriculum by the Secretary of State posed a threat to internationalism in the curriculum because it has to be seen in a context where 'the prevailing philosophy is one that does get excited about Christianity being absolutely predominant in RE, about the need to make sure British history prevails over other sorts of history and to stamp on anything that has the label anti-racism attached to it'.[58] Part of this context was the well-orchestrated political pressure from the neo-conservative Hillgate Group to 'ensure a solid foundation of British and European history and . . . no concessions to the philosophy of the global curriculum currently advocated by the multi-culturalists'. Its influence on the Secretary of State was evident in Kenneth Baker's instructions to the history curriculum working group that 'the programmes of study should have at the core the history of Britain',[60] and in his successor's reaction to their interim report that the British experience should be given a 'sharper focus' and greater emphasis placed on 'historical facts'.[61]

However, although the National Curriculum is being developed through attainment targets and programmes of study for the core and other foundation subjects, even the Thatcher government recognised that a broad and balanced curriculum requires that attention be given to a variety of issues that are not easily encapsulated within individual school subjects. Once, late in the day, it had superimposed a set of aims onto its crude curriculum model, it became increasingly obvious that that model was not necessarily well-suited to the promotion of 'the spiritual, moral, cultural, mental and physical development of pupils at school and of society' and to the preparation of pupils 'for the opportunities, responsibility and experiences of adult life', as required by the Education Reform Act.

The National Curriculum Council has now been given the task of giving coherence and relevance to the curriculum by addressing the question of cross curricular issues. In its initial thinking the NCC distinguished between cross curricular dimensions, cross curricular skills and cross curricular themes. These are to be dealt with both in areas of the curriculum outside the scope of the basic curriculum as defined by the Act and through forging links between elements of the different programmes of study being developed by foundation subject working groups. Task groups have now made some specific recommendations on various themes and guidance has recently been published on education for economic and industrial understanding, careers education, health education, environmental education and citizenship.

These might appear to offer a new context for the work of the initiatives discussed in this paper and some individual schools and LEAs are planning to use them in this way. However, critics have suggested that in practice the government's approach to curriculum planning will still marginalise cross curricular issues. The more pessimistic among them argue that the National Curriculum will effectively outlaw some of approaches favoured by the integrated humanities and world studies lobbies. Given that the knowledge, understanding, skills and attitudes to be taught to pupils at each key stage are being defined piecemeal by a series of separate subject working groups, these are expected to drive the curriculum of most schools. There is also a widespread preception that, to date, the programmes of study finally approved by the Secretary of State have emphasised specific subject content at the expense of broader process skills and that the official curriculum is therefore largely being defined in terms of subject-specific attainment targets rather than its relevance to the developmental needs of pupils and the responsibilities of adult life.

Nevertheless, the heavy pressure on the curriculum, belatedly acknowledged by John McGregor, Baker's successor as Secretary of State, has led to a reconsideration of the role of history and geography in Key Stage 4, and there is now some expectation that curriculum organisation under the National Curriculum will prove somewhat more flexible than was originally anticipated. Furthermore, some of the working group reports have seemed to endorse certain elements of progressive practice, and the fact that even the final report of the History working group did not entirely capitulate to the government's pressure to emphasise ethnocentric factual content, offers some scope for teachers to maintain alternative approaches to curriculum planning.[62] Some of the ideas contained in the curriculum guidance documents on the cross curricular themes also seem to reflect the influence of progressive practice, though their marginal role in the curriculum as a whole limits the opportunities they can provide for radical innovation.[63]

This limited success of professional educators in defending elements of progressive practice even in the context of a concerted political onslaught against the power of the 'liberal educational establishment' does not anyway compensate for the failure of the labour movement to claim a voice in the debate about the nature of the comprehensive school curriculum. This must not just be a matter of claiming to have thought of the National Curriculum first, or arguing merely about what particular subjects or elements of subjects should be in the curriculum, but one of establishing, and arguing for, the principles which should inform curriculum planning. Of course, there can ultimately be no single arbiter of the curriculum and it will all be much more complicated than claiming, as do different elements of the right, that tradition or the market (whether industry or the individual consumer) should be the criterion of judgement.

Yet it is clear that some approaches to curriculum planning are more consistent with the political project of the left than others. Even that, of course, begs a great many questions, especially about the appropriateness of some of the cruder models of a common curriculum. Modern socialism seeks to build on and unite new social movements, such as those of feminism, ecology, peace and black politics, as well as the more traditional elements of the labour movement. A radical approach to planning the curriculum will therefore need to embrace differences as well as commonalities in a way that is denied both within the traditional curriculum and the Conservative government's version of a National Curriculum.[64] The curriculum movements discussed in this paper offered some glimpses of how to achieve this but they showed too little awareness of the broader context in which they were operating.

If professional and political movements are now to come together to implement the elusive curriculum of the public educators, they will need to recognise the changing nature of the public sphere. Some people would argue that it is too much to expect the labour movement to recognise the implications of this for education when it is still struggling to make sense of its implications for its overall political project. Yet, these matters are not resolved in a linear manner (or even resolved in a final sense) and, while the left struggles with its own uncertainties, the school curriculum is being largely shaped by the spurious certainties of the right. Recent suggestions that the Labour Party will maintain most of the current National Curriculum arrangements if it ever comes to power are hardly grounds for optimism that the 1990s will prove any more conducive than the Thatcher years to a radical rethink of the school curriculum.[65] Some comfort can however be taken from the fact that the National Union of Teachers has made an important, if belated, start on rethinking the principles that would need to inform any alternative to the National Curriculum.[66] In taking that exercise forward, there are important lessons to be learned from a careful study of the curricular approaches advocated by the integrated humanities and world studies movements, as well as from an awareness of the shortcomings of the professional and political strategies they employed to further their cause.

NOTES

I am most grateful to David Halpin, University of Warwick and Nick Clough, Bristol Polytechnic, for their helpful comments on an earlier draft of this paper.

1. B. Moon (ed) *Comprehensive Schools: Challenge and Change*, NFER-Nelson, Windsor 1983.
2. C. Benn and B. Simon, *Half Way There*, McGraw-Hill, London 1970.
3. M.F.D. Young, 'On the politics of educational knowledge', *Economy and Society*, Vol 1, 1972.
4. M.F.D. Young (ed), *Knowledge and Control*, Collier Macmillan, London 1971. N. Keddie (ed), *Tinker, Tailor . . . The Myth of Cultural Deprivation*, Penguin, Harmondsworth 1973.
5. M. Levitas, *Marxist Perspectives in the Sociology of Education*, Routledge, London 1974.
6. R. Williams, *The Long Revolution*, Penguin, Harmondsworth 1965, pp 171-2.
7. G. Whitty, *Sociology and School Knowledge*, Methuen, London 1985.
8. D. Gleeson and G. Whitty, *Developments in Social Studies Teaching*, Open Books, London 1976.
9. D. Warwick, 'Ideologies, Integration and Conflicts of Meaning' in M. Flude and J. Ahier (eds) *Educability, Schools and Ideology*, Croom Helm, London 1974.
10. D. Halpin, 'The Sociology of Education and the National Curriculum', *British Journal of Sociology of Education*, Vol II, No 1, 1990.
11. D. Lawton, *Class, Culture and the Curriculum*, Routledge, London 1975.
12. M. Holt, *The Common Curriculum: Its Structure and Style in the Comprehensive School*, Routledge, London 1979.
13. D. Hargreaves, *The Challenge for the Comprehensive School*, Routledge, London 1982.
14. CCCS, *Unpopular Education*, Hutchinson, London 1981.
15. J. North (ed), *The GCSE: an Examination*, Claridge Press, London 1987.
16. Gleeson and Whitty, *op cit*; Whitty, *op cit*.
17. I. Lister, 'Global and International Approaches in Political Education', in C. Harber (ed), *Political Education in Britain*, Falmer Press, Lewes 1987, pp 51-2.
18. G. Whitty, 'Integrated Humanities', in C. Lacey and R. Richards (eds), *Education, Ecology and Development*, Kogan Page, London 1987.
19. HMI, *Curriculum 11-16: a Review of Progress*, HMSO, London 1981.
20. Whitty, *op cit*, p 143.
21. K. Joseph, 'View from the Top', *Times Educational Supplement*, 13.1.1984.
22. I. McNay, 'GCSE and the New Vocationalism', in T. Horner (ed), *GCSE: Examining the New System*, Harper and Row, London 1987.
23. S. Ball, *Politics and Policymaking in Education*, Routledge, London 1990.
24. D. Hargreaves *et al*, *Improving Secondary Schools*, ILEA, London 1984.
25. D. Holly, *Humanism in Adversity*, Falmer Press, Lewes 1986.
26. Ball, *op cit*.
27. North, *op cit*, p 22.
28. HMI, *An Inspection of GCSE Humanities Courses in 20 Secondary Schools*, DES, London 1989.

29. D. Hicks (ed), *Education for Peace*, Routledge, London 1988.
30. Lister, *op cit*.
31. Hicks, *op cit*, p 11.
32. *Ibid*, p 17.
33. C. Harber, 'Political Education and Peace Education', in C. Brown, C. Harber and J. Strivens (eds), *Social Education: Principles and Practice*, Falmer Press, Lewes, 1986.
34. C. Cox and R. Scruton, *Peace Studies: a Critical Survey*, Institute for European Defence and Strategic Studies, London 1984.
35. See, for example, British Atlantic Committee, *Peace and Conflict Studies*, BAC, London 1983.
36. See, for example, D. Heater, *World Studies*, Harrup, London 1980.
37. *Peace Education Network Letter*, 1984.
38. Hicks, *op cit*.
39. Cox and Scruton, *op cit*; C. Cox *et al*, *Whose Schools? A Radical Manifesto*, Hillgate Group, London 1986.
40 Cox and Scuton, *op cit*.
41. D. Aspin, ' "Peace Studies" and "Education": a rejoinder to Scruton', *Cambridge Journal of Education*, Vol 17, No 1, 1987.
42. P. White, 'Countering the Critics' in Hicks, *op cit*.
43. Aspin, *op cit*.
44. R. Hatcher, 'The Construction of World Studies', *Multiracial Education*, Vol II, No 1, 1982.
45. S. Berry, Review of *Minorities, World Studies Journal*, Vol 2, No 3, 1981.
46. See Huckle's contribution in C. Lacey and R. Richards, *op cit*.
47. G. Whitty, 'Political Education: Some Reservations', *The Social Science Teacher*, Vol 8, No 3.
48. Aspin, *op cit*.
49. S. Fisher and D. Hicks, *World Studies 8-13: A Teacher's Handbook*, Oliver and Boyd, Edinburgh 1985.
50. R. Richardson, 'Elephant Education: A Cautionary Tale', in Fisher and Hicks, *op cit*.
51. Hatcher, *op cit*.
52. Lacey and Richards, *op cit*.
53. DES, *The National Curriculum: A Consultation Paper*, London 1987.
54. C. Barnett, *The Audit of War*, Macmillan, London 1986; M. Wiener, *English Culture and the Decline of the Industrial Spirit*, Cambridge University Press, 1981.
55. I. Jamieson and T. Watts, 'Squeezing out Enterprise', *Times Educational Supplement*, 18.12.1987.
56. *Times Educational Supplement*, 24.3.1989.
57. R. Johnson, 'Thatcherism and English Education', *History of Education*, Vol 18, No 2, 1989; G. Whitty, 'The New Right and the National Curriculum', *Journal of Education Policy*, Vol 4, No 4, 1989.
58. *Education*, 8.7.1988.

59. Hillgate Group, *The Reform of British Education*, Claridge Press, London 1987.
60. *The Times*, 14.1.1989.
61. *Independent*, 11.8.1989.
62. DES, *History for ages 5 to 16*, DES, London 1990.
63. National Curriculum Council; *Education for Economic and Industrial Understanding; Careers Education and Guidance; Health Education; Environmental Education; Citizenship;* all published by National Curriculum Council, York 1990.
64. J. Donald, 'Interesting Times: Education and Broadcasting in the 1990s', *Critical Social Policy*, Vol 9, No 3, 1990.
65. Labour Party, *Aiming High*, Labour Party, London 1990.
66. National Union of Teachers, *A Strategy for the Curriculum*, National Union of Teachers, London 1990.

FEMINIST INTERVENTIONS IN SCHOOLING 1975-90

ROSEMARY DEEM

INTRODUCTION

In this chapter I want to look at some of the developments which have taken place in the field of gender and state schooling in England and Wales since 1975. I will attempt to assess what has been achieved, consider just how radical feminist interventions have been, explore what has constrained those interventions and discuss what some of the remaining challenges are. I have chosen 1975 as a starting point because it marked the passage of the Sex Discrimination Act, which provided a minimal legislative framework outlawing certain forms of sex discrimination across a number of areas of public life, including education. The date chosen, therefore, is not intended to suggest that there were no feminist interventions into state education prior to 1975; clearly these have a long history in the nineteenth as well as twentieth century.[1]

Although I want to concentrate on feminist interventions (that is those that both recognise the subordinate position of woman and set out to change it), as I have pointed out elsewhere,[2] it is not always possible to clearly differentiate between feminist and non-feminist interventions. Of course radical changes may be aligned to the political right or left; in this chapter I concentrate on those radical changes which address social inequalities, particularly of gender but also social class, ethnicity and special need, and changes which are concerned with the life chances of all those who pass through the education system. Interventions themselves tend to take place in two very different contexts; relatively unfavourable political climates and relatively favourable ones. Many of the interventions referred to here have taken place in the relatively unfavourable climate of Thatcherism, from 1979 to 1990.

CHANGES FOR THE BETTER, CHANGES FOR THE WORSE

As I write in 1990 there has already been a great deal of change in education emanating from a Tory government. The speed of changes to education prompted by the right and mostly contained in the 1988 Education Reform Act (and the frequency of the U-turns on previously supposedly unchangeable policies) has been immense. This is despite the fact that at first sight the ground conditions for any change in state education are far from promising. There is a massive teacher supply crisis in many areas, teacher morale and pay remain low, many schools are inadequately resourced (which is being exacerbated by schools who find themselves net financial losers under delegated budgets) and hundreds of school buildings are in need of proper repair and maintenance. The pace of change in itself presents certain difficulties for anyone wanting to suggest further changes, a factor not fully recognized, for example, by the 1989 Labour Party Political Review on education.[3]

The ambiguous nature of many of the changes being brought about (or supposedly being brought about) by the 1988 Education Reform Act and other recent legislation (the 1986 No 2 Education Act, the 1987 Teachers Pay and Conditions Act, etc) also present certain obstacles. The simultaneous move to both decentralized control under governing bodies,[4] and to centralised control under the Department of Education and Science and the National Curriculum Council have wrong-footed several left strategies for change based on critiques of the failure of the state education system.[5] Other left interventions have focused their hopes on Local Education Authority based changes. Both of these 'solutions' may simply not address all the problems which we currently face nor fully recognise the present climate for educational change. Firstly, we are now faced with the need to support, before the state system of schooling as we know it disappears, the notion that the state should fund, as well as ensure the quality of, primary and secondary education, at a point when the real mechanisms for influencing schools have never been further from our control. Secondly, despite Brian Simon's[6] argument that Local Education Authorities historically have been a progressive force in education, it is evident both that this has only ever been partially true and that it has only been possible in periods where LEAs have had room for manoeuvre. In the current conditions, as many local authorities who have been poll tax capped, face lopping thousands of millions of pounds off their education budgets, that local authority autonomy has almost entirely gone. Thirdly, Thatcherism may also have affected the motivation of many of those who enter local politics, which is fast becoming an arena for the building of personal reputations rather than one in which serving the community is a prime motivating force. It is now possible to argue that issues to do with social justice and inequality in education may equally well be addressed in schools which are outside the LEA system, but still within the state system, as by LEA schools, especially as the line between local management of schools and Grant Maintained schools is increasingly being blurred.[7] Not only do all these relatively new provisos apply; at the same time we have to argue support for a cause (equality) when the pursuit of equality rather than differentiation is apparently deeply politically unpopular.[8]

In the 1990s, we are in the midst of a far more ambitious Conservative attempt to change education than anything that has ever been attempted by the left. Why is it that left interventions have never attempted anything so radical? Of course it remains to be seen whether the right-wing endeavours encompassed in the Reform Act will actually achieve the desired outcome.[9] But many left interventions which have been radical in intent, have not proved to be so in practice. In relation to feminist interventions, this has sometimes been because of the difficulties of overcoming widespread apathy or hostility to gender issues in the state system of schooling. Furthermore, many of the factors which affect and induce sexism in schools, are products of wider social and economic relations which cannot possibly be changed by interventions confined to schooling. Also, the schooling system we are attempting to change is located not only within patriarchal social relations but also capitalist social relations. This may limit the kind of left radical reforms that are possible in practice because of the interconnections between schooling, the economy and the state. Capitalists may be willing to allow the right to engage in radical change, especially if they see that change as operating in directions which are favourable to the generation of profit, but historically they have been much less willing, even in different political conditions, to allow the left to do the same. Nevertheless, in periods of labour shortage, employers may prove to be supporters of changes which make the supply of labour more flexible and adaptable.

FEMINIST INTERVENTIONS INTO GENDER AND SCHOOLING

Not all of the interventions made to combat gender discrimination in schooling over the last two decades have been made by feminists. There is in any case no one variety of feminism. As Arnot and Weiner[10] have pointed out, there are at least four different versions of feminist theory and politics, which can be seen to have shaped particular interventions into gender and schooling. These are liberal feminism which focuses on individual rights, radical feminism which concentrates on overcoming patriarchal power wielded by men over women, Marxist and socialist feminism which tries to tackle both class and gender power relations, and black feminism which focuses on power relations based on race, class and gender. Within these limits, I therefore regard a feminist intervention as one in which those making the intervention believe women and girls to be subordinate and see the intervention as helping to overcome the social relations, processes and power structures by which female subordination is secured. However this does not necessarily mean that all feminist inspired or feminist supported interventions will fit neatly with their theoretical and philosophical origins nor that they always achieve the desired outcomes.

Arnot and Weiner[11] suggest that feminists working in education during the 1980s have been involved in four main types of activities. First there are teacher-initiated changes, often small scale and short-lived. Second there are action research projects involving either independent teacher research or collaboration with academic researchers, which are longer in duration but may also be relatively modest in terms of immediate size and effect. A third variety is teacher contact networks like the Schools Council Sex Differentiation project.[12] Finally there are teacher union initiatives such as setting up women's committees, developing research and running courses. It is clear that this categorisation does not exhaust all the possibilities; feminists have also been involved in other kinds of interventions. These include encouraging LEAs to establish gender policies through pressure groups or political parties[13] and taking on posts in LEAs connected with equal opportunities.[14] Now some commentators would argue that the latter two interventions may involve compromising feminist principles[15] in order to achieve anything. Hence Weiner talks about LEA equal opportunity posts being taken by 'career teachers within the existing school power structure rather than by the pioneering and radical teachers who had first taken action'.[16]

However the question of the relationship between political principles and political action is a complex one which may apply just as much to the activities undertaken by a group of teachers in a school as to initiatives taken by LEAs or governments. It is not, I think, always helpful or accurate to say that one kind of intervention is more likely to have to compromise its principles than another. All interventions may come up against existing structures which are resistant to change, may meet hostility and may be faced by problems of inadequate resources. This is admitted by Arnot and Weiner. Although they say of feminist interventions that 'Clearly teachers wanted to be agents of change rather than instruments of an oppressive system',[17] and they point to choices such as teachers and LEAs choosing not to set up special advisory posts for gender as these could be elitist, they also accept that compromises to feminist principles such as anti-elitism may sometimes have to be made, in order to develop alliances and support for interventions from those who are not feminist but who have access to power.

Several writers have tried to establish criteria for judging whether or not interventions are feminist. This often involves making a distinction between equal opportunities or girl-friendly initiatives and feminist or girl-centred approaches to changing education. For example Weiner suggests that girl-friendly approaches are moderate interventions which seek to tinker with girls' opportunities without causing conflict and do not try to do anything very fundamental to the structure of education.[18] An example would be rewriting school option choice booklets to emphasise that both girls and boys could take any subject they wanted. Girl-centred approaches, on the other hand, seek radical alterations in the balance of power between women and men and are prepared to risk the conflicts and hostility these may bring in their wake. Hence a girl-centred approach might initate girl-only physics teaching or girl-only tutorial groups as a way of addressing sexism, sexual harassment and the tendency of male students to put down female students.

Yates, writing about the Australian experiences of feminist interventions in education, is very critical of so-called girl-friendly approaches.[19] Yates argues that the use of posters of women scientists in science labs to give science a more girl-friendly image, or the changing of questions in maths lessons to reflect so called feminine interests such as clothes or cooking as well as male interests like cars or football, is of limited value. Yates is arguing that such changes may alter how girls feel about education but do not fundamentally change the gender power relations involved in schools. She also argues that girl-friendly approaches tend to operate with a model of girls as deficit boys, who simply need strategies for remedying the deficiencies. Arnot, reviewing recent developments in gender policy, argues that many national policy initiatives, such as the Sex Discrimination Act, the brief mention of gender issues in some HMI and DES documents and the setting up of a handful of DES courses on gender stereotyping, have paid lip service to the issues of gender equality rather than seeking any radical reforms.[20] Wolpe goes even further than this in castigating feminist approaches and interventions themselves for their focus on middle-class girls and the labour market.[21] Instead, says Wolpe, such interventions ought to focus on issues like developing alternatives to the nuclear family, reshaping the domestic division of labour and trying to change the male balance of power in sexual relationships and in the definition of female sexuality. Most of these critiques make important points but all of them fail to recognise the constraints within which feminists must work.

Although feminist interventions have become widespread over the past two decades, they have not always received general support from the left. The left in Britain still sees class inequality as a bigger priority in education than gender, although it is gradually conceding that race and ethnicity may also be important. As a strategy, the focus on class has been in any case defeated and all the initiatives on class inequality characteristic of the 1960s and 1970s debates about comprehensive schools have largely disappeared from view since the advent of Thatcherism.

Although I am well aware that the Labour Party does not represent the whole of the political left in Britain, for electoral purposes it is the only significant force. If we look at Labour Party education policy, the perceived insignificance of gender issues in schooling is immediately apparent. This is despite the commitment of the Labour Party to setting up a Ministry for Women had they won the 1992 general election. The 1989 Labour Party Policy Review documents on education pays little heed to gender. Hence a whole paper was devoted to multicultural issues, but it did not even recognise that the controversy over separate schools for Muslim students has a gender dimension to it.[22] The major document on schools certainly mentions gender but then goes on to talk as though all school students were homogeneous, distinguished by neither gender nor ethnicity.[23] If we are to expect major changes on gender and education from the Labour Party they have yet to surface in its discussion documents. Labour, in general, is strong on words about gender equality but weak on action, even in relation to issues like selecting women candidates for parliamentary elections. In the Labour Party it has only been at grass-roots level that gender issues have really been seen as an important concern.[24] Even there, as Barry has shown, the concern is more often for a moderate women-centred approach rather than a more radical feminist stance.[25] If this is true of Labour, it is also true of other left groupings as well. Even the growing interest in exploring gender issues from the standpoint of masculinity has not really spread beyond a minority in the male left. There are still many who think that all gender inequalities can be laid at the door of class divisions. Until this misconception is overcome, many left radical initiatives will continue to ignore the gender dimension, much to their detriment.

THE ACHIEVEMENTS OF INTERVENTIONS INTO GENDER AND SCHOOLING

The late 1970s saw a number of books and articles published, mostly by feminist researchers and writers, documenting the extent of sexism in schools both for pupils and teachers,[26] and this literature continued to be produced into the early 1980s, gradually placing as much emphasis on explaining the situation as on describing it.[27] The 1970s focus was on describing how and where gender differentiation in schools occurred. Thus writers like Byrne and Deem, working from different perspectives, both looked at the curriculum, the hidden curriculum, women teachers and resource distribution between male and female pupils.[28] Work such as that of Spender examined how male power was evident in the ways schools worked, with a particular focus on the extent to which teachers spent time on male rather than female pupils and on the differential language use of male and female speakers.[29] Macdonald tried to develop Marxist theories of reproduction to explain the patterns of gender discrimination found in schools. None of these books spelt out in detail how changes might occur.[30]

But already by the early 1980s the problems of gender

differentiation in schools were being more widely recognised, by Local Education Authorities, the Manpower Services Commission, the Department of Education and Science and Her Majesty's Inspectors, as well as by many feminist teachers themselves. Gradually the descriptive focus of writings on gender and schooling began to shift towards a more practical orientation, describing initiatives which had been taken and action research carried out.[31] A few local authorities started to appoint people with a specific responsibility for implementing equal opportunities with a focus on gender, and also developed policy guidelines (for example Brent, Sheffield and ILEA). A number of LEAs now have equal opportunities policies (which may cover race and ethnicity as well as gender) and so do many individual schools, although the effectiveness of these varies considerably.[32] But 1989 and 1990 saw retreats from this position in councils where control changed from Labour to Tory (Bradford, Ealing, Brent), and the ILEA, the largest authority with equal opportunity policies, was abolished on 30 March 1990.

What we have learnt from the last ten years is that intentions are not enough. A policy statement, at LEA, school or departmental level, is useful but still needs acting upon if it is to have any impact at all, even a moderate one.[33] Policy, as we have begun to realise, is a process not a statement and words have to be turned into deeds and the changes monitored and evaluated. Specific tasks have to be set (increase number of women teachers in senior posts; get more girls to study A level physics) if anything concrete is to be achieved. Furthermore, changes can only occur when people are willing to admit that in the past, along with everyone else, they may have been less than perfect, and when people can see things they regard as real problems involving gender.[34] There has also begun to be the realization that gender is not just an issue for women but one which crucially concerns men as well.[35]

Some limited progress has been made in achieving gender equality, so far as white middle-class girls are concerned (for example improvements in the proportions of girls taking chemistry and maths in GCSE and other exams for 16 year-olds, more girls taking A levels and entering higher education).[36] But at the same time there has also been regression (for example there are now fewer female secondary heads than in the 1960s). Furthermore there has been a failure to address gender issues that are not consistent with feminist philosophy, such as the fate of the working-class boy. Yet there is a range of contradictory issues involved here. Working class boys are under-achieving, but they also have access to a gender divided education and often occupy a large percentage of teacher time. It is no good changing girls unless we also change boys and men.

Limited progress of gender equality has occurred in several fields, not just education, and has included a greater involvement of women of all ages, including mothers of young children, in the labour market,[37] as well as in the sexual division of labour in the household.[38] But progress in one direction is often marked by backward steps in another, so that many of the women now in employment face massive childcare problems, still have to do most of their own housework, may have to care for elderly dependents, are often in part-time insecure jobs and receive poor wages. In any case a greater awareness of gender issues and the development of 'gender policy' does not necessarily always lead to change of the kind desired, especially if goals and mechanisms for change are incorrectly identified or if legislation is intended to change attitudes as well as practices;[39] hence the results may, in the end, disappoint. It is also possible that the very existence of gender policies and equality legislation leads to complacency of the kind which says 'we have a policy, what else do we need?' 'we've done gender and are "doing" race now' or, 'women are all equal nowadays aren't they, there's the Sex Discrimination Act that says so'.

The achievements which have occurred include the following:

1. Recognition at all levels of schooling that gender inequality not only exists in education but is detrimental in its effect upon girls *and boys*, women *and men*. Much of this recognition is due to the efforts of feminists working in small groups to persuade others to take the issues seriously. However we should recognise that economic pressures and demands for labour power also often lie behind changes in attitude and that such pressures are constantly changing.

2. An awareness that gender differences are socially and economically constructed and not natural or innate. Equally important, as Yates notes, is the recognition that within education gender issues are extremely complex ones, affected not merely by sex-role socialisation (which is a simplistic formulation assuming that all children are effectively indoctrinated with an unchanging and clearly differentiated gender identity) but also by interpersonal relations, wider social relations and a host of factors outside schools altogether.[40] Feminist work by academics and practitioners has been crucial to more sophisticated awareness.

3. The development of a more 'gender-inclusive' curriculum affecting exams, materials and learning resources as well as syllabuses. Thus the content of some school subjects has been changed to include more

about the achievements of women and exam questions are generally less sexist. The impact of the National Curriculum on this remains to be seen but the curriculum documents published so far suggest that there will be a wide variation between subjects with regard to how seriously gender issues are taken.

4. The development of many national, international and local policy initiatives on gender and education, even though these have had variable results and certainly have impacted little on female/male power relations in school.[42] These have included EC directives on gender equality, criteria about gender equality in national initiatives like the Technical and Vocational Education Initiative,[43] and the adoption of the statement 'we are an equal opportunities employer' by many LEAs. Not all of these have been radical in any shape or form. Feminists have nevertheless frequently tried to help implement these initiatives, however ill-considered or poorly resourced they may have found them, in the absence of progress on anything more radical.

5. A high level of applied and action research has been carried out by teachers themselves as well as by academics, on the problems of sexism in education. This has included a good deal of project work, as for example on the Open University MA module on gender and education and other Masters Degrees in education. Much but not all of this research has been done by feminists. Such research has not been extensively financed by funding agencies, with a few exceptions, such as the nationally funded Manchester based Girls into Science and Technology project, which tried to undertake action research in schools to increase the take up by girls of science, and attempted to change the content of 'masculine science'.[44] Some of the work however has at various points been helped and facilitated by organisations like the Schools Council[45] and the Manpower Services Commission (now the Training Agency).

6. The development by feminists of many useful strategies and initiatives to try to overcome the problems of sexism in education. Some initiatives taken by schools are documented in Weiner.[46] Another good example of an initiative subsequently used by many teachers, has been *Genderwatch*, the collection of self assessment schedules for use in schools by teachers wishing to document the extent of gender discrimination, which was developed by Kate Myers in the London Borough of Merton when she worked for the now defunct Schools Council.[47] Although many of the strategies have adopted a liberal model, focusing on individuals and on access/ outcomes rather than on redistribution of power relations,

nevertheless significant changes have occurred and many lessons have been learnt.

7. Some positive shifts have occurred in the patterns of female achievement in school, higher education, adult education and training, for example more women entering higher education, more girls taking chemistry and maths in school exams, and some blurring of the sexual division of labour in the labour market. But in the main these changes remain considerably determined by race, ethnicity and class.

8. More women are remaining in or returning to the labour market for longer periods of their lives. Not all feminists however, see this as a positive development.[48]

9. There has been a slight but perceptible shift in the domestic sexual division of labour, with more men at least 'helping' with children and household chores.[49] Again this shift has been affected by factors other than gender, including class and ethnicity and its impact and extent should not be exaggerated.[50] Although feminists outside education have shown much concern about the domestic division of labour, Wolpe argues that few of those within education have considered strategies to change that division.[51]

10. There has been a realisation that gender issues cannot be tackled effectively, either at the theoretical or the practical level, without also taking fully into account the effects of race and ethnicity and social class.[52] Regrettably this greater realisation of the complexity of social and educational disadvantage has not very often extended to special needs and students with disabilities.

AREAS WHERE INTERVENTIONS HAVE YET TO SUCCEED

There is still much scope for further change, even in areas where a lot of interventions have already been made. The curriculum is one such area. Curriculum divisions between the sexes in the UK are now largely confined to the secondary rather than primary sector (although there are certainly areas of work, for example computing and football, which are likely to be boy dominated even in the primary school). Many of the remaining problems are not about across the board under-achievement by girls. What remains a problem is under-achievement by many working-class and black girls, for example in relation to science, craft, design and technology and computer studies. Some subjects, like PE, have been little considered by feminist work, as noted by Scraton in her own pioneering research.[53] Yet as that research has noted, physical education is one of the most gender-divided subjects in the secondary school curriculum.[54] Mixed PE has many potential problems, including low teacher expectations of girls' performance and actual under-achievement by many girls, and girls frequently 'give up' on PE as soon as they can, despite its potential for reducing male-female power relations based on physical power and strength.

Other areas of major concern are: the under-representation of women teachers in the senior levels of teaching especially in secondary schools; the sustained existence of very hierarchical authority structures, especially in secondary schools; the virtual absence of black women teachers;[55] and the continuing failure of initial teacher training to tackle gender issues.[56] Some of the remaining feminist concerns about female teachers are explored in two recent books[57] but there is still a great deal of scope for research and change in this area. Also, many interventions have rightly been targeted at teaching staff but this has often meant forgetting about ancillary workers. The latter group therefore have the potential to undermine many initiatives on sexism through ignorance of or opposition to the issues. In many classrooms male students still dominate, although Randall and Wolpe suggest that girls are far from passive in the classroom and that the subject being taught and the environment affect the interaction of girls with teachers.[58] Thus girls may do better in humanities than in craft, design and technology and may be more confident when teachers are aware of gender issues than when they are not.

Sexual harassment remains a key problem which, despite many efforts by feminists, persists in many mixed schools.[59] Sexuality itself, as recent work by Holly[60] and Jones and Mahony[61] demonstrates, remains a massively problematic area for girls and women in schools and one in which unequal power relations are very much manifest. Such power relations affect not only sex education lessons, general social relations between the sexes and the way girls and boys treat and regard each other, but also affect sexual behaviour and the use of contraception. The extent to which schools adequately prepare male as well as female students for parenting and domestic life and for alternatives to the conventional sexual division of labour in the nuclear family, is another major area where much still needs to be done by feminists.[62] Women's sport and leisure facilities and opportunities, allowing for wide variations between women of different ages, ethnicity and social class, continue to display marked inequalities compared to those for male leisure, and are often heavily constrained by male power.[63] Few educationists have seen this as a priority for action but it has a major impact on women's lives, and, as Scraton shows, schools play a part in constraining women's sport and leisure.[64] There is then, little room for complacency.

TEACHER HOSTILITY TO CHANGE

Although, as I have already pointed out, feminist teachers have been at the forefront of those trying to rid schooling of sexism, they have not always done so with the support of their colleagues. School-based interventions have frequently met with hostility from other teachers[65] and LEA initiatives have also had to take account of indifference, apathy and extreme sexism from those working in schools.[66] Considerable differences in the ability of teachers to identify personally, as well as professionaly, with issues of sexism, have been found amongst female and male teachers attending courses about equal opportunities, with male teachers often unable to see the issues as relevant to their personal lives.[67]

Women teachers themselves, whether feminist or not, have often been the victims of individual discrimination and have collectively had to grapple with strong patriarchal power relations and structures in schooling.[68] Often this has produced very contradictory attitudes in women teachers themselves. So Hicks, in a study of women teachers, found that many of them had considerable personal ambivalence about the appropriateness of their dual roles as teachers and mothers/ housewives and sometimes regarded men as 'better' teachers than women.[69]

But not all the problems stem from female teachers' ambivalence about gender equality. Spear noted that male science teachers (science remains a significant area of under-achievement for girls) were often extremely hostile to tackling issues about sexism and had attitudes which supported the notion that women should play a subordinate role to men.[70] Davidson found that many male teachers harboured all kinds of myths about women teachers and their inability to pursue careers in teaching.[71] These included the beliefs that women worked only for pin money, were not interested in or properly qualified for promotion and were frequently absent from school. Kelly discovered that science teachers in the schools used by the Girls into Science and Technology project very often did not see girls' under-achievement as a problem worth pursuing.[72] In addition, notions about what it is professionally appropriate for teachers to do are also crucial. Pratt, Bloomfield and Seale, in a study of option choices in secondary schools, found that it was often possible for those teachers who were not committed to gender equality to subvert strategies designed to reduce sexism.[73] So there is abundant evidence of the lack of support for initiatives on gender and education from amongst teachers themselves.

It would be easy to interpret some of this hostility as relating to ideologies of teacher professionalism impeding changes in schooling which would help children, parents and employers. Such evidence exists. Hence, for example, some teachers in the Pratt, Bloomfield and Seale study felt it was 'unprofessional' to intervene in subject choice by pupils, even where this resulted in considerable gender inequality. Such choices were considered to be 'natural', resulting from personal decisions by individuals and any teacher intervention would affect the school's neutral position in such matters. Riddell, researching two rural comprehensive schools, discovered that some teachers voiced beliefs in gender equality but that their teaching and actions belied these.[74] Other teachers in her study felt, as in the Pratt study, that altering gender divisions was not the proper concern of teachers and schools.

Attacking professional power is very much on the political agenda these days. The 1988 Education Reform Act itself is couched in terms of shifting power from self-interested professionals or producers, to altruistic consumers, who are rarely, if ever, defined as pupils or students, but rather as parents and employers. However, quite apart from some concerns about the extent to which a heavily controlled, poorly paid teaching force constitutes a profession, concerns which have been especially raised by Ozga[75] in her discussions of the proletarianisation of teaching and its similarity to the labour process in other working-class jobs, it is also difficult to understand why notions of the need for professional neutrality in matters to do with gender should affect some teachers but not all. Middleton has attempted to explore this through life history interviews with feminists.[76] Clearly as Arnot and Weiner demonstrate, some teachers have been extremely prominent in tackling gender issues.[77] It is, however, apparent that teachers in England and Wales are often deeply conservative (as evidenced at least partly by their voting preferences in general elections during the 1970s and early 1980s). It is also clear that initial teacher training has not always broached issues of gender and education.[78]

In the end, teachers may be no different from the rest of the population. If society is deeply sexist and many people hold

old-fashioned views about the role of women and the desirability of their subordinate status, it is hardly surprising that teachers also hold such views. I have argued elsewhere that, no matter how much we may dislike the apparent economic determinism, women's equality has been most supported at times of labour shortages.[79] This view is confirmed by Weiner, who points out that vocational initiatives supporting equal opportunities have often done so because of the need to attract female labour.[80] Thus at such times, employers may be enthusiastic supporters of moderate equal opportunities initiatives. But such pragmatic views are not always shared by the rest of the population. The continued prevalence of sexism in the population as a whole, teacher conservatism and the failure to raise fully issues about gender in initial training courses, do help explain why only a minority of teachers have taken action on gender and why their interventions have often met hostility.

STUDENT RESISTANCE TO GENDER INITIATIVES

Hostility, of course, has not just come from teachers but also from students themselves. There is a great deal of evidence that male students in particular cause huge problems for female students and teachers and are also heavily resistant to changing their behaviour. Whereas female pupils, whatever their personal ambivalence to gender equality, can often see the benefits of its pursuance, boys can seldom see anything to be gained and much to be lost. Evidence on boys' dominance of the classroom abounds.[81] This evidence is not easily argued away by the claim that girls are not just passive victims.[82] Girls may well be more assertive in the classroom, although calls for teacher help often reflect lack of confidence rather than the reverse.[83] But boys, in general, often occupy more teacher time than girls; they answer and ask more questions and are generally more likely to demand help from teachers.[84] Boys, whatever their actual level of achievement, are confident and as a result often over-estimate their own abilities and under-estimate those of girls; the reverse is true for girls who tend to lack confidence, especially in areas of the curriculum which they regard as male preserves, and hence under-estimate their own capabilities and over-estimate those of boys.[85] Boys frequently use girls as a negative reference group.[86]

Language use and interaction in classrooms also reveal boys' hostility to girls having any kind of classroom equality. Spender's researches reveal that girls and women are less likely to be taken seriously when they speak in mixed groups, that female talk is often regarded as trivial by males, that women are more tentative and often more muted in their use of language, that men frequently interrupt women who are speaking, that women who actually say very little are often seen as speaking too much by men, that women defer to men in conversations and that women are much more co-operative in their use of language than men.[87] French and French point to evidence that there is often a gendered division of labour in conversation, with women being supportive of others and men less so.[88] Like Spender, who finds female language usage more co-operative, French and French suggest that women are more likely to be collaborative, taking shorter turns with others, whilst men are more likely in mixed groups to take long turns in which others must simply listen. The potential for sabotaging feminist interventions here, whether in the classroom or staffroom, is immense. Even in boys-only schools, males may still display sexist attitudes. In such schools, Askew and Ross argue, weaker boys may take on the role of girls; there is violence, bullying, seeking of power and prestige, a lack of trust and support between pupils, and certain kinds of teaching such as collaborative and discussion based work are, the authors suggest, very unpopular.[89] This kind of finding however is still far from fully documented so we cannot assume that it is universal.

THE PROSPECTS FOR THE FUTURE – GENDER AND THE REFORM ACT

It will not be possible here to give a full discussion of gender issues and the 1988 Reform Act.[90] The Reform Act itself is hardly geared to dealing with gender issues. Insofar as it does so, as Miles and Middleton note, it does so purely from a liberal perspective of equal rights. No positive discrimination or other radical action is proposed by the Act in respect of gender or race. The main reasoning for including equal opportunities criteria in aspects of the Reform Act at all, relates to labour shortages and the need to comply with existing national legislation and EC directives.

So far as equal opportunities interventions in Local Education Authorities are concerned, the Act is not good news. It has abolished the Inner London Education Authority, which, whatever the criticisms of its equal opportunities policies, had gone a very long way down that particular route. And its introduction of delegated budgets means it is less likely that we will see the continued existence of national and local equal opportunities policies which can be fully implemented and monitored. It will be largely up to individual schools. Against this of course, one has to set the fact that many LEAs have never developed any initiatives on equal opportunities. Contrary to the arguments of some,[91] it is not more likely that opted out schools will fail to develop or sustain equal opportunities policies than LEA schools, since there are so many more variables than this influencing what happens in an individual school. Monitoring equal opportunities policies, where they exist, will be largely in the hands of heads and governors in all state schools.[92] This means there is likely to be wide variation in what happens. Employer governors may well favour equal opportunities, whilst other governors retain more conservative attitudes. In some state schools feminist interventions will ensure that gender remains on the agenda; in others, it will sink without trace.

Employment and promotion of women teachers will be affected by the Act too. In 1988 there were 288 complaints from teachers to the EOC about alleged sex discrimination in selection and appointments procedures and some successful industrial tribunal cases have identified unlawful and discriminatory practices by governors.[93] Current research suggests that governor training is not routinely tackling this issue[94] and that equal opportunities is a long way down the priority list of many governing bodies.[95] Other things too will affect women teachers' promotion; in primary schools the requirement to be good at science and technology may limit promotion prospects for those women who find these subjects hard themselves. With the advent of Local Management of Schools, especially in large secondary schools, financial skills will increasingly be demanded of those who reach the senior management ranks; again for women who lack confidence in maths and handling finance in public, this will be a disadvantage in seeking promotion.

The National Curriculum at first sight, by contrast, looks promising in terms of equal opportunities. The notion of an entitlement curriculum does at least draw attention to the need not to discriminate between students on gender or other social grounds and the importance of gender as a cross curricular theme has also been stressed. The National Curriculum will make it compulsory for schools to teach core and foundation subjects, including science and technology, at least up till the end of the key stage 3, for all students. In theory at least this could lead to girls being less likely to drop out of subjects like physics and maths and boys being less able to drop out of subjects like languages. In practice however, since there will probably continue to be some choices within the core subjects, patterns of gender discrimination may well persist. Further, the National Curriculum itself may leave little room for students to discuss changing roles for women and men in the home and in employment and little scope for preparing boys as well as girls for parenthood and domestic life.

Assessment will also present many potential problems. Testing is not always culture fair, yet there is no guarantee (despite the evidence of the EOC to the National Curriculum Task Group on Assessment and Testing)[96] that the Standard Assessment Tests will take full account of gender (or race and class) in every subject area. Doing poorly in tests in subjects where either sex lack confidence will not boost that confidence either. As Gipps has noted, the current decision that test results will make no reference to social differences (class, gender, ethnicity) means that there will be no opportunity for the much vaunted parent power and parental choice of schools to be based on knowledge of whether a school appears to be particularly good, for example, at teaching working-class girls.[97]

CONCLUSION

The 1988 Education Reform Act has paid scant attention to gender issues and does not provide a good backdrop for future feminist interventions in schooling. More worryingly, few feminists seem to be amongst those looking carefully at the room for manoeuvre within the ERA. There are possibilities for change which lie within the inherent contradictions of the legislation itself and these sometimes lie in quarters, such as opting out, which the left may too quickly rule 'out of bounds'. The Labour Party itself needs to give much more thought to policies which not only relate gender, race, ethnicity, class and disability more closely together, but which also tackle those issues across the whole range of economic and social policies, from the shape of the economy to whether there should be separate Muslim schools in the state system. We also need to make sure in future that radical interventions into schooling are properly thought out, are translated into specific and achievable tasks and are carefully monitored and evaluated. In the past this has not always been the case. Even though this attention to the rational aspects of the process will not solve all the problems, they will certainly help.

This article has reviewed the often unsystematic nature of a wide range of feminist interventions in education over the past two decades.

It has pointed to the small extent of many of these, but at the same time noted the achievements so far made. These are limited in scope, sometimes contradictory and many are far from radical. But even what has already been achieved may be lost unless gender issues are firmly incorporated into future left radical policies on education. Furthermore, feminist interventions and attempts to eliminate sexism, and even non-feminist endeavours to improve the surbordinate status of women and girls in the schooling system, need to emanate not just from female teachers and researchers but also male teachers and educational researchers, school governors, pupils, school ancillary workers and parents. Women have struggled for many decades for a rightful place in education and for an end to the contribution of education to the reproduction of their subordinate status. It would be nothing short of a disaster if the provisions of the Reform Act and the failure of the left to recognise the central place of gender alongside class, race and special needs, in tackling inequality, meant that the 1990s saw gender disappear from the educational agenda altogether.

NOTES

Thanks are due to Kevin Brehony and Ali Rattansi for their comments on earlier drafts. During the time that the various drafts of this chapter were being written, I was heavily involved in the move of Stantonbury Campus, Milton Keynes, towards Grant Maintained Status. This has involved me in a great deal of rethinking of my position on a range of issues to do with schooling and educational innovation, including my ideas about gender. Although none of them have seen or commented on this paper, Maggie Constable, Mike Davies, Jo Kilby, Gill Mullis, Gill Molloy, Lynn Norfolk, Gay Smith, Penny Westwood and John Wilkins have all helped, in different ways, to shape the thinking that has gone into the final version.

1. J. Purvis, *Gender and Education*, Unit 25, Course E205, Open University, Milton Keynes 1984.
2. R. Deem, 'Bringing gender equality into schools', in S. Walker and L. Barton (eds), *Changing Policies, Changing Teachers*, Open University Press, Milton Keynes 1987.
3. Labour Party, *Multi-cultural Education – Labour's policy for schools*, London 1989; and *Children First – Labour's policy for raising school standards*, London 1989.
4. R. Deem, 'The reform of school governing bodies – the power of the

consumer over the producer?', in M. Flude and M. Hammer (eds), *The 1988 Education Act: Origins and Implications*, Falmer Press, Lewes 1989.

5. Centre for Contemporary Cultural Studies, *Unpopular Education*, Hutchinson, London 1981.

6. B. Simon, *Does Education Matter?*, Lawrence and Wishart, London 1985.

7. R. Deem, 'The new school governing bodies – are race and gender on the agenda?', *Gender and Education*, Vol 1, No 3, 1989; and 'Governing by gender? School governing bodies after the Reform Act', in P. Abbott and C. Wallace (eds), *Gender, Sexuality and Power*, Macmillan, London 1991.

8. B. Simon, *Bending the Rules: The Baker 'Reform' of Education*, Lawrence and Wishart, London 1987.

9. Flude and Hammer, *op cit*.

10. M. Arnot and G. Weiner, *Gender and Education*, E813, Open University, Milton Keynes 1987.

11. M. Arnot and G. Weiner, 'Teachers and gender politics', in Arnot and Weiner (eds), *Gender and the Politics of Schooling*, Hutchinson, London 1987.

12. G. Weiner, 'The Schools Council and Gender: a case study in the legitimation of curriculum policy', in M. Arnot (ed), *Race and Gender*, Pergamon, Oxford 1985.

13. J. Headlam Wells, 'Humberside goes neuter: an example of an LEA intervening for equal opportunities', in J. Whyte, R. Deem, L. Kant and M. Cruickshank (eds), *Girl Friendly Schooling*, Methuen, London 1988.

14. C. Adams, 'Teacher Attitudes towards issues of sex equality', in Whyte *et al, op. cit*; H. Taylor, 'INSET for equal opportunities', in Whyte *et al, op cit*.

15. M. Arnot, 'Political lipservice or radical reform? Central government responses to sex equality as a policy issue', in Arnot and Weiner (eds), 1987 *op cit*; G. Weiner, *Just a Bunch of Girls*, Open University Press, Milton Keynes 1985.

16. G. Weiner, 1984, *op cit*, p 5.

17. Arnot and Weiner, 'Teachers and gender politics', *op cit*, p 360.

18. G. Weiner, 1985, *op cit*.

19. L. Yates, 'Is girl friendly schooling what girls need?', in Whyte *et al, op cit*.

20. M. Arnot, 'Political lipservice . . .', 1987, *op cit*.

21. A. Wolpe, 'A socialist education for girls', in H. Lauder and P. Brown (eds), *Education in Search of a Future*, Falmer Press, London 1988.

22. Labour Policy, *Multi-cultural education*, 1989, *op cit*.

23. Labour Party, *Children First*, 1989, *op cit*.

24. H. Wainwright, *Labour: A Tale of Two Parties*, Hogarth Press, London 1987.

25. A.M. Barry, unpublished PhD thesis, 1990.

26. See, for example, R. Deem, *Women and Schooling*, Routledge and Kegan Paul, London 1978; E. Byrne, *Women and Education*, Tavistock, London 1978.

27. See, for example, M. Macdonald, 'Socio-cultural reproduction and

women's education', in R. Deem (ed), *Schooling for Women's Work*, Routledge, London 1980; E. Sarah and D. Spender, *Learning to Lose: sexism and education*, Women's Press, London 1980.

28. R. Deem, 1978 *op cit*; E. Byrne, 1978, *op cit*.
29. D. Spender, *Manmade Language*, Routledge and Kegan Paul, London 1980; and *Invisible Women: the schooling scandal*, Writers and Readers, London 1982.
30. Macdonald, *op cit*.
31. Whyte *et al*, *op cit*; Arnot, 1985, *op cit*.
32. Arnot, *op cit*.
33. Whyte *et al*, *op cit*.
34. A. Kelly, 'Changing schools and changing society: some reflections on the GIST project', in Arnot 1985, op cit.
35. R. Connell, *Gender and Power*, Polity, Cambridge 1987.
36. *Social Trends*, 1990.
37. S. Dex, *The Sexual Division of Work*, Wheatsheaf, Brighton 1984; J. Martin and C. Roberts, *Women's Employment: A Life time Perspective*, HMSO, London 1984.
38. J. Gershuny and S. Jones, 'The changing work/leisure balance in Britain: 1961-1984', in J. Horne, D. Jary and A. Tomlinson (eds), *Sport, Leisure and Social Relations*, Routledge, London 1987.
39. D. Kirp, M. Yudof and M. Franks, 'Gender in the house of policy', in Arnot and Weiner (eds), 1987, *op cit*.
40. Yates, *op cit*.
41. *Ibid*.
42. Whyte *et al*, *op cit*; J. Whyte, *Girls into Science and Technology*, Routledge and Kegan Paul, London 1986; H. Burchell and V. Millman (eds), *Changing Perspectives on Gender*, Open University, Milton Keynes 1989; Arnot, 'Political lipservice', *op cit*.
43. Burchell and Millman, *op cit*.
44. Whyte, *op cit*.
45. Weiner, 'The Schools Council and Gender', 1985, *op cit*.
46. Weiner, *Just a Bunch of Girls*, *op cit*.
47. K. Myers, *Genderwatch*, SCDC/EOC, London 1987.
48. Wolpe, *op cit*.
49. Gershuny and Jones, *op cit*.
50. R. Deem, *All Work and No Play: the Sociology of Women and Leisure*, Open University Press, Milton Keynes 1986.
51. Wolpe, *op cit*.
52. A. Brah and R. Minhas, 'Structural Racism or Cultural Difference: Schooling for Asian Girls', in Weiner, *Just a Bunch of Girls*, *op cit*; K. Riley, 'Black girls speak for themselves', in Weiner, *Just a Bunch of Girls*, *op cit*; Arnot, 1985, *op cit*; H. Carby, 'Black feminism and the boundaries of sisterhood', in Arnot and Weiner (eds), 1987, *op cit*.
53. S. Scraton, 'Shaping up to womanhood', unpublished PhD thesis, Open

University 1989.

54. S. Scraton, 'Images of Femininity and the teaching of girls' physical education', in J. Evans (ed), *Physical Education, Sport and Schooling*, Open University Press, Milton Keynes 1986; and 'Boys muscle in where angels fear to tread: girls' subcultures and physical activities', in Horne, Jary and Tomlinson (eds), *Sport, Leisure and Social Relations*, Routledge, London 1987; and 'Gender and P.E.: ideologies of the physical and the politics of sexuality', in Walker and Barton, *op cit*.

55. B. McKellar, 'Only the fittest of the fittest will survive: Black women and education', in S. Acker (ed), *Teachers, Gender and Careers*, Falmer Press, London 1989; S. Bangar and J. McDermott, 'Black women speak', in De Lyon and Mignolio (eds), *Woman Teachers: issues and experiences*, Open University Press, Milton Keynes 1989; P. East *et al*, 'Access to teaching for black women', in De Lyon and Mignolio, *op cit*.

56. Equal Opportunities Commission, *Gender Issues: The Implications for Schools of the Education Reform Act 1988*, EOC, Manchester 1989.

57. De Lyon and Mignolio, *op cit*; Acker, *op cit*.

58. G. Randall, 'Gender differences in pupil-teacher interaction in workshops and laboratories', in Arnot and Weiner (eds), *Gender Under Scrutiny*, Hutchinson, London 1987; A. Wolpe, *Within School Walls*, Routledge, London 1988.

59. C. Jones, 'Sexual tyranny: male evidence in a mixed secondary school', in Weiner, *Just a Bunch of Girls, op cit*; J. Halson, 'The Sexual Harassment of Young Women', in L. Holly (ed), *Girls and Sexuality*, Open University Press, Milton Keynes 1989.

60. *Op cit*.

61. C. Jones and P. Mahony, *Learning Our Lives: Sexuality and social control in education*, Women's Press, London 1989.

62. Wolpe, *Within School Walls*, op cit.

63. Deem, 1986, *op cit*.

64. Scraton, 1989, *op cit*.

65. Weiner, 1985, *op cit*.

66. H. Taylor, 'A Local Authority Initiative on Equal Opportunities', in Arnot, 1985, *op cit*.

67. Adams, *op cit*.

68. De Lyon and Mignolio, *op cit*; Acker, *op cit*.

69. L. Hicks, *op cit*.

70. M. Spear, 'Teachers' attitudes towards girls and technology', in Whyte *et al*, *op cit*.

71. H. Davidson, 'Unfriendly Myths About Women Teachers', in Whyte *et al*, *op cit*.

72. Kelly, *op cit*.

73. J. Pratt, J. Bloomfield and C. Seale, *Option Choice*, NFER/Nelson, Slough 1984.

74. S. Riddell, 'It's nothing to do with me': Teachers' views and gender

divisions in the curriculum', in Acker, *op cit*.

75. J. Ozga, *Schoolwork*, Open University Press, Milton Keynes, 1988.
76. S. Middleton, 'Streaming and the politics of female sexuality: case studies in the schooling of girls', in Arnot and Weiner (eds), *op cit*; and 'Educating feminists: a life history study', in Acker, *op cit*.
77. Arnot and Weiner, *Gender and Education*, *op cit*.
78. EOC, *op cit*; D. Leonard, 'Gender and initial teacher training', in Acker, *op cit*; C. Skelton and J. Hanson, 'Schooling the teachers: Gender and initial teacher education', in Acker, *op cit*.
79. R. Deem, 'State policy and ideology in the education of women 1944-1980', *British Journal of Sociology of Education*, Vol 2, No 2, 1981, pp 131-144.
80. Weiner, 1989, *op cit*.
81. Stantonbury Campus Group, 'The realities of mixed schooling', in R. Deem (ed), *Co-Education Reconsidered*, Open University Press, Milton Keynes 1984; P. Mahony, *Schools for the Boys*, Hutchinson, London 1985; Spender, 1982, *op cit*; S. Askew and C. Ross, *Boys Don't Cry*, Open University Press, Milton Keynes 1988.
82. Wolpe, 1988, *op cit*.
83. Randall, *op cit*.
84. Spender, 1982, *op cit*; C. Buswell, 'Sexism in school: routines and classroom practices', *Durham and Newcastle Research Review*, Vol 9, No 46, 1981, pp 195-200; Mahony, *op cit*.
85. M. Stanworth, *Gender and Schooling*, Hutchinson, London 1983; J. Shaw, 'The politics of single sex schools', in R. Deem (ed), *Co-education Reconsidered*, Open University Press, Milton Keynes 1984.
86. Shaw, *op cit*; Mahony, *op cit*; S. Lees, *Losing Out*, Hutchinson, London 1986.
87. Spender, 1980, *op cit*, and 1982, *op cit*.
88. J. French and P. French, 'Sociolinguistics and gender divisions', in S. Acker, J. Megarry, S. Nisbet and E. Hoyle (eds), *Women and Education: World Yearbook of Education*, Kogan Page, London 1984.
89. Askew and Ross, *op cit*.
90. A more detailed discussion may be found in: EOC, *op cit*; S. Miles and C. Middleton, 'Girls' Education in the Balance: the ERA and inequality', in Flude and Hammer, *op cit*; and NUT, *The Education Bill and Equal Opportunities*, NUT, London 1987.
91. NUT, *Grant Maintained Schools*, NUT, London 1987.
92. Deem, 'The new school governing bodies – are race and gender on the agenda', *op cit*; and 1990, *op cit*.
93. EOC, *op cit*.
94. D. Streatfield, *School Governor Training and Information for Governess*, NFER-Nelson, Slough 1988.
95. R. Deem, 'The reform of school governing bodies', *op cit*; 'The new school governing bodies – are race and gender on the agenda', *op cit*; R. Deem and K. Brehony, 'Restructing state education after the Reform Act: social

justice, social divisions and the governing of schools', paper given to British Sociological Association, April 1990.

96. DES, *National Curriculum Task Group on Assessment and Testing*, HMSO, London 1988.

97. C. Gipps, 'The social implications of National Assessment', paper given to British Sociological Association, April 1990.

COMMON EDUCATION AND THE RADICAL TRADITION

CAROLINE BENN

The Left's radical tradition in education cannot be understood apart from the dynamic contest between equality and elitism, as cycles of reform and counter-reform rotate in educational history, often giving the false impression that history is repeating itself. Activity from one spurs the other into reorganising its forces, and although it often seems as if ideas of hierarchy and differentiation are more entrenched, their development invariably over-reaches, while radical reform, ever inching forward, maintains its steady historical momentum.

Commitment to greater human equality is a central feature of this tradition – and one of its basic constituents is common education: all members of a society educated together. Common education's first objective is a broad and balanced learning experience that develops all human beings to their full capacities, its second to act cohesively on those who live together to one society. Its origins are in the 17th century reforms of Bishop Comenius who was faced with social havoc caused by wars between Christian sects in the wake of the Reformation. Before this time the different denominations controlled formal learning, but Comenius proposed a new education system: common to all, regardless of religious affiliation. As well as learning together, everyone in his system also proceeded in steps – or grades – from earlier to later years, and from lower to higher forms of enlightenment. Most modern education systems descend in part from these proposals.

That everyone could be equally well educated was – and remains – a revolutionary idea. For this reason common education has always been opposed by conservatives and elitists who fear it will lead to changes in class and productive relations in favour of new social groups. Their counter-proposals always favour different types of education according to a person's social or economic level (and lately, innate 'intelligence'), their motives no less political than those behind

142

common education. Lately, opposition has also come from those who resist mass production in education as leading to state manipulation, patently also a social concern. One modern educator – Ivan Illich – even blamed Comenius's original plan for the compulsory schooling systems which he believes strangle genuine education in all advanced nations today, where the institution has come to define the purpose of education rather than the other way around.[1] However, Illich's main complaint – that 'no matter how much each generation spends on schools, it always turned out that the majority . . . were certified unfit for higher grades of enlightenment and had to be discarded' – is exactly the starting point of those who have advocated common schooling in modern times.

That the majority should have the same rights as an elite minority to enjoy the full range of education available to each generation, was an idea that dawned in the industrial revolution, as artisans were struggling to understand their political and class predicament in early 19th century Britain. Soon Chartists and other reformers were asking for common schools – to break down class barriers and give the majority 'better opportunities', as Richard Cobden put it.[2] When the 1870 Act brought universal basic education, the radical tradition, now augmented by a socialist movement and the 'new unionism' of workers in the skilled trades, immediately sought to advance it in a common direction. Thus Keir Hardie, at an 1896 International Socialist Congress, successfully moved for the same educational provision for everyone without regard to any individual's test score or exam qualifications,[3] while a Trades Councils and Cooperative Societies' representative, appearing before the Bryce Commission investigating secondary education in 1894, made another of common education's basic demands: that the system be organised on the basis of age divisions rather than those of social class.[4] Neither demand was likely to be conceded by the bourgeoisie (let alone the old aristocracy), who feared the surge of equality – and demand for public services – that universal basic education would foster. Indeed, the forces of elitism were already hard at work to mitigate the latest reforms by devising new types of segregation.

'It mattered not that the teacher had no training so long as the house possessed a respectable exterior', wrote Frederick Rogers, trade unionist, self-educated social reformer and university extension lecturer, about middle-class attempts to escape social contact with the working class after 1870. 'I have seen schools . . . with the legend "Middle Class School" cut out of white paper and pasted on a window glass', he wrote; more than enough to attract parents 'who pinch and save to pay high fees to schools like this in order that their children should not associate' with children in Board or Voluntary schools, which often had a far 'superior education'.[5] At the upper end of the middle class, professional parents were busy starting new private enterprises, their own 'public' schools. Some of these had been founded specifically as common schools – in the cases of Winchester and Eton as 14th and 15th century neighbourhood schools for poor children without clerical backing, to help them compete with the well to do of the day. In the 19th century this practice of 'enclosing' once-common institutions for the use of elite groups – so closely parallelled by the enclosure of the common land going on at the time – was even more pronounced in the case of the much larger group of endowed schools. These had often been established by religious bodies specifically to provide free, local education for the poor. The Endowed Schools Commission of 1867, reviewing their operation, made several key changes in response to the growing claims to education of the bourgeoisie – all entirely at the expense of the working class. These included empowering such schools to charge fees.

DIVIDING SCHOOLS AND MINDS

For the majority of the working class it was a case of starting all over again, as it so often is in the drama of common schooling, where a new divided system replaces an old, and has to be countered anew. In the late 19th century pressure for change came particularly on behalf of skilled workers' children for the kind of education which the middle classes took for granted for their sons (daughters everywhere had a much harder struggle). This led to 'scholarships' for the poor – provided they were few in number, industrious, capable of passing tests, and working strictly out of individual ambition to advance in the existing system – in other words, 'deserving'. Radicals opposed this idea of education as a privilege, a 'ladder' for the few; they believed it was a right for all, and should be a 'broad highway', an extension of basic common schooling to promote the collective advance of working-class communities. The heart of it was a growing belief in the educability of everyone. They had to face not only traditional elitism from the middle and upper classes, but from their own ranks as well. Most Fabians, for example, were strongly in favour of a segregated education for Labour's own aristocracy of leaders. They supported the establishment of local grammar schools brought in by the 1902

Education Act: mirror-image public schools offering classical education to the less affluent. It was at this precise date, as Brian Simon and David Rubinstein point out, that divisive 'differentiation of the types of school . . . was built into the national system' in Britain.[6] It was also at this point that radical reformers began the lengthy task of combating the determinism inherent in the concept of 'intelligence' – a formidable new criterion that was to regulate educational opportunity for at least half a century.

From the Ministry of Education, men like Cyril Burt, the high priest of IQ, set the new determinist view: 'intelligence . . . is inherited . . . not due to teaching or training . . . uninfluenced by industry or zeal . . . (and) measured with . . . ease.'[7] Segregation was justified by science in the form of the IQ test, claimed to be value free, fair, and nothing to do with social status or wealth. It came unstuck in the end not because the 'science' was flawed (although Cyril Burt's dishonest manipulation of data did not help his cause), but because it was socially unacceptable. As large scale analyses of school entry statistics became possible in the second half of the 20th century, IQ's claims to be without social bias did not stand up. Put simply, too many of those who turned out to have 'intelligence' were also middle class, wealthy or culturally well-endowed.[8] Once again the elite had commandeered a route originally designed – at least in part – for the poor.

Meanwhile, however, a divisive secondary system had been entrenched in Britain after the 1944 Act at a time when countries with educational histories very similar to Britain's were beginning to move away from crude academic selection. Ironically it was the work of a supposedly 'reforming' British Labour government, which, despite protests from its own supporters, insisted not only on retaining the old system of different 'types' of schools, but adding to it a national IQ test at 11-plus. It assumed that a radical remit had been discharged with the introduction of a new Secondary Modern School for the majority and the abolition of fees for grammar schools – illustrating the way partial reforms can often prolong inequalities rather than end them. Behind this failure to reform radically in 1945 was the same powerful civil service and educational establishment which had just produced a national report (and was later to produce the government's own pamphlets) suggesting that only a minority had the intelligence for a mainstream education, while the majority, who 'found abstraction had little meaning', were happier working with their hands in applied activity.[9] This majority, it was confidently stated on behalf of those who would live and work in the second half of the twentieth century, needed no qualifications of any kind from their schooling.

COMPREHENSIVE REFORM

Those who opposed this elitist orthodoxy were the supporters of comprehensive education – as common schooling had come to be called in Britain after the Second World War. Aware of education's social motivation and consequences, and including educationalists like Fred Clarke, Shena Simon, Brian Simon, and Robin Pedley,[10] they were largely concerned with those sectors of education with least prestige and influence: secondary modern and primary schools. Secondary schools saw first hand what talent had been unable to show itself at an earlier stage, and primary schools, watching comprehensive primary education developing so successfully, wanted it extended, abolishing altogether the hated examination that decided children's futures at the absurdly early age of eleven. They were opposed by the majority of teachers in the prestige areas of secondary education, the grammar and public schools, who supported selection. So too did the media, particularly influential journals like the *Times Educational Supplement*, whose editorials for most of the 1950s and 1960s were intensely anti-comprehensive. As for the universities, only one vice-chancellor ever supported the comprehensive cause, and even as late as the 1970s the principals of all Oxford colleges signed a letter deploring the comprehensive change.[11]

Yet by the 1970s, common secondary schooling was well established, having accelerated after 1945 when Labour local authorities like Middlesex and London, defying a Labour government, applied to develop comprehensive schools rather than a divided system. Over the thirteen years after 1951, Conservative governments also had to deal with growing numbers of local authorities of all political hues wishing to 'go comprehensive'. Though teachers in unions like the NUT were originally divided, they were won over by experience during the 1960s.[12] Parent groups and campaigning organisations such as The Campaign for Comprehensive Education, The Campaign for the Advancement of State Education, and the education journal, *Forum*, were supported by relentless pressure from those parents and pupils injured by selection (those just below a cut-off line always exerting the greatest thrust). These organisations added their weight to those challenging the claims of the IQ scientists who ran selection. All were able to point to research that showed the divided system denied opportunity to the majority and wasted talent;[13] by the mid 1960s even a Conservative Minister of Education was able to talk about intelligence not as a genetic trait but as that which could be 'acquired' by everyone.[14] As William James once noted, the most revolutionary fact in life is that people can change things simply by changing the way they think about them. This was the radical tradition's great achievement: it changed the way people thought about human mental capacity and its relationship to educational opportunity.

THE COUNTER-REFORMATION

This change bred a counter-reformation which did not begin in 1979, when a Conservative majority was elected, but long before in initiatives like the Black Papers and the groups formed to 'save' grammar schools from serving the whole attainment range. Incessant media coverage was given to their claims that comprehensives lowered behavioural and academic standards and restricted 'choice' – much of it thinly disguised objections on behalf of those previously accustomed to being able to move away from predominantly working-class schools for their children's education. Comprehensive schools were always well defended (though never with the same media coverage) and in the late 1980s even a Conservative Education Minister had to admit that standards had not declined. But for nearly two decades agitation about comprehensive education was never out of the public's eye. The result was not so much that popular opinion set against it – since experience of the new schools began turning the tide in their favour after 1970 – but that there was a widespread assumption that enormous changes were being made in the education system when in fact this was not the case. The reform was always partial, and its first phase was eventually to run into the ground. Labour governments of 1964 through to 1979 – with 13 years in power – were as timid as they had been in 1945 when it came to radical educational reform.

Despite strong support for comprehensive reform from successive Labour Party conferences for over twenty years, there was still the old Fabian/Labourist commitment to the grammar school to overcome. Harold Wilson's automatic response in 1964, that its abolition would be over his dead body, spoke to a well defined interest group. Persuading communities to make a move towards comprehensive education in some local education committees was often better accomplished by radical education officers than senior Labour politicans.[15] Nationally, most Labour leaders and education ministers, though committed to a degree of social mixing, privately believed in the limited availability of intelligence and the necessity of protecting an academic elite – if not in grammar schools, at least within the comprehensive. Their comprehensive reforms were consequently strictly limited to external structural reorganisation. This was itself a large task – all the more reason to ensure it was achieved effectively. There were doubts whether a single short circular in 1965, sketching current suggestions for external restructuring, was enough to effect so major a reform, and these were amply confirmed within a year. Half the authorities requested to send in reorganisation plans failed to do so.

Lack of effective legislation mattered because the persistence of 11-plus selection throughout this time caused doubt and demoralisation about how many comprehensives were 'genuine' when half were not receiving comprehensive intakes. There was also no positive definition of a comprehensive school, still less of how education inside such schools was supposed to develop. From the start there were worrying signs that the retention of a selective assessment system like GCE O level, especially where streaming was used to buttress the process, had the effect of collapsing a grammar and modern school into one and, did not always produce a vastly changed educational outcome and this was made worse, not better, by the addition of a 'second class' CSE exam.[16]

Although discussion was constant in all comprehensives about the forms of grouping, curriculum, and assessment most appropriate to a common school, lack of guidance from the top meant that some new schools carried on the old divided system under a new roof, while others sought to develop new forms of education that enhanced learning and had social impact. The latter began unstreaming; they entered all pupils for external exams – despite the fact that the system was only designed to cater for 60 per cent. Many developed a common curriculum for the earliest years, and in time a common core after 14-plus. These developments had their advantages, for they meant changes were well grounded in practice. But it was not enough. Legislation to secure reorganisation became more and more urgent so that all these changes could proceed rationally – and eventually universally. They needed a context free from the corrosive effects of continuing selection, and from delaying action by vigilante groups who were able to bring lightning legal actions on obscure technicalities which related to the old law still in force. From the late 1960s there was pressure on Labour's education policy-makers to act on unstreaming, common curricula, and above all, a single assessment system at 16-plus. The response from Labour governments was at best equivocal, at worst stony. This failure to act to end selection in the state system was compounded by lack of action on public schools (except for the partial measure of ending the direct grant, which merely served to increase the private sector by 100 schools). Thus this other much heralded Labour reform, in spite of the massive Public Schools Commission's fact-gathering activity, which began in 1965, had petered out completely by the 1970s. Matters were most crucial for comprehensives in the big cities, where polarisation occurred not only on selective and social lines, but also on grounds of race and religion.[17] Properly pursued comprehensive legislation – difficult though it would undoubtedly have been – could have mitigated many of these problems before – inevitably – they came home to haunt the system.

When comprehensive legislation was eventually brought forward in 1976, it was not the major education act promised in the late 1960s but a one-clause bill that did not end selection after all. Instead it merely gave the Secretary of State power to require non-selective planning. Even so, counter-reformers called it a 'jackboot' measure and no Labour minister ever used it. Nor did it help in guiding comprehensive development, since comprehensives were defined entirely negatively as schools 'not entered as the result of selection tests', a definition which applied equally to secondary modern schools. Such caution might have been justified if there was evidence that local authorities, parents and teachers were turning away from comprehensive change. But they were not. Pressure to 'go comprehensive' grew throughout this period (and agitation within Conservative controlled authorities continued right up through the 1980s).[18] It was strongest of all during the three-year period of Conservative rule under Margaret Thatcher's ministry in the early 1970s, when more comprehensive schools were approved than at any other period in history – a fact some Conservatives cited later to imply their party had always favoured this popular reform.[19]

The consolation for radical reformers was in having won so many of the arguments, but to secure developments in practice, forward planning was required, particularly after 14-plus. This had already occurred in countries like Scandinavia through twenty-year rolling programmes of comprehensive legislation that saw an ordered changeover with streaming abolished and education and training curricula reformed and extended to the age of 18 by the late 1970s. Comprehensive development was also proceeding in almost all of the rest of Europe, both eastern and western – as well as in Japan from 1945, and, after the Cultural Revolution, in China as well.

The two world giants, the USA and the USSR, had legislated for comprehensive systems after the First World War to bring social cohesion to their diverse populations – and to raise mass standards in anticipation of technological change. In the USA by the 1970s it was being pushed up to the age of 20 through the community college movement. Even in those few countries not going over to full comprehensive systems – like Germany – a high standard of skilled training was available to half the age group after 16. In Britain the training system was still rudimentary – largely confined to apprenticeships, mostly going to white males, while the percentages staying on in education after school-leaving – or going on to higher education – were nearly the lowest of all the major industrial nations.

But Labour left office in 1979 without taking decisive legislative action on this major reform. In 24 years of Labour governments from 1924 there had been no major Labour Education Act. For a Party committed to change through the Parliamentary process rather than extra-Parliamentary action, this legislative abdication is highly significant, and points yet again to a radical educational tradition in Britain that has repeatedly lacked translation into positive political action at the top. Behind it is a failure by Labour to formulate change in terms of the values and objectives of egalitarian social change – a failure that was to loom all the larger as Conservatives swept through the 1980s enacting legislative change in every corner of the education and training system – pursuant to a well defined and articulated political ideology of elitism and market-led restructuring.

RECESSION CRISIS

Mere government inaction might have characterised comprehensive reform until the end of the Labour government in 1979 had not economic events forced a reactionary second phase into being and – after a period of deep retreat – the eventual renewal of radical forces in education. The crisis, heralded by the oil price problem in 1973, came to a head in the World Bank's intervention in Labour Policy in 1976, bringing capitalism's latest economic failings to bear on all policy, education included. Labour was unprepared – in education as in every other field of government – when unemployment began to rise.

Instead of proceeding to end selection and integrate training with education, extending both up to 18 (and thus catch up with reforms the majority of advanced industrial nations had already made), a Labour government abruptly closed the comprehensive book. It was plain that behind this move was concerted corporate pressure from the business and civil service establishments. Through a single set speech delivered by the prime minister at Ruskin College and a private government publication released only to selected editors (but never to parents, teachers or the general public),[20] the government suddenly claimed that the comprehensive reform's aims had been achieved and that virtually everyone was now assured of comprehensive secondary education – a manifest untruth[21] but widely repeated.

Almost overnight comprehensive-compatible criteria for educational development were abandoned. When long overdue discussion – for example, on the curriculum – was encouraged, it came instead through an engineered 'great debate' on schools' 'relevance' to work – selectively confined to pupils outside GCE streams. The government implied that these young people were out of work because the schools failed to teach them basic skills, when it was plain they were workless because employers could offer them no work (and without qualifications because the system could offer them none). Unemployment was structural and was going to get worse. The 'great debate' suggested it could all be managed by getting schools closer to employers' needs. Even the trade unionists invited to take part appeared to believe the cause of worklessness lay in schools – rather than a misfunctioning economy where large scale unemployment was soon to become an epidemic. They spoke as one with their employers (in pointed contrast to the continuing disputes going on between them in the industrial field). In particular, they were at one about the need for schemes of training. The first, YOP, was introduced in 1977 by the Manpower Services Commission of the Department of Employment. The scene was thus set for another round of divisive development akin to the secondary modern/grammar divisions of the 1944 Act – but starting at the age of 14, when a hierarchical exam system sorted pupils into separate streams in every subject. After 16, GCE A level would continue for the 'academic', while an equally large section of youth was to be diverted to 'schemes' of work, most with little educational content. The policy that inevitably evolved was reminiscent of nothing so much as the Charity Schools of the 18th century, created to give education to the poor. As Joan Simon shows, these merged with the workhouses at the first sign of economic trouble, so that what began with children learning to read 'ended with the spinning wheel'.[22]

Had comprehensive criteria been reinforced in 1976 and over the next ten years encouraged through a common curriculum for 14-18 (which included training), the long-awaited extension of schooling could have mitigated some of the worst features of 'training' schemes which were to follow. Using the billions available later to the MSC – plus a matching contribution from employers – real skills training could have been extended, and eventually integrated with continuing education, allied to the long overdue reform of post-16 qualifications and courses. This would not have created jobs but it would have put education and training in a better position to meet unemployment (and take part in recovery from it later), and given those worst affected by it a better chance to defend themselves and the social programmes upon which so many depended. Looked at internationally, it was not an impossibilist goal by any means.

But not only was this course not implemented, it was not even argued. In the ideological vacuum that followed, some of the radical left came out in favour of training as a more suitable means than education of engaging the commitment of working-class young people, while others on the left rounded on training's narrow instrumentalism and hostility to the values of liberal education. Thus the left fell into dispute about whether training itself was good or bad rather than discussing the way education for and about work – both professional and skilled – could be successfully developed within a common system that related education and training to true social and community need. Having lost the comprehensive keystone that would have resolved these issues, the radical movement was divided by the 'great debate' and its aftermath. Again there had been a measure of political failure, for apart from a vague commitment to promote more social mixing, the kind of society comprehensive change might have helped to achieve was never discussed as part of the politics of social change in Britain. The positive virtues of common schooling for changed social or productive relationships were not allied to the new ideology being promoted – what one set of observers has called the shift from 'an egalitarian ideal ... into (the) talent generating expedient of the Parliamentary leadership'.[23] As time went on, adherents were increasingly confined to a narrow educational compound – with a defensive approach that ill equipped them to deal with an increasingly aggressive counter-reform. Conservatives took full advantage of the radical left's ideological disarray and Labour's failures to end selection and define the criteria of comprehensive reform. Legislation was used repeatedly: introducing the 11-plus into law for the first time to keep grammar (and any voluntary-aided schools that wished it) selective; protecting private education through assisted places, promoting new forms of differentiation through City Technology Colleges and 'opted out' schools; and, lastly, ensuring that as some schools filled up, 'open enrolment' meant others would decline and close – inevitably those serving working-class areas, whose pupils would be dispersed on long journeys to join the schools next due to close. By these multiple means involving replacing the old, open compulsory 11-plus by a new, hidden, optional 'parental choice' between increasingly unequal schools, academic and social selection would grow insidiously. Instead of a common curriculum which guaranteed an equal learning experience, the government imposed a quite different National Curriculum allied to a renewed national programme of enforced mass attainment testing throughout school life, which would insure it was applied increasingly differentially. Alongside, this, educational expenditure cuts were being ruthlessly enforced.

Few of these policies had popular support, but they were not as unpopular as reconvening an overt policy of grammar schools and secondary modern schools would have been. This was the government's preferred option but it was not possible because the argument on common education had been won. Herein lay the counter-reformation's deeper problem: the majority now believed in the concept of equal opportunity for everyone. Permanent new foundations had been laid for a democratic involvement of the majority in their own learning within a system of education that could well lead to thinking that encouraged the redistribution of power and resources more equally throughout society. Conservatives concluded that urgent action was required to try to turn both system and thinking around, and to curb mass demand for continuous improvement in educational opportunities, inevitably stimulated by advances in common schooling. To do this, not having won the argument, required escalating state intervention and dictation to promote social control through a return to academic hierarchy. This involved a vast array of legislation to exert the strictest control of the majority's destinations – even their thinking – as well as protection for existing social relations and their re-assignment to rigidly differentiated institutions, qualifications and curricular pathways. As Brian Simon noted, when commenting on the objectives of ministry mandarins controlling these draconian reforms, their most significant, if inadvert, comment on why this 'change' was needed, was that education had to teach people 'to know their place once more'.[24]

MIRROR-IMAGE POLITICS

Policy from the left during this time zig-zagged between radical fightback activity, including initiatives to promote race and gender equality, and attempting to outflank Conservatives at their own game. Taking the latter course, the Labour Party, for example, turned from advocating a universal and unified education service in policy papers prepared by the whole party at the beginning of this period, to the promotion of consumers' rights, concentrating heavily on 'choice' and 'standards', in a series of education 'charters' and policy proposals prepared by the Parliamentary leadership.[25] Labour leaders also accepted the *de facto* segregation of training, with policy jointly formulated with the TUC, making the MSC's Task Group Report of 1982 their base line.[26] Their main complaint was that the Task Group provisions were never properly implemented by Conservatives. But MSC thinking under the Conservatives promoted a three-tiered division throughout education after 16 and was completely incompatible with the general long term trend of radical reform towards the extension of comprehensive education and its integration with training. Radical reform would have meant that GCE A level and YTS would give way to a reorganisation of all post-16 courses on credit-transfer lines which would unify the education and training curriculum, making it flexible and accessible throughout adult life. Despite several excellent critiques and forward looking initiatives from Labour and other sections of the left over a long period and in relation to all sectors, there was no unifying ideology and thus no basis from which to challenge the socio-political thinking that counter-reformers were advancing throughout this time. Some of the counter-reform was uncannily reminiscent of the separate-types-of-mind thinking from 1945 about the majority being unable to understand 'abstractions' and needing to work with their hands. In 1986, for example, David Young of the MSC justified YTS on the grounds that many young people were much better off outside mainstream education because their minds simply 'couldn't grasp . . . concepts.'[27] No one even asked by what means nature wrought conceptual capacity in most middle class youth, but not in those more likely to be unemployed, less affluent or from ethnic minorities. Just as there was no official opposition to the solidifying tripartite structure after 16 and its internal divisions, which included such self-fulfilling projects as 'Low Achievers Programmes'. It was a low ebb.

Although Conservatives kept the initiative, their reforms were gradually brought to a halt by the contradictions of their position on comprehensive education. They argued for – and undoubtedly wanted – improvements in mass education and training that competitor countries had already achieved, and ironically, sanctioned the 'single'

16-plus exam that Labour had refused. But their hierarchical approach meant that the new GCSE still kepts its grading and final examination, and after 16 the A level was retained with only minor modifications. This, plus the continuing elitist dedication to differentiation between institutions, courses, qualifications and 'schemes', blocked the effectiveness of any policies purporting to improve common schooling. Nowhere was this contradiction more evident than in the organisation of the 16-19 sector, where cutbacks and falling population began to force school amalgamations, and tertiary colleges had became popular among rationalising administrators and 'bottom line' Conservatives because they were so much more efficient than a lot of scattered sixth forms. The problem was that such colleges cut across counter-reformers' determination to retain the sixth form, particularly in prestigous and selective schools. Tertiary reorganisation threatened the tripartite division which suited counter-reformers so well: academic courses segregated in the sixth and limited to a minority of the age group, predominantly middle class and vocal, YTS in place for about the same number of mainly working-class leavers with little voice, and a middle tier of vocational education that expanded and contracted according to employment figures. By sanctioning opting out for schools threatened with reorganisation tertiaries were virtually halted. Attention was concentrated on vocational and training tiers in a way that was comparable to the attention the secondary modern and technical schools received in 1945. This time the 'technical' tier was rapidly developed into a confusing jungle of BEC and TEC and CPVE and City of Guilds – with a National Council on Vocational Qualifications charged with bringing order out of the chaos. But it was a policy of proliferation rather than change, and, together with training schemes, was designed to serve another function of the counter-reformation: the reorientation of education and training to meet the needs of employers and the market – rather than those of society and individuals. Run mostly by the Manpower Services Commission rather than the DES, training schemes in particular were designed to help meet employers' short term needs, tiding them over recession, while low training allowances restructured wages downwards to discipline youth into accepting long periods of unemployment or poorly paid intermittent work – which was all that capitalism had to offer. When they rebelled – as in the riots of the early 1980s, some specifically related to training – further pressure was brought to bear in the form of cuts in social welfare, housing and other youth benefits. When criticism from trainers, educators and unions grew about any particular training programme, the 'scheme' was often withdrawn and another introduced with the promise of improvement. Over a dozen schemes came and went in as many years.[28] But instead of improvements, each change generally brought poorer funding, lower allowances, fewer rights , and diminished quality. By 1990 even the TUC had dismissed the schemes.

Yet in the 1970s unions and Labour had welcomed training schemes, seen as a means to secure the skills required to keep Britain in business and meet the needs of young people. All of which they might have achieved had they been integrated with education in a comprehensive reform that also provided everyone with meaningful educational qualifications as well as real skills training. But only a small fraction of the new 'schemes' fulfilled these criteria – and for them there was selection so blatant it made the 11-plus look like an open door. One area listed 35 selective tests employers operated for places on the few sought after YTS schemes which replaced the old apprenticeships and led to jobs.[29] One result was that the few 'good' schemes were often commandeered by males, whites or the middle class. Without the comprehensive principle to guide its development, mass schemes of training fell to differentiation and elitism even more surely than education, leaving the YTS majority with mere 'workfare' activity. Despite much MSC jargon, there was little real skills training, much narrow male and female work patterning, racial inequality, health and safety failures, lack of accountability, and impoverished educational input.[30] Only a minority got any meaningful educational qualifications and many went straight back on the dole. Schemes were not popular and to maintain numbers required increasingly costly advertising or heavy policing with threats of total benefit withdrawal. Over-weighted with working-class and ethnic minority youth, trainees suffered a shocking lack of rights, and no redress when employers failed to deliver their side of the training bargain, a frequent occurrence.[31] This made uneasy reading compared to the fuss being made of parents' and pupils' rights in schools, often for young people of exactly the same age: 16 and 17. The inequality between top and bottom in a supposedly comprehensive secondary system was too self evident to ignore. Elitism had badly over-reached itself yet again.

The Radical Revival

Despite – or rather because of – the juggernaut of counter-reformation activity, and the inequalities it revealed and fostered, many opportunities appeared for radicals to develop their own initiatives and thinking in both schools and colleges, taking advantage of the fact that at least there was funding for some of this activity – not all of which could be controlled from Whitehall or monitored by censoring MSC bureaucrats. As a result, many teachers and trainers found space to innovate and extend opportunity during this period. One example was the explosion of enquiry-based course work associated with the GCSE, its success mainly due to comprehensive schools responding positively to pressure upwards from the common curriculum and making use of earlier experience of school-based assessment under the discarded CSE Mode III. TVEI was another example. Although designed to operate selectively (and in many schools becoming merely a low-status tech stream), wide-awake comprehensives commandeered it to power the engine of comprehensive curricular and assessment change, motivated by the need to benefit all pupils, not just some. Many innovations – like several new modular curricula for GCSE – had nothing to do with technology; local areas merely used the money to implement reforms that were waiting in the wings. In Scotland a modular vocational curriculum at 16-plus – albeit within a divided system – pioneered a unitary 'credit' principle.[32] In new college courses and on training schemes – despite their narrowness and market-orientation – expenditure on curriculum development offered chances for innovation in course content and teaching methods – as did funding for training initiatives of all kinds under YTS. In all these areas educators and trainers promoted ideas of self development, critical enquiry, group advance, race and gender equality and co-operative working.

Because the changes taking place were arguably more extensive than those of the comprehensive reform of the 1960s and 70s, they were accompanied by an explosion of critical research and analysis, particularly centred around post-16 education and training. This received almost no attention in the mass media – in striking contrast to the attention given to criticisms of comprehensive reform earlier, when even a single pupil smoking a cigarette on the way home from school was given headline and peak-viewing coverage as a sign of imminent national collapse. For the scandals of training, however, including the deaths of young people on schemes with inadequate safety provision – there was little investigative journalism. A bibliography on training and education complied by university and other researchers for the trade union movement in 1987[33] showed that out of 2000 items on education and training in the previous four years (a larger output than even the comprehensive reform had generated) only 2 per cent related to the mass media, heavy or light, broadcast or written. With the mass media throughout the counter-reformation acting merely as tame conduits for Conservative government policy pronouncements, the left's radical thinking and policy promotion was confined to a network of specialist groups, research units, voluntary bodies, trade unions, unemployment centres, government departments, and to individual teachers, lecturers, youth workers, and trainers. Many began campaigning for reforms in the post-16 arena of further education colleges and workplaces. Left with the least qualified young people to 'discipline' into the new social relations required by the counter-reformation, they experienced at first-hand, some for the first time, the ultimate selection process – the one for employment. A bond developed between them and their learners as it had in the despised secondary moderns forty years earlier. As in that earlier time too, both resistance to divisive schemes and transformational initiatives were coming from those sectors with the least prestige: non-advanced FE, training boards, the Youth Service, adult education, YTS workshops and unemployment centres, often involving – as before – the least influential groups in education: the 'general' educators from the technical colleges, the part-time tutors in adult and extension education, ethnic minority educators determined on justice for deprived minorities in a system manifestly failing them, women determined to resist the training strait-jacket that was limiting them once again to a narrow range of options in service and caring work. Supporters from mainstream comprehensive schools took a longer time to join in, particularly those locked in struggles to resist tertiary reorganisation, under the illusion that preserving the sixth form in the all-through school was somehow defending comprehensive education. Many have heard little of vocational and training developments involving the rest of the age group, though it was obvious that their dream of 'new sixth formers' with their special CEE exam, had never really materialised. Imperceptibly, some became defenders of a new status quo built around a widened A level, another example of how a partial reform can sometimes prolong inequality rather than end it. But others have moved on to explore new alternatives. One think-tank concluded that even the Labour Party's most up-to-date policies on 16-19 could become divisive and backward looking. It proposed a new unified qualifications and assessment system for Britain.[34] In many sectors, including the National Curriculum Council and the Training Agency, initiatives proliferated in the race to devise a new common core for the 16-plus. Meanwhile, not surprisingly, the tertiary college became the flagship of a new generation of common education reformers who saw in its combined academic and vocational education – together with a neighbourhood commitment, links with local employers and its capacity to provide for adults of all ages – the institutional basis for a renewal of comprehensive reform: what one tertiary principal has called 'a new national network of People's Colleges'.[35] Common education was on the move again.

LEARNING THE LESSONS

The comprehensive reform has been the left's only truly popular educational initiative this century. As its failings have been shown to stem largely from incomplete development, policy priorities start with its continuation. After the counter-reformation of the 1980s, institutional change at secondary level alone, would be inadequate. What is required – and what will be expected – is an immediate initiative to extend comprehensive reform to the rest of the system – downwards to the years below five and upwards to the years beyond 16. These changes would be phased in over a considerable period of time – and this should be made clear – but the terms have to be set down early, if only to engender the required public support. But a renewed comprehensive reform has to learn the lessons of its own past, and the first is that institutional change alone is not enough, even supported by effective legislation. A simultaneously planned programme of reform in curriculum and assessment is equally necessary. Lacking this, the first comprehensive reform was limited to the external 'comprehensive school'. This led to diversionary arguments about its 'ideal' age range or siting, or prolonged comparisons with 'the grammar school' – by definition a sterile exercise, postponing society's commitments to a national non-selective education system that involved all schools in the delivery of comprehensive education, however various – based on the positive principles of an equal education taken in common. But a second lesson is that these basic principles need constant reinterpretation, as the reform moves slowly to each new age group. Practices appropriate for the compulsory years of education need modification before age 5 and after 16-plus where participation is voluntary. A single new type of nursery or college is not required so much as the coordination and extension of existing provision within a single new system with simultaneous development of the curriculum. If each geographical area is to have comparable provision as well, not only will careful planning be necessary but a whole new range of venues and forms of education – many undreamed-of, will need to be available for people to choose, as and when it suits their lives.

PARLIAMENTARY PRIORITIES: BACK TO BASICS

All future policy from the left – wherever local and national electoral results bring it power – should be based on a firm decision to strengthen the public education service in Britain – in conscious contrast to the market model that recent governments have tried to introduce, treating education as a by-product of profit accumulation. As a result, schools and colleges have become 'businesses' required to compete to the death for dwindling resources, and people are treated as inherently unequal beings whose educational opportunities can be left to market forces. This model would be replaced by a return to a commitment to support all institutions of education and training – and all people – as equally potentially successful and deserving of support. To achieve this nationally, some existing legislation would need early repeal, including that underwriting 11-plus selection. Other recent changes – for example, those permitting more autonomy to schools and colleges in the management of their day to day running – could be redirected to positive democratic ends – provided legislative priority was also given to reviving local (and regional) education authorities with new powers and duties, including the duty to keep the needs of all institutions in equal balance. This in turn would require a new legal harmonisation of all schools and colleges in such matters as admissions, finance and governing body powers. It could also include new legal rights for parents and students: including the right to attend a named local school or college.

An equal legislative priority would be the immediate requirement that all local authorities prepare new comprehensive reorganisation plans. One set would be for a new publicly co-ordinated nursery and pre-school care service, uniting and expanding the wide variety of child services already developing; and the second (preferably given to new post-16 regional authorities) would be for rational plans after 16, bringing schools and colleges and workplaces into a new national network under a single set of regulations, initially to extend comprehensive opportunity for education and training for everyone up to 19, and thereafter, and in stages, from 18 onwards throughout life. Many local authorities and individual institutions – alone and in consortia – have already blazed small nursery or tertiary trails, and these rank as some of the most popular developments in recent years, many – especially those after 16 – rigorously discouraged by Conservative governments. As well as giving funds to authorities to forward such reorganisation overall, there might also be ear-marked grants to individual institutions to encourage innovation and desireable change, while avoiding coercion – made available for such diverse objectives as schools wishing to unstream or universities wishing to expand their local adult programmes beyond any national requirements. Simultaneously, curriculum reform should be pursued as a third equal priority, including a complete overhaul of curriculum and assessment from 16 plus, transmuting A level, vocational education, and training programmes, into a unified system of flexible and modular accreditation, combined with a common core for everyone in the 16 to 17 year group. In time, courses and degree structures for the years after 18 would need similar unification.

RESTORATION OF THE COMMUNITY INTEREST

But it isn't just a matter of equality in meeting individual needs; comprehensive education is also about a more cohesive social structure. Just as urgent is the restoration of the criterion of the common good as an arbiter in a system planned to serve the whole community – not just the professional elite or employers' short term needs. Willing the means (from public and private finance) to guarantee comparable standards in terms of available courses and facilities at all levels in all areas, would be the long term objective. But if equality as a positive objective is to be reinstated, another lesson from the past is that it is more complex than merely removing academic selection or increasing funding, however necessary both are. Without redistribution of resources – for example, to fund a greatly enlarged range of access courses – the finest system-on-paper falters. So too if there are no positive initiatives to meet the needs of gender, race, religion, culture, age, disability and low income levels. Which is why monitoring educational access and outcome – on all these criteria – should become another new duty for authorities. In this way new 'standards' reflecting actual service to people – would replace the present narrow definition of 'standards' limited to mass 'scores' on questionable tests or the exam 'results' of elite institutions. Definitions of 'choice' should also be reframed: to apply to the range and quality of education and training actually available to people in their local educational institutions or workplaces – and the support services that permit these to be taken up – thus replacing the present differential and institutionally based definition that limits 'choice' to those with money, cultural advantages, or luck. Any system has to have the capacity to balance equality for everyone with attention to the differing needs of individuals, groups or areas – avoiding uniformity on the one hand and, on the other, a variety that degenerates into pandering to the already advantaged. But it also requires the capacity – so lacking in the past – to stand up to those powerful few who will resist the rededication of their institutions to the wider community. Only the community as a whole – through its own renewed commitment to a common education service – can make this stand.

In advanced nations labour shortages mean a new generation will find itself in demand by an economy staggering from the failures of the narrow market approach. This new generation will be in a stronger position to ask for genuine choice of mainstream educational opportunity throughout adult life, and help with child care earlier. And industry will find it increasingly necessary to contribute a greater share of the costs, as it must. As the value of education and training for self-fulfilment as well as for social and economic advance – both individual and collective – is increasingly appreciated, hewers of wood and drawers of water will gradually become extinct, and there will be a debate on the whole issue of work – both professional and skilled – and the way jobs are distributed in society. For common education's next great historic advance must involve tackling the selective processes that divide and oppress in the occupational structure. This will force us to look at the kind of society that education and work are both supposed to serve – in short, rediscovering education's social and political purposes. These purposes will be forced upon society in any case, as, on a daily basis, through the educational services and elsewhere, we seek to redistribute resources to mediate the world's economic and cultural diversity, and to negotiate the planet's social and environmental welfare. Only a common education service can hope to educate for success in these crucial tasks. Far from being over, as elitists prematurely conclude, it is more than possible that common education's greatest contribution is yet to come.

NOTES

1. I. Illich, *Tools For Conviviality*, William Collins, Glasgow 1973, p 32.
2. Quoted in D. Rubinstein and B. Simon, *The Evolution of the Comprehensive School*, Routledge and Kegan Paul, London 1969, pp 3-4.

3. Keir Hardie, speech to the International Socialist Congress, London, 27 July 1896, reprinted *Westminster Gazette*, August 1, 1896.

4. Bryce Commission on Secondary Education, 1894, quoted in Simon and Rubinstein, *op cit*, p 5.

5. F. Rogers, *Labour, Life and Literature*, Smith Elder and Co, London 1913, p 59.

6. Simon and Rubinstein, *op cit*, p 3.

7. C. Burt, *How the Mind Works*, Allen and Unwin, London 1934, pp 28-9.

8. See Public Schools Commission, *Second Report*, Vol 1, p 51, for the figures of direct grant schools, including social composition of free place holders; *DES Statistics*, Census Supplement, Tables 12 and 13, 1961, for social composition of grammar schools; and for social composition of holders of Assisted Places in the 1980s, see G. Whitty, J. Fitz and T. Edwards, 'Assisting Whom? Benefits and Costs of the Assisted Places Scheme', *BERA*, 1986.

9. Secondary Schools Examinations Council, *Curriculum and Examinations in Secondary Schools*, Norwood Report, 1943; see also for example, *The Nation's Schools, Their Plan and Purpose*, No 1, 1945, *The Organisation of Secondary Schools*, Circular 73, 1945 and *Examinations in Secondary Schools*, Circular 103, 1946.

10. See F. Clarke, *Education and Social Change*, Sheldon Press, London 1940; S. Simon, *Three Schools or One?*, Muller, London 1948; B. Simon, *Comprehensive Education: A New Approach*, Gollancz, London 1956, *Intelligence Testing and the Comprehensive School*, Lawrence and Wishart, London 1953, and *The Common Secondary School*, Lawrence and Wishart, London 1955; R. Pedley, *The Comprehensive School*, Penguin, Harmondsworth 1963.

11. The exception was E.G. Edwards of Bradford University. For the principals' letter, see *The Oxford Times*, 27.2.1976, and *Comprehensive Education* Issue 42, 1981.

12. The NUT came out for comprehensives several times in the 1960s, and in 1969 agreed to 'abolishing selection and ending the grammar school'.

13. See, for example, The Central Advisory Council for Education, *Early Leaving*, 1954.

14. Edward Boyle, Foreword, Central Advisory Council for Education, *Half Our Future*, (Newsom Report), 1963; See also I.G.K. Fenwick, *The Comprehensive School*, Methuen, London 1976, p 118.

15. R. Batley, O. O'Brien, and H. Parris, *Going Comprehensive*, Routledge and Kegan Paul, London 1970, passim.

16. J. Ford, *Social Class and the Comprehensive School*, Routledge and Kegan Paul, London 1969.

17. See C. Benn and B. Simon, *Half Way There*, Penguin, Harmondsworth 1972; *Coexistence or Comprehensive?*, NUT 1973; J. Ford, *op cit*, and A. Dummet, and J. McNeal, *Race and Church Schools*, Runnymede Trust, 1981.

18. Campaigns still continued in parts of Kent, Norfolk, and Wiltshire, for example.
19. P. Halls-Dickerson, 'Comprehensive Education in the Modern World', *Comprehensive Education*, No 51, 1989.
20. *School Education in England: Problems and Initiatives*, DES, July 1976.
21. When Labour left office in 1979, half the local education authorities in England had some form of 11-plus selection still operating (House of Commons, 12.7.1970). Only 50 per cent of comprehensives were judged genuine in the same year (C. Benn, 'The Return of the 11-plus', *Forum*, November 1979).
22. J. Simon, 'From Charity School to Workhouse, in the 1720s: the SPCK and Mr Marriott's Solution', *History of Education*, Vol 17, No 2, 1988, pp 113-129.
23. D. Reynolds and M. Sullivan, *The Comprehensive Experiment*, Falmer, Lewes 1987.
24. B. Simon, 'Lessons in Elitism', *Marxism Today*, Sept. 1987, quoting from P. Broadfoot (ed), *Selection, Certification and Control: Social Issues in Educational Assessment*, Falmer, Lewes 1984.
25. See, for example, the Labour Party's *Charter for Pupils and Parents*, 1985; *New Skills for Britain*, 1987, and *Meet the Challenge, Make the Change*, 1989.
26. MSC, *Youth Task Group Report*, 1982; Labour Party and TUC, *Plan for Training*, 1984.
27. David Young speaking at an ILEA conference on the MSC, London 16 February 1986.
28. Youth Opportunities Programme (YOP), Special Temporary Employment Programme (STEP), Training Opportunities Programme (TOPS), Training For Skills Programme (TSP), Work Experience Programme (WEP), Work Experience on Employers Premises (WEEP), Wider Opportunities for Women (WOW), Work Experience (WE), Community Enterprise Programme (CEP), Community Industry (CI), Youth Training Scheme (YTS), Modes A and B, one year and two year, Community Programme (CP), Employment Training (ET), Young Workers Scheme (YWS), and Youth Training (YT)
29. B. Gibson, *Employers' Selective Criteria in YTS Schemes*, MSC Forum Report, Newcastle Trades Council, 1984.
30. See *Report of the National Labour Movement Inquiry Into Youth Unemployment, Training and Education*, Vol 7, Birmingham Trades Union Resource Centre 1987; and C. Benn and S. Fairley, *Challenging the MSC on Jobs, Training and Education*, Pluto Press, London 1986.
31. See NATFHE, *The Great Training Robbery: An interim Report on the Role of Private Training Agencies within the YTS*, Birmingham Liaison Committee, BTURC, 1984.
32. D. Raffe, 'Modules and the Strategy of Institutional Versatility: The First Two Years of the 16-plus Action Plan in Scotland', in D. Raffe (ed),

Education and the Youth Labour Market, Falmer, Lewes 1988.

33. *Report of the National Labour Movement Inquiry, op cit*, Vol 1.
34. D. Finegold *et al*, *A British Baccalaureat?*, Institute for Public Policy Research, No 1, London 1990.
35. K. Wymer, *Peoples' Colleges*, Centre for the Study of Tertiary Education and Training, Birmingham 1989.

PART II

RETHINKING RADICALISM: PAST TIMES, NEW TIMES

Capitalism, Patriarchy and the Origins of Mass Schooling: The Radical Debate

Ian Davey

One of the more interesting aspects of the writing of the history of education in the past decade has been the retreat from grand theory. In contrast to the decade before, historians of education in the 1980s have been much more circumspect about making generalisations. In part, this reflects an uneasiness about social theories of causation and a penchant for the particular and the narrative form. In part, it reflects an increasing theoretical sophistication and disenchantment with the explanatory power of the various social theories employed to explain educational change. This disenchantment is especially apparent in discussions about the origins of 19th-century school systems – the subject of much debate in the 1960s and 1970s. A decade later, historians are much less sanguine about the efficacy of theories of social control and class domination associated with earlier revisionist and neo-Marxist social histories. If recent historians have attempted to generalise at all, the theories have been more tentative and the explanations more pluralist.

In one sense, the reasons for this retreat are simple – the theoretical debates about school and society became more complex. The major source of theoretical inspiration in the 1960s and 1970s, Marxism, was itself riven with debates as historically-minded contributors struggled to distance themselves from the abstract theoreticist concerns of Althusserians. At the same time, Marxists were forced to confront the increasingly sophisticated theoretical contributions of radical feminists and poststructuralists. To many historians, for whom the debates seemed remote and ahistorical, the temptation to get on with the business of writing history rather than get mired in the theoretical bogs was irresistible. There is, however, a second reason why the debates about the origins of state schooling foundered. Those progressive historians who remained committed to the development of a theory of the role of schooling in social change came under attack from the New Right which became increasingly powerful politically in the 1980s. As Richard Johnson correctly points out, this attack has been difficult to counter because the New Right has built on and reworked many of the critiques of the form of state school systems pioneered by revisionists and neo-Marxists in the preceding decade.[1] This has had the dual effect of forcing some historians into a defensive posture regarding their analyses and, at the same time, focussing the attention of some of the leading contributors on the urgent political challenges of the current situation.

However, the question why relatively similar state school systems were established in 19th-century western societies remains centrally important in the history of education, particularly in the current political climate, and it is unlikely that purely parochial interpretations will provide an adequate explanation. Fortunately, there are signs of renewed interest among radical historians and sociologists in the historical relationship between capitalism and schooling first espoused by Marxists like Brian Simon in England and revisionists like Michael Katz in the United States. These contributions, which include commentaries on their earlier work by both Katz and Simon, have begun to reflect the impact of recent critiques of Marxist theory. Nevertheless, as I will suggest in the following review of the key contributions by English-speaking historians to the debates about the origins of state schooling, recent developments in the theory of state formation and in the anlysis of patriarchal relations need to be incorporated into the analysis.

MARXISTS AND REVISIONISTS

In the 1960s historians on both sides of the Atlantic began the task of revising the dominant whig explanation of the rise of mass schooling in the 19th century. Influenced by developments in social history they discarded what Edward Thompson called 'Pilgrim's Progress' theories of history – the ransacking of the past to find predecessors of the present – and began to explore broader social explanations of the interpolation of the school between the family and the workplace, between the infant and the adult.[2] In the process, the logic of the explanation regarding the origins of mass schooling offered by historians shifted from debates about church and state to the changing social relationships associated with the rise of industrialisation and urbanisation. The historiographical triggers in both Britain and the United States were published in 1960. In Britain, the strength of Marxist social history was reflected in the publication of Brian Simon's *Studies in the History of Education, 1780-1870*, which firmly focussed the analysis of the politics of educational reform in the 19th century on the class struggle during industrialisation.[3] Simon's contribution established the centrality of the analysis of working-class education for subsequent British historians of education, be they neo-Marxists or social democrats. In the United States, where Marxist social history was less influential, historians of education were more influenced by anthropological notions of culture, and structural functionalist sociological theories of socialisation and social control. Bernard Bailyn's *Education in the Forming of American Society* established the context by urging historians to move beyond a narrow institutional approach towards a much broader cultural definition of education and to seek social explanations for the rise of schooling.[4] Moderate revisionists, like Lawrence Cremin, emphasised specialisation and role differentiation in a more complex urban, industrial society. The radicals, particularly Michael Katz, emphasised the changing social structure and problems of social order and effectively turned the earlier whig argument about the origins of public schooling on its head – the schools were forced into existence as a means of social control by the newly ascendant urban middle class.[5]

There were two important outcomes of the initial focus on the relationship between urbanisation, industrialisation and education reform. First, historians of education became much more self-conscious about the theoretical underpinnings of their research. Second, the relationship between social class and the origins of school systems assumed a central position in the debate, although it was a much more contentious issue in North America where class-based historical and sociological analyses were much rarer. By the 1970s the debate centred on the recasting of the class forces at work in the development of state schooling by the radical social control theorists who argued that the new school systems were the coercive instruments of control of the ascendant middle class in urban industrial society. Although some more conservative historians invoked modernisation theory and others explored psycho-history, the real challenge to the radical social control theories in the 1970s came from the left.[6] On both sides of the Atlantic scholars influenced by European theory, and in particular Marxism – most notably Althusser's and Bourdieu's theories of reproduction and Gramsci's theory of hegemony – began to question the adequacy of explanations of the origins of schooling which were based on urbanisation and industrialisation. Essentially, these scholars accepted the reconfiguration of the class forces at work expounded by the radical social control theorists, but argued that the rise of schooling was associated with the controlling interests of the capitalist class. Accordingly, it was the particular nature of capitalist industry and capitalist society which was the motive force behind the establishment of mass school systems.[7]

In 1976 three significant publications brought the debate about the relationship between schooling and capitalism into clearer focus. The first, and most influential, was *Schooling in Capitalist America* in which the Marxist economists Bowles and Gintis posited a theory of reproduction to establish a 'correspondence principle' between the social relations of work and the social relations of schooling.[8] In their account, the public school systems came into existence to induct children into the new set of roles and routines required of a productive workforce under industrial capitalism. The argument rested on a much more sophisticated theoretical foundation than social control theory and it generated widespread debate and influenced research programmes. Yet, despite its apparent emphasis on class conflict, the central argument about the role of schooling in reproducing the social relations of capitalism was just as functionalist in its structure as the class domination thesis at the heart of social control theory. Moreover, as the critics pointed out, Bowles and Gintis' argument posited a very mechanistic relationship between schooling and the economy, emptying the school experience of content and leaving little room for tension, contestation and human agency.[9]

A number of key criticisms of *Schooling in Capitalist America* were anticipated in articles by Richard Johnson and Michael Katz published in the same year.[10] Johnson's schematic 'Notes on the Schooling of the English Working Class' provided the building blocks for a critique of Bowles and Gintis' economism. He drew on Gramsci's notion of hegemony and recent analyses of the transformation of popular culture in the transition to industrial society and emphasised the relationship between a 'crisis in capitalism' and the rise of mass schooling. For him, the struggle over education in England in the late 18th and early 19th centuries represented a 'class cultural' conflict in which the critical question was related to the particular form mass schooling assumed.

The period was characterised by 'an extended war over the winning of consent, a prolonged crisis in hegemony' in which 'schooling as a public if not a state apparatus was actually forced into existence . . . by the collapse of older systems of control'. Johnson's argument and subsequent work on oppositional practices, along with the work of other historians of English education such as Frith and Lacqueur, focused the discussion of the origins of mass schooling on cultural forms in a way which overcame the limitations of earlier, more economistic, base and superstructure Marxist formulations.[11] This work, coupled with the critique of Althusserian structuralism and reproduction theory and the increasing emphasis on contradiction, resistance and human agency since the late 1970s, has helped to cement the significance of class analysis in the debate.

In North America, the publication of Katz' 'The Origins of Public Education: A Reassessment' in 1976 also represented a very important contribution to the debate. In this article, Katz provided a critique of his earlier argument which had generated much of the enthusiasm for the radical social control thesis. As with Johnson, he drew on Gramsci's notion of hegemony to explain the success of the bourgeois school reform programme. At the same time, he agreed with Bowles and Gintis that the central dynamic in the explanation was not urbanisation or industrialisation as such but capitalism. Katz' argument is remarkable for its attempt to integrate the findings of much of the 'new social history' in North America in the 1970s into a theoretically eclectic, but persuasive, argument about the rise of mass schooling. Its significance, however, lies beyond this because it raised a number of issues which historians of education are only now beginning to explore. First, Katz drew a distinction between capitalism as a system of wage labour and industrial capitalism and located the origins of public education in the former, noting that outside of England the apparent correlation between industrialisation and school reform was not very tight. As well as addressing the problem of timing in the theories associated with urbanisation and industrialisation or industrial capitalism, Katz also incorporated two other important elements into his revised analysis. He discussed the role of the state and its relation to particular institutional forms and he examined the significance of changes in family formation for educational reform.

In the decade after 1976, English-speaking revisionist and Marxist historians of education did not contribute much directly to the debate about the origins of mass schooling. In England most of the essays in the McCann reader on popular education and socialisation relied on versions of the social control thesis to explain the origins of schooling, while Nasaw's attempt to provide a synthetic account of school reform in the United States fell short of its avowed goal of emphasising class struggle rather than domination.[12] Graff's very important revisionist study of literacy in Ontario with its emphasis on the moral economy represented a synthesis of the class control and hegemonic arguments of Thompson, Johnson and Katz in particular.[13] In fact, the most sophisticated theoretical interventions from the left have come from those working on late 19th and 20th century education. Hogan's emphasis on the process of class formation and Reese's analysis of the agency of subordinate groups in the area of progressive reform in North America were both critical of the social control thesis. Hogan, in particular, develops a complex framework for the analysis of class processes which draws on the work of Connell on class practice and, to a lesser extent, Giddens on class structuration to argue that classes are 'made, unmade and remade in a continuous process of class formation, decomposition and reformation'.[14]

At the same time, the theoretical work of Apple in the United States and Johnson and others at the Centre for Contemporary Cultural Studies in England have expanded our understanding of the relationship between ideology, culture and educational forms.[15] Although its primary focus is post-1945 schooling in Britain, *Unpopular Education*, in particular, has been very influential because the theoretical introduction identifies the weaknesses in earlier formulations of the relationship between schooling and capitalism, focusing on the connections between the family, the school and waged labour and the politics of educational reform. It is particularly useful because of the authors' conceptual clarity in their discussion of the differences between 'culture, public representation and ideology' and their characterisation of the role of schooling in the establishment of capitalist hegemony as a succession of historical crises and educational 'settlements'. As well, their argument draws on Johnson's earlier work on 'really useful knowledge' to distinguish between radical alternative or 'substitutionist' strategies and 'statist' strategies in working-class educational politics.[16]

Significantly, both Apple and Johnson and his colleagues have attempted to incorporate elements of the feminist critique of class theory in their reformulations. Without doubt, since the late 1970s the development of feminist theory and explorations in women's history have provided the most incisive challenge to the dominance of class analysis of educational reform. Initially, much feminist theory related to schooling developed from class analysis. It provided critiques of Marxist categories and emphasised the necessity of analysing modes of reproduction as well as production. The early Marxist-feminist accounts portrayed the patriarchal relations characteristic of modern societies in terms of their functional importance for capitalism, gender relations being subordinated to class relations in the final analysis. Radical feminists, on the other hand, asserted the primacy of patriarchy whether it was understood as a set of material relations (such as men's appropriation of women's domestic labour) or derived from more ideological forces. In many of these early accounts the reproduction of patriarchal relations was represented as unproblematic in a way reminiscent of the reproduction of class relations in Althusserian theory.[17] In the 1980s both streams of feminist theory learned much from critiques of their earlier formulations and developed more sophisticated accounts of the historical nature of patriarchal relations, focusing particularly on the material relations between men and women, on ideology and on subjectivity.[18] At the same time, feminist historians have advanced rapidly beyond 'great woman' approaches to history and have begun to redefine the questions historians of education need to address. The work of Prentice and Danylewycz in Canada, Clifford and Hoffman in the United States, Davin, Purvis and Dyhouse in England, and Mackinnon and Theobald in Australia has challenged our understanding of such issues as the 'feminisation of teaching' and curriculum reform in the late nineteenth century.[19] Their explication of the critical role women played as teachers prior to the establishment of state school systems and their emphasis on the gendered nature of vocational education provide an important corrective to the conventional 'malestream' accounts in the literature. Some historians like Purvis in England and Miller in Australia have explored the interconnections between class and gender relations and 19th-century school reform.[20] Yet, at this stage, we do not have a fully developed theory of the implications of patriarchal relations for the origins of mass schooling. The most comprehensive account, so far, is contained in Beasley's analysis of a 'crisis in patriarchy' in late 19th-century South Australia during the period when the state school system was established.[21]

Marxist explanations came under attack from a different quarter at the same time as the feminist challenge gathered momentum. The increasing availability in English of the work of Foucault and other French poststructuralists from the late 1970s provided historians with accounts of social regulation and power which criticised class (and gender) based analyses and emphasised the complex of overlapping and sometimes contradictory forces at work in the emergence of institutional and state forms of social control.[22] Foucault's analysis of the formation of 'disciplinary societies' in his account of the emergence of the prison in *Discipline and Punish* was particularly influential in early adaptations of his argument to the history of education such as Jones and Williamson's 'The Birth of the Schoolroom'.[23] This account and others drawn from Foucault challenged notions of unitary and linear development in explanations of the rise of schooling such as the relationship between educational reform and industrial capitalism posited by the neo-Marxist. However, the focus on 'discursive fields' and 'dominant discourses' and the ambivalence about class and gender relations at the heart of Foucault's analysis raised more questions than it answered for radical historians. As Rothman pointed out as early as 1971, there is a tendency to conflate discourses about the apparatuses of social regulation with actual practices and the absence of an analysis of the latter makes it difficult to account for the constitution of interests in power relations. This has led to a focus on 'the strategies of the powerful' at the same time as the emphasis on the dispersed nature of power relations has obscured the role of the state in the construction of institutional forms. As one recent commentary has suggested, the work of Foucault and his followers has identified important mechanisms of state action without providing an account of its dynamics.[24]

If the feminists and poststructuralists have created problems for Marxist class analysis at the theoretical level in the decade after 1976, the empirical work of mainstream historians of education since then has demonstrated the inadequacy of the industrialisation/industrial capitalism explanation for the rise of schooling. Historians such as Silver in England have criticised the revisionist and neo-Marxist argument for its simplicity and called for more work on popular education.[25] Cremin's second volume on American education took the revisionists to task for their presentism while continuing to map the increasingly complex configurations of educational provision in the nineteenth century.[26] In Canada, Gidney and Lawr pointed out that rural reformers were equally enthusiastic about centralised school systems as their urban counterparts.[27] However, the most detailed rebuttal of the industrialisation thesis is contained in the massively quantitative study by the American historians Kaestle and Vinovskis, *Education and Social Change in Nineteenth Century Massachusetts*.[28] The detailed empirical studies in this work indicate that educational reform was associated with increasing population density and urbanisation rather than the level of manufacturing activity although the authors stress the complexity of the forces at work. The importance of Kaestle and Vinovskis' findings should not be underestimated, because they focused on Massachusetts which was both the site of early school reform in the United States and the subject of detailed revisionist and Marxist studies which emphasised the relationship between industrial capitalism and the rise of schooling.[29] However, the study reflected the limitations of the debate that it addressed. In subjecting the work of Bowles and Gintis and others to detailed criticism, it tended to equate capitalism with industrial capitalism rather than with wage labour. At the same time, although it paid considerable attention to differential male and female patterns of enrolment and teaching participation, the study did not consider the importance of patriarchal relations at all.

The state of the debate over the origins of mass schooling in the mid-1980s reflected the theoretical and empirical criticisms levelled at the revisionist and Marxist explanations advanced in the early 1970s. Those few historians who attempted syntheses acknowledged the importance of the 'new social history' in revitalising the field, concurred with the revisionists that capitalism and class relations were important, criticised the social control arguments at the heart of the functionalist analysis and confirmed the complexity of the processes at work. Kaestle's *Pillars of the Republic*, for example, is a fine attempt to draw together the various strands of his earlier work into a coherent account of the rise of common schooling in the United States. He provides no mono-causal explanation based on the experience of the cities of the north-eastern seaboard and pays due attention to regional differences in his account. In essence, he argues that state-regulated common schooling came about because those in power were infused with a reform ideology which welded together a commitment to republican, protestant and capitalist values.[30] Similarly, Maynes' synthesis of recent research on the social history of schooling in western Europe weaves together a complex set of arguments about literacy rates, institutional and pedagogic reform, and socio-economic development.[31] While broadly endorsing 'the revisionist emphasis on the character of schools as implements of a new style of class domination', she maps out the different trajectories of educational reform in the various western European countries, acknowledges the agency of the popular classes, and reminds us of the significance of state intervention in 'pre-industrial' societies like 18th-century

Prussia. Importantly, she devotes a chapter to the consideration of family strategies regarding education which others, like Wilson in Canada, have noted as being an increasing pre-occupation of historians of education.[32] Useful as these works are, though, they did not really engage with the theoretical critiques of Marxism and revisionism nor did they posit any new theory of social change which would account for the rise of school systems in the 19th century.

NEW QUESTIONS

The search for new explanations of the origins of 19th-century state school systems in the late 1980s has been led by radical scholars working in peripheral societies outside of Britain and the United States. Interestingly, recent discussions by key contributors to the establishment of the dominance of class analysis in the 1960s and 1970s reflect the criticisms of their earlier positions without engaging with the more recent feminist and poststructuralist critiques. Simon, for example, in his essay on England in *The Rise of the Modern Educational System* provides a fine account of the relationship between class formation and educational restructuring in the mid 19th century which incorporates a critique of the economic reproduction theory of Bowles and Gintis and the social reproduction theory of Bourdieu. He correctly points out that the utility of reproduction theory is limited because of its inability to explain historical change and suggests that Gramsci's theory of hegemony provides the most useful model to interpret educational developments in England in the period.[33] Katz has also recently published a revised version of his 'Origins of Public Education' which addresses the criticism that the new social history in the United States had neglected politics. He draws on the work of Katznelson and Weir to argue that working-class commitment to democratic politics played a key role in shaping the development of public education.[34] However, the most significant new advances in our understanding of the origins of state schooling have emanated from scholars working on the establishment of school systems in the predominantly agricultural societies of Canada and Australia, as for them the questions left unanswered in the 1970s debate about class and educational reform remain of critical importance.

As the critics have pointed out, any explanation of the establishment of state-controlled school systems which attributes causality to the social transformations associated with industrial capitalism founders on the question of timing. States like Prussia and the British colonies in

Canada and Australia introduced compulsory schooling long before they industrialised. Moreover, state intervention in schooling occurred after the rise of industrial capitalism in England. The weakness of the connection is clearly indicated by the disclaimer in *Schooling in Capitalist America*:

> A similar response to the expansion of capitalist production – though with important variations reflecting differing economic, political and cultural conditions – occurred in other countries. In England, both working people and employers supported some kind of educational expansion, although their objectives were radically different. An effective stalemate among the proeducational strategies of capitalist employers, the powerful and more conservative Church of England, and land-owning interests postponed the implementation of public education on a national scale until the 1870s. In a few areas – such as Prussia and Scotland – where military or religious purposes dominated educational policy, mass instruction was implemented considerably before the impact of capitalist expansion was felt.[35]

However, this does not mean, as some critics have suggested, that historians of education should abandon consideration of theories of capitalist development in our search for an explanation of the origins of provided schooling. It means that we need to develop a much more comprehensive understanding of the rise of capitalism. If we accept that capitalism as a system of property relations associated with wage labour encompasses much more than its mature form of modern industry, we need to examine the transformation of agriculture, commerce and handicraft production in the period prior to the 19th century.

The Canadian sociologist Curtis has addressed the problem of the timing of educational reform in a very instructive way. He juxtaposes the relationship between the level of economic development and the establishment of state school systems in Ireland, Upper Canada and England to criticise the ahistorical and functionalist limitations of Marxist reproduction explanations based on the industrial capitalism thesis. In the process, he argues against base/superstructure formulations of the relations between capitalist development and institutional forms and directs our attention to the role of the state. Significantly, he emphasises the international nature of the capitalist economy and concludes that 'without an analysis of relations among nations, uneven educational development is unintelligible'. For him, the 'pre-industrial' development of state schooling in Upper Canada and Ireland is explicable in terms of their colonial status and 'the relative independence of the colonial state' in contrast to the class struggles and sectarian divisions which blocked educational reform in England.[36]

More recently, Curtis has made a major contribution to the debate about the origins of state schooling in his book *Building the Educational State*. His analysis is particularly interesting because of his use of the theoretical insights of Marxism and of Foucault. Curtis' educational state is built on a foundation of Marxist accounts of state formation and cultural forms, topped by a superstructure drawn from Foucault's analysis of power and subjectivity, and held together by the bricks and mortar of a detailed rereading of archival sources. His central argument builds on Marxist cultural theory, elaborated by Johnson and others, insofar as he posits that the primary concern of the 'governing classes' in their support for state education was the reconstruction of popular character and culture to buttress their own political authority, property relations and the Christian religion. For Curtis, however, the educational reforms associated with the rise of state schooling had less to do with the transformation of Ontario's economy than the consolidation of class power and the reconstruction of political conflict in the establishment of a state. Educational practice 'was centrally concerned with political self-making, subjectification and subordination; with anchoring the conditions of political governnance in the selves of the governed; with the transformation of rule into popular psychology'.[37] In this sense, Curtis argues, the new state school system was directly involved in state formation, producing citizens imbued with bourgeois moral values of self-regulation and self-government through a seemingly neutral process of education which, because of the bureaucratic nature its administration, claimed to occupy a domain above politics and class conflict.

Curtis' use of Foucault's analysis of power and subjectivity in his account of the role of schooling in state formation adds a significant new dimension to our understanding of the politics of 19th-century educational reform. However, although *Building the Educational State* provides many illuminating insights into the construction of forms of masculinity and femininity in the period, gender relations are not central to the analysis. This provides an interesting contrast with Miller's important recent account of the development of state schooling in another 19th-century British colony, South Australia.[38] Miller's starting point in *Long Division: State Schooling in South*

Australian Society is very similar to that of Curtis in its theoretical orientation. Essentially she draws on the neo-Marxist analyses of Johnson and others to argue that the centralised state school system was established in 1875 because of ruling class concern over the failure of the previous policy of 'judicious intervention in a free education market' to ensure the regular attendance of working-class children at school. Accordingly, the new state form of schooling was designed to transform the culture of working-class children by compelling them to attend the newly defined efficient schools with vastly increased central control over teachers, the curriculum and school discipline.

However, two features of Miller's argument differentiate it from earlier accounts. First, she draws on the insights of the sociology of knowledge to argue that the form of efficient schooling constructed a definition of intelligence which condemned most working-class children to failure as it conflicted with many aspects of the culture and routines of working-class life. Second, she incorporates feminist critiques of class analysis in her account and systematically explores the impact of the sexual division of labour and patriarchal relations on the development of the institutional forms of schooling. For example, she posits the importance of gender and race as well as class relations in South Australia, a colony established according to Wakefield's theory of systematic colonisation, from its inception:

> Sometimes in conflict, often in concert, the structuring processes of class, gender and race entered into the making of virtually every aspect of colonial life: the division of labour, wealth and poverty, patterns of land use, colonial architecture, trade unions, the design of manufactured products, the shape of the educational system, industrial legislation, child-rearing practices, the physical and psychological development of individuals and government economic policy.[39]

Long Division is particularly significant precisely because Miller, like Purvis in her studies of 19th-century England, focuses on the interconnections of class and gender relations in her analysis of the origins of state schooling. It is theoretically sophisticated and meticulously researched and probably provides the best Marxist-feminist account of the history of schooling available.

However, in an important sense, *Long Division* represents the culmination of an historiographic era rather than the beginning of a new one. Miller's analysis subordinate gender to class and cannot easily accommodate the more recent feminist critiques which stress the often contradictory dynamics between capitalism and patriarchy and the concomitant need to acknowledge that gender relations are at least as powerful as class relations in the structuring of social forms. Like Curtis, Miller provides a stimulating account of the development of state schooling by incorporating aspects of recent critiques of Marxism into a framework based on class analysis. Unlike Curtis and some other social historians, though, she does not accord religion a particularly significant role in the process of class formation and educational reform. In *Building the Educational State*, Curtis argues that the incorporation of the moral regulatory dimension of 'our Common Christianity' was a key component in the construction of self-government through individual self-discipline in educational practice.[40] Given Miller's interest in the connections between patriarchy and capitalism, it is unfortunate she did not include a similar analysis of the role of Christianity in her account, particularly as recent studies by feminist historians such as Ryan and Davidoff and Hall have shown that religion played a critical role in the reconstruction of gender relations in the 18th and 19th centuries as well. Ryan's brilliant study of Oneida County, New York, is especially significant as it clearly demonstrates the role of religion in the transformation of family, class and gender relations associated with the expansion of capitalism.[41]

Ryan's account of the transformation of familial relations in Oneida in the first half of the 19th century argues that the religious revivalism which accompanied the development of capitalism in the period had as much to do with age and gender relations as it did with class: 'age, gender, family . . . were seen to operate as causal as well as derivative forces in the shaping of society, politics and economics'.[42] She analyses the processes whereby the corporate family subsistence economy, in which subordination to patriarchal authority was synonymous with social order, crumbled when the county no longer contained enough unimproved land to sustain a second generation of farmers. The penetration of market relations into the region marked a period of experimentation with new forms of social practices and association out of which the 19th-century middle-class family emerged. Importantly, she indicates that fundamental changes to the family were underway before the emergence of industrial capitalism. While public schooling is only tangential to Ryan's complex argument, she does comment in passing that the school system, 'the major public institution to be expanded and systematised' in the period, was 'designed to facilitate the passage of children out of the house and into society and the economy'.[43]

While the focus of Ryan's study is the emergence of the middle-class

182

family, its significance is much broader because of the rapidity of capitalist development in the period. In a little more than half a century the economy of Oneida County was transformed from subsistence farming to industrial capitalism triggering massive changes in age and gender, as well as class, relations. The economic, social and religious ferment described by Ryan involved a challenge to traditional forms of patriarchal authority in the household, the church and the wider community at the same time as the social relations of production were revolutionised by the development of capitalism. In short, the upheavals in early 19th-century Oneida were part of the process whereby the institutional forms of governance and social order of a non-capitalist society were reworked in the face of the spread of market relations. By the middle of the century new family and institutional forms of patriarchal authority, more attuned to the changed conditions of a wage labour economy and the separation of home and work, had emerged. It seems likely that Ryan's account of the reordering of social life in Oneida County is an instance, albeit in a very compressed time-frame, of a process underway throughout the western world in the same period. This suggests a possible reconfiguration of the explanation of the origins of mass schooling which overcomes the problem of timing associated with the industrial capitalism thesis. Importantly, it incorporates an analysis of both the transformation of class relations in the transition to capitalist society and the reconstruction of age and gender patriarchal relations in the same period.

The work of historians on 'proto-industrialisation' in England and Europe provides a more comprehensive picture of the processes at work. Medick and others in Germany and Levine in England have analysed the relationship between family formation and rural manufacturing prior to the 19th century.[44] They argue that this early form of capitalist industry gave rise to a new transitional family form as rural populations increasingly began to rely on manufacture for a market for their means of subsistence. In contrast to peasant and smallholding families, proto-industrial families depended almost entirely on wage labour rather than ownership of, or access to, land for their existence, although the family continued to labour as a unit. In consequence, Medick argues, the source of patriarchal power in peasant and small-holding families – control over productive property – was destroyed:

> marriage and family formation slipped beyond the grasp of patriarchal domination; they were no longer 'tangibly' determined by property relationships.[45]

183

The demographic implications of this crisis in patriarchal age relations were enormous. The age of marriage fell as children, no longer dependent on patriarchal sanction, established their own households earlier. At the same time, in proto-industrial households the number of children increased, reflecting both the earlier age of marriage and the need to expand the family's supply of labour as wages were so low. It has been estimated that the adult male contributed only about one-quarter of the total income, making him dependent on his dependents for his subsistence in the family wage economy.[46]

In subsequent work Levine and Tilly have drawn out the demographic implications of the proletarianisation of Europe prior to the rise of factory production, including in their analysis the expansion of agricultural capitalism as well as proto-industrialisation. Tilly, in a series of demographic projections regarding natural increase, social mobility and migration concludes, significantly, that natural increase must have played the major role in the proletarianisation of European populations from 1500 to 1800 – the proletariat made itself rather than was made. In a 'modified Marxist account', he makes concessions to Malthus pointing out that the old patriarchal system of enforced celibacy for large numbers of servants and labourers disintegrated as wage labour expanded. Malthus' errors, he concludes, were 'to inflate the particular circumstances of capitalist expropriation into general laws, to misunderstand the incentives to high fertility, and to neglect the importance of capitalist farmers, merchants and manufacturers to the increase of the proletariat'.[47]

Levine looks in more detail at proletarianisation in England where captitalist wage relations in agriculture and rural industry were most developed. He sketches out the implications of the demography of proletarianisation – whereby the proletariat grew from about 2.5 million in 1700 to 16.5 million in 1871 – for our understanding of industrialisation. In an analysis essentially derived from Marx's distinction between the formal and real subsumption of labour under capital, he proposes a two stage model of industrialisation in which the first stage from 1700 to 1850 involved the expansion of handicraft and manufacturing production and the second stage, driven by the railway boom of the 1840s, saw the rise to dominance of machinofacture in industries beyond the textiles factories of the north. The first phase was based on the more intensive exploitation of the wage labour of men, women and children in a family wage economy and was associated with 'explosive growth' in the birthrate in the proto-industrial villages between 1760 and 1815. This growth, which helped fuel the development of capitalist industry, was followed by a 'precipitous' decline in the period to 1845 as these rural proletarians moved into the cities to search for work when more intensive forms of manufacture began to replace domestic industry. The urban proletarians sold their labour, not the products of their labour as in the proto-industrial villages, and the age form became increasingly individuated, although devices like sub-contracting meant that the family wage economy lingered on.[48]

Individuated wage packets characterised Levine's second stage of industrialisation from the mid-19th century – capital-intensive machinofacture which we traditionally associate with the 'Industrial Revolution'. This was the classic period of proletarianisation in which many artisans were deskilled and lost control over the labour process. It was also the period when, as in the textile industry earlier, production was increasingly centralised in large-scale factories, separating home and work for the vast majority of the population. As Levine points out, the shift from labour-intensive manufacture to capital-intensive machinofacture had profound implications for proletarian families. Whereas 'the first phase of industrialisation led to the duplication of wage-earning hands . . . the second phase, with the notable exception of the northern textile factories, began to tie the family's fortunes to the achievements of the male breadwinner'.[49] That is, the dissolution of the family wage economy was accompanied by a 'surge of patriarchalism' which involved a redefinition of the age and sexual division of labour. In consequence, 'wealth flows within the working class family changed direction' and the cost of children soared leading to declining birthrates. In Levine's terms, stripped of its productive role, the working-class family, like its bourgeois counterpart, became 'the locus of reproduction and consumption' with the respectable working man's wife at home and children in school.[50]

The triumph of the patriarchal working-class family ideologically, if not in practice, has been the object of considerable debate among feminist historians and theorists. Much of the discussion has centred around the sexual division of labour, the domestic ideology and the construction of the male breadwinner's wage form in the 19th century.[51] It is possible to conclude from this debate that the construction of the breadwinner's wage form and its accompanying domestic ideology arose from patriarchal rather than capitalist imperatives. Delphy and others have argued that the locus for the subordination of women lies in the continuity of their domestic role in a 'family mode of production' which provides for men's control of women's labour through the marriage form.[52] As Tilly and Scott have demonstrated, the sexual division of labour in the family economy remains fairly constant throughout the period of industrialisation and women's pre-capitalist responsibilities for maintaining familial functions did not decrease as they were increasingly drawn into wage labour. Conversely, the intensification of the sexual division of labour associated with the breadwinner's wage and the domestic ideology in the 19th century cannot be seen as a functional necessity for capitalist development. In fact, the exclusion of women (and children) from the labour market can be seen as antagonistic to capital accumulation as the history of sweated labour in the later 19th century demonstrates.[53]

If we accept that patriarchy operates independently from capitalism then, as Beasley argues, historians of education need to look carefully at the gender, as well as class, relations implicit in mass schooling because the timing of the establishment of school systems is coterminous with a 'crisis of patriarchy' centering on struggles around the intensification of the sexual division of labour:

> In establishing school systems men thus gained a far greater degree of control over children. Public schooling did not simply represent the development of a system of class hegemony but also a system of patriarchal hegemony, i.e. it constituted the development of a society-wide institution which complemented direct control within the family.[54]

Implicitly, Beasley's argument acknowledges the significance of the other dimension of patriarchy – control over age relations. However, with the notable exception of Anna Davin, most feminists have not really explored the construction of tighter distinctions between adults and children, although they have pointed out the gender-specific nature of many reforms.[55] Yet, as the discussion of the proletarianisation process suggests, it had dramatic implications for patriarchal controls over children and the subsequent struggles to establish the breadwinner's wage involved a campaign against (male and female) juvenile labour as well as women's waged work. That is, just as it was too simplistic to collapse all arguments about the origins of schooling into arguments about class relations and capitalism, it is not sufficient to collapse all arguments about patriarchal relations and schooling into arguments about gender relations. It is absolutely essential that we grant the struggle over age relations a degree of autonomy in our analyses.

At this point it is possible to sketch out a general argument about the origins of mass schooling which focuses on a protracted crisis of patriarchy associated with the rise of capitalism. In essence, the argument posits that the transition from feudalism in Europe, and from subsistence farming in the colonies, to mature forms of capitalism was accompanied by an extended crisis in patriarchal relations which reverberated through all levels of society and shook the foundations of governance in all social institutions including the state, the church and the family. Initially, it involved a challenge to patriarchal age relations, which is not to suggest that age relations are not gendered, but to emphasise that the crisis focused on the rule of the father rather than the husband. The struggle for control of the political state, involving the debate between the patriarchalists and social contract theorists and the eventual overthrow of the rule of kings and the triumph of bourgeois liberalism and democracy, is well known. The obvious fact that this triumph was a triumph for men, for brothers, is also increasingly acknowledged now that feminists have focused our attention on 'fraternity' as well as 'liberty' and 'equality'.[56] We also know that this political struggle was accompanied by ferment in the other site of patriarchal power, the church, spawning more egalitarian forms of religion throughout the period. We also now know, from the work on proto-industrialisation, that the crisis in age relations associated with the early stages of capitalism had a material reality which reached into the households of farming patriarchs, as their children, no longer dependent on access to land for their livelihood, could leave to establish their own households without the patriarch's consent. Moreover, insofar as the family wage in proto-industrial households was generated by the combined labour of the husband, wife and children, the crisis intensified since the household head's authority was conditional, particularly in relation to his children who, as he had done beforehand, could withdraw their labour when they reached 'adulthood', and establish their own households. In colonial areas like Canada and Australia patriarchal authority was even more tenuous as the availability of land 'further out' weakened the father's hold on his children's labour, and the transition from subsistence to capitalist forms of farming and industry was much quicker as settlement coincided with, and fueled, the rapid expansion of British economic imperialism and the growth of the international commodity market.

If the crisis in the governance of age relations had deepened by the end of the 18th century because of the rapid growth in capitalist wage relations, it was exacerbated by the challenge to patriarchal gender relations which gathered momentum in the later years of that century. The beginning of the battle to extend the newly ascendant bourgeois notions of individualism and citizenship to middle-class women was coterminous with a similar struggle in working-class households associated with the individuation of the wage form and the separation of home and work in the transition to manufacturing capitalism. There are two important things to note about the resolution of this crisis in patriarchy in the 19th century. The first is the fusion of age and gender relations through the exclusion of women and children from the world of commerce and industry and the creation of separate spheres for both – the domestic world for women centering on morality, mothering and the management of the household, and the world of childhood and schooling for juveniles involving the new concept of the school-age child. Both spheres, of course, were dependent on the household head and subject to his authority. The second point is that the resolution of the crisis occurred much earlier in middle-class households.[57] The resolution of working-class age and gender relations had to weather the storm of early capitalism's appetite for women and children's labour and the resultant struggle over the wage form. Working-class patriarchy was only stabilised after the struggle for the male breadwinner's wage was largely won and notions of proletarian male respectability, associated with the dependent wife and child, were realised in the late 19th century.[58]

I want to suggest that the origins of mass schooling can only be understood if we take account of this dual crisis in patriarchal relations associated with the development of capitalism. For the ascendant middle class, the gendered nature of patriarchal relations was of paramount importance and the institutional forms they developed to educate their children in the late 18th and 19th centuries reflected these separate spheres. For the great mass of the people, though, whether they lived in Britain, Europe, North America or Australia, the patriarchal crisis induced by the development of capitalist wage labour relations and the explosive growth in the number of children was both more complex and more complex to govern. The social ferment in class, gender and age relations unleashed by this process produced a crisis in obedience within farming and proletarian communities which, coupled with their increasingly democratic religious temper, spurred the traditional bastions of patriarchal order, the churches, to explore new forms of governance of children. The Church of England's National Society, for example, observed in its first annual report that its form of monitorial schooling was created with:

the sole object in view being to communicate to the poor generally, by the means of a summary mode of education . . . such knowledge and habits, as are sufficient to guide them through life, in their proper stations, especially to teach the doctrines of Religion, according to the principles of the Established Church, and to train them to the performance of their religious duties by early discipline.[59]

It is important to note, however, that this essentially defensive new institutional form, aimed at schooling all children, was forged in a period of intense gender as well as class struggle as Barbara Taylor has demonstrated.[60] It is also important to note that the reworking of this new instrument of mass tuition as a state form in the more secular and democratic politics of the mid-19th century coincided with the beginnings of the resolution of the patriarchal crisis through the male breadwinner's wage form. At the same time as the proletarian struggle for manhood suffrage was being won, the burgeoning powers of the state were brought to bear on the struggle for proletarian patriarchal respectability. The reforms which emanated from this intervention reflected the age and gendered nature of the conflict as women and children were swept from the labour market in a campaign that saw the elaboration of ideologies of dependency for each group and the development of new institutional forms, both familial and educational. Women's lives were increasingly defined by the ideology of domesticity centering on their roles as wife and mother in the working-class family. Children of both sexes above the age of infancy were defined as school children and compelled to attend the new state institutions designed to prepare them for their future adult roles.

There is an irony in this analysis of the origins of early school reform. In the heady days of revisionism in the early 1970s it was customary to ridicule the focus on the relations between church and state of the more conventional historians of 19th-century education. Now, refracted through the classed and gendered lenses of the ensuing debate about the relationship between schooling, capitalism and (more recently) patriarchy, we can acknowledge that they were right in choosing the objects of their analysis even if they asked the wrong questions. The challenge for radical historians of the 1990s is to incorporate an analysis of age and gender patriarchal relations, and their intersections with class relations, into our accounts of the establishment of state school systems.[61]

NOTES

This essay is a revised version of two published articles: 'Capitalism, Patriarchy and the Origins of Mass Schooling', *History of Education Review* 16, No 2, 1987, pp 1-12, and 'Rethinking the Origins of British Colonial School Systems', *Historical Studies in Education* 1, No 1, 1989, pp 149-159. I would like to thank my research collaborator Dr Pavla Miller, for her comments and criticisms. Her recent article, 'Historiography of Compulsory Schooling: what is the problem?', *History of Education* 18, No 2, 1989, pp 123-144, addresses the same question in more detail; and the argument is further elaborated in P. Miller and I. Davey, 'Family Formation, Schooling and the Patriarchal State' in Marjorie R. Theobald and R.J.W. Selleck (eds), *Family, School and State in Australian History*, Allen & Unwin, Sydney 1990, pp 1-24.

1. R. Johnson, 'Thatcherism and English Education: breaking the mould, or confirming the pattern?', *History of Education*, Vol 18, No 2, 1989, p 93.
2. E.P. Thompson, *The Making of the English Working Class*, Penguin, Harmondsworth 1968, pp 12-13.
3. Simon, *Studies in the History of Education 1780-1870*, Lawrence and Wishart, London 1960 (republished in 1974 as *The Two Nations and the Educational Structure 1780-1870*); see also Richard Johnson, 'Educational policy and social control in early Victorian England,' *Past and Present* 49, 1970, pp 96-119.
4. B. Bailyn, *Education in the Forming of American Society*, University of North Carolina Press, Chapel Hill, 1960.
5. M.B. Katz, *The Irony of Early School Reform*, Harvard University Press, Cambridge 1968; L.A. Cremin, *American EducationL The colonial experience*, Harper and Row, New York 1970; C.F. Kaestle, *The Evolution of an Urban School System, New York 1750-1850*, Harvard University Press, Cambridge 1973; David Tyack, *The One Best System*, Harvard University Press, Cambridge 1974. For a comparison of the origins of mass schooling in Britain and North America, see Kaestle, 'Between the Scylla of Brutal Ignorance and the Charybdis of a Literary Education' in L. Stone (ed), *Schooling and Society*, Johns Hopkins University Press, Baltimore 1976, pp 177-189. There are numerous discussions of American revisionism, such as: M. Lazerson, 'Revisionism and American educational history', *Harvard Education Review*, 43, 1973, pp 269-273; and C.F. Kaestle, 'Conflict and consensus revisited', *Harvard Education Review*, 46, 1976, pp 350-396.
6. See for example R.F. Butts, 'Public education and political community', *History of Education Quarterly*, Summer, 1974, pp 165-184; and B. Finkelstein, 'In fear of childhood', *History of Childhood Quarterly*, 3, 1976, pp 321-335.

7. See, for example, A.J. Field 'Educational expansion in mid-nineteenth Century Massachusetts', *Harvard Educational Review* 46, 1976, pp 521-552.

8. Bowles and Gintis, *Schooling in Capitalist America: education and the contradictions of economic life*, Basic Books, New York 1976.

9. See 'Schooling in capitalist America', *History of Education Quarterly*, Summer 1977; and David Hogan, 'Capitalism, liberalism and schooling', *Theory and Society*, 8, No 3, 1979, pp 387-413. For Bowles and Gintis' later thoughts on the book, see S. Bowles and H. Gintis, 'Contradiction and Reproduction in Educational Theory' in I. Barton, R. Meighan and S. Walker (eds), *Schooling, Ideology and the Curriculum*, Falmer Press, Lewes 1980, pp 51-65. See also M.W. Apple, 'Standing on the Shoulders of Bowles and Gintis', *History of Education Quarterly*, Summer, 1988, pp 231-241.

10. R. Johnson, 'Notes on the schooling of the English working class, 1780-1850', in Roger Dale *et al* (eds), *Schooling and Capitalism: A sociological reader*, Routledge and Kegan Paul, London 1976, pp 44-54; M.B. Katz, 'The origins of public education: A reassessment', *History of Education Quarterly*, Winter, 1976, pp 381-408.

11. Johnson, p 50; S. Frith, 'Socialization and rational schooling: elementary education in Leeds before 1870', in P. McCann (ed), *Popular Education and Socialization in the Nineteenth Century*, Methuen, London 1977, pp 67-92; Thomas Laqueur, 'Working class demand and the growth of elementary education', in L. Stone (ed), *Schooling and Society*, pp 192-205. See also, P. Gardner, *The Lost Elementary Schools of Victorian England*, Croom Helm, Methuen, London 1984; David Vincent, *Bread, Knowledge and Freedom: A study of nineteenth-century working class autobiography*, Methuen, London 1982; and David Hamilton, 'Adam Smith and the Moral Economy of the Classroom System', *Journal of Curriculum Studies* 12, 1980, pp 281-298.

12. See, McCann, *op cit*; D. Nasaw, *Schooled to Order: a social history of public schooling in the United States*, Oxford University Press, New York 1979.

13. H.J. Graff, *The Literacy Myth: literacy and social structure in the nineteenth century city*, Academic Press, New York 1979.

14. D.J. Hogan, *Class and Reform: school and society in Chicago 1880-1930*, University of Pennsylvania Press, Philadelphia 1985; and W.J. Reese, *Power and the Promise of School Reform: grass roots movements during the progressive era*, Routledge and Kegan Paul, Boston 1986. See also, R.W. Connell, *Which Way Is Up?*, Allen & Unwin, Sydney 1983; and A. Giddens, *The Class Structure of the Advanced Societies*, Hutchinson, London 1973.

15. See M.W. Apple, *Education and Power*, Routledge and Kegan Paul, Boston 1982; and *Cultural and Economic Reproduction in Education*, Routledge and Kegan Paul, Boston 1982; and *Teachers and Texts: A Political Economy of Class and Gender Relations in Education*, Routledge, New York 1986; J. Clarke *et al* (eds), *Working Class Culture: Studies in history and theory*,

Hutchinson, London 1979; and S. Barron *et al, Unpopular Education: schooling and social democracy in England since 1944*, Hutchinson, London 1981.

16. Barron *et al*, Ch. 1 & 2; see also, R. Johnson 'Really Useful Knowledge', in Clark *et al* (eds), *Working Class Culture*, pp 75-102. This exploration of the radical opposition tradition owes much to the earlier work of Simon and Silver in the 1960s.

17. See, for example, R. Deem, *Women and Schooling*, Routledge and Kegan Paul, London 1978; A. Kuhn and A-M. Wolpe (eds), *Feminism and Materialism: women and modes of production*, Routledge and Kegan Paul, London 1978; M. MacDonald, 'Schooling and the reproduction of class and gender relations', in R. Dale *et al* (eds), *Education and the State*, Vol 2, Falmer Press, Lewes 1981, pp 159-178.

18. M. Barrett, *Women's Oppression Today: problems in marxist feminist analysis*, New Left Books, London 1980; C. Delphy, 'A materialist feminism is possible', *Feminist Review*, 4, 1980, pp 79-105; L. Sargent (ed), *Women and Revolution*, South End Press, Boston 1981; S. Rowbotham, 'The trouble with "patriarchy"', in R. Samuel (ed), *People's History and Socialist Theory*, Routledge and Kegan Paul, London 1981, pp 364-369; Sally Alexander and Barbara Taylor, 'In defence of "patriarchy",' in Samuel, pp 370-374; J. Allen, 'Marxism and the man question: some implications of the patriarchy debate', in J. Allen and P. Patton (eds), *Beyond Marxism? interventions after Marx*, Intervention Publications, Sydney 1983, pp 91-112; Mia Campioni and Elizabeth Gross, 'Love's labours lost: marxism and feminism', in Allen & Patton, *op cit*, pp 113-142; C. Beasley, 'The Patriarchy Debate: Should we make use of the term "patriarchy" in historical analysis?', *History of Education Review* 16, No 2, 1987, pp 13-20; C. Pateman and E. Gross (eds) *Feminist Challenges: social and political theory*, Allen and Unwin, Sydney 1986.

19. See, for example, M. Danylewycz and A. Prentice, 'Teachers, gender and bureaucratizing school systems', *History of Education Quarterly*, Spring 1984, pp 75-100; G. Joncich Clifford, ' "Daughters into teachers": educational and demographic influences on the transformation of teaching into "women's work" in America', *History of Education Review*, Vol 12, No 1, 1983, pp 15-28; N. Hoffman, *Women's 'True' Profession: voices from the history of teaching*, Feminist Press, New York 1981; J. Purvis, 'Women and teaching in the nineteenth century' in Dale *et al, op cit*, pp 359-376; Carol Dyhouse, *Girls Growing Up in Late Victorian and Edwardian England*, Routledge and Kegan Paul, London 1981; A. Davin, 'Imperialism and Motherhood', *History Workshop Journal*, Spring 1978, pp 9-65. A. Mackinnon, 'Women's education: linking history and theory,' *History of Education Review*, Vol 13, No 2, 1984, pp 5-15; M. Theobald, ' "Mere accomplishments": Melbourne's early ladies' school reconsidered ", *History of Education Review*, Vol 13, No 2, 1984, pp 15-28.

20. J. Purvis, 'Towards a history of women's education in nineteenth century

Britain: A sociological analysis' in J. Purvis and M. Hale *et al.* (eds), *Achievement and Inequality in Education*, Routledge and Kegan Paul, London 1983, pp 153-192; P. Miller, *Long Division: state schooling in South Australian society*, Wakefield Press, Adelaide 1986. See also, R.W. Connell *et al*, *Making the Difference: schools and social division*, Allen and Unwin, Sydney 1982.

21. See C. Beasley, 'Educating Rita's Grandmother: the social relation of the sexes and South Australian curriculum reform, 1870-1915', Unpublished M.Ed. Thesis, Flinders University of South Australia, 1984, in which she introduces the concept of a 'crisis in patriarchy'.

22. See, especially M. Foucault, *Discipline and Punish*, Allen Lane, London 1977; Michael Foucault, *The History of Sexuality*, Vol 1, Allen Lane, London 1979; and Jacques Donzelot, *The Policing of Families*, Pantheon, New York 1979.

23. K. Jones and K. Williamson, 'The Birth of the Schoolroom', *Ideology and Consciousness* 6, 1979, pp 59-110.

24. D.J. Rothman, *The Discovery of the Asylum*, Little Brown, Boston 1971, pp xvii-xviii; S. Franzway *et al*, *Staking a Claim: Feminism, Bureaucracy and the State*, Allen and Unwin, Sydney 1989, pp 18-19. For critical commentaries on Foucault and Donzelot, see Barrett and McIntosh, *The Anti-Social Family*, Verso, London 1982, pp 95-105; and M. Crane (ed), *Towards a Critique of Foucault*, Routledge and Kegan Paul, London 1986.

25. H. Silver, *Education as History*, Methuen, London 1983, Introduction.

26. L.A. Cremin, *American Education: The National experience, 1783-1876*, Harper and Row, New York 1980.

27. Gidney and Lawr, 'Bureaucracy vs. community? the origins of bureaucratic procedure in the Upper Canadian school system', *Journal of Social History*, Spring 1980, pp 438-457.

28. C.F. Kaestle and M.A. Vinovskis, *Education and Social Change in Nineteenth Century Massachusetts*, Cambridge University Press, New York 1980.

29. See Katz, *Irony*; Bowles and Gintis, *Schooling*; and Field, 'Educational expansion in mid-nineteenth-century Massachusetts', *op cit*.

30. C.F. Kaestle, *Pillars of the Republic: common schools and American society, 1780-1860*, Hill and Wang, New York 1983.

31. M.J. Maynes, *Schooling in Western Europe: A social history*, State University of New York Press, Albany 1985.

32. J.D. Wilson, 'From social control to family strategies: some observations on recent trends in Canadian educational history', *History of Education Review*, Vol 13, No 1, 1984, pp 1-13.

33. B. Simon, 'Systematization and Segmentation: The Case of England', in D.K. Miller *et al* (eds), *The Rise of the Modern Educational System*, Cambridge University Press, 1987, pp 88-108.

34. M.B. Katz, *Reconstructing American Education*, Harvard University Press, Cambridge, Massachusetts, 1987, pp 5-23; and I. Katznelson and M. Weir,

Schooling for All: Class, Race and the Decline of the Democractic Ideal, Basic Books, New York 1985.

35. Bowles and Gintis, *Schooling, op cit,* pp 159-160.
36. B. Curtis, 'Capitalist development and educational reform: comparative material from England, Ireland and Upper Canada to 1850', *Theory and Society,* Vol 13, No 1, 1984, pp 41-68. For an interesting discussion of state formation in England, see P. Corrigan and D. Sayer, *The Great Arch: English state formation as cultural revolution,* Blackwell, Oxford 1985.
37. B. Curtis, *Building the Educational State: Canada West, 1836-1871,* Falmer and the Althouse Press, Lewes, Sussex and London, Ontario, 1988.
38. Miller, *Long Division, op cit.*
39. *Ibid,* p 5.
40. Curtis, *Building the Educational State, op cit,* pp 108-112. See, also, Kaestle, *Pillars of the Republic, op cit;* P.E. Johnson, *A Shopkeeper's Millenium: society and revivals in Rochester, New York, 1815-1837,* Hill and Wang, New York 1978; A.F.C. Wallace, *Rockdale: The growth of an American village in the early industrial revolution,* Norton and Co, New York 1972, 1978.
41. M.P. Ryan, *Cradle of the Middle Class: The family in Oneida County, New York, 1790-1865,* Cambridge University Press, 1981; and L. Davidoff and C. Hall, *Family Fortunes: Men and Women of the English Middle Class,* 1780-1850, Hutchinson, London 1987.
42. Ryan, *op cit,* p 15.
43. *Ibid,* p 234.
44. See P. Kreidte *et al, Industrialization Before Industrialization,* Cambridge University Press, 1981; D. Levine (ed), *Proletarianization and Family History,* Academic Press, Orlando 1984. See also, C.C. Harris, *The Family and Industrial Society,* Allen and Unwin, London 1983; and W. Seccombe, 'Marxism and demography', *New Left Review,* No 137, 1983, pp 22-47.
45. Cited in Harris, *op cit,* p 121.
46. Cited in D. Levine, 'Industrialization and the proletarian family in England', *Past and Present,* 107, 1985, p 189.
47. C. Tilly, 'Demographic origins of the European proletariat', in Levine (ed), *Proletarianization, op cit,* p 54.
48. Levine 'Industrialization', *op cit,* p 187; See D. Levine *Reproducing Families: The political economy of English population History,* Cambridge University Press 1987, for a more extended discussion. See also, W. Seccombe, 'Patriarchy stabilized: the construction of the male breadwinner wage norm in nineteenth century Britain', *Social History,* 11, 1986, pp 53-76.
49. Levine, 'Industrialization', *op cit,* p 179.
50. *Ibid,* p 189.
51. See, for example, S. Alexander *et al,* 'Labouring women', *History Workshop,* 8, 1979, pp 174-192; Barrett, *Women's Oppression, op cit,* Chapter 5; C. Hall, 'Early formation of Victorian domestic ideology', in S.

Burman (ed), *Fit Work for Women*, Croom Helm, London 1979, pp 15-32; B. Taylor, *Eve and the New Jerusalem1, Virago*, London 1983, Chapter 4; W. Seccombe, 'Patriarchy stabilized', *op cit*; Tilly and Scott, *Woman, Work and Family*, Holt, Rinehart and Winston, New York 1978.

52. C. Delphy, *Close to Home: A materialist analysis of women's oppression*, Hutchinson, London 1984.

53. Allen, 'Marxism', *op cit*; Beasley, 'Education', *op cit*; Raphael Samuel, 'Workshop of the world: steam power and hand technology in mid-Victorian Britain, *History Workshop*, 3, 1977, pp 6-72.

54. Beasley, 'Educating', *op cit*, p 60.

55. A. Davin, 'Child labour, the working-class family, and domestic ideology in nineteenth century Britain', *Development and Change*, Vol 13, 1982, pp 633-652. See also, Beasley's discussion of Wimshurts's work on street children in Beasley, 'Educating', *op cit*, pp 98-100.

56. See, for example, C. Pateman 'The Fraternal Social contract: some observations on patriarchial civil society' in J. Keane (ed), *Civil Society and the State: new European Perspectives*, Verso, London 1988; and C. Pateman, *The Sexual Contract*, Polity Press, London 1988.

57. See, especially, Davidoff and Hall, *Family Fortunes, op cit*.

58. Levine, *Reproducing Families, op cit*; Seccombe, *op cit*, 'Patriarchy Stabilised'.

59. Quoted in Silver and Silver, *The Education of the Poor: the history of a national school 1824-1974*, Routledge and Kegan Paul, London, 1974, pp 8-9. For patriarchalism and Sunday Schools, see M. Dick, 'The myth of the working-class Sunday School', *History of Education* 9, No 1, 1980, pp 27-41.

60. Taylor, *Eve and New Jerusalem, op cit*.

61. Several useful texts draw on a Foucault's insights into power and subjectivity to make these connections, most notably: Curtis, *Building the Educational State, op cit*, and J. Donald, 'Beacons of the Future: Schooling, Subjection and Subjectification', in V. Beechey and J. Donald (eds), *Subjectivity and Social Relations*, Open University Press 1986; also David Hogan, 'The Market Revolution and Disciplinary Power: Joseph Lancaster and the Psychology of the Early Classroom System', in *History of Education Quarterly*, Vol 29 No 3, 1989, pp 381-417. However both Hogan and Donald tend to share Foucault's blindness to the importance of gender relations. For an interesting use of Foucault by a feminist historian see M. Theobald, 'Discourse of Danger: Gender and the History of Elementary Schooling in Australia, 1850-1880', *Historical Studies in Education* 1, No 1, 1989, pp 29-52.

WHAT'S LEFT OF PROGRESSIVE PRIMARY EDUCATION?

KEVIN J. BREHONY

In a recent analysis of the educational programmes of the New Right it was argued that progressivism is a 'modernising tendency of a broadly left-wing kind'.[1] In this chapter I intend to scrutinise this characterisation of progressive educational ideology with particular reference to the history of elementary and primary schooling in England and Wales. I shall look critically at the evidence for the assumption, widely held on both left and right, that there is something specifically left-wing about progessivism. I shall do this through a necessarily brief examination of the ideas and practices which have been subsumed under the label of progressive education and by teasing out some of the links and connections which have persisted over time between progressivism and a number of individual and collective actors who have occupied a variety of positions on the left. My purpose in doing this, over and above that of presenting new evidence concerning the extent and nature of those links, is to try to draw some conclusions, from a left perspective, about the nature of the relationship between the left and progressivism in education. I shall argue that the left has either been hopelessly optimistic about the power of progressive education to bring about social change or, conversely, it has considered that education has little or no role to play in the process of social transformation. My task is made somewhat difficult by the fact that I have restricted myself to the field of primary schooling. This is partly because of my personal professional involvement in this sector of education, but, more importantly, it is because, ever since Callaghan's speech at Ruskin in 1976, state educational policy has either been directed towards, or has unintentionally resulted in, the destruction of the conditions in which progressivism managed to obtain an, admittedly limited, institutional base within the primary school. Hostility towards progressivism in primary schools has consequences which go beyond the primary sector. Arguably, the limited foothold which progressivism managed to obtain in primary schools has had an effect in other sectors, because it has, for many years, constituted an important source of alternative ideas and practices for the relatively few secondary schools and departments which have attempted in their curriculum and pedagogy to make a radical break from the traditional grammar school mould. For the left, as it goes through the process of rethinking its future strategies in education, as well as across the whole spectrum of social policy and practice, the assault on progressivism raises important questions about whether it is desirable to defend it in its current form and, if it is, the way in which that defence should be mounted. Alternatively, if it should be concluded that progressivism is indefensible, the question is raised of whether it could be modified or, if it is beyond reconstruction, what kind of pedagogy should replace it. An adequate discussion of all these questions and the issues to which they give rise is beyond the scope of this chapter; rather, it is intended as a contribution which begins to clarify the uneasy relationship between the left and progressivism.

It is by now customary, almost obligatory, to commence any discussion of educational progressivism with an investigation into the various meanings that the term has, over time, been made to bear.[2] Such an activity is not without value as it helps to counteract any tendency towards an unthinking acceptance of the existence of something simply because a term is in circulation which appears to describe it. Even the most cursory glance at the history of what is held to be progressive education ought to be enough to counteract any tendencies towards the reification of the label 'progressivism'. It has been used to refer to so many diverse, and often conflicting, ideas and practices in education that it is not unusual to question whether it has any meaning at all.[3] A phenomenon such as progressivism does not possess a fixed, timeless essence which, after a certain amount of poking around by historians among the accumulated dusty layers of educational ideas and practices, may be revealed in all its purity. As Dale has reminded us,[4] educational progressivism is simply not like that. Almost as soon as its ideas and practices condense and crystallise as a recognisably distinctive discourse, they tend rapidly under the pressure of ideological conflict among other things, to become fluid again. However, I am going to depart from the usual practice of mapping the meanings of progressivism, and state here at the outset that I shall take as my object that which has widely been called 'child-centred education'.[5] In addition, I shall treat the child-centred view as an educational ideology, broadly in the sense proposed by Skilbeck,[6] but with the qualification that the sense in which ideology is to be utilised here is an inclusive one. That is to say that all knowledge is potentially socially determined and may, as a consequence, express social interests.

It is usual to broadly define child-centred education as taking as its starting point the educational needs of the child in a particular stage of its development rather than beginning with the intention of transmitting that knowledge which is held to be most worthwhile at any given time by those with power to define it. This, I shall argue, has been a relatively constant feature of progressive education within the primary school sector throughout the 20th century. Moreover, as Wright has pointed out, progressive education and radical education are not mutually exclusive but occupy positions along a continuum.[7] If this is so, then it may be argued that for most of this century the form that radical educational thought and practice in the primary sector has taken has been that of child-centred education. But radical education in this context is a relative concept, because the radicalism of child-centred education has frequently arisen out of the fact that it has been as much defined by what it has opposed as by what it has stood for. It should be borne in mind that the notion that there is a relatively unified child-centred position, which has a long history, is valid only at a high level of abstraction, and in an article of this length necessity dictates that much must be left unsaid or conveyed only in generalities. For these reasons I shall deal mainly with the more visible, and the more widespread, manifestations of child-centred education in texts and public discourse rather than in classrooms.

SOCIALISM AND CHILD-CENTRED EDUCATION

The longstanding relation between child-centred education and socialist politics is a particularly complex one because, despite a common hostility to dominant relations of power and authority, neither logically entails the other. Moreover, there is, in some respects, a quite striking lack of congruence between them. This is, perhaps, most apparent in the centrality given to individualism by many child-centred educationalists, with their subsequent lack of sympathy for the collectivist thrust of most forms of socialism. The principal role of repulsion for child-centred education for over a century has been the standardisation which unavoidably accompanies bureaucratised, mass education systems. Against the uniformity of the group, child-centred education has posed the particular needs of the individual. It is at heart, then, a liberal conception which places above all other considerations the rights of individuals. Nevertheless, there may be a principle of articulation which exists outside the ideologies of progressivism and socialism, which renders the nature of the historical relation between them less opaque. Arguably, the concept of modernity is such an articulating principle. Child-centred education and socialism may both be seen to be part of the project of modernity, which was born from the Enlightenment, and which, among other things, consists of the idea that human happiness, freedom and progress can be increased by means of the application of reason, and particularly reason in the form of science. Socialism and child-centred education, because of their apparently rational foundations, and because they hold out the promise of an improvement in the human condition, may both be seen as firmly linked to the project of modernity. It is this common assumption, that social amelioration is both possible and desirable, which might go some way towards explaining the attraction of child-centred education for the left.

There are strands in both child-centred education and socialism which have held out the possibility that the consciousness of individuals may be transformed through education, broadly conceived, and that as a consequence society may be transformed. And, even if much socialist thought has consistently held that changed individuals can only result from changed circumstances, both child-centred educators and socialists have believed in the possibility of the production of new kinds of individuals through education. While this belief in 'person-making' is not the exclusive property of socialists and progressive educationalists (religious denominations, for example, have been engaged in a similar enterprise for quite some time), it has been a prominent feature of much socialist and progressive thought.[8]

At first sight, the claim that 'person-making' is a prominent objective of child-centred education may seem perverse: there is a common association of progressive child-centred schooling with a hostility to anything approximating to 'moulding' the child (a position which was most forcefully articulated by A.S. Neill, who was ably supported on this issue, at some distance from pupils and schools, by the Fabian dramatist G.B. Shaw).[9] However, there is much evidence in the work of Froebel, Montessori and other leading child-centred educators to support it. For example, this position is to be found in the work of E.G.A. Holmes, an influential figure in the progressive, 'new' education movement in the early years of this century, who argued that a change in human nature by means of education was a necessary condition for the building of socialism.[10] It is perhaps significant that the kind of person that Holmes wished to see produced through a reconstructed system of education differed little from the type of individual admired by enthusiasts and apologists for the Soviet Union in the inter-war years, a type of individual, so they claimed, that was emerging from the Soviet school system.[11] As with the Webbs, what most distinguished Holmes and other child-centred educationalists from Marxist socialists was not ends but means.[12]

Within the state system – the elementary school, and the primary school which officially replaced it after 1944 – it is not often possible to discern a connection between child-centred ideas and figures on the left. But in the progressive private school, that other area of schooling where progressivism gained an institutional foothold during the 20th century, such links are more easily revealed. Whatever direction Cecil Reddie's allegiances took subsequently, Abbotsholme, the school of which he was head, was founded by socialists who were members of the Fellowship of the New Life.[13] Among the small group of left progressive schools in the 1920s there was also Beacon Hill, the school of Bertrand and Dora Russell.[14] A.S. Neill, with whom Bertrand Russell corresponded, occupied a place somewhere within the left spectrum, or sufficiently within it for the leading Marxist historian A.L. Morton to teach at his school, Summerhill – as did his wife, Vivien and his brother Max.[15] Similarly, King Alfred's school, which counted socialist educationalist like J.J. Findlay among its founders, had on its staff until 1948 Vera Hyett, the founder of the Anglo-Soviet friendship society, as well as six members of the left-wing Teachers Labour League.[16] These examples virtually exhaust the category of the left progressive school and although they were different in many respects, they had in common the fact that they were established primarily to test the theories and practices of child-centred education. It would not be all that misleading to suggest that they were also established so that middle-class liberals and leftists, distrustful of the public school system, could reproduce their own ideological stances in their children.[17]

In the field of nursery schooling, until 1918 an unwilling part of the private sector, there was Margaret McMillan, who by virtue of her work in the ILP is generally regarded as a socialist, despite her support in later life of the Conservative MP, Lady Astor.[18] In this field it is also significant that Sylvia Pankhurst, with whom Lenin polemicised on account of her 'infantile disorder', organised a Montessori nursery during the First World War.[19] Her main intention, like McMillan, was to rescue the slum child, but she made clear that her choice of the Montessori system was motivated by its apparent effectiveness in disciplining the children who attended the Mothers' Arms nursery.[20]

Like the Froebelians, Montessori offered a rational 'system' of education, but hers was more loudly proclaimed to be based on scientific principles and to be, as a consequence, more modern. A commitment to scientism as well as, paradoxically perhaps, a pervasive religiosity are particularly noticeable features of her writings. This paradox may be explained by the fact that the 'science' of child development has always been shot through with romanticist and other 'irrational' elements which privilege sensibility over sense; and it has also contained many dubious notions derived from theories of evolution, which have acted as a powerful template for thought in education for so long. Montessori, in seeking rational solutions to problems of pedagogy, was no different from any of the other child-centred educators in her adoption of a method grounded in conceptions that were often far from scientific. Montessori, like many of the Froebelians at the turn of the century, situated her practice firmly in the geographical and social location of the slum. Hers was a practice which, like the settlement movement to which it and the Froebelians were allied, sought the transformation of the condition of the urban poor. This was to be achieved through the reconstruction of the homes of the slum dwellers by the education of young children and, through them, their supposedly inadequate mothers. Not surprisingly, this stance attracted the attention not only of liberals, who were becoming increasingly fearful of the East End slum dwellers who, particularly on Mafeking night, had shown their propensity for jingoism and other reactionary causes, but also of socialists who were trying to ameliorate the condition of the people of the abyss.

In the left progressive schools, the reproduction of ideologically desirable attitudes among the children of the middle class left was their most important objective; in the nursery school movement in the early part of this century, however, the left was engaged principally in rescuing the children of the poor in order to transform them, their families and society.[21]

While of interest and importance in forming the educational vision of the left, particularly that part of the vision which lay outside Labour Party policy, these rather exotic figures were, in the main, peripheral to developments in state elementary education system of the late 19th and early 20th centuries. Although socialists with a relatively high profile were to be found in the private sector, developing innovatory pedagogies and curricula, few were to be found working in, let alone guiding, the educational apparatus of the state.[22] (There were some exceptions however, for example the biographer of William Morris, J.W. Mackail, who was an Examiner in the Education Department and who lectured frequently at Fabian and ILP meetings).[23]

This absence might in part be explained by the fact that state education at this period was largely confined to elementary schooling, and was subject to a highly bureaucratic regulatory regime which was unattractive to most socialists, particularly middle-class ones who had to face the deep divisions of class.[24] Alongside the system provided for the working class there existed the realm of secondary, or as it was originally often termed 'middle-class', schooling. This adhered, in varying degrees, to a version of the classical education purveyed in the leading public schools. Faced with such seemingly inhospitable ground, child-centred innovators concluded, as Neill did, that the only place to go was the private sector.[25] There, the progressives adopted a prefigurative strategy, intending that the ideas and practices which they developed would be those of education in a transformed society, as well as constituting a route to it. The state was not ignored in this strategy, as these practices were, in an often indirect way, to spark off a great wave of modernising reform in the state sector. Not for nothing were the private progressive schools, of which Abbotsholme was the first, called by their supporters 'New Schools'; they aimed at nothing less than the production of a new, modern education which would, they hoped, herald the modernisation of the entire education system and would therefore, by extension, lead to a modernised or, what in their view was virtually the same thing, socialist society.

MODERNISATION IN STATE EDUCATION: THE FIRST WAVE

Modernisation, like progressivism, is a term susceptible to many usages. But in one sense, it connotes in education a continual struggle to adapt the schooling of the working class to what are perceived to be the requirements of industry. Within the state sector, which until 1902 was almost entirely composed of the elementary schools, there was an attempt at modernisation in the late 19th century which was related to the major transformations in the sphere of production that began to take place from the late 1880s. An alliance of modernisers emerged, many of whose members could be described as being on the left in education, by virtue of their attachment to a collectivist version of liberalism. This modernising bloc, referred to by Williams as the 'industrial trainers',[26] was also supported by people who tended to be in favour of women's suffrage, Irish Home-Rule and the cause of labour. Their enthusiasm for the latter, however, was strictly within the limits set by their adherence to the interests of industry and manufacturing; their view of a modernised education system was one in which opportunity was to be broadened, but there was no commitment to any kind of equalisation of the life chances of its pupils. This grouping initially favoured a form of modernisation of the elementary school which consisted of a 'marriage' between a programme of manual training and child-centred Froebelian ideas and practices.

Put baldly, the Froebelians advocated a child-centred position which held that, in the determination of infant pedagogy and curriculum, the characteristics and dispositions of young learners should over-ride the needs of a traditional 'society' which were expressed in the elementary school Code. With respect to infants in the elementary schools, the Education Department had in the 1890s endorsed this view through the medium of a number of Circulars, and had recommended the adoption of selected Froebelian ideas and practices by infant schools and departments. The Education Department made this endorsement because of the lack of a policy on a suitable curriculum for young working-class children; it did not, as the modernisers wished, endorse a handwork-centred curriculum to extend throughout the elementary school. Opposition on ideological grounds to this aspect of the modernisers' programme was particularly intense from traditionalists. But entangled with this opposition was the voluntarists' contention that a modernised curriculum, or for that matter modernised school accommodation, would be beyond the bounds of what they could afford.[27]

Thus one outcome of the attempt to modernise the schooling of young children was that there came into existence two broadly distinct versions of child-centred education. One, the property of the educational movement which nurtured it, possessed alternative and even oppositional elements relative to the existing forms of pedagogy, curriculum and educational ideology. The other, the official version, stripped the former of its transformative goals, and harnessed it to the objectives of the 'moralisation' of the working-class child and the production of forms of skilled labour power. It was in this latter form, as simply a technique or method, that child-centred education was imposed in the state sector, upon largely unsympathetic teachers, and on a system which lacked the material resources and conditions for it to be practised effectively.

Despite the adoption by the state's education apparatus of a modern rhetoric of infant schooling, the progress of modernisation was severely curtailed by the settlement which found legislative expression between 1899 and 1902. At the same time the progress of child-centred education also faltered as the conditions upon which its practice depended failed to be brought into being. Large classes, the pressure of the need to prepare pupils for subsequent stages of schooling, the growing importance of selection, lack of resources and unsympathetic teachers and inspectors were some of the obstacles which ensured that child-centred education remained, by and large, an official discourse without a corresponding practice.

However, in its Froebelian form, child-centred education became hegemonic in the sphere of the theory of infant education. In part this was due to the rationalisation of Froebelian theory brought about by educationalists open to developments in the United States. This new Froebelianism substituted for Froebel's metaphysics a legitimising rhetoric drawn from psychology. This progressive rationalisation of the world of Froebel, by figures like Dewey and G. Stanley Hall, constitutes a second type of modernisation, and while this form of modernisation was related to the programme of the industrial trainers, it is not necessarily reducible to it.

The settlement of 1902 left elementary schooling firmly wedded to a conception of education best described as traditional rather than modern, in the sense that it was badly adapted to meeting the needs of industry as defined by the industrial trainers. Proof of this is to be found in Morant's Code of Regulations for Public Elementary Schools which were issued in 1904. An old Harrovian himself, it was perhaps predictable that the habits he wished the elementary school to cultivate had a traditional flavour. The objectives, of forming and strengthening character, that he wished the elementary school to pursue were situated in a highly diluted version of a liberal, that is to say a non-vocational, conception of education. It may be described as diluted principally because, although individual development to the greatest extent possible was for Morant a desirable end of elementary schooling. So too was the selection of those who showed 'promise of exceptional ability'. He also felt another end should be the making of 'upright and useful members of the community'. These latter objectives clashed rather violently with the liberal notion of individual development because, under the selective system which was initiated by the Board of Education under Morant, the opportunity for self development was only permitted to the very few. Moreover, in Morant's view as in that of the Webbs, individual development was subordinated to social requirements such as the need for upright citizens. Morant was a moderniser in the field of administration and in his enthusiasm for the notion that the many weak should submit themselves to the leadership of the few strong, in order to fend off the challenge of foreign industrial and military competition – his vision of the modern was not one in which the dissolution of the boundaries of social class had even a minor part to play. His embrace of what would now be regarded as neo-fascist ideas suggests that Morant was a moderniser of the right, whose main concern was preparing the nation for a new stage of imperialist rivalry.[28]

Like his erstwhile Fabian allies, the Webbs, Morant was an advocate of differentiation in education. That is to say, each social class, and even layers within classes, should have provided for them in separate institutions an educational diet deemed appropriate to their future station. In this there was little that was democratic, leaving aside his support for a scholarship route that was a little broader than T.H. Green's ladder from 'the gutter to the university'. What was radical about his view of education was his support, expressed in a letter to the socialist activist and educator Margaret McMillan, for the notion that for certain categories of the working class it did not much matter what they were taught, as their physical and emotional needs were such as to render irrelevant and grossly inappropriate most of the watered down liberal curricula purveyed in the elementary schools. Here Morant made contact with the child-centred view which also prioritised the physical needs of the child over the requirement to transmit 'school knowledge'.

While Morant, in common with many Froebelians at the time, thought that child-centred prescriptions were suitable only for the children of the labouring poor, some of the contributors to the section on schools in the New Year Book of the Workers' Educational Association (WEA) of 1918, for example the campaigner for nursery schools, Grace Owen, saw them as suitable for all young children. Margaret McMillan's contribution to the same volume suggests, however, that there was quite a lot of oscillation in progressive discourse between the position embraced by Morant and that by Owen. Arguably, this was because attempts to get child-centred approaches accepted as being best suited to all young children had generally met with little success, and the child-centred educationalists felt that they might gain an institutional base for their practices by taking advantage of the widespread anxiety about racial degeneracy and imperial decline.

The WEA Yearbook was part of organised labour's contribution to the great debate on educational reconstruction which took place during the latter stages of the First World War. It was not, as its editors stressed, sufficient to demand more education, they needed also to demand an education which harmonised with 'their social ideals'.[29] However, as in the case of the Board of Education's policy on the schooling of young children, questions of practice in the WEA Yearbook were left to those who had constructed themselves, and had been constructed by the state, as experts. The contributions of Owen and McMillan, acknowledged experts on the education of young children, did not directly address the 'social ideals' of the workers but instead dealt largely with the techniques and practices of a child-centred education.[30] The contrast between their contributions and that of Holmes, another expert by virtue of his having held the position of Chief Inspector, is indicative of the problem of translating generalities which seemed to harmonise with the workers' social ideals into educational practices. His prescription for a child-centred education for democracy was simple:

> Give a child freedom for self-development, release him from the cramping and deadening pressure of autocratic authority, rigid discipline and mechanical instruction, and two things will happen. The spirit of liberty, equality, fraternity will begin to germinate in his heart, and his capacity . . . for making the most of his natural aptitudes and inclinations will at least be kept alive.[31]

The state, in the sphere of infant schooling, had accepted a version of the child-centred message partly by default; and the WEA Yearbook reflected a similar attitude of leaving pedagogy to the experts within the labour movement.

MODERNISATION IN STATE EDUCATION: THE SECOND WAVE

As is well known, the Geddes Axe of 1922 signalled the end to the era of reform and modernisation heralded by the Education Act of 1918.[32] Nevertheless, the post-war period was marked by an upsurge in interest in child-centred education which was not to recur to the same extent until the late 1960s. Both periods were also, of course, marked by widespread political opposition to the state and to the capitalist system. Arising out of this ferment in education in the 1920s were a proliferation of progressive movements such as the New Education Fellowship, and of methods which included such approaches as the Dalton Plan and the Project Method. As Labour, which had replaced the Liberals as the party of state education, edged closer to government if not to power, the attitudes of its education experts, like R.H. Tawney, to child-centred approaches were at best ambivalent. In part this was due to their preoccupation with access to, and the establishment of, a more broadly defined secondary schooling. Such a focus did not encourage much debate about pedagogy and curriculum, although the Labour Party's Advisory Committee on Education did from time to time consider these matters.

Much has been made of Percy Nunn's membership of this committee.[33] Nunn, a leading advocate of a highly individualistic version of child-centred education, did not however play a prominent role in the committee and resigned not long after his appointment. Of more significance, from the point of view of Labour's perception of child-centred education, was the presence on the committee of Beatrice Ensor, the dominant figure in the New Education Fellowship, which began as a front organisation for Theosophists with an interest in education. Ensor produced for the committee a classic statement of the child-centred position,[34] which Tawney then proceeded to dilute until it lost all its impact. By the time the policy statement 'From the Nursery School to the University' appeared in 1926 the child-centred position was unrecognisable. This incident permits the inference that for Labour electoral success was not to be jeopardised by the advocates of fanciful education programmes. But while the official Labour line eschewed the incorporation of child-centred prescriptions in its pronouncements, the Commission on Education appointed by the Bradford ILP did not. On the contrary, it promoted them with enthusiasm. Regarding the desirability of the nursery school the Commission proclaimed that 'every child born has a right to the fullest individual growth and development'. Growth or the 'natural unfolding in a natural order of latent capacities' required for its fulfillment teachers who were able to display 'a vigilant passivity' and 'the minimum of authority'. In infant schools, according to the Commission, education was unsatisfactory partly because teachers were trained to 'teach actively, and not to watch, vigilantly indeed but passively'.[35] The stance is that of Froebel, with additional material from Montessori and McMillan, but the conclusion was given a left nuance observable in the claim that 'a working class trained in the Nursery School spirit would not tolerate existing conditions, economic or social'.[36]

Other sections of the left were less enthusiastic about child-centred education. To the left of Labour in education in the 1920s stood the Teachers' Labour League (TLL), which for much of the period of its existence was a grouping of socialists active in education. From the late 1920s it was largely a front for the Communist Party. The TLL's collective position on child-centred education was never made clear in its journal *The Educational Worker*, but it was critical of the private progressive schools and the Conference of New Ideals in Education[37] led by the former Chief Inspector of Schools, E.G.A. Holmes. For the TLL, the mysticism which pervaded much of the utterances and discussions of the Conference of New Ideals was too much to take, as was its middle-class composition. The supporters of New Ideals were characterised by the TLL as favouring 'class-collaboration to check class struggle'. Critiques of progressive schools and of progressive methods, including those which had initially been favourable received in the Soviet Union,[38] were as far as the TLL got in producing anything in the nature of what Jones refers to in this context as, 'a detailed elaboration of "socialist pedagogy" '.[39] This absence of a socialist pedagogy which commanded a measure of agreement on the left meant that, for a self-declared Marxist teacher like Beryl Pring, much of what she considered for the constitution of methods of socialist education would still have to be 'borrowed from the ideas of progressive schools'.[40]

Unlike the Teachers' Labour League, the Bradford ILP pursued a strategy of reform through the existing state institutions. In oral evidence to the Consultative Committee on the Board of Education which was preparing its report on the primary school, the Bradford ILP Commission of Education argued for experiments similar to the American project method or the Soviet 'complex' system.[41] In its written evidence it recommended that the demand for instruction in the primary school should be 'severely and decisively limited, and encroachment by the result-monger sternly repressed'. What mattered most was 'the spirit and vitality of the children, the vividness of their games and dramatic work, the freshness and sincerity of their drawings', and not that which was measured by examinations.[42] Similar views were expressed in the evidence of other organisations from within the labour movement. The TUC stressed the importance of individual work as opposed to listening passively to the teacher[43] and the National Union of Agricultural Workers thought that the child should not 'be regarded as a receptacle to be crammed with facts but rather as a personality to be developed to the full'.[44] These instances of the adoption of child-centred positions by organisations on the left and within the labour movement are cited not in order to claim that the Consultative Committee was heavily influenced by their evidence – the child-centred case was in any case presented by Percy Nunn and Cyril Burt who together dominated the Committee's report – but to illustrate the extent to which they had become the received wisdom of the left regarding the schooling of young children.

In the development of the primary school the Hadow reports of 1931 and 1933 are of central significance. This is because they announced a new conception of schooling for young children which broke decisively with previous practice in the elementary schools. Above all, unlike the elementary schools which were established expressly for the purpose of schooling the children of the labouring poor, the primary school in the Hadow conception, as it appeared in its 1931 report, was to be a school for all social classes.[45] It was intended to lead to secondary schooling, in all its bewildering variety, for all;[46] this was the birthright of the citizens of the representative-interventionist state without exception.[47] It was thus a modern schooling appropriate to a modern state. It was modern in other ways too, in particular in its embrace of the notion that children develop in identifiable and distinct stages and that a school's pedagogy and curriculum should be organised around that recognition. Supplying the theoretical props for these notions was the task of Percy Nunn, who gave evidence on the curriculum,[48] and the psychologist Cyril Burt.[49] Confirmation of the significance of the stages in physiological terms was provided by Professor Harris, an assistant professor of anatomy at University College. The Hadow Reports depended very heavily upon science, and psychology in particular, for the legitimation of its proposals. Nevertheless, despite the seemingly scientific arguments for an age-related system of school organisation, the age of transfer was chosen on grounds of administrative convenience. Burt and Nunn simply provided legitimacy for the decision to create a specific form of schooling for pupils aged seven to eleven. Evidently, the extent to which scientific evidence was taken into account in Hadow's recommendations was somewhat limited. One of the reasons that such knowledge played the restricted but by no means unimportant role of legitimation, was that it was limited in scope. Partial confirmation of this is provided by Burt's memorandum on the mental characteristics of children, which is included in the report as an appendix. Burt mixes what he claims to be objective knowledge about mental characteristics with a number of child-centred, commonplace notions, the relation of which to his psychology is far from clear. Perhaps the kindest explanation is that the kind of psychology practised by Burt, which abstracted pupils from the conditions which existed in elementary schools, was simply incapable of generating proposals to guide the practice of their teachers.

By the time of the outbreak of the Second World War, official discourse on the schooling of young children borrowed heavily from child-centred ideology. The reports in which that discourse is enshrined are complex documents which bear the marks of their collective authorship. Like all official discourse, they were produced for particular audiences in a determinate political context. A consequence of this is that by selective quotation any number of contradictory messages may be seen to have been produced by Hadow; but a sustainable case can be made that Hadow stripped the child-centred ideology of its moral prescriptions and retained only its technical ones. Evidence that Hadow saw the main purpose of the school as 'person-making' is not apparent, particularly as, in true liberal humanist fashion, and in marked contrast to Morant's view, the report on the primary school maintained that the most desirable end of education in this stage was education.[50] The left in the same period, transfixed as it was by the rise of fascism and the imminence of war, appeared to lose faith in person-making through education. For the Labour Party, with its statist strategy of widening access to post-primary schooling and its concern with the generally appalling condition of much publicly provided schooling, questions of pedagogy and curriculum were held to be best left to the experts. In the moral prescriptions of child-centred education, as has been seen, it had apparently little interest.

While the Hadow reports were the annunciation of the birth of the modern primary school, it was the Act of 1944 which finally brought it into being. In another sense also the immediate post-war years marked a turning point in the fortunes of child-centred education. Coinciding with the war years were the deaths of a whole generation of progressive educationalists. The following years of reconstruction were in a very real sense ones in which the child-centred ideology was rediscovered.[51] Some like Alec Clegg, the Chief Education Officer of the West Riding of Yorkshire, claimed that subsequent developments in primary schooling had nothing to do with the work of previous child-centred educators.[52] There were of course some continuities, and among these was the National Froebel Foundation, which was deeply implanted in the training colleges which produced infant school teachers, and which vigorously promoted Piaget's developmental psychology. With Labour's gaze firmly fixed upon access to the grammar school, and subsequently to the generalisation of its supposed benefits through comprehensive schools, the connection between the left and the child-centred ideology became even more tenuous. At odds with widespread and deep-seated notions about the nature of childhood and the purposes of schooling, the child-centred ideology became, in the 1950s and early 1960s, as Cunningham charts, an almost exclusively professional ideology.[53] This ideology, as Alexander has suggested,[54] gave purpose and identity to countless primary school teachers even when, as was so often the case, they were unable because of unfavourable material and ideological conditions to adopt the kinds of practices which that ideology supported. Nevertheless, despite its appearance of radicalism which stemmed from its opposition to mental testing, it was an ideology which by no means 'stood unequivocally outside, let alone against, the Establishment'.[55]

PLOWDEN AND MODERNISATION IN STATE EDUCATION: THE THIRD WAVE

Although Plowden found that some all-age primary schools had still not been reorganised in the post Hadow of 1926 mould, by the late 1960s changes in primary schools of a modern kind, in several senses, were becoming visible. School architecture was but one area in which change took place, as not just new buildings but radically different ones replaced those built in the 19th century. Innovation was also observable in the practices of primary education. The 11-plus, as the trend towards comprehensivisation quickened, began to lose its stranglehold on the primary school curriculum, and there were many sources of theory and practice which were utilised to fill the spaces created by its decline. Streaming also began to loosen its grip, mainly as a consequence of the demise of the 11-plus. Taken together these, and many other changes both planned and unplanned, were beginning, along with the long post-war boom, to create conditions which were, for the first time on a fairly large scale, favourable to the practice of child-centred education, if only in its official, Hadow version. These changed conditions created opportunities for new work which were seized upon by child-centred teachers, inspectors, college lecturers and others. The effects of this activity were cumulative. Around the time of the publication of the Plowden Report, in 1967, an impression was created by a somewhat disparate set of sources that something in the nature of a revolution had occurred in English primary schools. A central element in that supposed revolutionary upheaval, it was said, was the child-centred ideology to which Plowden had given its somewhat ambiguous approval. As Simon has shown,[56] the more sweeping claims about the implementation of child-centred practices were not supported by the evidence of the Primary Survey, ORACLE and other research.

Alongside the further confirmation in the official discourse of Plowden that child-centred techniques, largely legitimated by selections from Plaget's psychology, were the most desirable for the promotion of learning, there was a recrudescence on the left of support for child-centred education. The reasons this occurred are many, as Wright has demonstrated,[57] although their consideration is beyond the scope of this discussion. But as Jones as argued,[58] the proposal of a strategy by Plowden which not only had as its object the time-honoured, child-centred objectives of active learning and an end to restrictive subject divisions, but also aimed to use the school as a lever with which to close the deep fissures of social class, helped to create days of hope among a left in education which by this time was largely outside the Labour Party. Optimism sprang less from a belief that the state could lessen the effects of class divisions through education policy, than from the fact that Plowden took seriously the massive role played by such divisions in the determination of educational outcomes. Plowden also offered teachers on the left an answer to the question of 'what to do on Monday?', which it had failed to confront in previous decades. While for all teachers that is a major consideration, once more, almost by default, sections of the left assumed child-centred education to be, as Jones puts it, 'synonymous with socialist change'.[59] This assumption was not long lived, and in the primary sector it is doubtful if it ever existed. There was, nevertheless, one place in the sector where such an assumption was widely thought to be held, and that was at William Tyndale Junior School. However the progressive teachers at Tyndale were rather circumspect about the relation between child-centred education and socialist political action in their account of the affair that engulfed them in the mid 1970s.[60] Nothing is to be found in this account which is manifestly about person-making. Like the Hadow report, the account of the teachers at William Tyndale stresses educational ends but it evades the question of why they adopted a philosophy which 'was democratic, egalitarian and non-sexist' if they had no aims external to the process of schooling itself.

As was typical of the left by the mid 1970s, the progressive William Tyndale teachers were critical of what they perceived to be the limitations of progressive or child-centred education, and were seeking to transcend it. A similar reaction among teachers on the left during the mid 1970s is chronicled by Wright who, in relation to their attitudes to child-centred education, makes a distinction between radical and progressive teachers. This distinction holds perhaps at the level of the analysis of the relation between school and society, and that of the ends of education and schooling, but is less evident at the level of pedagogy and learning. Sharp and Green, whose work was based specifically on research in a primary school, went further by arguing that child-centred education was not only not radical, but that its effects were highly conservative. They also maintained that child-centred progressivism failed to comprehend the realities of a stratified society, and that in comparison with traditional educational ideologies it was a more effective form of social control.[61] Despite her unhappiness with Sharp and Green's use of the concept of ideology,[62] this is essentially the burden of Walkerdine's critique of child-centred ideology in primary schools.[63] Although pointing it out clearly does not disprove Walkerdine's case, it still seems somewhat ironic that the Black Paperites and their new right successors have failed to see the supposed conservative potential of child-centred ideology. This does not mean that the approach of Walkerdine is the same as that of the Black Papers, but that they share a dislike of child-centred education.

For child-centred education, as has been emphasised, it is science in the form of developmental psychology which promised to lead the way to the emancipation of the pupil from ignorance, and of society from intolerance and repression. It is therefore not surprising that child-centred education has come under attack from the post-structuralist quarter. It may very well be the case that the political implications of leading poststructuralist and postmodern thinkers, like Foucault, from whose work Walkerdine's critique draws extensively, are, as Sarup claims, 'neo-conservative'.[64] Sarup's judgement notwithstanding, in recent years poststructuralism has generally been regarded as radical, and consequently poststructuralist critiques of child-centred education have had that appearance also.

Novelty, intellectual fashion and radicalism are often conflated, but in this particular instance there are other determinants at work which help give to Walkerdine's poststructuralist critique of child-centred education its appearance of radicalism. Foremost among these are the fact that in her work the poststructuralist rejection of the modern project of child-centred education has been harnessed to a feminist critique of its ideas and practices. It is in this context that she observes that the 'natural child', which child-centred pedagogies take as their point of departure, can only be made possible by 'the servicing labour of women' teachers.[65] Added to this feminist critique is the familiar poststructuralist theme that liberation through the application of reason is a 'sham' because in classroom practice informed by the child-centred approach . . . 'freed from coercion, the child is much more subtly regulated into normality.'[66]

In Walkerdine's view, child-centred education, and the developmental psychology with which it has been underpinned, cannot lead to the liberation of children and a subsequent transformation in the 'social domain'.[67] Instead of children's development producing a child-centred pedagogy, she claims that the apparatuses of child-centred pedagogy produce development.[68] Furthermore, there are no empirically-verifiable facts of child-development which stand outside discursive practices, and children are therefore, in contrast to the belief of the child-centred educators, unknowable.

Leaving aside the problem of whether any pedagogy can ever produce liberated individuals in the sense that she once thought it could, Walkerdine's poststructuralist critique of child-centred ideology is interesting in the way that it parallels the critique which poststructuralists make of the Englightenment.[69] In these critiques the road to rationality leads not to freedom but to slavery and domination. Little wonder that she finds it difficult to formulate political strategies on the basis of this analysis.[70] By way of a contrast, Skidelsky, although starting with a similar critique of the ideals of the Englightenment, has found little difficulty in proposing political strategies which run contrary to child-centred education.[71] Skidelsky also highlights the tension between romanticism and rationalism in child-centred ideology but, as has been noted in relation to Montessori, feeling and reason have not always been as sharply distinguished as he implies.

CONCLUSION

Walkerdine's critique of both child-centred pedagogy and the promise of rationalism represents one strand in the historical record of reaction to both phenomena. The optimism of Holmes and others considered here represents an opposite response. It would appear, then, that when the left, broadly conceived, has not been attributing to child-centred education the power to change society, it has either been trying to destroy it or in some way to supersede it. Much of the hostile reaction has had to do with the fact that at times the educational apparatus of the state has appeared to give legitimacy and encouragement to aspects of child-centred education. From this it has been concluded that if the state adopted aspects of the child-centred approach it must demonstrate that such an approach is inextricably bound up with state apparatuses of control and repression. Nevertheless, if it were as efficacious in terms of social control as Sharp and Green suggested, the puzzle remains as to why the state – in the form of the Board of Education and its successors, the Ministry of Education and Department of Education and Science – has never got beyond the point of granting child-centred education lip-service approval. This is not to say that the state's half-hearted support for child-centred education makes it beyond criticism. It does suggest, however, that Walkerdine and Sharp and Green may have exaggerated the extent to which child-centred education is functional to the state's strategies of social control. When they produced their critiques, the discourse of child-centred education was the official discourse of the primary sector, but, as Sharp and Green among others noted, it was not often evident that the practice was child-centred. Indeed it could be argued that much of the confusion on the left regarding the most appropriate stance to adopt towards child-centred education stems from the fact that it has never been tried to any significant extent. It could be argued that the conditions in which child-centred education could take place on a wide scale have not been created because of the failure of repeated attempts to modernise the education system, and particularly its primary school sector. By the failure of modernisation I mean the limited nature of the transformation of the conditions and practices within the primary sector which have been grossly inadequate to the needs of all the individual pupils with it, and which lag far behind the technological and social transformations which have occurred in recent decades. Two aspects of this failure may be singled out for emphasis. Firstly, the state has always been reluctant to spend sufficient money on publicly provided schooling to secure conditions in all schools equivalent to those which exist in the best schools. In a society divided by class it is unlikely that it ever will, despite the arguments of successive waves of modernisers on the left. The selection function of schools, and the need to secure the cultural reproduction of the directing and subaltern classes has always been paramount. Secondly, with regard to the particular circumstances of primary schooling, the state shows no sign, even in this current period of upheaval, that it is prepared to resource the schooling of primary school pupils to the same extent that it resources those in secondary schools. Whatever the received wisdom of education under Thatcherism says to the contrary, resources are important, as child-centred education is an expensive pedagogy in terms of staff, buildings and equipment. If every child's learning needs were to be put at the centre of the process of schooling, a massive transfer of resources would be required from the highest to the least attaining pupils. The political outcry that would follow would be deafening, as the radical Tyndale teachers found when they attempted the educational equivalent of socialism in one country.

It is precisely the parsimonious stance of the state, and the failure of successive modernising projects in the shadow cast by the overwhelming presence and imperatives of class divisions, that has been responsible for much of the left's support for child-centred education. But, as has been seen, that sympathy co-exists with a frequently expressed hostility to child-centred education. Many have held, as did the TLL, that the problems which socialists were seeking to resolve were not soluble through schooling. The converse of this was the position of the ILP. Common to both positions has been a lack of understanding regarding the nature of educational ideologies. In this regard Entwistle's distinction between the 'moral' and 'technical' prescriptions of child-centred education is useful.[72]

Moral prescriptions have to do with the narrower field of the teaching and learning of school knowledge. Broadly, this is a similar approach to that of Donald,[73] who has sought to distinguish between what he called 'educational ideologies' on the one hand and the 'practices of schooling' on the other. Like Entwistle's technical prescriptions, the latter consist of theories of child development and pedagogic techniques whereas the former are about the intended or expected outcomes of an educational practice.

When sections of the left have regarded child-centred education as a means for transforming society through person-making, they have often overlooked the primitive state of what passes for pedagogy and theories of learning generally. This failure to develop a pedagogy and theory of learning adequate to the conditions of mass schooling is not something specific to child-centred education, but, given the commitment of child-centred educationalists to methods rather than to forms of knowledge, this weakness is more than slightly ironic. For a long period, until quite recently, child-centred educators were content to cite Piaget when asked to explain how children learned. However, Piaget did not produce a model of how children in school learn. It was not his object. But he was taken to have produced a theory of learning which was highly individualistic and which took little account of the complexities of interaction in classrooms.

The issue of learning is a vitally important one. If, for instance, no coherent account can be given of how children learn to read, it is unlikely that one can be given of how children learn to be socialists or feminists or whatever. Without an adequate theory of learning it is not possible to develop an adequate theory of teaching. It might well be an Enlightenment fantasy to believe that outcomes of pedagogic practice may one day be predictable to a greater extent than is now possible, but few on the left today would deny that the principal function of schooling should be the promotion of learning in order to empower individuals and communities. If that is the case then, in this respect, Wright was correct to highlight learning as a major area of concern for the left in education.[74] A more adequate theory of learning which addresses real children interacting in primary schools, and not abstracted individuals, is an absolute necessity for the construction of a socialist pedagogy. Such a pedagogy would aim at person-making only in the restricted sense that the persons made can grasp all of the opportunities presented by society for self development and active participation in the polity. Without such a theory, and a practice based upon it, the left is condemned to borrow indefinitely from the child-centred ideology, which carries with it too much ideological baggage from romanticism to be of much utility in this task. What needs to be retained from the child-centred ideology is the stress on the creation of autonomous learners, on the provisional nature of knowledge, and on the objective of co-operative rather than coercive relations of schooling. This is not because such things necessarily produce better persons, but because they are valuable in their own right.

Putting learning at the centre of education may appear to reduce the problem of education to solely a technical question. But this does not mean that issues of value are thereby eliminated. What the child-centred educationalists have consistently failed to recognise is the social nature of school learning, and the fact that the major structural divisions within society of class, race and gender are frequently the seat of obstacles to learning. Thus commitment to the promotion of learning should require not ghettoised anti-sexist and antiracist initiatives, but the installation of those concerns right at the heart of every teacher's practice. Having said that, the review of the relation between the left and child-centred education which was been presented here illustrates a key point which was frequently made by educationalists at the beginning of this century, that education and schooling are not synonymous. In other words, however desirable the goals may be, unless the school is in harmony with the other educational institutions of society it is unlikely that they may be attained. In the case of young children, many of those educational institutions promote values which teachers, not always without good reason, reject, and there is thus created a contradiction which the system of schooling is powerless to resolve. For many this may be an unpalatable argument, as it underlines the relative powerlessness of the school system to effect major change, and to this extent the poststructuralists have been right to attempt the deconstruction of child-centred education and question its capacity to bring about the changes claimed by its supporters. On the other hand, for the left and for radicals generally, it may well be that the shedding of such illusions is long overdue and a necessary preliminary to the construction of a radical alternative.

NOTES

1. K. Jones, *Right Turn*, Hutchinson Radius, London 1989, p 87.
2. P. Cunningham, *Curriculum Change in the Primary School Since 1945*, Falmer, London 1988, pp 11-13.
3. R.J.W. Selleck, *English Primary Education and the Progressives*, Routledge and Kegan Paul, London 1972; L. Cremin, *The Transformation of the School*, Vintage, New York 1961.
4. R. Dale, 'From endorsement to disintegration: progressive education from the Golden Age to the Green Paper'. *British Journal of Education Studies*, Vol 27, No 3, 1979, p 206.
5. H. Entwistle, *Child-Centred Education*, Methuen, London 1974.
6. M. Skilbeck, 'Ideologies and Values'. *Unit 3, E203, Curriculum Design and Development*, Open University Press, Milton Keynes 1976.
7. M. Wright, *Assessing Radical Education*, Open University Press, Milton Keynes 1989, p 16.
8. A. Gramsci, 'Americanism and Fordism' in Q. Hoare and G. Nowell Smith (eds), *Selections from the Prison Notebooks of Antonio Gramsci*, Lawrence and Wishart, London 1971, pp 279-316; and L. Trotsky, 'Literature and Revolution' in I. Deutscher, (ed), *The Age of Permanent Revolution*, Dell, New York 1964, pp 315-326.

9. J. Croall, *Neill of Summerhill*, Ark, London 1984, p 174.

10. E.G.A. Holmes, *Give Me the Young*, Constable, London 1921, p 139; E.G.A. Holmes, *Freedom and Growth and other Essays*, J.M. Dent, London 1923, p 26.

11. P. Sloan, *Soviet Democracy*, Victor Gollancz, London 1937, p 42. H. Johnson, *The Socialist Sixth of the World*, Victor Gollancz, London 1939, p 347.

12. B. and S. Webb, *Soviet Communism*, Longmans Green, London 1937 (2nd ed).

13. W.A.C. Stewart, *The Educational Innovators*, Vol II, Macmillan, London 1968. W.H.G. Armitage, *Heavens Below*, Routledge and Kegan Paul, London 1961. J. Darling, 'New life and new education: The philosophies of Davidson, Reddie and Hahn; *Scottish Educational Review*, Vol 13, No 1, 1981, pp 12-24.

14. D. Russell, *The Tamarisk Tree*, Vol 1, Virago, London 1977, pp 197-210.

15. R. Hemmings, *Fifty Years of Freedom*, George Allen and Unwin, London 1972. Croall, *op cit*.

16. *The Education Worker*, Vol 1, No 7, 1927, p 8.

17. D. Russell, *The Tamarisk Tree*, Vol 2, Virago, London, pp 6-7.

18. C. Steedman, *Childhood, Culture and Class in Britain: Margaret McMillan*, Virago, London 1990.

19. V.I. Lenin, *'Left-Wing' Communism, an Infantile Disorder*, Progress, Moscow nd; E.S. Pankhurst, *The Home Front*, Century Hutchinson, London 1987, pp 425-429.

20. E.S. Pankhurst, *The Home Front, op cit*, pp 425-426.

21. C. Steedman, *op cit*, p 161.

22. K. Kean, *Challenging the State? The Socialist and Feminist Educational Experience 1900-1930*, Falmer, London 1990, p 2.

23. G. Sutherland, *Policy-Making in Elementary Education 1870-1895*, Oxford University Press, 1973, p 41.

24. P.B. Ballard, *Things I Cannot Forget*, University of London Press, 1937, pp 70-74.

25. A.S. Neill, *Neill! Neill! Orange Peel!*, Quartet, London 1977, pp 139-142.

26. R. Williams, *The Long Revolution*, Penguin, Harmondsworth 1965, pp 161-164.

27. G. Kekewich, *The Education Department and After*, Constable, London 1920, pp 86-87.

28. B.M. Allen, *Sir Robert Morant*, Macmillan, London 1934, pp 125-126.

29. G.D.H. Cole and A. Freeman, *Workers' Education Association Yearbook*, WEA, London 1918, p 56.

30. G. Owen, 'Day Nurseries and Nursery Schools', *Workers' Education Association Yearbook*, WEA, London 1908, pp 145-148; M. McMillan, ' "Treatment" versus "Training" ', *Workers' Education Association Yearbook*, WEA, London 1918, pp 149-154.

31. E.G.A. Holmes, 'Laying in our schools the foundations of democracy',

Workers' Education Association Yearbook, WEA, London 1918, p 157.

32. B. Simon, *The Politics of Educational Reform 1920-1940*, Lawrence and Wishart, London 1976, pp 37-58.

33. R. Barker, *Education and Politics 1900-1951*, Clarendon Press, Oxford 1972, p 36.

34. B. Ensor, 'Curriculum and Methods', memorandum No 99, Labour Party Advisory Committee on Education, February 1924.

35. Commission on Education appointed by the Bradford Independent Labour Party *The Nursery School*, Thornton and Pearson, Bradford 1929, p 28.

36. *Ibid*, p 40.

37. Report on New Ideals Conference, Malvern, *Educational Worker*, Vol 13, No 28, 1929, p 12.

38. K. Jones, *Beyond Progressive Education*, Macmillan, London 1983, p 117.

39. *The Educational Worker*, Vol 5, No 65, 1933, pp 13-15.

40. B. Pring, *Education: Capitalist and Socialist*, Methuen, London 1936, p 201.

41. PRO ED 10/148 Paper S12 (48).

42. PRO ED 10/148 Paper S27.

43. PRO ED 10/148 Paper S12 (25).

44. PRO ED 10/148 Paper S51.

45. Board of Education, *Report of the Consultative Committee on the Primary School*, HMSO, London 1931, p xxviii.

46. B. Simon, *The Politics of Educational Reform 1920-1940*, Lawrence and Wishart, London 1976, p 129.

47. S. Hall, 'The representative-interventionist state 1880s-1920s', in *D209 The State and Society*, Open University Press, Milton Keynes, 1984; K.J. Brehony, 'Popular control or control by experts? Schooling between 1880 and 1902', in M. Langan and B. Schwarz, *Crises in the British State 1880-1930*, Hutchinson, London 1985, p 260.

48. PRO ED 10/148.

49. PRO ED 10/148.

50. Board of Education, *Report of the Consultative Committee on the Primary School*, HMSO, London 1931, p xv.

51. P. Cunningham, *Curriculum Change in the Primary School Since 1945*, Falmer, London 1988, p 13.

52. B. Simon, 'The primary school revolution: myth or reality?', in E. Fearn and B. Simon (eds), *Education in the Sixties*, History of Education Society, Leicester 1980, p 20.

53. P. Cunningham, *op cit*, pp 80-81.

54. R. Alexander, *Primary Teaching*, Holt Rinehart and Winston, London 1984.

55. P. Cunningham, *op cit*, p 217.

56. B. Simon, 1980, *op cit*, p 20.

57. N. Wright, *Assessing Radical Education*, Open University Press, Milton Keynes 1989, pp 5-14.

58. K. Jones, *op cit*, pp 44-49.

59. *Ibid*, p 125.
60. T. Ellis, J. McWhirter, D. McColgan, and B. Haddow, *William Tyndale the Teachers' Story*, Writers and Readers, London 1976.
61. R. Sharp and A. Green, *Education and Social Control*, Routledge and Kegan Paul, London 1975, pp vii-viii.
62. V. Walkerdine, 'Developmental psychology and the child-centred pedagogy: the insertion of Piaget into early education', in J. Henriques, W. Hollway, C. Urwin, C. Venn, and V. Walkerdine (eds), *Changing the Subject*, Methuen, London 1984, p 196.
63. V. Walkerdine, 'Progressive pedagogy and political struggle', *Screen*, Vol 27, No 5, 1986, pp 54-60.
64. M. Sarup, *An Introductory Guide to Post-structuralism and Postmodernism*, Harvester Wheatsheaf, Hemel Hempstead 1988, p 140.
65. V. Walkerdine, 1986, *op cit*, p 59.
66. *Ibid*, p 56.
67. V. Walkerdine, 1984, *op cit*, p 153.
68. V. Walkerdine, *Ibid*, p 162.
69. A. Callinicos, *Against Postmodernism*, Polity, Cambridge 1989, pp 9-11.
70. V. Walkerdine, 'Sex, power and pedagogy', *Screen Education*, 38, 1981, p 24.
71. R. Skidelsky, *English Progressive Schools*, Penguin, Harmondsworth 1969, p 247.
72. H. Entwistle, *Child-centred Education*, Methuen, London 1974, pp 17-18.
73. J. Donald, 'Beacons of the future: schooling, subjection and subjectification', in V. Beechey and J. Donald (eds), *Subjectivity and Social Relations*, Open University Press, Milton Keynes 1988, pp 216-217.
74. N. Wright, *op cit*.

WHEN CLASS BECAME COMMUNITY: RADICALISM IN ADULT EDUCATION

SALLIE WESTWOOD

INTRODUCTION

Adult education, throughout its history, has been contested terrain in which diverse ideologies have sought hegemony. In the 1980s the ground had shifted again, in response to Thatcherism in Britain and, more recently, the events in Europe. Adult education in the last decade has been restructured in order that it might be more securely tied to the market and become part of 'enterprise culture'. The generation and reproduction of an 'enterprise culture' in Britain has been a major part of the ideological project for Thatcherism and the 'free marketeers'. At the heart of this project is a deep contradiction: in order to secure enterprise culture the state must intervene not only in economic life but in the ideological sphere, through training and educational ventures which, it would seem, the market would not otherwise sustain.[1] Contradictions are not new to adult education, but those raised by the demise of the socialist vision go to the very heart of radicalism in adult education. Even the term 'radical' has to be reassessed in relation to the rise of the New Right and the development of a postmodern politics which seeks to overturn the 'grand narratives' developed from the Enlightenment projects for human progress. The history of radicalism in adult education is intimately bound up with one of these grand narratives, the struggle for socialism in Britain. This essay considers, all too briefly, the early struggles within adult education and the way in which, consistent with the vision of socialism as it developed, a class-based view of radicalism became central, until the resuscitation of community which came to be privileged in radical discourse on adult education in the 1970s – although class and community were specifically linked for some writers. The 1980s brought discourses from feminism, antiracism and the new social movements for peace, gay rights and green issues onto the adult education agenda while, at the same time, adult education struggled with the state over restructuring and resources for adult learning. Struggles in relation to the state, and debates concerning its role in adult education, are an old and continuing story, a point of continuity throughout the history of radicalism in the field. The debate has moved on again in relation to the current interest in 'New Times' and the ways in which left politics can be recast for the 1990s.[2] This essay closes with a consideration of this issue and the ways in which the new politics has specific resonances with the political concerns of adult education as they have been elaborated historically.

CLASS IS PRIVILEGED (I)

There were several key issues that were part of the debate within radical adult education as it developed from the 19th into the 20th century. The first of these concerned the role of the state and the relationship between the state, 'schooling' and emancipatory education. The second was the issue of gender which was allied with the debate between feminism and socialism. The third was the issue of 'Really Useful Knowledge' which, in the 20th century, became a debate about the role of Marxism in independent working-class education; and the fourth, exemplified in the debates between the Plebs League and the WEA, was the complex relationship between the political project of socialism and radical adult education. The argument of the paper is that these complex issues were discussed, to their detriment, within a reductionist account of socialism – an account that emphasised a unitary view of the working class which was itself homogenised through the emphasis on white, male workers whose politics was tied to production. This socialist vision was further emasculated by its parochialism and its construction as an English tradition at a time when the power of Empire developed a nationalism that defined most of the world as 'Other'. A consideration of the development of working-class politics is essential to an understanding of the early history of radicalism in adult education.

As Ali Rattansi points out, towards the end of the 18th century, the vocabulary of 'class' developed in response to the need to conceptualise economic and political relations in an emergent social order which was rapidly obliterating old communities and loyalties for which the terminology of 'stations', 'estates', and 'ranks' had been more appropriate. The arrival of the property-less 'free' labourer heralded the naming of 'the working class'.[3] But, despite Thompson's confidence that the working class was in formation by 1832,[4] our current understanding is of a far more discontinuous history, which is equally marked in the development of socialist ideas. For, as Barbara Taylor reminds us, far from following a steady path of theoretical and strategic progress, socialist development has been characterised by fundamental ruptures.[5] As Taylor points out, 'no aspect of socialist tradition more clearly reveals this uneven, fractured history than its relationship to feminism'.

The Owenites were a part of the early socialist movement which struggled with feminism and 'the woman question'. Owenism was separated from other aspects of developing working-class politics in its commitment to collective family life and equality between women and men. This was not a consensus view but attracted a minority of radical activists who constituted 'an iconoclastic vanguard'. The commitment to the rights and liberation of women was part of a socialist ideal that was humanitarian in its concerns, but not yet located with the revolutionary potential of the working class as it came to be in later Marxist accounts. There is nothing in the writings of the early socialists about expropriating the bourgeoisie or a revolutionary class politics. However, the radical commitment to women's rights subsequently became invisible, submerged within working-class politics just as it was removed from the Chartist call for citizenship rights. The Owenites wanted an end to all oppressions whether based on class, creed, sex or race. William Thompson and Anna Wheeler produced their celebrated *Appeals of One-Half of the Human Race* which undermined the idea that women and men shared common interests. Instead, women were subjected to oppressions and humiliations which demanded redress . . . 'Women are more in need of political rights than any other portion of human beings'.[6] It was the Owenites who challenged the notion of the innate inferiority of women and who saw in marriage a model of a relationship located in slavery. This was elaborated by Owen in 1835 when he called for easy divorce and simple civil marriages, demands he shared with others of his day. But he went further in his critique of the family as a bastion of self-concern and social inequalities, and a real impediment to radical change. However, for Owen there was no critique of the family as a site for patriarchal power vested in the husband/father. These were not his major concerns – he was far less concerned with the question of women's emancipation than many of his followers. From his followers, alongside the plea for a more liberated sexuality (on a heterosexual model), came a strikingly feminist view of social and family life which was to be organised on communal lines. Housework, childcare and education would be collectivised, reproductive tasks would no longer be the responsibility of individual wives and mothers but would be shared and organised to benefit not only women but children, who would be inducted into the new world and fashioned in relation to socialist ideals.

The 1830s were a time of general agitation in which the Owenites, including many women, came onto the political stage. Anna Wheeler, a famous Owenite, commented on the 1832 Reform Bill that it clearly ignored the claims of women for political rights alongside most working men. Instead, the Benthamites, she wrote, offered education, 'since they acknowledge that Women would make better Servants if they were better instructed'.[7] Benthamite education was clearly for domestication, not emancipation of autonomy.

In 1834, however, the Grand National Consolidated Union was formed and women were active in the union, the co-ops that were set up and as part of the tailors movement. But none of these working peoples movements was to succeed and Owenism moved into a new phase, more ideologically to the liking of Owen who had been troubled by the militancy of his followers and the analysis of developing capitalism as a world of class antagonisms.

The Owenites were passionate educators. As Silver points out they placed enormous emphasis on the rational power of knowledge and truth; they looked to education, and to their own educational efforts to transform society to the extent that education became the political project.[8] It was an education that shared with the popular education of the time an informality, integrated with everyday life, available to children and adults, men and women and which incorporated the notion of 'Really Useful Knowledge'. The Owenites were fiercely critical of 'schooling', rote learning, individual and competitive forms and the role of discipline: they stressed, instead, the role of co-operation and a collective experience of education which should extend the powers of the individual within an educational process that was conceived of as celebratory. It was a deeply emancipatory view of education that inducted people into the social science, sciences and arts and literary world of the day.

The Owenites and the Chartists were deeply suspicious of the state and state intervention, and they distrusted all forms of paternalism and philanthropy, emphasising independence and a clear distance from state initiatives. The state was conceived as a controlling and manipulating power and was placed in opposition to 'the people' and later 'the working class'. Thus the notion of popular education had, as part of its conception, independence from the state and state interference. The Chartists in their struggles for citizenship were 'up against the state' in the same way that other radical workers, who tried to form unions, were. The repressive power of the state in relation to these early attempts to organise was all too familiar to those involved. The separation between state and independent working-class education was to re-emerge sharply in the early decades of the 20th century, in the dispute between the state supported WEA and The Labour College.

The struggles waged during the 1830s and 40s which brought the Co-op Movement to the fore, followed by the Chartists, created populist ferment and generated the galaxy of stars that pervade the annals of adult education histories: Owen, Brougham, Lovett and others, who, in conjunction with the popular press, brought a new meaning to the dictum Knowledge is Power. The relationship between knowledge and power documented by Simon, Johnson and Thompson on a broader canvass is not an articulation entirely without women, as Taylor's work has clearly shown, but women had to be excavated from the accounts of popular struggles where they were subsumed, alongside black and Irish people, within the movements that shaped the working class as constituted in the late 19th century. For the adult education map these times remain as a beacon to independence in the search for working-class education. They are incorporated into the vision of what ought to be and have helped to shape later projects.

As the strength of the Chartist Movement waned in the 1850s, the importance of combining around economic issues came to the fore. This ushered in skills-based craft unions and foregrounded the divisions between skilled and unskilled workers, which combined with gender divisions to render women outside union organisations, tied, instead, to a domestic ideology which emphasised the family wage in opposition to equal pay for women and men. And as Dorothy Thompson writes:

> The Victorian sentimentalisation of the home and the family, in which all important decisions were taken by its head, the father, and accepted with docility and obedience by the inferior members, became all pervasive and affected all classes . . . the moves towards a more equal and co-operative kind of political activity by both men and women, were lost in the years just before the middle of the century . . . One of

the losses of this process . . . was the potential contribution to politics and society generally of the women of the working class communities'.[9]

Thus, the ideology of domesticity which pervaded the Victorian landscape and schooling for women and girls in this period (and afterwards) presented a dichotomy between the home and femininity and the public realm of work and labour which was male. Women were part of the specific space, in mind and place, which was the home and which related to consumption whereas production and the world of class relations was tied to masculinity. The resonances of this have been part of the history of adult education ever since, generating in mainstream adult education 'the women's interest curriculum' and leaving the struggles over working-class education to be constructed as a male world. But neither socialist ideals nor feminist demands died. They were reconstructed in the light of the changing relations between capital and labour and the state through the 19th and into the 20th century.

CLASS IS PRIVILEGED (II)

It was the Chartist leader, Ernest Jones, who said, 'A People's education is safe only in a people's hands,[10] but as the 19th century progressed, and the state became more interventionist in relation to the growing power of organised labour, it became more and more difficult to maintain this position and the contradictions between state support and independence finally erupted in the 20th-century struggle over the Central Labour College. This was preceded by the founding of the working men's colleges (and the settlements) in the 1850s which were motivated by paternalistic and philanthropic ideals. Maurice, the founder of the first Working Men's College in London, was a Christian socialist who, like many of his day, was imbued with the notion of moral and social uplift through education. Similar ideas fuelled the development of extension education which took Oxford and Cambridge dons to 'the people'. As Rée notes, 'To be excluded from the University was to be debarred from full citizenship'.[11] Rée's work traces the importance of the autodidact in working-class history, while the extensionists brought both a notion of one nation and the idea of a consensus generated through a shared literary and scientific culture into which the working classes would be inducted. As I have argued elsewhere this vision of nationhood and consensus through education was located with white 'English' men, one class extending their patronage to a specific section of the working class, the respectable, skilled and organised fraction.[12] But it was clear that by the 1890s the extension movement was dominated by the middle classes.[13] It was from this background that university adult education developed and the Workers Educational Association (1903), which was born out of the visionary ideals of Albert Mansbridge, himself a celebrated autodidact and Christian committed to self-improvement and the individual advance of working-class men.

The problem was that by 1870 the radical impulse among the developing working class had waned. The early co-operative movement had been superseded by one in which education was of minor importance and in which socialist ideals had given way to thrift, dividends and the notion that somehow co-operation could buy out capitalism. Later, however, it was the Women's Guild and the Co-operative Movement that kept alive the radical impulse, with its critique of women's oppression and its attention to the everyday lives of its members.[14]

The last quarter of the 19th century marked a new era for British capitalism, the growing power of empire and a profound period of restructuring ensued which involved a shift in the role of the state to become a regulatory agency much more concerned with the 'management of populations'.[15] While labour continued to organise, the economy fell further into recession and the demands for citizenship both in a political sense and in terms of resources were louder. This was a forerunner to the demands generated by the labour movement and the Labour party which marked not simply a concern for living standards and the social wage but also for a place in the nation and a share in the nation's wealth.

It is clear from the early history of working-class development that the working class has never been a single unitary subject but has been simultaneously fractured by skill, gender, ethnicity, region and the cultures generated by these divisions. But the bifurcated vision, one radical and the other liberal, in adult education at the turn of the century was of *a* working class. The radical vision related to socialist ideals of collective goals and mobilisation for emancipation through working-class institutions, and the other, the liberal view, to gradual and individual development through education which marked the liberal tradition.

It was the liberal tradition, with philanthropic backing from America, that called into being Ruskin College with the avowed aim of bringing working-class people into Oxford. It was set up in 1899 and brought socialist activists, some from the trade unions, into full-time study. Not surprisingly, clashes soon followed with the Oxford establishment and when the socialist principal was dismissed the students went on strike in support of him and against the power of the university to define knowledge, access and assessment, and to impose non-socialist academics. The striking students joined with other Ruskin students who had formed the Plebs League, with its journal, *The Plebs*, as a vehicle through which to generate independent working-class education based on socialist principles. They established the Central Labour College in 1909, with funds from the National Union of Railwaymen and the South Wales Miners' Federation, as a key part of their strategy and as an antidote to Ruskin.

In the meantime Mansbridge had brought the WEA into being as another vehicle by which working-class people, but predominantly men, could benefit from university education. It was not, from the start, an avowedly socialist organisation, although G.D.H. Cole and Tawney were prominent among its members. The WEA accepted the liberal notion of impartial teaching, individual development through an education that was democratic in its forms, but which adhered to the university tutorial class model. As Armstrong notes, there was a polarisation of working-class educational viewpoints between those who followed the WEA's liberal, impartial education, rejecting 'socialist propaganda', and those who reaffirmed the socialist claim for an independent working-class education.[16] The issue was not simply about funding, but was a struggle for hegemony in relation to working-class education and politics. The struggle was to become a long protracted dispute between the WEA and the Labour College Movement carried on in the pages of *The Plebs* and centred around the key themes of the role of the state, the importance of Marxism and the relationship between education and the working-class movement; feminism, despite a number of prominent women in both the WEA and the Plebs League, and large numbers in classes, was not much on the agenda. Before I explore these debates I want to briefly outline the historical context.

In the lead up to the First World War and within the context of the consolidation of British imperial power, there was a new wave of militancy which fuelled debates about working-class education and its role in the socialist future, many of which were represented in the pages of *The Plebs*. Alongside was the call for women's votes and the growning unionisation of the workforce; union membership doubled between 1910 and 1914. But it was only the left of the ILP that heard the call for women's votes; for many socialists it was a diversionary politics, an aside from the central business of class struggle. But it was also clear that only an estimated two-thirds of the male population were eligible to vote and Hinton points to the fact that before 1918 of 670 MPs only 95 were elected by working-class constituencies.[17] The issue of citizenship, therefore, remained crucial, but the debates were forestalled by British entry into 'the war to end all wars' which changed the landscape of struggle irrevocably. Suffrage organisations called a truce and socialists, willingly or otherwise, were dragged or drawn into the war or jailed for their pacificism. The jingoism of the time did not, however, impress the women's Guild of the Co-operative Movement who campaigned against the war in opposition to their middle-class sisters and working-class brothers in the Co-op movement.

The period immediately after the war was one of reconstruction and political militancy, with socialists alive to the possibilities of the Russian revolution and organising through the unions, the Labour Party and the Communist Party, which came into being in 1920. The growing role of the state, in relation to the economy and the increased numbers of state sector workers, set new agendas for the labour movement and assisted in the politicisation of economic struggles. Thus, as Simon points out, by the start of the 1920s, the WEA, the Labour College and the Communist Party all had an interest in the development of independent working-class education and a battle ensued for hegemony on this terrain.[18] *The Plebs* continued as the major voice of the period and it was in its pages that the notion was elaborated and debated as the 1920s progressed and the class struggles of the period moved towards the general strike of 1926. In 1921 the National Council of Labour colleges (NCLC) was formed to integrate and generate educational work in the regions, and in South Wales, for example, the NCLC was an important part of the developing socialist culture. The WEA moved closer to the developing university extra-mural departments and the TUC in relation to the provision of workers education. By the mid-1920s the NCLC involved around 30,000 students but thereafter declined while the WEA involved 60,000 on an annual basis by 1930.[19]

There were, as I have suggested, several strands to the debates between the NCLC and the WEA. The first of these concerned the independent quality of working-class education and the paramount importance attached to this by the NCLC. Independent, in this context, meant independence and distance from the state and state support, because any involvement with the state would undermine the emancipatory project of working-class education and would incorporate the working class further into capitalism. These views, as Brown suggests, relate to Marx's 'Manifesto' view of the state as a management committee for the bourgeoisie, further reinforced by a Leninist conception of the capitalist state. This analysis, and the tenacity with which it was adhered to, meant there was no room for strategic engagement with the state and that educators, like the WEA, who were supported by the state were damned as 'capitalist lackeys', working not for emancipatory education but in the interests of capital for the incorporation and, thereby, emasculation of the working class. Brown's account points out that behind the public vitriolics the actual practices of the two organisations were not always in such sustained opposition. The WEA had state support, but it also raised its own funds, and did so especially when its grant was cut as it was, for example, in the East Riding of Yorkshire because it was accused of promoting socialism. On the other hand, the NCLC did seek and receive local state support in some areas.

The second major area of debate concerned the curriculum and pedagogic issues, in the language of the earlier radicals: what constituted 'Really Useful Knowledge' within the context of working-class struggle? The NCLC accused the WEA of offering 'bourgeois social science', tied to the university model of learning and thinking, which could not, by definition, be liberatory. The NCLC, on the other hand, provided a Marxist canon for working-class activists who would take the message back into the workplace and the community and were accused by the WEA, therefore, of 'propaganda'. The commitment to social science was common to both, but the content of the courses was very different in the two organisations. The WEA insisted it was essential to introduce students to a wide range of ideas, summed up in the notion that both Marshall and Marx must be taught, that could then be discussed by class participants. Students in the NCLC classes were taught the labour theory of value, studied Dietzgen's philosophy and Engel's anthropology and were, most importantly, taught by other working-class activists.[20] It is consistent with the historical context that Marxism should have been so central to the construction of independent working-class education. It brought science and reason together in a powerful critique of capitalist exploitation and offered activists crucial keys with which to unlock the processes of capitalist accumulation. It was, however, a Marxism of its time, centred on political economy and a reductionist account of politics and ideologies.

In assessing the debate and its importance to the development of working-class struggle Fieldhouse suggests that the WEA was crucial to the way in which Marxism was marginalised within the labour movement and he lays at the feet of the WEA a major repsonsibility for the deflection away from Marxism of working-class leaders and activists.[21] It is easy to see why this would have happened within the WEA because, although Marxism was on the agenda and clearly formed part of many classes, Marx's ideas were taught as one possible analysis among others, not as a truth or a key to unlocking capitalism, nor a specific proletarian knowledge. In contrast, Brown points to the pedagogic processes of the two movements and highlights the importance of class discussions and debate in the WEA against the more authoritarian teaching mode of the NCLC.[22] But, given the students, it is difficult to envisage a class in either organisation which was not marked by debate and discussion.

As Simon records, one of the problems for the Labour College was its separation from a political base, which tended to generate isolation.[23] It saw itself as the educational wing of the labour movement and its work in the regions was often well integrated with local trade councils and union branches. But the situation as Brown suggests was not as simple as the public polarisation between the WEA and NCLC made out. In some areas, like Yorkshire, the WEA was a more openly socialist and Marxist inspired educational venture than the NCLC would admit. And on the other hand the NCLC, as the 1920s waned, had to negotiate with, and place themselves in relation to, trade unions that shifted to the right. To the point, writes Simon, that the *Plebs* became, in later years, the voice of the right of the trade union movement.[24] By the end of the 1920s the Plebs League had become part of the NCLC, and the Labour College, faced with severe financial constraints had closed. The General Strike of 1926 had generated severe economic pressures on the main funders and in the decade that followed recession deepened and union membership declined.

In the 1930s, the NCLC began to lose support. And after the Second World War, its commitment to Marxist theory, according to Armstrong, was only superficial as its views moderated to make its ideology virtually indistinguishable from that of the Labour party and the TUC. As he points out, the demise of the NCLC was ironically parallelled by the strengthening of the WEA, which by this time had all but lost its socialist purpose.[25] It is a double irony that according to Brian Simon there was probably more Marxism as part of the WEA and university extra-mural programmes in the 1940s and 1950s than in the NCLC as it survived.[26]

The questions that independent working-class education tried to address were, as Armstrong suggests, much more complex than was believed at the time, and the tools with which to work were not complex enough. There was no analysis of hegemony to assist the NCLC in building a counter-hegemonic educational movement, and that it did not succeed is as allied to this, and to the problems encountered by the trade union movement and the Labour party in generating a socialist culture in Britain as the 'common sense' of the age. The fractures within the working class, economism and welfarism, indeed the very seductions of capitalism, worked against the development of independent working-class education but, so too did the conception of 'radical' as a Marxism in its more unsophisticated guise, tied to a notion of the vanguard within the working class. For as Phillips and Putnam point out the conditions which made the movement for independent working-class education will not be re-created – it would be romantic to simply present this experience as a lesson for contemporary British socialists.[27]

The adult education subsequently generated through the state via the local authorities and the university sector was dominated by the liberal tradition with a stratified curriculum that generated practical skills in the LEA sector, and cerebral pursuits from the 'responsible bodies', the universities and the WEA. Funding for trade union education was secured from the state and courses continued, but the early radicalism survived only in pockets, within the spaces generated by the marginal position of adult education. It was within these spaces that a discourse on community education was generated which once again brought the issue of knowledge and power, 'really useful knowledge', to the fore, and replayed in some part the debates on state intervention and autonomy, but in relation to a much more local focus which denuded the power and centrality of class as the main focus for political engagement.

WHEN CLASS BECAME COMMUNITY

The impulse to community education in adult education was generated from a number of sources. One source was the development in the 1930s of the village colleges by Henry Morris, who saw a way to stem the depopulation of rural areas and who offered a high minded educational vision in the liberal mode. A more important source was the state sponsored strategy for community regeneration within the inner cities, subsequently expressed in the Plowden Report (1970), and following from the so-called 'rediscovery of poverty' in the 1960s that impressed itself upon adult education. The latter tied the regeneration of working-class communities to an educational intervention which was to be cheap, local and participatory. In fact, as a system of compensatory education it was never fully realised, partly because the sums of money involved were derisory. The two seemingly distinct directions actually shared a number of important, and often opaque assumptions. One shared premise was a situation conceptualised as a 'deficit', rural depopulation or inner city deprivation, that required remedy by an interventionist strategy which, in the model of community development (with its colonial history) would engage the state and local communities in a partnership for renewal and regeneration. It is a familiar theme and one which has resurfaced with new vigour in the 1980s.

The notion of compensatory education based on the deficit model re-emerged within the discourses of mainstream adult education in the language of 'the disadvantaged', a central theme of the 1973 Russell Report. And, interestingly, the organisation thought most appropriate to work with 'the disadvantaged' was the WEA. This juxtaposition itself repositioned the WEA, divorced from 'the working class' and central to the community regeneration strategy.

The other major underlying premise that informed the community approach was the ideological construction of homogeneous communities. Thus, within working-class neighbourhoods community became a place and space within class; or, without reference to class, it transformed geographical space, that is locality, into the social space of community. The contradictions and fractures of gender, ethnicity and age divisions, to name the most important, melted and were not constructed as a central part of 'communities'. Thus, community was located withinin a consensus constructed around the hegemony of white Englishness and homogenised as 'the community', becoming itself the subject/object of educational interventions. This looks, on the face of it, unpromising ground for radical adult education with its history in class struggle and the development of working-class and labour movement organisations. In many respects this proved indeed to be the case, and as Cowburn notes, the analysis of education offered by many community education writers seems to operate in a political vacuum with no sense of the historical, and takes no cognisance of the political implications of education and community education.[28] But the attention to community education given by adult educators was, perhaps, as contradictory as community education itself.

For the school-based sector during the 1970s it was the work of Eric Midwinter in Liverpool that provided the model of community education with its emphasis upon parental involvement, home-school links, the relevant curriculum and the community as context for schooling.[29] Little attention was given to the contradictions of the relations between parent power and professional ideologies and authority and, as I have suggested, class relations were conspicuous by their absence. Midwinter writes of 'people', or 'folk', but not of class, gender or ethnic subjects.[30] However, Midwinter did have a conception of 'educational guerillas' who were part of the fight to democratise education, and of the need to educate local people so that they might become political activists and thereby exercise power rather than simply participate in the community education enterprise. Midwinter's work was much debated, criticised simultaneously for not being radical enough and for being too radical. In the 1980s the debates surrounding community education were carried on through the pages of *Network*, the publication from the Community Education Development Centre in Coventry. For adult educators it was the work of Tom Lovett in Liverpool which, through the WEA, provided the adult education component of the community education package.

Lovett worked away from educational institutions, taking education to the community, and was self-conscious about his role as a professional, and the ways in which community adult education can be one part of the community development approach.[31] The problem with what was generated in this context, despite the settings, like the pub, was that the content of the education look remarkably the same as any other liberal adult education programme which was taught in a conventional manner. Women were much in evidence in Lovett's account of his work, on the doorsteps and in their homes being interviewed about classes, or as students in classes, bringing into sharp relief that community education and community development work involves working with women. But, there was no attempt to problematise or prioritise the role of adult education in women's lives. Lovett's work was very much marked by his role as a WEA tutor, there as provider and stimulator of educational demands.

There were alternative ways of working which were more highly politicised, like the work of Ashcroft and Jackson, who brought educational skills to bear upon a political problem and who used the vehicle of the mass meeting, which they saw as an essential part of working-class labour history, as an educative forum in relation to the issue of housing which was on the agenda in the locality where they were working.[32] Their perspective was self-consciously in the tradition of independent working-class education, using the understanding that politicisation relates to real, material issues in people's lives and that people are organised and galvanised by these issues. From this comes a form of education which is 'experimental', but through which working-class people learn about the dynamics of capitalism, the role of the state and the local state and their position as citizens within this. Yarnit also worked in Liverpool on a 'second chance' project, forerunner to access courses, which challenged the notion that working-class people want a 'relevant' curriculum related to their immediate lives and tied to experiential, informal learning modes in the classroom.[33] What working-class people in Yarnit's classes wanted was the knowledge and skills that would taken them into higher education, the very things that form part of the cultural capital of the middle classes.

Community education projects proliferated through the 1970s and into the 1980s; many were low budget interventions related to informal approaches, while the community school model was introduced in many counties, which shifted the focus to suburban localities and further reinforced the homogenised view of community. In the community school movement there was no account of sexism, racism or class politics; instead they worked within the state provided model – focusing on the dual use of buildings and the participation of local people in management committees for community education. The emphasis was on locale and a consensus on what constituted local issues and concerns, but these were most likely to be articulated by white, middle-class participants whose constructions of community may not have matched those of young people or the elderly, for example. Underlying this was the assumption that 'community' was tied to consumption and thereby divorced from production, and this produced a form of familialism in which family and community were brought together in a series of discourses that emphasised common interests and goals alongside forms of housekeeping in relation to resources. There was nothing here about the power relations or abuses of family life and the interests of women and young people were subsumed within a cosy conception of family and community.

On the other hand, however, community based adult education did in part revive elements of the earlier radical tradition, but in new circumstances related to state education. The aim of much community education was to democratise education through the participation of local people in management committees, education councils and on governing bodies, but participation rarely generated real power in relation to the state structures. There was some attention to curriculum and modes of learning and to the knowledge base of community education in relation to 'Really Useful Knowledge'. But it was only where class relations became part of the account of community education that the issues of power relations in liberal capitalism were addressed. Thus it was only where the earlier concerns of the radical tradition came together with the later class privileged account that community education brought a critical and political account to education, as in the work of Ashcroft and Jackson cited above and, for example, in Jane Thompson's work with women in Southampton.[34]

A new impetus to community education was provided by the work of the educator Paolo Freire, who, working in the repressive conditions of Chile, advanced an account of popular education which drew on an eclectic array of sources that often bewildered his readers.[35] But the message of his work was clear – education was either for domestication or liberation, and a liberatory view of education had at its centre the knowing subject with whom educators must engage. Freire worked to generate a literacy scheme that made the politics of language and symbols central, and which forcefully denied the conception of literacy simply as a technical and functional skill. His work has had a major impact on adult education in the 1980s, introducing a discourse of empowerment. But his own analysis of class relations, the role of the state and political organisation in the periphery nations was weak, despite his references to Mao Tse Dong, Che Guevera and Gramsci. His interest in their struggles and writings was centred on the emphasis that they placed on *cultural* struggles as part of politics and on the relationship between revolutionaries and 'the people'; his was a conception born out of liberation theology, which emphasises the human subject and the empowerment of the people within the Latin American context. When he ventured to Guinea Bissau, after liberation, and worked in the context of a state sponsored education system, his work became much more clearly located in Marxism and political economy and the relations between production and education.[36] In the West, Freire's work has been domesticated through its piecemeal inclusion in literacy projects and community and informal educational ventures. But his radical humanism connects strongly with the issues of the power of people to intervene in their own lives and to work co-operatively, and makes problematic the relationship between knowledge and power in forceful and illuminating ways. It also connects more strongly with the politics of the new social movements for women's rights, gay liberation, racial justice, peace and ecology.

Alongside Freire's work, Antonio Gramsci's analysis of ideological hegemony and the generation of counter-hegemonic cultures also became important, offering adult educators new ways of posing the old problems of their work. Thus, Lovett, Clarke and Kilmurray, in providing an account of their work in Northern Ireland, invoke Gramsci as an alternative to Illich and the de-institutionalisation of society (presumably because they represent to them separate strands of radicalism) and suggest that 'Gramsci wanted to extend the traditions of cumulative knowledge based on secular rationalism, by expanding established educational institutions to incorporate the whole population'.[37] And in order to secure Gramsci for adult education they continue, 'Gramsci is the Marxist, escaping the brutality and narrowness of peasant Sardinia, imprisoned by Mussolini, trying to realise the dreams of Hardy's Jude – a curious view of Gramsci's powerful analysis of the generation of counter-hegemonic forms in education and his insistence on education as an arena of contested terrain.

Working in Northern Ireland added a powerful cultural and ethnic dimension to the class analysis of adult education, and Lovett and his collaborators try to weave this dimension into their account of adult education and community action. In concluding they point to the central issues for community education in relation to political action and suggest four main axes – 'choice, authority, relevance and purpose.[38] It is a language redolent of the liberal tradition in adult education, and tied to the main concerns of the WEA tradition, choice related to democracy 'which also involves upholding the best of the past in terms of human enlightenment and organising affairs with a view to achieving democratic control over the whole of society'.[39] Thus authority enters the equation, again invoked in relation to 'tradition': 'Authority and tradition would not disappear; they would become more firmly rational and universal'.[40] Relevance relates firmly to the curriculum, but the authors acknowledge that 'it is too blunt a category to be much use in shaping educational programmes'.[41] They also acknowledge the complexities and contradictions of heterogeneous purposes, and that it is important to work with and through

238

these in terms of the longer term aim which is securely tied to 'a progressive unfolding of the enlightenment'.[42] In a later essay Lovett reasserts these themes, and by so doing underlines the hegemony of the liberal tradition in adult education and the ways in which radical writers like Gramsci are incorporated into its vision in part because the liberal and the socialist projects share the Enlightenment goal of rational progress.[43]

In the 1980s radical adult education has become more diffuse, and more clearly allied to the new social movements, generating curricular innovations like women's studies programmes and a feminist critique of adult education.[44] The pressing issue of racism and its articulation with gender and class relations has received much less attention, but is foregrounded in Avtar Brah's work in London through the urban community studies courses, the summer school programme and antiracist work with the local state. Work with the unemployed reintroduced the notion of class politics, but in ways that emphasised and attempted to counter the disenfranchisement of working-class people through unemployment.[45] Fraser and Ward point to the alignment between work with unemployed people and community action and set up, with local people, courses on welfare rights and community organising, alongside specific discussion groups with women. In part, the adult education contribution was intended to be a counter to the instrumentalism of the MSC (now Training Agency) courses with their proscriptions against the discussion of the causes of unemployment and the role of the state.

Given the development of equal opportunities policies in education more generally, adult education responded through the work of access courses, which encouraged and provided a route through education to black and white working-class adults, women and men. Black people were conscious of the need for access courses to address the histories of empire and migration to Britain, and to examine the issue of racism, both historically and in Britain today, and it is they who have politicised access work through the demand for black tutors and black studies courses, much in the way that women's studies had done previously. These initiatives were, however, often marginal within a marginal sector, funded differently and in short term ways, with contract workers which could not guarantee continuity. Now, however, access is becoming part of mainstream funding at the very point that mainstream funding has been securely located with the market. Alongside these developments were those of the then Manpower Services Commission which had a major impact on adult education work in the further education sector and will continue to do so through the inception of the TECs.

Radical adult education in the 1980s found itself up against the state in the same way as mainstream adult education, not least the WEA and the universities whose 'Responsible Body Status', and with it guaranteed funding, has now disappeared. At the same time, restructuring in the local authority sector and the demise of the ILEA have jeopardized learning opportunities for adults overall. As I suggested at the beginning of this paper, the irony of current policy is that in order to roll back the state and place adult education securely in the market place, the state has intervened to restructure the field. Local Management of Schools will present new struggles for community educators in community schools. Not surprisingly it has been difficult for radical adult educators to mount an effective campaign to defend the meagre resources now involved, let alone to provide a new and more radical agenda for adult education. Because the radical impulse was historically tied to the strength of labour and the labour movement, and this strength has been depleted in the 1980s, these have been difficult times for adult education generally and radical adult education in particular. The discourses within which community education was sited have become part of the discourse of the Right, with an emphasis on the active citizen participating in the governance of schools and in control of school-based community resources. Equally, the curriculum has been nationalised, leaving little space for local initiatives and geared more fully to the technical function account of the relations between education and production. But equally important for the radical tradition are the debates underway concerning the very nature and future of socialism itself. It is to these debates that I now turn.

ADULT EDUCATION AND 'NEW TIMES'

The current period is one of profound changes for adult education and the current debate on 'New Times' is one attempt to provide a language within which to situate these changes. The debates have a special resonance with the shifting terrain of adult education especially at a time when the discourses, conservative, liberal and radical, that comprise adult education are undergoing a process of reassessment and the politics of Europe is manifestly entering a new phase. 'New Times' is no more homogeneous than adult education and should not be understood in a unitary way.[46] It is one attempt to grapple with the processes of economic restructuring that have characterised capitalism since the Second World War, while simultaneously considering the political shifts attendant upon this which have generated debates about socialism as a political project.

Economically, the post-war period has been marked by processes of globalisation of capital and profound restructuring which has effected manufacturing and distribution.[47] The changes are marked by the move away from Fordist production processes and mass production generally in the Western economies. Using assembly line techniques, Fordism generated standardised products for mass markets in the post-war boom years. The labour process deskilled workers and centralised managerial control through the use of Taylorist time and motion techniques. But it also generated workers' organisation and resistance. Now the shift is away from this form of manufacturing and towards a system of flexible specialisation, pioneered by the Japanese, where there is no longer a major investment in large plants and large workforces, but a series of interconnected operations organised around small firms that produce the materials for the production process and relate to a core. Firms can be globally separated and managed by a complex and less centralised management system using computer technology and both vertical and horizontal forms of integration. Companies, like Toyota for example, then generate a core of highly skilled and adaptable workers who receive high rewards. The underside of these developments in the generation of a periphery of low paid, insecure workers in part-time and discontinuous work who are often women or black workers. Benetton has provided a model of the use of these forms of working in the clothing industry, through the use of sub-contractors and homeworking. The shifts in working practices can be seen in the employment statistics for Britain which show that 60 per cent of jobs are now in the service sector, and 1 in 4 jobs is part-time. Women workers now constitute 50 per cent of the labour force and are concentrated in services.

But the changes are not uni-directional as, for example, the continued success of McDonalds, the Fordism of food shows. These are contradictory tendencies working out differently in diverse social formations; thus mass production is very much a part of the economies of the Newly Industrialising Countries, the NICs. Those of us working in education in Britain might be forgiven for thinking that Fordism has just arrived in the state sector, complete with measured day work in the form of competency measures and performance indicators. The public sector appears to want it both ways, the flexibility of the market with the control of Fordist managerial techniques. The implications of this for adult education are, as yet, unknown, but it raises some important questions for the field. Given the increase in flexible specialisation, what will be the meaning of vocational education in the 1990s? The new methods of working and the skills involved point to a massive initiative in education and training, one which needs to listen to the demands of workers alongside those of employers, and that needs to respond to the rapidity with which skills and jobs will change. There is also the question of the peripheral workers: how will they be able to move into the core and away from casualised employment? Equally important for the radical tradition in adult education is the role of trade unions and trade union education. Fordism produced powerful unions and vibrant shopfloor cultures with which adult education could connect, but the trend is away from the shopfloor; workers are now divided between core and periphery workers with an increasing number who are non-unionised. The response from some of the major unions has been merger, and more mergers are currently being negotiated in the public sector (NALGO, NUPE and COHSE, for example), but the educational and political task for generating relevant strategies for the 1990s has barely begun. The optimistic view of the current changes sees in flexible specialisation moves towards worker democracy, an enhanced role for workers in management and control, new working practices, and ways in which the active citizen will become part of the workplace rather than being tied to consumption. Thus, for the optimists, a movement of global capitals will have profound radical-humanising effects at the local level. Adult education in Britain, especially through the community education variant, has consistently looked to locality and region in order to develop specific practices appropriate to local areas; it should, therefore, be well placed to intervene.

The profound changes in production have major implications for politics in Europe and especially for the politics of the left. The socialist agenda is currently being recast, partly as a response to these changes, and partly as a result of the popular movements for democracy in what was Eastern Europe. This does not mean that the complex discourses which formed socialism have overnight melted away, but they are being subjected to an interrogation which had already begun in relation to the new social movements for racial justice, women's rights, gay rights and green and peace issues, which have set political agendas not rooted in production and the white, male working class. The concerns of the new politics, like the economic changes, have been simultaneously global and local and have been concerned as much with process as with ends. The new politics has emerged in response to what Lyotard has called 'the death of the grand narratives'[48] of which Marxism is exemplary, and an end to the Enlightenment project of rational progress towards a better world: this has shown itself to be doubled-edged, a project that can produce both fascism and Stalinism. Thus a new politics is marked by local narratives, a point of special interest to those in community education. For some there is an intermediary position that maintains the importance of meta-narratives as a way to situate local ones, because the central premises in the movements for feminism, racial justice and socialism cannot be so easily superseded.[49] However, the important point is that these premises, like the oppression of women for example, cannot be understood in essentialist terms, through an overarching theory of patriarchy, or an appeal to the essential sisterhood of women; such theories mask difference. Instead, our politics must be forged in relation to difference, which allows among women distinctive class, racial, ethnic and sexual identities that generate similarity and difference simultaneously. The politics of difference has been crucial to the experience of European politics in the recent period; there has been an explosion of national and ethnic consciousness, a 'return of the repressed'. This process is deeply contradictory because it regenerates pluralism and culturalism, which has major implications for the politics of citizenship, but at the same time reasserts old chauvinisms and racisms. But the message to radical adult education is a very clear one: homogeneous conceptions of the working class, women, black people and community require deconstruction if they are to be in any way effective starting points for a politicised adult education.

Citizenship has once again returned to the political agendas of both right and left. But the right has given citizenship a high profile and inflection in relation to consumerism, which generates a new politics of consumption in conditions where the gap between rich and poor in Britain is widening. The response from the left has been an attempt to generate a discourse on citizenship that links the individualism of formal citizenship rights with democracy, and links the concept of a socially conscious active citizen to the new social movements. Radical adult education (and adult education more generally) has had an historical interest in citizenship and political education for democracy, grounded in the notion of knowledge as power. But the labour movement model of earlier times now needs revision in the light of new ideas about the politics of difference, and a deconstruction of the unitary view of the working class; this is essential for the important work of political education in the 1990s. In other ways too the old and the new have to come together to consider the political implications of the relationship between access to knowledge and citizenship in the realm of culture. Thus far this has been little debated in adult education, despite the new broadcasting bill and its implications for the media. The new politics raises fundamental questions for radical adult education. It is no longer possible to do as Lovett and his co-authors did, and place one's faith in the unfolding of reason and progress as in the Enlightenment project, and most especially in the socialist vision.[50] We need to look instead to the contradictions and diversity of the socialist tradition in the light of the present conjuncture. As events unfold in Hungary, Poland and Czechoslovakia, it will be possible to see a new diversity, and the ways in which it relates to the new democracies of Europe will produce important lessons for the old democracies. The right may claim a victory in terms of the power of the market and capitalism, and assist in its birth and sustenance in these countries, but there are other, socialist, discourses on the political terrain and within the histories of these nations they will also have a bearing on their future development. Radical adult education will, perhaps, become less parochial as it engages with the new Europe, less concerned with what has effectively been the hegemony of the English tradition. This tradition has been a major problem, I would argue, for the variants of socialism in play in Britain.

Crucial to the new politics, and foregrounded by the economic changes and the politics of difference, is the issue of identity and with that, the politics of subjectivities. This is a politics consistently foregrounded by feminism, expressed in the phrase 'the personal is political'. But the resurgence of a new politics of ethnicity has drawn attention to the enduring nature of culture, language and place as sources of political identification. At the same time, however, there are new theorisations of the subject. The notion of the essential, unitary subject, aligned with the englightenment view of 'rational man' (*sic*) has given way to an understanding of the subject as shifting terrain, bringing together 'multiple selves' that seek forms of political and cultural expression within the politics of difference.[51] This new view of the self speaks to the complex biographies that form part of Europe, bringing together a colonial past and a multiracial present and focusing attention upon post-coloniality. An understanding of the ways in which these new selves are constructed and reconstructed is an important part of the 'New Times' debate. In Britain attention has focused on the debate around British identity, because it is contested terrain in which the hegemony of white Englishness has been fractured by the claims of an ethnically diverse population no longer willing to be marginalised in relation to the ideological construction of the nation.

Alongside these developments have been the debates that have centred around consumption, and the ways in which individuality is expressed through consumption and life style, always difficult areas for the British left. This is linked to the current divisions in consumer power, between those who can effect consumer choices and those who cannot, and the ways in which this is articulated with debates on citizenship and democracy. The consumption of culture, and with that representations, and the ways in which these representations are produced and read, is also related to the politics of style which has been foregrounded by writers associated with the 'New Times' thesis. This interest in style and consumption has been dismissed by some critics as nothing more than a 'designer socialism' for 1990s, fashioned in response to the individualism of the Thatcher years and the failing commitment of ageing socialists.[52] Far from generating a radical vision, critics suggest that postmodern politics of which the 'New Times' project is to a certain extent a part, is de-radicalising and domesticating; that, rather than providing an alternative to the right, it answers them in their own language.

The criticism and debate will continue, but the major insights offered by a de-centred view of the subject cannot be ignored by adult educators. Such a view has profound implications for the ways in which both 'the adult' and 'the learner' are constructed in adult education discourses and, consequently, for the practice of adult education. It leads us to examine, once again, the knowledge/power complex in adult education and to start a work of excavation in relation to the discourses that construct adult education and place subjects as subjects/objects of knowledge. The Foucauldian perspective acknowledges the micro-politics of social life, and the diffuse nature of power, in ways which have some resonance with the work of Freire and his attempts to un-pack the relationship between knowledge and subjects. Freire's project was to intervene in the power relations and make them more democratic in ways that some radical adult educators have sought to follow. But Freire's politics has in many ways been a politics of transcendence, a visionary politics often divorced from the micro-politics of institutional life and the power of the state.

In conclusion, therefore, the debates around 'New Times' raise in novel ways many of the enduring issues of radical adult education, re-cast for a world where certainties seem in short supply. But this world of flux, fracture and transformation requires a series of new engagements by adult education, not least in setting a horizon beyond British borders and in the New Europe. Similarly, the old conceptions of Britishness need a radical revision; one which takes account of the politics of difference, and of a world known through difference. Thus, while the British have historically been adept at creating the 'Other', it is now time to address Britain's own 'Otherness' in relation to the diversity of the postmodern world, and to construct ethnicities in Britain that take their place in this diversity, without the privileging of any one identity. Ethnicities are but one moment in the transformative process, alongside the economic and political spheres where economic positions that called into being class subjects are shifting, and political alliances are being remade. Radical adult education has, historically, worked at the interface. It is precisely here that the language of 'New Times' makes its intervention, and this is why it has such powerful resonances for radical adult education and a place in the future account of radicalism in the field.

NOTES

The final part of this paper, 'Adult Education and "New Times"' was first presented at the Standing Conference of University Teachers on the Research and Education of Adults, Sheffield 1990. I am grateful to Kathryn Noble for wordprocessing the paper.

1. S. Westwood, 'Adult Education and Enterprise Culture', *Adults Learning*, September 1989.
2. I am using 'New Times' as a term to describe a set of ideas, associated with *Marxism Today*, about the deep-rooted changes that have taken place in culture, economics and politics in the last two decades, and which are linked to a democratic left politics that repudiates fundamentalism and essentialism.
3. A. Rattansi, *Marx and the Division of Labour*, Macmillan, London 1982.
4. E.P. Thompson, *The Making of the English Working Class*, Hutchinson, London 1963.
5. B. Taylor, *Eve and the New Jerusalem: Socialism and Feminism in the Nineteenth Century*, Virago, London 1983. I am indebted to Barbara Taylor's analysis for her work on feminism in the working-class movement of this period, from which much of my analysis here is drawn.

6. Taylor, *op cit*, p 21.
7. *Ibid*, p 61.
8. H. Silver, *English Education and the Radicals: 1780-1850*, Routledge, London 1975, p 61.
9. D. Thompson, 'Women and Nineteenth Century Radical Politics: A Lost Dimension', in Mitchell and Oakley (eds), *The Rights and Wrongs of Women*, Penguin, Harmondsworth 1976, p 138.
10. K. Worpole, 'Educating the Labour Movement', *Socialism and Education*, Vol 9, No 3, 1952, p 11.
11. J. Ree, *Proletarian Philosophers: Problems in Socialist Culture*, Clarendon Press, Oxford 1984.
12. Westwood, *op cit*.
13. B. Simon, *Education and the Labour Movement: 1870-1920*, Lawrence and Wishart, London 1965.
14. Westwood, *op cit*.
15. Hall and Schwarz, 'State and Society: 1880-1930', in M. Langan and B. Schwarz (eds), *Crises in the British State: 1880-1930*, Hutchinson, London 1985.
16. P. Armstrong, 'The Long Search for the Working Class. Socialism and the Education of Adults, 1850-1930', in T. Lovett (ed), *Radical Approaches to Adult Education: A Reader*, Routledge, London 1988.
17. J. Hinton, *Labour and Socialism: A History of the British Labour Movement 1867-1974*, Wheatsheaf, Brighton 1983.
18. B. Simon, *The Search for Enlightenment: The Working Class and Adult Education in the Twentieth Century*, Lawrence and Wishart, London 1990.
19. G. Brown, 'Independence and Incorporation: The Labour College Movement and the Workers' Educational Association before the Second World War', in J. Thompson (ed), *Adult Education for a Change*, Routledge, London 1980.
20. A. Phillips and T. Putnam, 'Education for Emancipation: The Movement for Indpendent Working Class Education 1908-1928', *Capital and Class*, Spring 1980.
21. R. Fieldhouse, *The Workers' Educational Association: Aims and Achievements, 1903-1977*, Syracuse University, New York 1977.
22. Brown, *op cit*.
23. Simon, 1990, *op cit*.
24. *Ibid*.
25. Armstrong, *op cit*, p 53.
26. Simon, 1990, *op cit*, p 63.
27. Phillips and Putnam, *op cit*, p 40.
28. W. Cowburn, *Class, Ideology and Community Education*, Routledge, London 1986, p 212.
29. E. Midwinter, *Patterns of Community Education*, Ward Lock, London 1973, and *Education and the Community*, Unwin, London 1975.
30. Midwinter, 1975, *op cit*.

31. T. Lovett, *Adult Education, Community Development and the Working Class*, Ward Lock, London 1975.
32. B. Ashcroft and K. Jackson, 'Adult Education and Social Action', in Jones and Mayo (eds), *Community Work One*, Routledge, London 1974.
33. M. Yarnit, 'Second Chance to Learn, Liverpool: Class and adult education', in Thompson (ed), *op cit*.
34. J. Thompson, *Learning Liberation: Women's Response to Men's Education*, Croom Helm, London 1983.
35. P. Freire, *Cultural Action for Freedom*, Penguin, Harmondsworth 1972, and *Pedagogy of the Oppressed*, Penguin, Harmondsworth 1972.
36. P. Freire, *Pedagogy in Process: The Letters from Guinea Bissau*, Seabury Press, New York 1978.
37. T. Lovett, C. Clarke and A. Kilmurray, *Adult Education and Community Action*, Croom Helm, London 1983, p 140.
38. *Ibid*, p 147.
39. *Ibid*, p 149.
40. *Ibid*, p 151.
41. *Ibid*, p 153.
42. *Ibid*, p 156.
43. T. Lovett, 'Community Education and Community Action', in Lovett (ed), *op cit*.
44. Thompson, 1983, *op cit*.
45. K. Ward, 'A University Adult Education Project with the Unemployed', *Studies in the Education of Adults*, Vol 1, September 1983; Fraser and Ward, Education
46. *Marxism Today*, Special 'New Times' Issue, October 1988.
47. R. Murray, 'Fordism and Post-Fordism', *Marxism Today*, October 1988.
48. J.-F. Lyotard, *The Postmodern Condition*, University of Minnesota Press, Minnesota 1984.
49. N. Fraser and L. Nicolson, 'Social Criticism Without Philosophy: An Encounter Between Feminism and Postmodernism', *Theory, Culture and Society*, Vol 5, Nos 2-3.
50. T. Lovett, C. Clarke and A. Kilmurray, *Adult Education and Community Action*, Croom Helm, London 1983.
51. S. Hall, 'Brave New World', *Marxism Today*, October 1988.
52. A. Callinicos, *Against Postmodernism*, Polity Press, Cambridge 1990.

The Historiography of British Education: A Feminist Critique

June Purvis

Feminist history is now a booming area of study, both in this country and in the USA.[1] Yet many of the critical issues that feminists are debating about the social construction of knowledge are slow to infiltrate the history of education, especially in Britain. Indeed, in this country there has been little debate about the historiography of educational histories generally since Harold Silver's 1977 complaint that only those structures, events, ideas, campaigns, successes and failures in Victorian education that have meaning in 20th-century terms have been admitted to the British definition of the history of education.[2]

My aim in this chapter is to bring the issue of historiography to the forefront by offering a feminist critique of British history of education. As we shall see, the issues that feminists are raising and exploring hold important implications for how we define history, how we write history and the intellectual practice of the discipline generally. Throughout my critique I shall focus especially upon histories of the 19th century.

Male Centred Histories of Education

Histories of 19th-century education offer a wealth of data – and also a range of differing and often conflicting interpretations. However, since historians rarely make explicit to their readers the perspective which is guiding their selection, analysis and interpretation of the so-called 'facts', it is somewhat difficult to categorise the various accounts.

It is now common, though, to find references to 'liberal', 'socialist' and 'Marxist' histories' while, at the same time, acknowledging the diversity of interests and views within each broad approach.[3] Such labels are useful to the feminist since they help one to untangle the complexities of the various accounts and to analyse the differing interpretations. In particular, the broad approaches identified above adopt certain paradigms that govern what is included and excluded when actually 'doing' the history of education. Having said that, however, the one theme that unites these varying approaches is their focus upon male experiences. In the following discussion I shall illustrate this point by examining three recurring preoccupations within British history of education – the emphasis upon men as makers of educational history, the focus upon education as being mainly for boys and men and the trivialisation of girls' and women's experiences.

Men as makers of educational history
A liberal perspective has been the dominant tradition within histories of the 19th century generally, and such accounts have concentrated upon the activities of 'great' individuals in political, economic, intellectual, literary and artistic circles. However, as the Australian feminist Jacquie Matthews points out, this emphasis upon individualism has been confined to great men and to the most powerful male elites.[4] What is immediately apparent is that most educational histories of the 19th century work within this mainstream liberal paradigm and focus upon the role of 'great men' in making national policy and in the administration and provision of education. Such an approach is found in an early account of 19th-century education, Birchenough's 1914 book *History of Elementary Education in England and Wales from 1800 to the Present Day*.

For Birchenough, 19th-century educational history was made by elite men. There are no heroines in his tale, only heroes. We follow throughout the book reference after reference to one man or another who made his mark through the various reforms he introduced, supported or opposed. These heroes then become established as the subjects of educational history for subsequent writers. Dr Kay (later the word Shuttleworth was also added to his name), for example, as secretary to the Committee of Council on Education, initiated in 1846 a pupil-teacher system; under this system, the brightest scholars in elementary schools might be apprenticed to the headteacher for five years from 13 to 18, provided the teacher was competent to conduct the apprentice through the stipulated course of instruction and that the school conformed to certain requirements.[5] Robert Lowe, Vice-President of the Education Department, introduced in 1862 a Revised Code which stipulated, amongst other things, that all future grants to schools were to be made on the basis of a single capitation payment of 12s per child per annum; grants could only be earned for pupils under 12 years of age, and were dependent upon a child's regular attendance and satisfactory results in an annual examination in reading, writing and arithmetic conducted by a government inspector. 'If the new system will not be cheap', pronounced the Vice-President, 'it will be efficient, and if it will not be efficient it will be cheap'.[6] The plan attracted much hostility and, comments Birchenough, made Lowe 'one of the best hated men of the day. He was subjected to attacks on all hands, and in 1864 was (unfairly) driven from office'.[7]

Such 'first' histories have a special power that extends far beyond the initial date of publication. As the radical feminist Jane Marcus points out, first histories invent the narrative and historical plot. The choice of decisive events and the naming of key figures sets the scene for the drama; the next generation of historians has to struggle hard if it wishes to break the grip and force of the first account.[8] An examination of educational histories written in subsequent decades reveals that the 'grip' of Birchenough's account is still strong.

Barnard, for example, in *A History of English Education from 1760*, an influential book that was first published in 1947 and which reached a sixth impression (with amendments) in 1969, continues in the same tracks. Once again, we hear of the schemes introduced by Kay-Shuttleworth and Lowe. While the former is regarded as a hero – 'one of the most important figures in educational history', Lowe, with his emphasis upon 'payment by results', is one of the few villains of the story, a 'Liberal free-trader . . . prepared to apply to education his economic theories'.[9] Similarly, other mainstream educational histories published in the 1970s and 1980s are framed within a liberal paradigm with an emphasis upon the role of great men as makers of educational policy.[10]

The interpretative framework of liberal history contrasts sharply with that of socialist and Marxist historians. As an editorial in a 1982 issue of *History Workshop Journal* notes, socialist history means not merely the history of socialist movements or labour movements, but the 'reinterpretation of all dominant social and cultural institutions in terms of a class perspective'.[11] Within such a broad definition of socialist history one may place both non-Marxist and Marxist approaches. Marxist histories, for example, may offer a materialist analysis in which political, cultural and ideological dimensions are related to the economic mode of production. Furthermore, the relationships between social classes, class struggle and class consciousness are central to such analyses. Yet, despite the contrast with liberal history, Marxist history shares with the latter an unspoken assumption – that history is made by men, although this time it is working-class men rather than elite men.

The most prominent orthodox Marxist in British history of education is Brian Simon, whose especial concern with working-class education has a particular focus:

> The story of the working-class struggle for education is itself chequered because it is . . . interrupted or forced underground by persecution and intimidation. But if newspapers are suppressed, books censored and those who attempt to disseminate them gaoled, there is nothing like a period behind bars for writing a book. So from Dorchester gaol in the 1820s, from Warwick prison in the 1840s, come books which express the ultimate optimism and belief in *education of men who have espoused the cause of the working class and are looking towards socialism.* (My emphasis)[12]

The scene is set, and the drama of working-class men making history is enacted. As I have argued elsewhere, Simon's books inspired a generation of scholars and are widely used in higher education, becoming part of the 'accepted' paradigm of what a Marxist account of working-class education in the 19th century should entail.[13]

More recent Marxist writings, such as those by the Centre for Contemporary Cultural Studies Education Group, are similarly male centred. Thus, adopting a Gramscian perspective, the CCCS Education Group identifies various compromises and settlements in education which result from power struggles and confrontations between the different social classes. Although the relations between the various groups 'confer unequal powers to achieve desires or satisfy needs: class over class, *men over women*, white over black, adult over child'[14] (my emphasis), the nod in the direction of acknowledging the power relations between the sexes and the presence of women is not followed systematically through the book. Yet again, 'popular' struggles are male struggles.

Education is mainly for boys and men

Another common theme in educational histories of the 19th century is an emphasis upon education as an activity where the recipients are mainly boys and men. In regard to working-class children, for example, both boys *and* girls attended a range of educational forms such as dame schools, Sunday schools, charity schools, ragged schools, day schools of the British and Foreign School Society (largely supported by religious dissenters) and of the much larger National Society for the Promotion of the Education of the Poor in the Principles of the Established Church (the Church of England), and elementary board schools founded after the passing of the 1870 Education Act. Yet the focus of research has been upon the experiences of boys. Such a male centred perspective is further compounded by the common use of a sexist language that hides and marginalises the presence of girls. For example, Phillip McCann in the introduction to his 1977 edited book *Popular Education and Socialization in the Nineteenth Century* speaks of 'the working-class pupil and *his* parents[15] (my emphasis)'. a usage that is frequently adopted by other contributors to this volume. Similarly, John Hurt in his study of elementary schooling and the working classes from 1860-1918 discusses the provision of a schools meals service in the following terms:

> The predominant fear throughout the period . . . was that too lavish a provision of food would pauperise the parent. *The boy* receiving free dinners while *his brother* was being treated by the doctor for overeating was part of the mythology of the social worker. Again in a part of Bermondsey described by Charles Booth as one of the most poverty stricken in London, the local Charity Organisation Society man clung to the axiom that every meal given to a child meant another half pint of beer to a dissolute parent.
>
> However difficult *the Bermondsey boy* may have found it to obtain a meal, he had one advantage over the *rural lad*. School feeding agencies were mainly urban institutions, 55 of the 71 county boroughs and 22 of the large urban authorities controlling elementary education had some means of feeding children by 1905.[14] (My emphasis)

In extracts such as these, one presumes that the references to 'the working-class pupil' and 'a child' *includes* girls; but if this is so, the presence of girls is made invisible by a language which prioritises male experience as the norm.

The male centredness of educational histories of the 19th century is evident also in studies of middle-class schooling. In 19th-century England, middle-class children were largely schooled outside the evolving state elementary system; thus when they were young, middle-class girls and boys might be educated at home, by a governess, parents or tutor, or some combination of all three. However, once the boys were old enough, they were sent away to fee-paying public secondary schools. The girls, on the other hand, continued their secondary education at home and possibly attended a small, private school managed by middle-class ladies. In mainstream educational histories, however, whether general overviews or specialised accounts, it is common for references to middle-class girls to be conspicuous by their brevity.

S.J. Curtis, for example, in his general account of the history of education in Great Britain, first published in 1948 and reaching a sixth edition in 1965, has one chapter on school reform and state intervention in secondary education, 1805-95. But only three and a half pages out of forty four refer to the education of middle-class girls.[17] A few of the specialised histories on middle-class schooling do devote a whole chapter to girls; this is so, for example, with R.L. Archer's 1921 text *Secondary Education in the Nineteenth Century* and with Margaret Bryant's 1986 publication *The London Experience of Secondary Education*.[18] But such space devoted to girls is a rarity.

The specialised literature on fee-paying public schools also usually omits any reference to such institutions for girls, even though a number of girls' independent schools were founded, mainly by the Girls' Public Day School Company, in the decades after 1870. What is common is for the word 'public school' to be automatically defined as a *boys'* public school. A typical example here is Honey's 1977 book *Tom Brown's Universe: The Development of the Public School in the 19th Century* where the author makes it clear in the introduction that his focus is the 'day-to-day lives of Victorian schoolboys'.[19]

The trivialisation of girls' and women's experiences
When girls and women are mentioned in educational histories of the period, we often find that their experiences are trivialised in some way. Curtis, for example, includes in his chapter on *secondary* schooling from 1805 to 1895, a discussion of the education of *middle-class women* in various colleges that were established in the 19th century, such as Girton and Newham Colleges, at Cambridge University. Yet there is a separate chapter on 'The modern universities and the ancient universities in the modern world' where such a discussion should have been located![20] Similarly, Richard Aldrich in *An Introduction to the History of Education* includes no material on women students in his chapter on higher education, but like Curtis places the struggles of the 19th-century pioneers to become university students in the chapter on

secondary schooling.[21]

To conflate the categories of 'girl' and 'woman' in this way, is to represent the latter as vulnerable, immature, childlike, dependent beings rather than as mature individuals in their own right. In particular, it shoud not be forgotten that although women at Oxford and Cambridge could not be awarded degrees on the same terms as men until 1919 and 1947, respectively, the female students at Girton and Newnham *were* studying for university degrees. Emily Davies, generally regarded as the founder of Girton, had always insisted that the women students should study the same subjects as men. As an old student of the 1860s, Constance Maynard, recollected:

> No allowance whatever was made for our colossal ignorance of the special subjects required . . . Three years and one term was in those days the time allowed to men in which to take the Tripos, and Miss Emily Davies scorned all compromises and her students must conform to the same rule.[22]

The representation of members of the female sex in some other educational histories is even more dubious. Thus one of the two chapters on girls' schools in Jonathan Gathorne-Hardy's 1977 publication *The Public School Phenomenon* is titled 'The "crush": sex and love at girls' schools and some other considerations'. The content of this chapter is remarkable to read. Gathorne-Hardy suggests that a large number of women were attracted to teach in these girls' schools because they were lesbians or thwarted and aggressive 'old maids' seeking revenge on the men who did not marry them, or feeling envious of men's privileges:

> As with boys' schools, only in reverse, teaching at girls' schools attracted a considerable, but quite incalculable, number of lesbians. And just as homosexual men often fear and dislike women, so lesbians, and for the same reasons, often fear and dislike men. Again, women who entered teaching sometimes did so because they could not get married; subconsciously part of the attitude of some of them to men would include desires for revenge. Often these pioneer liberationists resented (quite understandably) the privileged and dominant position of men in society. They envied men and wanted to equal or surpass them. But there is aggression here too. All these forces help to explain the quite noticeable elements of fear, disgust and hatred towards men which girls' schools often manifest during this period.[23]

It is hard to imagine the entry of single men into schoolteaching being described in this way! For single men, entry into an occupation is usually seen in terms of commitment to a career. But in this example, single women became teachers for highly dubious 'motives'; there is no sense in the passage quoted that women actually *chose* to become public schoolmistresses and saw the job as a means of acquiring professional status while earning a living.

Similarly, it is difficult to envisage the same language being used in regard to headmasters that is reserved for headmistresses. Thus the head of the Godolphin School in the late 19th century, Miss Douglas, is criticised by Gathorne-Hardy in the following way for introducing into her own school features of the boys' schools of her time, such as houses, the prefect system, games, uniforms, discipline, house and school 'spirit':

> And Mary Alice Douglas, the 'great' headmistress who oversaw these changes, has changed in tune with them. In 1890, it is certainly a strong face, but it is a feminine one; she has long hair pulled back and piled up, a long skirt, fine bosom and a slender waist. In 1919 she is wearing collar and tie, a pin-stripe coat, a waistcoat, a skirt (or are they trousers? It is impossible to see); she has the short-cut hair, greying at the temples, and the level gaze of a successful headmaster.[24]

Would a 'great' headmaster be described as having the gaze of a 'successful' headmistress?

A FEMINIST CRITIQUE

It is hardly surprising that such male centred histories are now being carefully scrutinised by feminist historians. The re-birth of the women's political movement in Britain, the USA and Western Europe in the late 1960s, provided the impetus for such a questioning. As women in the 1970s and 1980s analysed and discussed their own unequal and subordinate position, interest grew in understanding women's lives in the past. Had women's subordination been common throughout history? What were the experiences of our foremothers in past centuries and past decades? As women began to hunt for replies to these questions and many more, it became clear that women were largely absent in mainstream histories, outside and not a part of the official record.

In 1972, Anna Davin, for example, pointed out that in a male-dominated society, history meant the history of men; men's activities in war, courts, politics, diplomacy and administration were the 'real' drama while women's activities were excluded.[25] This theme of the invisibility of women within a male defined *history* received more prominence in 1973 with the publication of Sheila Rowbotham's influential text *Hidden from History: 300 Years of Women's Oppression and the Fight Against it*.[26] The spark had ignited. Soon many women were researching primary rather than male centred secondary sources for knowledge of our foremothers, especially in the 19th century. From such activity, women's history was nurtured.

As research proceeded in the 1980s and 1990s, the differentiation between women's history and feminist history became more pronounced. Women's history is defined by its subject matter rather than its perspective and involves, as I have argued elsewhere,[27] putting women back into the historical record without necessarily challenging the assumptions and parameters of male centred history. Feminist history, on the other hand, requires a rewriting of the past, a constant questioning and reworking of that malestream record that has been written mainly by men and through the eyes of men. Feminist history is infused with the ideas, beliefs and theories of the feminist movement. Though there are many definitions of 'feminism' and many divisions within it,[28] at a general level it centres around the belief that women are oppressed by men; furthermore, as a political movement, feminism seeks to end this oppression and to liberate women from the social injustices that they experience because of their sex.

Feminism therefore holds important implications for the writing of history, and I shall now attempt to draw out some of these implications in regard to British history of education.

Making women visible as agents of educational change
We need to challenge the accepted orthodoxy that it is men who were the key figures in making educational policy and in the administration and provision of education. Liberal histories, for example, focus primarily on those forms of education that have meaning for the present. A more realistic picture is offered if we include a range of institutions that were popular in the 19th century and have long disappeared, eg, factory schools, schools of industry, ragged schools, workhouse schools, poor law schools. And once we do this, we bring women into the realm of policy-making, provision and administration.

Elite and middle-class women in 19th-century England had a long tradition of unpaid, philanthropic work amongst the poor, including the support and running of schools.[29] Mary Carpenter, the daughter of

Dr Lant Carpenter, a Unitarian minister, opened her first ragged school in 1846 and thus began her long involvement in the ragged school movement.[30] Louisa Twining, whose father was a tea merchant and philanthropist, was a well known workhouse visitor who advocated and promoted the training and supervision of workhouse girls: indeed, in the 1858 meeting of the influential National Association for the Promotion of Social Science she read a paper on the latter subject.[31] Yet such important figures who were influential in educational policy making and administration are notable for their absence in most histories of the period.

The distorted view of Marxist historians, who in their concern to document history 'from below' ignore any part that working-class women might play as agents in seeking their own self improvement, has been particularly challenged in my own research.[32] Thus in my study of working-class women's education in the two main adult education movements of 19th-century England I emphasise the importance of integrating a social class *and* gender perspective. Although these two adult education movements were aimed specifically at working-class men, I reveal that working-class women did become students within the mechanics institutes and working men's colleges, often struggling for admittance to such male places. At Birmingham in 1840, for example, a group of women unsuccessfully petitioned the local mechanics' institute for classes. 'Such a thing would ruin the Atheneum in a month', the middle-class directors announced. So the women looked elsewhere, to the local Owenite branch, which not only met the request but also delighted in the fact that they could provide something which their middle-class competitors could not.[33] At Bingley Mechanics' Institute, on the other hand, a deputation of young factory women was successful in 1850 in having their demands for a class met,[34] and at Holbeck, in the same year, another group of women were granted permission to become students by an all-male committee.[35] As such examples demonstrate, working-class women were not passive beings, but frequently actors in educational history, *demanding change*, and sometimes being successful in having these demands met.

Making women's education visible
The task of making women's education visible in the 19th century has already begun. Thus, as a result of feminist research, we now know much more about the education of both working-class and middle-class girls and women. An early contribution to this debate was

the article published by Carol Dyhouse in 1977 in which she highlighted the way that state educational provision for working-class girls from 1880 to 1920 was influenced by a pervasive domestic ideology that aimed to help these schoolgirls become 'good wives and little mothers.'[36] The way that ideas about femininity, wifehood, motherhood and domesticity could influence a girl's or woman's access to education, as well as the content of that education, has now been widely researched.

Sara Delamont points out that the feminist pioneers who pushed for improvements in the educational standards of middle-class girls and the entry of women into that preserve of masculinity, the universities, were caught in a snare of double conformity. The pioneers knew that for their schemes to be successful, their students must conform to strict traditional standards of ladylike behaviour; after all, few parents would be willing to support a daughter's education if they thought it would 'de-sex' her. At the same time, however, the pioneers insisted that their students adhered to the standards of the male academic academy.[37] Joan Burstyn links the opposition of the entry of women into higher education in the 19th century to the prevalent beliefs about the relative spheres for men and women. Middle-class men enjoyed access to higher education since it was seen as a means of preparing them for a career in the market-place; university education for middle-class women, on the other hand, was seen as irrelevant since women should be educated for domesticity as daughters at home, wives and mothers. The admittance of women to higher education, asserts Burstyn, was grudgingly accepted by the end of the 19th century not because the idea of middle-class womanhood had changed, but because it became an ideal that many financially hard-pressed middle-class families could no longer uphold.[38] Similarly, Anna Davin vividly illustrates how ideas about the sexual division of labour permeated reading textbooks used by working-class children in board schools in London. Women's work in such textbooks was presented as being in the home, either as a wife and mother or as a domestic helper of some kind in someone else's. Although, as Davin points out, it is impossible to decide how far the assumptions and prescriptions of such gender roles influenced the children who laboured through them, we must note that the situations presented as 'natural' to women and the behaviour advocated – unselfishness, compassion, devotion to housewifely industry and family duty – had a tendency to direct girls towards an exclusively domestic role, even at the expense of school.[39]

While our knowledge about female education in the 19th century is expanding, much still remains to be done. For example, we still have no in-depth study of women higher education students. What was student life like for a woman at this time? Did she find herself marginalised within the male context of the university? Did she experience many of the problems that women students complain about today, including sexual harrassment? Similarly, we have no informed, in-depth research on 19th-century women academics as a professional group. Were female lecturers the academic proletariat? Did women lecturers 'network' with each other? How did lesbians survive in academe? How did women with dependents, such as elderly parents or young children, juggle the demands of home and professional life? How did feminist academics survive within the male oriented and male dominated world of the university?

Although making women's education visible is an important task for the feminist historian, as the discussion here illustrates, it does not necessarily produce a 'feminist' history. At the heart of feminist history lies an examination of the power relations between the sexes as well as the task of exploring women's experiences.

Examining the power relations between the sexes
A key element of feminist thought is that the unequal power relations between the sexes is balanced in favour of men, and that this male power over women helps to explain the oppression and subordination of the female sex. Thus often the term 'patriarchy' is used by feminist historians since, at a most general level, patriarchy refers to those complex processes whereby men dominate and exercise control over women. The degree of emphasis given to an analysis of the power relations between men and women tends to divide the two main feminist groupings in Britain today. Thus socialist feminists may attempt to give equal weight to both patriarchal and social class relations while radical feminists mainly concentrate on the former. While the identification of such groupings may be useful to readers attempting to locate the perspective of a feminist writer today, not all feminists may be easily allocated to any one camp. In my own work on the education of working-class and middle-class women in 19th-century England, for example, I try to integrate a social class and gender perspective. While some would argue that this places me within the socialist feminist camp, others disagree and believe that my work is much more in tune with radical feminist thinking. I would place myself somewhere between the two.

Thus in my writings on the mechanics' institutes and working men's college movements, I argue that the institutes and colleges were not merely shaped by class cultures but also, more often than not, controlled by men and shaped in their interests; women had to struggle to enter such places and, once admitted, their presence still caused considerable controversy.[40]

In the mechanics' institutes, for example, we begin to hear about the admission of women from 1830; but women rarely, if ever, attained full membership with equal access to all facilities and privileges granted to men. It was common for women to be excluded from newsrooms and reading rooms; this was the case at London, Manchester and Colchester.[41] Even in the Manchester lyceums, institutes of a more popular kind that hoped to attract working-class men and women, women were admitted to 'all the privileges of the institution *excepting* the reading rooms'. (My emphasis)[42]

What is apparent is that newsrooms and reading rooms were regarded as men's clubs, comfortable retreats from the harsh world of work where the occupants could relax and discuss the affairs of the day. Women were regarded as belonging to the private sphere of the home and assumed to have no interest in the 'public' affairs of the world. As I point out, to examine the power relations between men and women in such educational forms is not to deny that for women the class context of their education was also critical. After all, both the mechanics' institute and the working men's college movements were largely initiated by the middle classes for the working classes.[43]

Investigating women's experiences

Feminist historians also place great store on trying to find women's voices in the past since it is hoped that this will especially challenge the interpretations that male centred histories offer. Finding women's voices in the 19th century is problematic however since, unless oral histories can be undertaken, one has to rely upon primary sources that have survived with the passing of time. And such written texts pose their own particular problems.

'Official' texts, such as government reports, for example, contain a mass of oral evidence given by women but the reader is given no information about the views of these women, nor of the way in which they acquired their information. Was the information acquired through first-hand experience, through observation, through listening to what other people said? In addition, any oral evidence submitted would be filtered through the particular perspective of those collecting and writing up the evidence who were nearly always middle-class men.

Similarly, 'personal' texts, such as letters, diaries and autobiographies contain their own problems. Autobiographies, for example, are subjective accounts of events that contain inevitable bias in the selection and presentation of content. And such texts were more likely to be written by middle-class than working-class women. Working-class women, on the other hand, might write a letter to the press. But when one reads such a letter, perhaps signed 'From a factory woman' or 'From a working woman', the researcher always has to question whether it is authentic. In addition, if the letter is written with correct punctuation and no spelling mistakes, one has also to question how the document was produced. Nevertheless, despite these and other problems presented by official and personal texts, such sources can be invaluable to the researcher concerned with finding women's voices.

Carol Dyhouse, for example, makes extensive use of autobiographical material in her account of the experiences of girls growing up, and of school and family life, in late Victorian and Edwardian society.[44] Similarly, I use autobiographical sources plus the oral evidence collected by other researchers, such as Stephen Humphries, when exploring the experiences of schooling for working-class girls. In trying to 'get inside' the 19th century classroom, I cite, for example, the autobiography of Ellen Wilkinson, born in 1891, who attended what she described as 'a filthy elementary school' where the masters often gave extra time and lent books to a 'bright lad'. Ellen bitterly recollected, 'I never remember such encouragement. I was only a girl anyway'.[45]

Other feminist historians have collected their own oral histories which they utilise with a range of documentary sources. Frances Widdowson uses such a technique in her study of women and elementary teaching, 1840-1914. She concludes that by the first decade of the 20th century the majority of elementary teachers came from the lower-middle classes. One schoolteacher, for example, born in London in 1888, remembered how her mother (an ex-nurse) had encouraged her to enter the occupation since it was a solid job:

> Mother was a very clever woman really, and she could see and understand quite a lot and she thought to be a teacher you'd get something solid – you can't be dismissed and it takes a pension . . . and if you lost your husband or anything you could always go back to it.[46]

Finding the voices of women in history helps the feminist to challenge mainstream historical thinking, in particular that commonplace assumption that one can generalise from the experiences of men for all humanity. As feminist historians have ably demonstrated, women's experiences are sharply differentiated from those of their menfolk; women's structural location within a patriarchal society where men oppress women, and masculinity is the dominant gender, generates a gendered experience.

Changing the way that women have been represented
It will be obvious from what I have said so far that a feminist critique of British history of education would also involve changing the way that women have been represented in most malestream histories. I shall illustrate this point by drawing upon an earlier example.

In this section on male centred histories of education, I discussed how women's experiences of education were often trivialised. Thus we must question the way that Gathorne-Hardy represents the headmistresses of the new academic schools for middle-class girls as unsexed, eccentric dictators. As Carol Dyhouse aptly comments, Gathorne-Hardy insinuates that one such headmistress, Miss Douglas, went through something approaching a personal sex-change.[47] It would be more appropriate to place any discussion of these reforming headteachers within the context in which they found themselves.

Joyce Senders Petersen stresses that these 'new' women were in direct contrast to the old-fashioned, lady-teachers of the small, private, family-like establishments that so many middle-class girls attended. The latter catered for a small, select clientele and did not judge pupils by impersonal standards of academic excellence but by the successful acquisition of social graces and qualities of mind and manner considered suitable for a domestic life. The private schoolmistress's social status therefore did not rest upon intellectual merit and academic achievement but upon ascriptive social characteristics – such as her own genteel background and the social standing of her clientele. The new reforming headmistresses had to break away from such a definition of their role if the academic goals that they upheld were to be taken seriously. The late 19th- and early 20th-century headmistresses were generally grand, remote, authoritative figures – professional women whose claim to elite status rested on their intellectual achievements.[48]

CONCLUSION

British history of education seems remarkably slow to respond to the challenges that feminist history poses. While feminist researchers document and chart the history of women's education, their findings remain ghettoised and isolated from what is seen as the 'main body' of work. Yet until feminist work is taken seriously, and the historical record re-written, there is little chance of restoring women to history and restoring history to women. Our foremothers deserve a better fate.

NOTES

1. The vast output of books is now being complemented by a number of journals in the field. The first issue of *Gender and History* appeared in Spring 1989, of *Journal of Women's Studies* in the Fall 1989, and a new feminist history journal titled *Women's History Review* appeared in April 1992.

2. H. Silver, 'Aspects of neglect: the strange case of Victorian popular education' *Oxford Review of Education*, Vol 3, No 1, 1977. For more recent discussions about historiography in the history of education see, for example, J. Hardin Best (ed), *Historical Inquiry in Education, A Research Agenda*, American Educational Research Association, Washington 1983, and G. Partington, 'Two Marxisms and the history of education', *History of Education*, Vol 13, No 4, 1984.

3. These terms are defined later in this chapter.

4. J. Matthews, 'Barbara Bodichon: integrity in diversity', in D. Spender (ed), *Feminist Theorists: Three Centuries of Women's Intellectual Traditions*, The Women's Press, London 1983.

5. C. Birchenough, *History of Elementary Education in England and Wales from 1800 To The Present Day*, University Tutorial Press, London 1914, p 272, pp 341-347.

6. *Ibid*, p 115.

7. *Ibid*, p 117.

8. J. Marcus, 'Introduction: re-reading the Pankhursts and women's suffrage', in J. Marcus (ed), *Suffrage and the Pankhursts*, Routledge and Kegan Paul, London 1987, p 3.

9. H.C. Barnard, *A History of English Education*, (1969 sixth impression with amendments, first pub. 1947), University of London Press Ltd, London, p 99, p 111.

10. See, for example, M. Sturt, *The Education of the People*, Routledge and Kegan Paul, London 1967; L. Lawson and H. Silver, *A Social History of Education in England*, Methuen, London 1973; P. Horn, *Education in Rural England 1800-1914*, St Martin's Press, New York; R. Aldrich, *An Introduction to the History of Education*, Hodder and Stoughton, London 1982.

11. 'Editorial', *History Workshop Journal*, Spring 1982.

12. B. Simon, *The Two Nations and the Educational Structure 1780-1870*, Lawrence and Wishart, London 1974, pp 14-15, first pub. in 1960 under the

title *Studies in the History of Education, 1780-1870*.

13. J. Purvis, ' "We can no longer pretend that sex stratification does not exist, nor that it exists but is unimportant" (M. Eichler). A reply to Keith Flett', *History of Education*, Vol 18, No 2, 1989, p 148.

14. Centre for Contemporary Cultural Studies Education Group, *Unpopular Education: Schooling and Social Democracy in England Since 1944*, Hutchinson, London 1981, p 32.

15. P. McCann 'Introduction' to P. McCann (ed), *Popular Education and Socialization in the Nineteenth Century*, Methuen, London 1977, p xi.

16. J.S. Hurt, *Elementary Schooling and the Working Classes 1860-1918*, Routledge and Kegan Paul, London 1979, p 105.

17. S.J. Curtis, *History of Education in Great Britain*, University Tutorial Press, London (1965 sixth ed., first pub. 1948), Chapter 5.

18. R.L. Archer, *Secondary Education in the Nineteenth Century*, Frank Cass, London (1966, first pub. 1921), chapter 9; M. Bryant, *The London Experience of Secondary Education*, The Athlone Press, London 1986.

19. J.S. de S. Honey, *Tom Brown's Universe: the Development of the Victorian Public School*, Millington, London 1977.

20. S.J. Curtis, *op cit*, Chapters 5 and 12.

21. R. Aldrich, *An Introduction to the History of Education*, 1982, chapter 5 and 6.

22. C.L. Maynard, *Between College Terms*, James Nisbet and co, London 1910, p 180.

23. J. Gathorne-Hardy, *The Public School Phenomenon, 1597-1977*, Hodder and Stoughton, London 1977, p 258.

24. *Ibid*, pp 249-250.

25. A. Davin, 'Women and history', in M. Wandor (ed), *The Body Politic: Women's Liberation in Britain 1969-1972*, Stage 1, London 1972.

26. S. Rowbotham, *Hidden from History: 300 years of Women's Opression and the Fight Against It*, Pluto Press, London 1973.

27. J. Purvis, 'Breaking the chains', *Times Higher Educational Supplement*, 30 October 1987.

28. Most writers distinguish between liberal feminism, radical feminism, socialist feminism, marxism feminism and black feminism. See the discussions offered in A.M. Jaggar *Feminist Politics and Human Nature*, Harvester Press, Brighton 1983; and R. Tong, *Feminist Thought, A Comprehensive Introduction*, Unwin and Hyman, London.

29. See, for example, F.K. Prochaska, *Women and Philanthropy in 19th Century England*, Clarendon Press, Oxford 1980; and A. Summers, 'A home from home – women's philanthropic work in the nineteenth century', in S. Burman (ed), *Fit Work for Women*, Croom Helm, London 1979.

30. See, for example, A Worker (Mary Carpenter), *Ragged Schools: Their Principles and Modes of Operation*, Partridge and Oakey, London 1850; M. Carpenter, *Reformatory Schools for the Children of the Perishing and Dangerous Classes, and for Juvenile Offenders*, C. Gilpin, London 1851; J.

Manton, *Mary Carpenter and the Children of the Streets*, Heinemann, London 1976.

31. L. Twining, 'On the training and supervision of workhouse girls', in *Transactions of the National Association for the Promotion of Social Science, 1859*, pp 696-703.

32. J. Purvis, *Hard Lessons, The Lives and Education of Working-Class Women in Nineteenth-Century England*, Polity Press, Oxford 1989.

33. B. Taylor, *Eve and the New Jerusalem: Socialism and Feminism in the Nineteenth Century*, Virago, London 1983, p 233.

34. Yorkshire Union of Mechanics' Institutes, *Report*, Edward Baines and Sons, Leeds 1850, p 24.

35. *Ibid*, p 37.

36. C. Dyhouse, 'Good wives and little mothers: social anxieties and the schoolgirl's curriculum, 1890-1920', *Oxford Review of Education*, Vol 3, No 1, 1977. an earlier article by Dyhouse was 'Social Darwinistic ideas and the development of women's education in England, 1880-1920', *History of Education*, Vol 5, No 1, 1976.

37. S. Delamont, 'The domestic ideology and women's education', in S. Delamont and L. Duffin (eds), *The Nineteenth-Century Woman, Her Cultural and Physical World*, Croom Helm, London 1978.

38. J. Burstyn, *Victorian Education and the Ideal of Womanhood*, Croom Helm, London 1989, p 172.

39. A. Davin, ' Mind that you do as you are told": reading books for Board School School girls', *Feminist Review*, 3, 1979, p 98.

40. J. Purvis, *Hard Lessons, op cit*, p 224.

41. *Ibid*, p 117.

42. B.F. Duppa, *A Manual for Mechanics' Institutions*, Longman, Orme, Brown, Green and Longmans, London 1839, p 143.

43. J. Purvis, *Hard Lessons, op cit*, p 224.

44. C. Dyhouse, *Girls Growing Up in Late Victorian and Edwardian England*, Routledge and Kegan Paul, London 1981.

45. J. Purvis, *A History of Women's Education in England*, Open University Press, Milton Keynes 1991; E. Wilkinson, 'Ellen Wilkinson', in The Countess of Oxford and Asquith (ed), *Myself When Young by Famous Women of To-Day*, Frederick Muller, London 1938, p 407, p 404.

46. F. Widdowson, *Going Up Into The Next Class: Women and Elementary Teacher Training, 1840-1914*, Women's Research and Resources Centre Publications, London 1980, p 67.

47. C. Dyhouse, 'Miss Buss and Miss Beale: gender and authority in the history of education', in F. Hunt (ed), *Lessons for Life, The Schooling of Girls and Women 1850-1950*, Basil Blackwell, Oxford 1987.

48. J. Senders Pedersen, *The Reform of Girls' Secondary and Higher Education in Victorian England, A Study of Elites and Educational Change*, Garland Publishing, New York and London 1987.

RADICAL EDUCATION AND THE NEW RIGHT

RICHARD JOHNSON

In 1972 Brian Simon edited a set of extracts under the title *The Radical Tradition in Education in Britain*.[1] This tradition was 'a unity, consistent within itself'. It was radical by virtue of its association with 'the long struggle' of the working class, first for democracy, then for socialism, and because it involved 'a fundamentally similar outlook' – education as a means to 'radical social change'. Radicals shared a faith in the formative power of education, a commitment to science and to secularism, and a conception of education that went beyond schooling to 'the totality of social influences'. These ideas flourished in the political excitements of the first half of the 19th century. All but one of the texts were from this period, though from different movements: Jacobinism (Tom Paine and William Thompson), post-war political radicalism and secularism (Richard Carlile), and Chartism (William Lovett). The 'basic ideas', however, 'found expression in later years'.

The radical tradition also figures in Simon's four-volume *History of Education*, especially in the first two volumes.[2] In volume 1 (*The Two Nations*), Simon argues that while ruling groups constructed a class-based educational hierarchy in the period up to 1870, 'the working class carried forward the ideas of the 18th-century forerunners and of the "practical philosophers" of "the age of reform" '.[3] In later essays the tradition is revisited more critically, but also used affirmatively in relation to contemporary issues. Coleridge's stress on self activity is preferred, for example, to the earlier mechanical environmentalism, though a fuller solution is found in Marx's *The Theses on Feuerbach*.[4] The radicals' optimism is cited against latterday conservatives (including progressivists) who believe in 'the determining character of inborn mental powers'.[5] Modern leftish critics of schooling also find themselves with an uncomfortable role in this historian's dialogue: their pessimism, based on the analysis of structure rather than struggle, aligns them with the knowledge-denying conservatives of the past![6]

The idea of a radical tradition is not unique to educational history. It has been a popular framework for history-writing on the British left. *The Two Nations* might be re-read in the context of the collective project of the Communist Party Historians' Group. Bill Schwarz has summed up the group's enterprise as follows: 'if a single common theme can be detected which bound the histories together it was the desire to demonstrate that the Communist Party was the inheritor of a long tradition of English popular radicalism'.[7] Hence that sequence of studies of peasant rebels, utopians, radical Puritans, 'primitive rebels', 18th-century rioters, early 19th-century popular radicals, and late 19th- and 20th-century socialists and trade unionists – all once expelled from the Conservative Nation – but now so prominent in our histories.

Within this sequence, Edward Thompson's *The Making of the English Working Class*, published three years after *The Two Nations*, came nearest to its preoccupations.[8] The books shared many themes, especially working-class self-education. Both took class relations as their explanatory thread. *The Two Nations* was mainly concerned with the institutional consequences of class outlooks and struggles, while *The Making* was about the process of class formation itself. Both books invited the reader to view early working-class movements as exemplary in some sense and to connect them with modern issues.

The radical education tradition and its historians interest me here for three reasons. First, *The Two Nations* and Thompson's *The Making* formed my own historical projects, so that revisiting them today is helpful at another turning point. In 1969, recently emerged from Conservative Cambridge history to Redbrick student radicalism, I decided to revise my PhD, finished the year before, from beginning to end.[9] It focussed on educational administration and policy-making. *The Two Nations* suggested a wider 'social' canvass, not as 'background' or even context, but as the generative matrix of policy. *The Making*'s electrifying accounts of radical culture showed there were sources much closer to popular experiences of learning, and offered ways of reading them. Both books explored a dynamic of struggles which might explain the growth of schooling.

Second, there is the problem of tradition as such. However much we strive to recognise the otherness of a past time, our historical projects remain irredeemably contemporary. But tradition constructs this past-present relation in a particular way, constituting the past as a guarantee for contemporary identities, or as legitimation for current projects. Traditions ('treasured memories'?) are always selective, working by exclusions, and are always invented, with original purposes in view.[10] I confess to suspicions about tradition-building, whether left or right, and also to real confusions. Are traditions irremediably conservative or ideological in some way? In which case we should constantly *de-construct* them, the better to recognise past complexities and current possibilities. Or are traditions essential to political identity of any kind, and do we just have the *wrong* traditions in command? In this case, we should *re-construct* traditions in order to dethrone the mighty and recognise the excluded. In this essay, I tend to deconstruction, but may well end up, surreptitiously, constructing a tradition of my own.

The third reason for revisiting radical education is to address contemporary dilemmas. The key issue is stated more directly elsewhere in this volume: what should the radical agenda be today? The difficulty of framing an answer comes, in part, from the intervention of a new claimant to radicalism on the political right. This is why this essay has a double focus: *two* 'traditions'. I want to revisit 'radical education' in the Simon sense; but I also want to place it alongside the New Rights's rise, to attempt some clarifications.

RADICALISM (1790-1850) AND THE HISTORIANS (1950-90)

The historiography of early 19th century radicalism is so dense and layered that a full archaeology is not possible here, only some probes. Early 19th-century radicals have figured in two late 20th-century conflicts: in the struggles of left and right, but also in the internal transformations of the left. Even in the 1950s and early 1960s, polarisations were sharp, partly because of the Cold War and the strength of Marxism among historians, and partly because of the salience of the first phase of industrial capitalism for both sides. Today we might mark this opposition through two texts: Thompson's *The Making*, of course, and *Capitalism and the Historians* which appeared in 1954.[11]

Capitalism and the Historians was edited by F.A. Hayek, later regarded as the New Right's key philosopher.[12] The collection stemmed from the Mont Pelerin Society, the first New Right 'think tank'. Hayek's preface showed his grasp of the political stakes involved:

Few men will deny that our views about the goodness or badness of different institutions are largely determined by what we believe to have been their effects in the past. There is scarcely a political ideal or concept which does not involve opinions about a whole series of past events, and there are few historical memories which do not serve as a symbol of some political aim.[13]

A key feature of the project was an alliance with economic historians based on a shared investment in the story of capitalism as a progressive process of 'growth'. This was a grand narrative to set beside the Marxist epic of the first working-class or the radical liberal or Fabian adventure of 'social reform'. It was not only the 'standard of living' of workers that was at issue here, but the 'rationality' of their politics in a period of economic 'improvement'. These challenges were directly met in *The Making*.

After *The Making*, this stark pattern of conflicts and arguments became more complex. Earlier skirmishes continued: hence that empiricist picking away at the thesis of class formation by Thompson's less sympathetic critics.[14] In the 1980s, after a period when left historians made the running, the historical right became more active and larger aims were realised in the radical right revival and in New Right governments. Increasingly, however, these conflicts were complicated by internal transformations in the left. Already Thompson had conducted his New Left critique of Stalinism by historical means. Now new political identities – around gender, race/ethnicity and sexuality especially – constituted themselves as social movements, and as historiographical projects. Early 19th-century radicalism became a battleground again; but this time on *many* fronts. Simultaneously, the conceptual frameworks – ways of representing culture and politics – shifted too.

A first area of revision was radicalism's theories or 'languages'. Thompson had described a range of radical frameworks, but made sense of this diversity as a developing consciousness of class. His critique of formal or 'categorical' thinking was powerful, but he preserved Marx's teleology – the movement towards a class-for-itself. The point was to show, from historical sources and with sensitivity to cultural traditions, that the working class really had made itself. Class was no romantic wish nor dogmatic theory; it actually happened. Later historians sought out the unevenness in the story. They did not narrate it as accomplished epic or melodrama.[15] They used cooler, less exciting forms, more ironic, tragic or academic. They stressed ambiguities, contradictions, missed chances, unfinished business. In one early revision, Patricia Hollis distinguished the 'old analysis' from 'the new', the Painite, Jacobin or 'political' theory of oppression and the later political economies.[16] She was sceptical about working-class evolutions and stressed, instead, the common ground between working-class and middle-class radicals.[17] Gareth Stedman Jones' much-discussed essay on 'Re-thinking Chartism' viewed radical traditions as 'languages' or political repertoires (discourses?) that were constitutive of political movements, not merely reflective of social conditions.[18] He stressed the resilience of the older 'political' (Painite) analysis, which accommodated aspects of political economy. Chartism was not the first working-class movement, class conscious and immanently socialist, but rather the outer limit of 'Radicalism' – a specific political form inherited from earlier times.

Similar arguments were developed by Gregory Claeys in books and articles on Paine, Painites and the Owenites, providing the most complex re-assessment of radical *ideas* to date.[19] Claeys followed Stedman Jones' reconceptualisation in terms of language or discourse and drew on earlier paradigm shifts in the study of political ideas. From Thompson and J.F.C. Harrison[20] he took a curiosity about the less familiar radical tributaries: not only the 'republican' mainstream and the oppositional political economies, but Christian millenarianism, theories of natural law and rights, agrarian radicalism, dissenting communitarianism and the democracy (and autocracy) of the sects.

Claeys clarifies the distinction between the 'old' and 'new' analysis.[21] Unlike Hollis (who stressed political economy), he ascribes the difference to Owenism. The difference is re-described as that between a 'political' analysis ('Republicanism') which explains oppressions in terms of law, taxation and aristocracy, and Owenism's stress on social relations and competition. These threads were differently combined in different movements. By the 1840s a 'social radicalism', incorporating Owenite elements, was dominant, but there were different variants: radical republicanism, anti-revolutionary, anti-statist, but sensitive to some social themes, and a home-grown socialism inclined to state intervention and social reform.[22] Both were in tension with the revolutionary socialist or Marxist tradition.

A second area of revision has been radicalism's social basis. There is rather general agreement that *The Making's* central thesis is not proven: that we cannot say a working class was made in this unified and inclusive sense.[23] Perhaps this has *never* happened, or not without some pattern of exclusion, hierarchy, hegemony inside the class itself. Alternatives to Thompson's view are divided, however, in two significant ways: between feminist and non-feminist accounts; and between those still concerned with the social basis of movements (artisans? male workers?) and those who put brackets round this question in order to bring out the role of language or discourse in constituting political forces in class, gender or other ways. The second division is becoming important; but I focus on the feminist work here.

The social historians' own 'old analysis' is being radically revised. Feminist historians are showing how most movements privileged the male worker/would-be citizen and marginalised women. Women were active but rarely on the same terms as men. This gender-structuring was a marked feature of the developing working-class 'public' (including its educational forms). It was reinforced by the adoption of 'respectable' forms of family relations, which policed women more firmly out of politics. Popular politics itself became more formalised, around masculine conditions, conventions and space.[24]

In the absence of a critical gender politics, these formations appear in the non-feminist histories not as explicit topics, but as premises: they have to be dragged out from the text by analysing its narrative and other conventions.[25] It is clear that 'the making' was also a making of unequal gender relations, and a formalising of political exclusions.

Where women's role has been researched, findings have been paradoxical: women, apparently marginalised, were indispensable to the movements. Barbara Taylor's *Eve and the New Jerusalem* has shifted conceptions of Owenism by showing how Owenite women (and some men) addressed questions of gender inequalities, sexuality, the family and the patriarchal character of religion. Women played a large part in Owenite campaigning and branch life. She suggests that the emergence of Owenite feminism was related to transitions in popular sexual relations.[26] Leonore Davidoff and Catherine Hall have shown the dependence of male middle-class public life (including its general missionary vocation) on the new gender formation of 'separate spheres'.[27] The implications for the social history of education are already enormous, but the differential positioning of men and women, boys and girls, in relation to literacy, self-education, teaching and schooling has also received attention, especially from June Purvis.[28] Women were important providers (as mothers, teachers, philanthropic organisers), but within relations that privileged men and boys here too.

Little connection has been made between accounts of the Claeys kind and feminist research, despite the salience of Owenism in both arguments. Has the bracketing out of the social composition of movements provided a new way to avoid gender issues? Feminist findings qualify even the complex account of a transition from 'political' to 'social' radicalism in *Citizens and Saints*. Owenism was, as we know from Taylor, the most 'feminine' of the movements: the public political sphere (with its exclusions) was less important than in republicanism, concerns of women were given space, and gender roles were less polarised. But Owenism was not 'social' *as opposed to* 'political': rather it politicised areas of social life (e.g. the sexual division of labour) which, for radical men, were not problems but supports.[29] It worked with a view of power as dispersed not focussed. In the older radicalism power was seen as concentrated in formally 'political' institutions, just as for later Marxism it was condensed in 'production' and the state. If we define the difference like this, it is harder to see a transition from 'old' to 'new'. Yes, a new form of 'social radicalism' emerged that allowed room for broader social and cultural themes, but the possibilities were soon boxed up again in more orthodoxly political-and-economic definitions of left politics. There was, therefore, a continuing *difference* rather than a *completed transition*. The perspective of gender was especially important because gender relations were – are – so diffused and omnipresent that it is hard to ascribe them to one source. So the feminism of Owenism, its stress on the social and cultural, and its view of power as diffused, were associated features which make it peculiarly interesting today – and claimable for a 'new' tradition?

The growing consciousnesses of gender and of nationality, race or 'ethnicity' necessarily challenges earlier evaluations of past episodes. They undermine the moral framing of class-based accounts; they point up their masculinity or Anglo-centricity.[30] This produces painful feelings and difficult dilemmas, as attachments to old heroes (radicals and historians) are qualified. Perhaps this is the crux of my problem about traditions. Left traditions in their old form are problems as well as solutions now, yet much of the writing which threatens to take their place is deconstructive rather than reconstructive. It often lacks a sense of political responsibility. It cares little for the identities invested in the older accounts and does not offer new hopes or homes. It leaves its (limited) readerships with only academic gratifications. Thus one main tendency is to stress the 1850s divide, and connect radicalism backwards to early modern times. This disrupts the older habit of hopeful forward projection. As Craig Calhoun puts it:

> In early nineteenth-century England, because of the strength of their traditions and their communities, many radical artisans, craftsmen and their fellows were in some ways more like the peasants and others who

have made revolutions than like the working class of today's advanced capitalist societies, which struggles for a variety of greater and lesser reforms.[31]

He concludes that it won't do to extend Marx's (proletarian) categories to these groups. Nor can the modern working class be expected to behave as artisans: 'New social foundations for radicalism may yet be made, but they are no longer inherited as they were before and during industrialization'. This argument makes much sense, though undialectical: were not the movements also about *becoming proletarian*? But that phrase, 'may yet be made', is also terribly bleak and politically agnostic! Taylor and Claeys are unusual in wanting to save something from their own critiques. Taylor's interest in Owenism is to trace 'the beginnings of a Communist-feminist project with which we still identify'.[32] Claeys hints at much unfinished business in the modern world to which older ideas may yet be relevant.[33]

In the two sections that follow I want to re-read the educational traditions in the light of these general perspectives.

EDUCATION AND JACOBIN THEORY

I start with 'Jacobin' writers of the 1790s because they present, in elaborated form, frameworks found in later radical practices and rhetorics, though they too were deeply indebted to earlier republicanisms in Britain and America.[34]

Jacobin writers were centrally concerned with political virtue or justice. According to Paine's classic statements, governments derived their authority from three sources: superstition and fraud, conquest or force, or from consent, common rights and thence from Reason. Only governments based upon the 'nature of man' were legitimate. Governments ought to guarantee the benefits of association and the natural rights which accompanied it. Oppression was not intrinsic to society; it was produced by illegitimate forms of government – monarchy, aristocracy and hereditary government, government by force and fraud. Properly representative government arising from the people was the answer.[35]

William Godwin's hostility to government was even more marked, though backed by utility not natural rights.[36] He began from the common assumption that the characters of human beings were shaped not by 'any original determination that they bring into the world' but were 'the offspring of circumstances and events'.[37] The problem was how to arrange circumstances to secure the greatest happiness. This utilitarianism was qualified, however, by a belief in altruistic intentions as the greatest human satisfaction. Since human beings could not be coerced into benevolence without substituting baser motives, all government was to some extent an evil. It eroded the independence which virtue required.

This political critique was linked to questions of knowledge. In Paine's typology of governments, reasonableness was a major criterion.[38] Monarchy was based on the great lie that abilities were hereditary; popular ignorance was necessary to sustain it. Mixed governments gave room for reason but this threatened the monarchical side. It was necessary to 'buy reason up' by bribery and to make government 'a continual enigma'.[39] Only representative, constitutional systems allowed reason full sway. They were inherently educative, eschewing secrecy, exploding ignorance, precluding imposition: 'the reason for everything must publicly appear'.[40] One important test of government was its educative value for citizens, its capacity to produce virtue. Paine's argument about religion was very similar:

> It has been the scheme of the Christian Church, and of all other invented systems of religion, to hold man in ignorance of his Creator, as it is of government to hold him in ignorance of his rights. The systems of the one are as false as are those of the others, and are calculated for mutual support . . . Christian theology . . . is . . . the study of nothing.[41]

So this analysis of knowledge and power focussed on the effects of politics in the narrower sense: political institutions and citizen morale. If mankind was essentially rational and civil society harmonious, power entered knowledge relations through 'artificial' attitudes and institutions. The knowledge/power problem came down to monopoly or deliberate mystification. Knowledge was witheld or falsified, out of self-interest or bad faith. 'Superstition' (a favourite term) was sheer ignorance, passivity, a lack of proper human agency.[42] Often, as in Wollstonecraft's attacks on conventional femininity, it was an over-evaluation of 'sensibility' or emotion as against careful, thoughtful judgement.[43] Since ignorance was ephemeral and lacked a 'rationality' of its own, Radicals were exceedingly optimistic about change. Knowledge for James Ensor was 'the universal monitor' of political affairs.[44] As Paine put it:

Those who talk of a counter-revolution in France, show how little they understand of man. There does not exist in the compass of language, an arrangement of words to express so much as a means of effecting a counter-revolution. The means must be an obliteration of knowledge; and it was never yet discovered, how to make man *unknow* his knowledge, or *unthink* his thoughts. (My emphasis)[45]

This unreasonable belief in Reason underpinned the fierce espousal of 'independence', the great social virtue. Again and again Paine asserted the value of intellectual self-activity: 'My mind is my own Church'; 'I do not choose to rest my belief on such evidence'; 'I had to form a system for myself;[46] and even 'I rarely ever quote; the reason is, I always think'.[47] Despite its universalist ring this ideal was not without contradictions. It has its own class character in these texts, part of the middle-class critique of aristocracy, patronage and social parasitism. Its popular applicability was as yet untested. It also had strongly masculine associations: the commonest qualifying adjective to 'independence' was 'manly'. Ensor, who took on some feminist themes, nonetheless wrote a whole book entitled *The Independent Man*.[48] Of government in 'a well-constituted republic', Paine wrote, 'the human faculties act with boldness, and acquire . . . a gigantic manliness'.[49]

So the Jacobins were far from immune to the masculinisation of citizenship in this period. One index of the resulting limitations is Mary Wollstonecraft's struggle to combine radicalism with feminism. She had to negotiate all this manliness. What was this complaint about masculine women, she asked. If this referred to women keen on hunting, shooting and gambling she might join the cry. If they meant the attainment of 'manly virtues', or more properly speaking 'human' ones, she hoped that women 'may everyday grow more and more masculine'.[50] She hoped they would put aside romantic fancies and dependence on men, and raise themselves out of 'perpetual childhood'. Her political-educational ideal was similar to Paine's and Godwin's, only she claimed it for women too:

The most perfect education, in my opinion, is such an exercise of the understanding as is best calculated to strengthen the body and form the heart. Or, in other words, to enable the individual to attain such habits of virtue as will render it independent. In fact it is a farce to call any being virtuous whose virtues do not result from the exercise of its own reason.[51]

This stress on independence helps to explain the extraordinary resonance of these radical middle-class writers within the popular movements of their day, composed as they were of the self-educated.[52]

Godwin explored the other side of this argument – the perils of dependence or patronage – with peculiar thoroughness. Some of the most incisive passages of his *Enquiry Concerning Political Justice* dealt with the control of thought, especially under monarchy or aristocracy. All religious or political provision of knowledge was to be opposed. Deliberately or not, established institutions would be used to perpetuate beliefs which inquiry would show to be false, but which would be supported for convenience. National or state education was especially perilous. Even Sunday Schools should be distrusted, for they taught 'a superstitious veneration for the church of England, and to bow to every man in a handsome coat'.[53] The true aim of education was self-activity:

> Refer them to reading, to conversation, to meditation; but teach them neither creeds nor catechisms, either moral or political . . . Whatever each man does for himself, is done well; whatever his neighbours or his country undertake to do for him, is done ill. It is our wisdom to incite men to act for themselves, not to retain them in a state of perpetual pupillage.[54]

Where radicals were concerned with more diffused social oppressions they had to 'stretch' their analysis to accommodate them. These tensions were clearest in Wollstonecraft's *Vindication*. Here she used the concepts of her radical circle while arguing with Paine, Rousseau and other theorists of the day.[55] Many of the ideas she used to understand the position of women were drawn from the critique of aristocracy as an unproductive class. Women were denied 'vigour of faculties', 'stability of character' and rational self-control ('manliness'); they were forced into parasitism and offered 'aristocratic' models for their aspirations. The dependence of women in the better off classes was an 'aristocratic' relation.[56] Middle-class sexual relations were more 'natural', but still unenviable. Women were not treated as rational human beings but as trivial creatures whose humanity was limited by their sex. Again Wollstonecraft stretched the radical categories: 'aristocracy' was extended to cover men's attitudes to women generally. On a different tack, she used the Godwinian critique of innate qualities to minimise the 'natural' disqualifications of women: dependence grew from 'circumstances', mis-education; and the early association of ideas.[57] Resourceful though these moves were, her practical insights were often in advance of her categories, the gaps defied by some energetic leap of speech or some telling analogy:

> Considering the length of time that women have been dependent, it is unsurprising that some of them hunger in chains and fawn like a spaniel.[58]

Her cause pushed her towards a more social and psychological analysis. These oppressions were subtle, dispersed, hard to capture in radical terminology. There was always something else:

> The preposterous distinctions of rank, which render civilisation a curse, by dividing the world beween voluptuous tyrants and cunning envious dependents, corrupt, almost equally, every class of people . . . Still there are some loopholes out of which a man may creep, and dare to think and act for himself: but for a woman it is an herculean task, because she has difficulties peculiar to her sex to overcome, which require almost superhuman powers.[59]

Education was a key solution for all radicals, but how should it be acquired? Godwin's arguments against institutionalising knowledge were clear. They put question marks against the idea of a tradition that starts with him and culminates in 'national education, universal, compulsory and free'. The problem intensifies when the right also lays claim to radicals – Paine as the first voucherite for example.[6']

Paine's views on state and education make either appropriation implausible. He shared Godwin's dislike of provision by state, church or philanthropy. Direct subsidies should be paid to parents to buy education themselves.[61] Ensor too hated philanthropic control: the people would seek knowledge themselves if 'treated decorously', presumably through the market. So far so good for neo-liberals! Paine, however, was no unqualified advocate of commercial society and financed his scheme by the progressive taxation of land; Ensor insisted that the distribution of property must be equal enough for all families to afford their schooling.[62] Mary Wollstonecraft supported 'National Education': a universal (and uncosted!) system of day schools where boys and girls from different classes would be educated together.[63] Perhaps this went along with her gender concerns. For if dispersed social arrangements and inherited psychologies subordinated women, not government nor law, why eschew government intervention so strictly? Reformed, might it not be a source of remedies instead?

THE LIMITS OF RADICALISM 1816-30

The post-war popular movements had a distinctively Painite agenda: faith in enlightenment and open educative campaigning, suspicion of philanthropic offerings, fierce intellectual independence, determination to go it alone.[64] The whole counter-educational impulse derived, as I have argued elsewhere, from practical dilemmas:[65] but the theory of the practice was Jacobin and Republican, stretched to popular circumstances.

Diffusion of the Painite message, or a version of it, was the great panacea. 'I was', wrote William Cobbett with characteristic immodesty, 'the teacher of the national; the great source of political knowledge'.[66] And on another occasion, writing in the *Political Register*, his paper, he stated, 'Just about the time that there needed something to take to school the young men who succeeded those who had been taught by Mr Paine, the Register made its appearance.'[57] The favourite half-humorous self-image of T.J. Wooler, editor of the popular *Black Dwarf*, was as 'public schoolmaster' guarding his reputation for good instruction, perhaps the first to coin the phrase 'the march of mind'.[68] John Wade, in the first edition of another radical newspaper, *The Gorgon*, expressed a similar aim:

> It is in order to promote the great work of enlightening the minds of the people, and preparing them for those changes which must infallibly come, that we have commenced the present publication.[69]

All radical journalists of 1816-30 urged their readers 'to get knowledge', and supplied resources accordingly.

Opposition to educational philanthropy was unremitting: 'all the jugglers of the world', wrote Wooler, 'calculate their gains in proportion to the intellect they can cloud'.[70]

> To teach the people to read, and to give them books to read is very proper. But the motives of such conduct must be understood, in order to give any credit to the parties.[72]

Orthodox schooling was not about 'rights', but was a kind of slavery. Witnessing charity school sermons, watching methodist Sunday School teachers 'shaking the brimstone bag', denouncing educationalists from Hannah More and 'Colquhouns' to Henry Brougham and even Robert Owen, Cobbett had no doubts at all:

> They wish to make cheap the business of *learning to read*, if that business be performed in their schools; and thus inveigle the children of poor men into those schools; and there to teach those children, along with reading, all those notions which are *calculated to make them content in a state of slavery.*[72]

Against mass schooling, radicals espoused a rational independence. Wooler advised his readers to think for themselves, never to suspend judgement in deference to superiors, to take nothing on trust. Some journalists, Richard Carlile particularly, took up Paine's secularism. Natural Science was the new educational paradigm. With his faith in Englightenment and brave struggles for press freedom Carlile seems sometimes to parody independence, individual to a fault.[73]

The weaknesses of the framework showed most in 'solutions'. The main implication was negative: opposition to state education. Resistance was almost unanimous, with proposals as diverse as Samuel Whitbread's, Robert Owen's and Henry Brougham's all opposed. So were more modest moves like charity reform or founding a British Museum.[74] Cobbett argued against state provision up to his death in 1835 (when other arguments were being heard). He justified his opposition to the educational vote of 1833 in terms he had used throughout. The money would pass through government hands. They would choose recipients and tie them to their will. Schoolmasters would be 'fifty-thousand more tax-eaters', 'two servile spies' in every parish. Any attempt to compel attendance would be 'an act of sheer tyranny'.[75]

The main problem with this framework was that it discouraged recognition of the difficulties faced by working people, especially working women, in obtaining an education of any kind. The most important positive recommendation – 'independence' – implied social conditions of its own, tended to individualism, and was beyond reach without communal provision. These limits were understandable at this stage in radical campaigns. With parliament unreformed and 'Old Corruption' still in place, why trust state provision? Nor did a longer-term educational strategy seem necessary, especially when, as Thompson puts it, ' "Multiplication" seemed to work'.[76] Would not radical reform resolve educational dilemmas too? The problem was what to do, educationally, to speed the outcome. All radical journalists supported the educational activities (for children and adults) of groups like Hampden Clubs and Political Protestants, but they had especial faith in their presses.

The achievements of the radical press in this phase are well-established, including the successes against legal control. They created the radical public. But the ways journalists wrote about their projects are also interesting. For Carlile, the printing press was 'like the true Messiah', come to emancipate all mankind: 'This Messiah is immortal and its saving powers must be universal and perpetual.'[77] Wooler was scarcely less optimistic. In the year of Peterloo he wrote an enthusiastic summation of the radical position:

> The public mind has undergone already a complete *revolution*. The ranks of reform have not only been swelled beyond *all expectations*; but the strength of the cause has gained amply by the accession of *so much mind*, and by that eager desire for information so conspicuous throughout the country. Men are no longer willing to be *blind agents* or *mere tools*, in the hands of any party, or any individual.[78]

The excitement was palpable; the framework was familiar, but how far did belief in the permanent, irreversible 'march of mind' weaken the search for realistic solutions? Did it make it harder to voice the everyday difficulties?

THE 1830s AND 1840s

The educational 'old analysis' persisted into the 1830s. New moves – like mechanics institutes, 'useful knowledge', infant schools, and the day schools of the Anglican revival – were slotted into the old rhetoric. A favourite target was 'the knowledge-diffusing gentry' of the Society for the Diffusion of Useful Knowledge. Cobbett often secured the continuities: he popped up at the London Mechanics Institute in 1827, for example, offering five guineas and a warning that patrons would 'put the mechanics on one side and make use of them only as tools'.[79]

Some radicals, however, were now rejecting Cobbett's 'brutalities' – including his conspiratorial model of knowledge and power. *The Poor Man's Guardian*, the leading pre-Chartist radical paper, attacked his theory of 'Heddekashun', incensed by his vote against the government education grant of 1833. He was accused of not caring 'a bean' whether labourers were educated or not. His family-based ideal of education was applicable to 'one man in a thousand'.[80] His views paled besides the Co-operative Congress which spoke 'of the formation of schools' and 'of scientifically educating the whole rising generation'. Education would 'unteach' Cobbett's crudities.[81] Actually Cobbett was in favour of *independent* education, even 'book-learning', but the challenge was a symptom of larger changes.[82]

Radicals had more to teach and 'un-teach' too. The 1830s saw a change in the strategies of leading groups: under the influence of middle-class educational agitations, the balance shifted from coercion to attempts to win consent. The struggle over knowledge intensified. Liberals popularised political economy, Anglicans sought to build a school in every parish, middle-class 'experts' promoted state education, and popular radicals adopted 'moral' or 'labour' economics, and the Owenite 'Science of Society'. Most modern commentators, pre-occupied with the relation to Marxism, have seen political economy as the leading edge here. Even Claeys, who identifies 'the new "social" vocabulary', gives Owenism's *economic* premises the key role.[83] It seems to me however that the broader expansion of politics was crucial: politics (in the sense of power relations to be struggled over) was extended beyond corrupt political institutions or everyday economic exchanges to social relations as a whole.

The first central insight was the educative force of social institutions, including production and distribution, but also the churches, conventional schooling, the family, sexual relations, 'the marriage system', and media directed at adults.[84] But beyond particular institutions lay the still more diffused 'formation of character' by circumstances – an insight owing much to Wollstonecraft and Godwin.[85] As new prominence was given to what today's critical theories call 'ideology' and 'subjectivity', the power-knowledge connection was re-theorised. Knowledge was not merely withheld or deliberately distorted; just to live in this old immoral world was to become irrational, to have your character shaped as competitive, disharmonious and violent, and your faculties undeveloped or distorted. It was also to learn that the blame lay with yourself. So it was not enough to spread reason around like a kind of manure. Conventional beliefs had a (social) logic of their own: they derived from the old immoral world. It was needful to 'unteach' them, tracing their social supports.[86] This teasing out and polemical confrontation of errors became a hallmark of Owenite campaigning. The word 'Rational' was copiously capitalised, but the 'irrational' was also attended to. Error extended to the rich and powerful. They did not use falsehood instrumentally, for their own purpose; they were as limited by the social conditions as anyone else.[87] Even Science was qualified: it could be skewed by 'circumstances' too.[88] More generally, Owenism's rather deterministic social environementalism was a rebuke to the earlier idealism.

A similar development occurred in the critique of orthodox schooling. To charges of 'surveillance' and 'slavery', Owenites added criticism of rote learning, of the neglect of 'affections and motives', of the inculcation of a mercenary spirit by rewards and prizes, of 'petty and vexatious regulations', of the absence of religious freedom and of the passivity imposed on children. Underlying this, as Silver argues, was disagreement about human capacities.[89] For Owenites, as for later socialists and Marxists, humans were deeply social or co-operative beings and had great possibilities for development: the tragedy was that the existing forms of sociality isolated, divided and stunted growth. Against this, conservatives of every hue continued to insist on the *inherent* limits or contradictions of human nature.

The first effect of Owenism was to raise radical ambitions. Political education had always figured in campaigning; the long-term extension of educational rights was an important demand. Education was integral to politics: 'knowledge is power' as the favourite slogan went.[90] Owenites agreed that education was a powerful (though not sufficient) strategy for change. But they loosened the connections between knowledge and citizenship, rationality and the public domain, and therefore the exclusive connection with 'manliness'. There were many social motives for education. This explains the extraordinary Owenite appetite for educational theory and pedagogic schemes.[92] So intense was it that there was a danger that Owenite would come to *mean* schoolteacher! Many individuals trod this path and the movement sometimes threatened to follow.[92] The impact on radicalism generally, however, was to raise the level of counter-education, and push towards more communal and institutionalised solutions, even, as in Lovett's 1840 plan, a whole alternative scheme.[93]

The second effect was to highlight barriers to popular education. This realism derived in part from changes in the relation of households to waged work. But these registered emphatically because Owenite discourse gave them priority. It was the Owenite press and the factory movement and Northern radical media generally that gave most space to this argument. Material difficulties – lack of time, leisure, money, books, freedom from employment – were stressed but also the need for quieter minds.[94] Some media (e.g. *The Pioneer*) brought out the particular difficulties of working-class women. As Owen himself put it to the middle-class educationalist Thomas Wyse:

> We urged the necessity of first satisfying the physical wants of the population, before offering them mental food. We said, that a stomach at ease, and a mind unharrassed by the cares and anxieties attendant upon a daily desperate fight with poverty and pinching want, are indispensable prerequisites to mental and moral instruction.[59]

So the practical dilemma deepened. As ambitions expanded, provided education looked more paltry still. Yet independent action was also vulnerable to underlying shifts and the lack of resources. In this context, national or state education began to be thinkable, inevitable even. As a long-term solution, counter-education had always been frail, so dependent on imminent success. As the movements wavered in the mid 1840s, even communal solutions were harder to sustain.

The process by which state education became 'inevitable' needs investigation. Three episodes seem important: calls for state intervention within Owenism, the history of the Factory Movement, and the debate over the Lovett/Collins schemes of 1837 and 1840. Larger dynamics of gender formation (especially around 'the family wage') and of class alliances (expecially around Liberalism) were crucial. In the later history of radicalism, the programme of the Chartist Convention of 1851 marked the key shift. Section 3 read:

> As every man [sic] has a right to the means of physical life, so he has to the means of mental activity. It is as unjust to withold aliment from the mind as it is to deny food to the body. Education should, therefore, be national, universal, gratuitous and to a certain extent, compulsory.[96]

After 1850, more surely by 1870, education came to be seen as something *provided for* the population by public agencies, to supply a deficiency or need. Power relations were thereby instituted which radicals had resisted. These gained legitimacy from another set of constructions – those around working-class childhood. But the 'natural' dependency of the child was articulated to specific social impulses: the desire to 'civilise' the working class, the drive to service an economy, the hope of promoting 'equality' or 'opportunity'. There have been many political variants of these themes and it is important to distinguish them, but all have shared a framework of assumptions very different from the pre-1850 radicalisms which have concerned us here.[97]

THE NEW RIGHT AND RADICALISM: BORROWED STRENGTHS

Tradition seems to involve a certain smoothing of the past by selective remembering and forgetting. By regarding early 19th-century radicals as forerunners of modern state education we have forgotten how critical they were of provided schooling and how strongly they believed in independence.

Never absent from popular experience, the knowledge that educational provision was a source of oppression or inequality resurfaced again in the 1970s, especially in the academic analysis of education.[98] As in the 1790s, however, broader political conditions were decisive. It was not parties of the left that took the insight on board. Instead, the critique of public education as a system of power and dependency was adopted by the New Right. Much of the vitality of its educational campaigning derives from this appropriation. New Right education is 'radical' only in this limited sense: it re-works some radical motifs. These appropriations in turn disorganise the left. Themes necessary for the renovation of the left are now associated with the other side. With lines of development blocked, resistance takes conservative turns – copying Thatcherite solutions or defending the past.[99]

There *are* parallels between Painite radicalism and the New Right. New Right theory resembles Cobbett's 'old corruption' in several ways.[100] Different writers, from Hayek to members of the Public Choice school, have developed their own class theory of the state, parodying the cruder figures of Marxism. Under 'Socialism' (including both Communist regimes and Western social democracy) new groups, a 'new class' perhaps, dominates the state: bureaucrats, 'liberal' or social-democratic politicians, public or state professionals. Hayek's arch-enemies are professional intellectuals employed by the state. The state is used for the security and self-aggrandisement of such groups; politicians buy votes by dispensing state benefits to client populations in new relations of dependency. Milton and Rose Friedman use a variant of this argument – their 'Iron Triangle' – to explain why President Reagan found it so difficult to restrict state expenditure in his early years.[101]

It is 'the ordinary taxpayer', not the worker, of course, who suffers from state and professional monopolies. Like Marx's peasants, taxpayers are politically passive in comparison with politicians and professionals: the point of New Right populism is to construct a voice for them and to harness it politically.[102] This voice demands what neo-liberalism prescribes: the restriction of public policy and the enhancement of market and of 'choice'. In educational politics, the attack focuses on the local state and the interests clustered around it. Public professionals and workers are in the front line, surprised to find themselves labelled as a kind of aristocracy. They are on the receiving end of strategies from 'cuts' to de-professionalisation.[103]

The comparison is imperfect of course. But it shows the need to re-evaluate public education (and the whole 'welfare' legacy). The shift in radical energies around 1850 was heavily overdetermined, but had long-term costs none the less. The advantages now seized by the radical right are reminders of political values lost in the move to statist or 'welfare' policies. Chief among these was a sense of popular agency traditionally associated with left-wing movements, but now articulated to the right through motifs like 'parental choice' and anti-professionalism.

THE NEW RIGHT: AN ANTI-SOCIAL AND ANTI-EDUCATIONAL MOVEMENT?

As we saw, Jacobinism involved a *combination* of beliefs hard to recognise today because ambiguously related to our political conventions. Tradition-builders on left and right have tended to misrecognise it. Certainly, it was strongly critical of what became a standard 'socialist' remedy (state intervention of various kinds) as furthering dependence and privilege. But it was also opposed to social inequalities of many kinds and, in the most persuasive reading, critical of some social consequences of the market.[104] This is the most obvious difference with the New Right.

Social injustice was central for Owenism of course, but political radicals deployed their Painite analysis expansively to account for new evils. On the New Right by contrast, a 'political' analysis is used restrictively to edit out evils which are diffused and social. Injustice is seen as a product of illegitimate state action or other encroachments on individual freedom by a monopolistic power. The routine coercions of economic relations are not recognised. Gender relations are seen as naturally harmonious. In this way, New Right theorists can deny the loss of freedom involved in unemployment or low pay or unequal forms of marriage, yet invoke draconic state intervention against trade unions or professions because they are monopolies.[105]

Does this mean there is no theory of the social in the New Right?

Not quite – for though this may be true of pure neo-liberalism, it does not match the kind of 'dirty' neo-liberalism which is Thatcherism. Here, via neo-Conservative theory, 'the social' returns with a vengeance.[106] 'Social' however does not refer to social practices or unequal social relations, but rather to principles of cohesion: tradition, authority, religion, 'the family', the Nation, properly evolved institutions. Hayek, in whose 'Whig' philosophy neo-liberal and neo-Conservative elements are combined, would restrict the legitimate use of the word 'social' to just these 'spontaneous' elements:

> It ['social'] was, of course, introduced to describe that order of human relationships which had developed spontaneously, as distinct from the deliberate organisation of the State . . . The truly social in this sense, is of its very nature, anonymous, non-rational and not the result of logical reasoning, but the outcome of a supra-individual process of evolution and selection, to which the individual, admittedly makes his contribution, but the component parts of which cannot be mastered by any one single intelligence.[107]

In this way a whole memory of Social-ism as a way of struggle is erased. It is not Paine nor Godwin that comes to mind but their antagonist Edmund Burke, not the Owenite project of using reason to change the world, but the orthodox 19th-century belief in providential causation (whether in religious, Smithian or social-Darwinist forms). In the same vein, the New Right attempts to re-naturalise a normative conception of 'the family' and the forms of sexuality it signifies. It counters radical politics – this time feminism – by abolishing the social, or by shielding it from legitimate contestation.

The New Right's conservatism may be specified further if we look to arguments about knowledge. Hayek is the obvious choice here, since epistemological issues are so central in his work.[108] His stress on relativity, the flux of time, the subjectivity of knowing, aligns him with contemporary criticisms of 'objectivity' and science, including those of modern radicals and feminists. He is a critic of 18th-century Reason and 19th-century Science. His scepticism is accompanied, however, by an appreciation of *implicit* knowledges, especially those carried in enduring institutions. His comparison between 'spontaneous' and 'constructed' organisations, and the implicit and explicit ways of knowing which correspond to them, underpins his attack on planning and his advocacy of the market – the 'spontaneous' institution *par excellence*. Again the Burkean echoes are resounding: his is a *conservative* scepticism.

The New Right's practical strength is its recognition of 'common sense' or of historically sedimented cultural forms.[109] This epistemological stance has close affinities with their preferred, populist, style of politics. The key political move is to seek out the already-existing popular beliefs that can be articulated to the New Right cause and to present them as good (British) common sense and as 'natural' too. I have in mind Mrs Thatcher's own politics, but also Conservative cultural agencies like *The Sun* and *The Daily Mail*.

How do these New Right orientations compare with those of modern left radicals? For Hayek the limits of knowledge are necessary or natural. It is dangerous to transgress them: 'constructivist rationalism' is a 'fatal conceit' which leads to over-government and to serfdom.[110] For contemporary left radicals, the limits are mainly social and cultural: all knowledge is socially constructed, according to specific rules, codes, frameworks. It is always produced from a particular point of view, constrained by premises and feelings. It is mixed up with social interests and power. It is formed in desire, including the desire for mastery or control. This is true of the Romance of Reason and of Science but of 'common sense', or less articulated knowledge too.[111]

From this point of view, it is as dangerous to endorse common sense as it is to enthrone Reason. The New Right's stance amounts to claiming that social values are non-negotiable, too 'deep', sublime or functionally necessary to be discussed. As one commentator on Hayek puts it 'the rational criticism of social life must come to a stop when it reaches the tacit component of our practices'.[112] Is this also a prayer that popular aspirations may not be stirred too deeply? Against this, some trends within the left argue for making things explicit, for raising consciousness, for talking things through, for analysing representations. This is no guarantee of truth, rather a means to negotiation and change. If oppressions are made conscious, collective action may remedy them.[113] It may well be that explicit knowing is overvalued here, but, of course, the implications are strongly pro-educational. This stance suggests, in fact, a whole constellation of new objects of study, with culture at their centre.

Conservative scepticism, by contrast, closes down intellectual ambitions and polices cultural diversities, just as it tries to take social issues off the political agenda. Some traditions (of the Nation, of the Family, of National Culture, of the academic map of 'real' subjects) are so hallowed, they are no-go areas for reason. It is wise not to be too self-reflexive about academic disciplines – hence the resistance to 'second-order disciplines' and interdisciplinary studies.[114] It is essential to maintain core values. New Right educational discourse – all 'cores', 'foundations' and 'bench-marks' – struggles to hold everything steady in a whirling cultural world.

In all these ways the New Right is a deeply anti-educational movement, setting its own limits to human possibilities. This explains much about the last ten years: the acceptability to Secretaries of State for Education of long-term deterioration in the facilities of public education, the exclusions of the National Curriculum, the impatience with educational professionals and 'intellectuals', the failure to modernise English education, even in capitalist terms, and the paucity of educational policy till the break-through of the mid-1980s. I am sure time-travelling Owenites would soon recognise the old Conservative enemy. But would they claim successors too?

NEW RADICALISMS AND OLD: AFFINITIES?

Classical republicanism in England and America was pre-occupied with political virtue and corruption. The project was to renew political life in the face of the diverse corruptions of court, aristocracy and commerce. The radicalisms of 1790-1830 adopted much of this framework. Paine, for instance, has been presented as a radical republican for whom public virtue under representative institutions was a restraint on commercial self-interest and who aimed for 'formal political equality' and 'relative economic equality'. Radical republicanism opposed those supporters of 'civilisation' who were willing to trade the moral effects of 'opulence' (which they sometimes criticised) for the benefits of unlimited commerce. As Claeys writes of radical republicans and conservative Whigs: 'two great languages of modernity thus clashed in this debate'.[115]

Early 19th-century radicalism pursued the dual aims of popular government and the just or virtuous society. 'Politicals' pushed towards manhood suffrage and popular government. Feminists insisted on women's inclusion in the political public and on the *general* importance of the personal and social. Owenites argued against reposing hope in 'merely political reform'; social arrangements and cultural conditions must be contested too, in ways that were fundamentally educational.

There is no simple continuity between these radicalisms and the socialisms and communisms of our own century: some continuities, perhaps, but also many ruptures. It is dangerous to view the past too narrowly through the lens of Marxism or the official socialist opposition. That is why historical deconstruction and recovery is so important: as a critique of the present not as confirmation of it. This is especially important today as the older socialisms are in crisis.

Can we construct a new tradition linking us with the educational radicals of the past – in all their diversity and difference? Perhaps not, but we might get encouragement from affinities, and take up certain tasks again. I am thinking of the renewed sense of corruption in public life: its many exclusions, the conflation of private interest and public service, the loss of civil liberties, the formality of parliamentary democracy, the erosion of public services. Unsurprisingly, demands for local participation, for fairer elections, for less official secrecy, for more open, less bullying, and more educative media and even for a written constitution, all grow apace. These are recognisable 'Republican' demands.

Social politics have re-emerged too. Contemporary critical theories favour dispersed models of power in efforts to grasp the multiplications. Feminists and the gay and lesbian movements have extended politics again, showing how power enters into sex, pleasure, intimacy and desire as well as into politics and work. Black politics and anti-racist agitations render problematic the political frame itself – the nation state and its ideologies of culture and race and warn against 'European' consolidations. Green politics highlight the ecological disasters which are undercutting the stories of 'Man's mastery of Nature' on left and right, and must end the commitment to perpetually increasing consumption. These movements have re-politicised areas which conventional left politics could not reach; and which the New Right protects in order to survive.

A common right-wing response has been to attack the politicisation of everything as 'totalitarian'.[116] This would make sense if, as in New Right theory, politics meant the state and the state meant coercion. But the right mistakes the post-war movements for its socialist familiars. The new movements are wary of deepening social regulation, though may not abjure state power. In this emergent model, politics itself is recast. Power is not repressive or coercive merely, but productive, positive, educative.[117] The range of remedies is extended. Collective self-organisation (often in small groups of networks) and alternative ways of living may be as effectual as law. Where law is invoked, negotiative or civil solutions may be sought. Many new features derive from an awareness that oppressions of all kinds, including those of class, have a deeply subjective side – problems of social misrecognition or misrepresentation, problems of identities narrowed or imposed. Culture is seen as a leading edge of change.

The New Right is an attack on socialism; it is also a defence against new 'Republicanisms' and 'Owenisms'. This second dialectic has many sites: the right's own tradition-building; its politics of identity around race, culture and nation; the revival of conservative moral movements. I focus here on the policing of politics itself. The New Right responds to the terror of political boundary-loss rather as it reacts to world-wide migrations – it tries to close borders. Key strategies are, first, to turn politics into economics; and, second, to use state power in pre-emptive, authoritarian ways.

Both tendencies are present in the 1988 Act. Parental choice evokes a fundamentally economic conception of participation. Parents participate as individuals, determining outcomes only through the unintended aggregate results of their decisions. They choose for 'their' children, with no broader public interest in view. Through these choices, according to the theory, a spontaneous wisdom operates, superior to the exposure and negotiation of differences. A minority also 'manage', another 'economic' function, within the terms of market forces.

This neo-liberal side of the Act erodes the public sphere, but is accompanied by centralisation. The apparent contradiction should not surprise unless the market is thought to be neutral, adjustive merely. As a system of social relations involving unequal powers, it requires supports, coercive and cultural. This is acknowledged in neo-liberal theory, *'laissez faire'* only on its anarchistic fringe. As many have noted, Thatcherism equalled free market *and* the strong state.[118] In education this meant parental choice *and* the national curriculum. The common element here is the limitation of educational politics, in the sense of public debate about future educational (which are also social) directions. The old system of educational administration ('part-nership', 'consultative bodies', negotiating rights – remember?) was inadequate but its limits were the work of history not nature, and were improvable.

It is important to reclaim the virtues of an open and active public life. Education ought to be a public service not a private speculation. In the meantime, even the new system provides opportunities to participate, especially in colleges and schools. At this point in the argument, however, we ought to be alerted again by the 'manly' language and listen to the social radical in us, who insists we attend to her agenda. Dispersed forms of power will determine who can be represented in the public spaces and who can benefit from provision. Formally democratic routines and 'equal' eductional access are not enough. We must shape new public forms in accord with our knowledge of the social; and there must also be ways of working, more directly, on the everyday inequalities themselves. That is why public education, which institutionalises particular social orientations to knowledge, should not be expanded without qualitative changes in its structures and practices. The social relations of education – its professionalisms, knowledges, institutional separations, its relations to wider cultural formations – have to be tackled too.

NOTES

1. B. Simon (ed), *The Radical Tradition in Education in Britain*, Lawrence and Wishart, London 1972. All quotations in this paragraph are from the Introduction, pp 9-20.
2. B. Simon, *Studies in the History of Education 1780-1870*, Lawrence and Wishart, London 1960. Retitled *The Two Nations and Educational Structure* in 1974 (cited hereafter as *Two Nations*); *Education and the Labour Movement, 1870-1920*, Lawrence and Wishart, London 1975.
3. *Two Nations*, p 367.
4. 'Samuel Taylor Coleridge: The Education of the Intellect', in B. Simon, *Does Education Matter?* Lawrence and Wishart, London 1985.
5. For example 'Education in Theory, Schooling in Practice: The Experience of the Last Hundred Years', *ibid*, especially p 46.
6. 'Can Education Change Society?', *ibid*.
7. Bill Schwarz, 'The Communist Party Historians' Group 1946-56' in R. Johnson, G. McLennan, B. Schwarz and D. Sutton (eds), *Making Histories: Studies in History-Writing and Politics*, Hutchinson, London 1982, p 71.
8. E.P. Thompson, *The Making of the English Working Class*, Gollancz, London 1963.
9. J.R.B. Johnson, 'The Education Department 1839-1864', Unpublished PhD Thesis, University of Cambridge 1968.
10. On 'selective tradition' see R. Williams, *The Long Revolution*, Penguin, Harmondsworth 1963, pp 66-70; on the invention of traditions see E. Hobsbawm and T. Ranger (eds), *The Invention of Tradition*, Cambridge University Press, 1983, esp pp 1-14.
11. F.A. Hayek (ed), *Capitalism and the Historians*, Routledge and Kegan Paul, London 1954.
12. For introductions see J. Gray, *Hayek on Liberty*, Blackwell, Oxford 2nd Edn., 1984; Eamon Butler, *Hayek: His Contribution to the Political and Economic Thought of His Time*, Temple Smith, London 1983.

13. Hayek (ed), *op cit*, p 3.
14. For a review of these see F.K. Donnelly, 'Ideology and Early English Working-Class History: E.P. Thompson and his Critics', *Social History*, 1 (2), 1976, pp 219-38.
15. For an analysis of *The Making* as melodrama see Renato Rosaldo, 'Celebrating Thompson's Heroes: Social Analysis in History and Anthropology' in H. Kaye and K. McClelland (eds), *E.P. Thompson: Critical Perspectives*, Polity Press, Cambridge 1990. For narrative and genre in history-writing see H. White, *MetaHistory*, The John Hopkins University Press, Baltimore 1973.
16. Patricia Hollis, *The Pauper Press: A Study in Working-Class Radicalism of the 1830s*, Oxford University Press, 1970.
17. Especially, *ibid*, pp 295-306.
18. G. Stedman Jones, 'Re-Thinking Chartism' in *Languages of Class: Studies in Working Class History, 1832-1982*, Cambridge University Press, 1983. For a useful conceptual critique see J.W. Scott, 'On Language, Gender and Working-Class History', in *Gender and The Politics of History*, Columbia University Press, New York 1988, pp 53-67.
19. See especially, Gregory Claeys, *Thomas Paine: Social and Political Thought*, Unwin Hyman, Boston, 1989; Gregory Claeys, *Citizens and Saints: Politics and Anti-Politics in Early British Socialism*, Cambridge University Press, 1989.
20. See especially J.F.C. Harrison, *Robert Owen and the Owenites in Britain and America*, Routledge and Kegan Paul, London 1969.
21. For what follows see Claeys, *Citizens and Saints, op cit, passim*.
22. *Ibid*, pp 285-326.
23. For a useful summary of issues and assessments see K. McClelland, 'Introduction' in Kaye and McClelland (eds), *op cit*. For different versions of the argument see E.J. Hobsbawm, 'The Making of the Working Class', in *Worlds of Labour*, Weidenfeld and Nicholson, London 1984; G. Stedman Jones, 'Class Struggle and the Industrial Revolution' in Stedman Jones, *op cit*; G. Stedman Jones, 'Re-Thinking Chartism', *ibid*, pp 90-178; C. Calhoun, *The Question of Class Struggle: Social Foundations of Popular Radicalism in the Industrial Revolution*, Blackwell, Oxford 1982; J.W. Scott, 'Women in the Making of the English Working Class', in Scott, *op cit*; R. Johnson, ' "Really Useful Knowledge": Radical Education and Working-Class Culture 1790-1848', in J. Clarke, C. Critcher and R. Johnson (eds), *Working-Class Culture: Studies in History and Theory*, Hutchinson, London 1979. For the notion of a 'working-class public', which I adapt below see the useful article by G. Eley, 'Edward Thompson, Social History and Political Culture: The Making of a Working-Class Public, 1780-1850' in Kaye and McClelland (eds), *op cit*.
24. See especially Dorothy Thompson, 'Women and Nineteenth-Century Radical Politics: A Lost Dimension', in J. Mitchell and A. Oakley (eds), *The Rights and Wrongs of Women*, Penguin, Harmondsworth 1976; D.

Thompson, *The Chartists*, Wildwood House, Aldershot, 1984; Scott, *op cit*; C. Hall, 'The Tale of Samuel and Jemima: Gender and Working-Class Culture in Nineteenth-Century England', in Kaye and McClelland (eds), *op cit*; S. Alexander, 'Women, Class and Sexual Differences in the 1830s and 1840s: Some Reflections on the Writing of Feminist History', *History Workshop Journal*, No 17, Spring 1984. For an exemplary analysis of this kind see Scott, *op cit.*

26. B. Taylor, *Eve and The New Jerusalem*, Virago, London 1984.
27. L. Davidoff and C. Hall, *Family Fortunes: Men and Women of the English Middle Class 1780-1850*, Hutchinson, London 1987.
28. For valuable openings up of these questions see J. Purvis, 'The Double Burden of Class and Gender in the Schooling of Working Class Girls in Nineteenth-Century England 1800-1870; in L. Barton and S. Walker (eds), *Schools, Teachers and Teaching*, Falmer, Lewes 1981; J. Purvis, 'Working-Class Women and Adult Education in Nineteenth-Century Britain', *History of Education*, 9 (3); J. Purvis, 'Women and Teaching in the Nineteenth Century' in R. Dale, G. Esland, R. Ferguson and M. Mac-Donald (eds), *Education and the State*, vol II, Falmer, Lewes. See also her essay in this collection, pp 249-66.
29. Scott has made a similar criticism of Stedman Jones which I have re-worked here.
30. For an example of the challenge on nation, race and ethnicity see P. Gilroy, *There Ain't No Black in the Union Jack*, Hutchinson, London 1986.
31. C. Calhoun, *op cit*, p 239.
32. Taylor, *op cit*, p 287.
33. Claeys, *op cit*, pp 325-6.
34. I focus here on four writers – George Ensor, William Godwin, Thomas Paine and Mary Wollstonecraft – because we find in their works elaborated versions of frameworks discernable also in popular radicalism. All four were well-cited in the post-war radical media.
35, Thomas Paine, *Rights of Man*, ed. Henry Collins, Penguin, Harmondsworth 1969, especially pp 181-206 (cited hereinafter as *Rights*).
36. My account of Godwin is based on D. Fleisher, *William Godwin: A Study in Liberalism*, Allen and Unwin, London 1951; M. Philp, *Godwin's Political Justice*, Duckworth, London 1986; H. Silver, *The Concept of Popular Education: A Study of Ideas and Social Movements in the Early Nineteenth Century*, MacGibbon and Kee, London 1965, pp 53-58, 84-95, 97-107; quotations from the text of *Political Justice* are from William Godwin, *Enquiry Concerning Political Justice*, ed. K. Codell Carter, Oxford University Press, 1971, (cited hereafter as *Enquiry*).
37. Godwin, *Enquiry*, p 28.
38. Paine, *Rights*, pp 194-206.
39. *Ibid*, p 163.
40. *Ibid*, p 206.

41. T.Paine,*TheAgeofReason*,ed.MoncureDanielConway,London,1896, p 191.
42. e.g. Paine, *Rights*, pp 140-41 and 162.
43. M. Wollstonecraft, *Vindiction of the Rights of Women*, Penguin, London 1975, pp 81-92 (hereinafter, *Vindication*).
44. G. Ensor, *On National Education*, Longman, London 1811, pp 14-23.
45. Paine, *Rights*, pp 140-41.
46. Paine, *Age of Reason*, pp 22, 24 and 63.
47. Quoted in Claeys, *Paine*, p 85.
48. G. Ensor, *The Independent Man*, J. Johnson, London 1806.
49. Paine, *Rights*, p 162.
50. Wollstonecraft, *Vindication*, p 80.
51. *Ibid*, p 103.
52. E. Thompson, *op cit*, especially p 711.
53. Godwin, *Enquiry*, p 236.
54. *Ibid*, p 237.
55. For her circle generally see H.N. Brailsford, *Shelley, Godwin and Their Circle*, Oxford University Press, Oxford 1913.
56. Wollstonecraft, *Vindication*, for example, pp 81-84, 101 and 144.
57. *Ibid*, pp 219-26.
58. *Ibid*, p 179.
59. *Ibid*, p 256-7.
60. See E.G. West, *Education and the Industrial Revolution*, Batsford, London 1975, pp 113-20 and compare Silver, *op cit* pp 91 and 104.
61. Paine, *Rights*, p 263 and 266-7.
62. Ensor, *National Education*, p 152.
63. Wollstonecraft, *Vindication*, pp 273-99.
64. Thompson, *op cit*, especially pp 710-20, 727-46.
65. R. Johnson, 1979, *op cit*, pp 76-9.
66. *Political Register*, 10 April 1830.
67. *Political Register*, 21 Dec. 1822.
68. *Black Dwarf*, 4 February 1818; 20 January 1819; 9 September 1818.
69. *Gorgon*, 23 May 1818.
70. *Black Dwarf*, 16 September 1818.
71. *Black Dwarf*, 20 May 1818.
72. Quoted in *Political Register*, 7 December 1833.
73. Simon, 1972, *op cit*, pp 91-138; and see the complex judgements in Thompson, *op cit*, pp 720, 723, 724-6, 762-68.
74. On charities see *Gorgon*, 30 May 1818 and 19 September 1818; on British Museum see *Black Dwarf*, 6 May 1818.
75. *Political Register*, 7 December 1833.
76. Thompson, *op cit*, p 77.
77. Simon, 1972, *op cit*, p 109 and J.H. Wiener, *The War of the Unstamped*, Cornell University Press, Ithaca (NY), pp 123-4.

78. *Black Dwarf*, 6 April 1819.

79. *Place Papers*, B.M.Ad. MSS 27824, vol 1, fols 16 and 23. Cuttings from *Mechanics Magazine*, 15 November 1823 and [*Morning Chronicle?*], 12 November 1823. For 'knowledge-diffusing gentry', see *Poor Man's Guardian*, 14 April 1832.

80. *Poor Man's Guardian*, 14 September 1833.

81. *Ibid*, 19 and 26 October 1833.

82. For general assessments of Cobbett on education see Johnson, 1979, *op cit*, pp 88-91; Hall, 1990, *op cit*, pp 92-94; Thompson, *op cit*, pp 746-62.

83. Claeys, *Citizens and Saints, op cit*, especially pp 142-66.

84. For Owenite theory in general see Claeys, *Citizens and Saints, op cit*; Taylor, *op cit*; Harrison, *op cit*; Silver *op cit*.

85. Silver, *op cit*, pp 84-5 and 90-91.

86. See, for example, the column written by 'The Un-Teacher' in *The Poor Man's Guardian* for example 25 January 1834). The author was probably William Lovett, a political radical deeply influenced by Owenism.

87. For example, on the subject of Lords Grey and Brougham and the Duke of Wellington, *The Crisis*, 19 May 1832.

88. See especially the critique of the over-development of natural science at the expense of social and moral understandings in William Thompson, *Inquiry into the Principles of the Distribution of Wealth most conducive to Human Happiness*, Longmans, London 1824 (reprinted Augustus Kelly, New York 1963) and published in part in Simon, 1972, *op cit*, pp 177-224.

89. Silver, *op cit*, pp 236-7.

90. See, for example, the masthead of *The Poor Man's Guardian* (where knowledge is represented by the printing press).

91. For which see Silver, *op cit, passim*.

92. For a fuller account of this tendency see Johnson, 1979 *op cit*, pp 98-100.

93. William Lovett and Henry collins, *Chartism: A New Organisation of the People*, 2nd edn., 1841, printed in part in Simon, 1972, *op cit*, pp 229-86.

94. For details see Johnson, 1972 *op cit*, pp 95-97.

95. *The New Moral World*, 16 November 1839, p 1.

96. Quoted in Ernest Jones, *Notes to the People*, No 7, p 131.

97. For a more elaborate version of this argument see CCCS, *Unpopular Education*, Hutchinson, London 1981, especially pp 34-40.

98. There were many versions of this argument in the 1970s and early 1980s, historical, sociological and 'ethnographic'. For a good review and assessment see G. Whitty, *Sociology and School Knowledge: Curriculum Theory, Research and Politics*, Methuen, London 1985, especially pp 7-55 and 76-98.

99. These and other arguments in the final section are developed more fully in Birmingham Cultural Studies, Education Group II, *Education Limited: Schooling, Training and the New Right since 1979*, Unwin Hyman, London 1990.

100. For general accounts of New Right theory see R. Levitas (ed), *The*

Ideology of the New Right, Polity, Cambridge 1986; S. Hall and M. Jacques (eds), *The Politics of Thatcherism*, Lawrence and Wishart, London 1983; D.G. Green, *The New Right: the Counter-Revolution in Political, Economic and Social Thought*, Wheatsheaf, Brighton 1987; N. Bosanquet, After the New Right, Heinemann, London 1983. In what follows I have drawn particularly on the works of F.A. Hayek and R. Scruton as cited below.

101. M. and R. Friedman, *The Tyranny of the Status Quo*, Penguin, Harmondsworth, 1985.

102. On New Right populism see especially S. Hall, 'Popular-Democratic versus Authoritarian Populism', in *The Hard Road to Renewal*, Verso, London 1988, pp 123-60.

103. For a fuller discussion of these strategies as they effect public professionals, especially in eduction see R. Johnson, 'My New Right Education', in Birmingham Cultural Studies, 1990, *op cit*.

104. See Claeys, *Thomas Paine, op cit*, especially pp 96-101.

105. For example, F.A. Hayek, *The Constitution of Liberty*, Routledge and Kegan Paul, London 1969, especially Ch 18. For a fuller version of this argument see Johnson, 1990, *op cit*.

106. For example, in the writings of Roger Scruton. See R. Scruton, *The Meaning of Conservatism*, MacMillan, London 1980 and M. David and G. Seidel's discussions of 'the family' and 'the Nation' respectively in Levitas, *op cit*.

107. F.A. Hayek, 'What is "Social"? What Does it Mean?' in *Studies in Philosophy, Politics and Economics*, Routledge and Kegan Paul, London 1967, p 241.

108. This seems the case from the beginning. Thus the famous anti-Communist manifesto – F.A. Hayek, *The Road to Serfdom*, Ark/Routledge and Kegan Paul, London [1944] 1986 – was published at about the same time as the essays collected in F.A. Hayek, *The Counter-Revolution of Science: Studies on the Abuse of Reason*, The Free Press, Glencoe, Illinois, [1942-44] 1952, which contains many of Hayek's characteristic epistemological arguments.

109. This is to redescribe New Right orientations in Gramscian terms. For an interesting New Right 'take' on Gramsci see R. Scruton, *Thinkers of the New Left*, Longmans, Harlow 1985, pp 76-86.

110. For the most recent statement of the theme see F.A. Hayek, *The Fatal Conceit: The Errors of Socialism*, ed. W.W. Bartley III, Routledge and Kegan Paul, London 1988.

111. This paragraph is an enormously compressed summary of key developments in social and cultural theory in the last 20 years! References defeat me!

112. J. Gray, 'Hayek', in R. Scruton (ed.), *Conservative Thinkers*, Claridge Press, London pp 256-7.

113. I am thinking of much feminist practice here, but also of the left and

feminist take-up of psychoanalysis and other 'technologies of the self' and Gramsci's insistence on making an inventory of our historical – Cultural making.

114. R. Scruton, 1980, *op cit*, pp 149-51.
115. Claeys, *Thomas Paine*, *op cit*, pp 155-56.
116. For example, Scruton (ed), *op cit*, editor's introduction, p 12.
117. This view of power is common ground between the new social movements and theorists as diverse as Gramsci and Michel Foucault. For a brave attempt at synthesis, decidedly 'republican' in style but inadequate on the 'social' side I feel, see E. Laclau and C. Mouffe, *Hegemony and Socialist Strategy: Towards a Radical Democratic Politics*, Verso, London 1985.
118. For example, A. Gamble, *The Free Economy and the Strong State: The Politics of Thatcherism*, Macmillan, London 1988.

BIBLIOGRAPHY

BRIAN SIMON

This bibliography covers books (written and edited), articles, contributions (or chapters) to books, pamphlets and other publications. It does not include reviews, and translations of books or articles.

BOOKS

A Student's View of the Universities (1943)
Intelligence Testing and the Comprehensive School (1953)
The Common Secondary School (1954)
Education in the New Poland (1954)
Psychology in the Soviet Union (1957) (editor)
New Trends in English Education (1957) (editor)
Educational Psychology in the USSR (1963) (editor, with Joan Simon)
The Challenge of Marxism (1963) (editor)
Non-Streaming in the Junior School (1964) (editor)
Education in Leicestershire, 1540-1940 (1968) (editor)
Half-way There: Report on the British Comprehensive School Reform (1970, 2nd edn 1972) (with Caroline Benn)
Intelligence, Psychology and Education: A Marxist Critique (1971, 2nd edn 1978)
The Radical Tradition in Education in Britain (1972) (editor)
The Evolution of the Comprehensive School, 1926-1972 (1969, 2nd edn 1973) (with David Rubinstein)
The Victorian Public School (1975) (editor, with Ian Bradley)
Inside the Primary Classroom (1980) (with Maurice Galton and Paul Croll)
Progress and Performance in the Primary Classroom (1980) (editor, with Maurice Galton)
Education in the Sixties (1980) (editor, with Edward Fearn)
Research and Practice in the Primary Classroom (1981) (editor, with John Willcocks)
Education in the Eighties (1981) (editor, with William Taylor)
Does Education Matter? (1985, 2nd edn 1988)
The Rise of the Modern Educational System: Social Change and Cultural

Reproduction, 1870-1920 (1987) (editor, with Detlef Müller and Fritz Ringer)

Bending the Rules: The Baker 'Reform' of Education (1988, 3rd revised edn 1988)

The Search for Enlightenment: The Working Class and Adult Education in the Twentieth Century (1990) (editor)

Studies in the History of Education

Studies in the History of Education, 1780-1870 (1960) – retitled (1974) *The Two Nations and the Educational Structure, 1780–1870*

Education and the Labour Movement, 1870–1920 (1965)

The Politics of Educational Reform, 1920-1940 (1974)

Education and the Social Order, 1940-1990 (1991)

ARTICLES

Title	Source	Date
'The Comprehensive School'	*Communist Review*	April 1949
'The Theory and Practice of Intelligence Testing'	*Communist Review*	October 1949
'Science and Pseudo-Science in Psychology'	*The Educational Bulletin* (Communist Party)	October 1949
'The Defence of Culture'	*Communist Review*	December 1949
'Activity Methods'	*The Educational Bulletin*	March/April 1951
'Educational Psychology in the USSR'	*Society for Cultural Relations with the USSR* (mimeograph)	1952
'Social Studies'	*The Educational Bulletin*	January 1952
'Educational Standards in Poland'	*The Educational Bulletin*	October 1952
'The British Universities'	*Arena*	1952
'Higher Education in Poland'	*Universities Quarterly*, Vol 7, No 2	1953
'Teacher Training in Poland'	*The Educational Bulletin*, No 30	1953
'Polytechnical Education in Soviet Schools, I'	*Vocational Aspect*, Vol VI, No 12	Spring 1954
'Leicestershire Schools 1625-40'	*British Journal of Educational Studies*, Vol 3, No 1	1954
'Spotlight on the GCE Plot'	*Education Today*	June 1954
'Are Children Equal?'	*Education Today*	July 1954
'Some Aspects of Research in Educational Psychology in the USSR'	*SCR Education Bulletin*	October 1955

'Polytechnical Education in Soviet Schools, II'	*Vocational Aspect*	Autumn 1955
'Psychology and Education'	*Marxist Quarterly*, Vol 3, No 4	1956
'Labour's Education Policy'	*Labour Monthly*	September 1958
'Has Crowther Wasted his Time?'(with Robin Pedley)	*Forum*, Vol 2, No 3	1960
'Selection and the Comprehensive School'	*Education Today and Tomorrow*	September/ October 1960
'An Open Letter to the Robbins Committee' (with Robin Pedley)	*Forum*, Vol 4, No 1	Autumn 1961
'Soviet Psychology and the West'	*Marxism Today*, Vol 6, No 3	March 1962
'A Visit to Soviet Psychologists' Psychologists'	*Anglo-Soviet Journal*, Vol 23, No 1	1962
'Soviet Psychology and the Learner'	*Bulletin of the British Psychological Society*, No 49	October 1962
'Education and Psychology'	*Marxism Today*, Vol 6, No 12	December 1962
'The Challenge of Marxism'	*Marxism Today*, Vol 8, No 1	January 1964
'The Future of Higher Education'	*Marxism Today*, Vol 9, No 4	April 1965
'Karl Marx and Education'	*Marxism Today*, Vol 9, No 8	August 1965
'Social Selection and the Doncaster Plan'	*Forum*, Vol 8, No 2	1966
'Anatomy of the Non-Streamed Classroom'	*Forum*, Vol 8, No 3	1966
'The Neighbourhood School'	*Comprehensive Education*, (Bulletin of the Comprehensive Schools Committee), No 4	Autumn 1966
'Non-streaming in Comprehensive Schools'	*Forum*, Vol 9, No 2	1967
'Content and Method in the Primary School'	*Forum*, Vol 9, No 3	1967
'Questions of Ideology and Culture'	*Marxism Today*, Vol 12, No 5	May 1968
'Marxism and Education'	*Marxism Today*, Vol 12, No 9	September 1968
'It Takes a War to Get Things Going'	*Sunday Times* Supplement	4 January 1970
'Egalitarianism Versus Education'	*Comprehensive Education*, No 14	Spring 1970
'Education: Owen, Mill, Arnold, and the Woodard Schools'	*Victorian Studies*, Vol XIII, No 4	June 1970
'Intelligence, Race, Class and Education'	*Marxism Today*, Vol 14, No 11	November 1970
'Streaming and the Comprehensive School'	*Secondary Education*, Vol 1, No 1	Autumn 1970

'The Labour Party and Education'	*Labour History Journal*	1973
'Losses of a Generation'	*Times Educational Supplement*	15 November 1974
'The James Report: A Rejoinder'	*British Journal of Teacher Education*, Vol 1, No 2	1 April 1975
'Theoretical Aspects of the PGCE course'	*British Journal of Teacher Education*, Vol 2, No 1	January 1976
'Contemporary Problems in Educational Theory'	*Marxism Today*, Vol 20, No 6	June 1976
'Observational Studies in the Primary School'	*Education 3-13*, Vol 4, No 2	October 1976
'Education and Social Change: A Marxist Perspective'	*Marxism Today*, Vol 21, No 2	February 1977
'The 1902 Education Act – A Wrong Turning'	*History of Education Society Bulletin*, No 19	Spring 1977
'Marx and the Crisis in Education' (The Marx Memorial Lecture, 1977)	*Marxism Today*, Vol 21, No 7	July 1977
'Educational Research and the Primary School'	*Forum*, Vol 19, No 3	Summer 1977
'Why Unstreaming?'	*Forum*, Vol 20, No 2	Summer 1978
'Problems in Contemporary Educational Theory: A Marxist Approach'	*Journal of Philosophy of Education*, Vol 12	1978
'Educational Research and Ideology: The Case of Psychometry'	*Nordisk Förening För Pedagogisk Forsknung – Information*, 5-78	1978
'Educational Research: Which Way?' (British Educational Research Association, Presidential Address, 1977)	*Research Intelligence*, Vol 4, No 1	1978
'HMI's and Mixed Ability'	*Forum*, Vol 21, No 2	1979
'Education and the Right Offensive'	*Marxism Today*, Vol 24, No 2	1980
'Where the Wild Men Aren't'	*Times Educational Supplement*	4 April 1980
'Inside the Primary Classroom'	*Forum*, Vol 22, No 3	1980
'Research and Educational Policy'	*Scottish Educational Review*, Vol 12, No 1	May 1980
'Thirty Years of Education in Leicestershire'	*Convocation Review* (University of Leicester)	1980
'Educational Change in the Twentieth Century'	*Leuvens Bulletin*, LAPP (University of Leuven, Belgium)	October 1980
'Comprehensive Reorganisation and the Primary School'	*Forum*, Vol 24, No 2	Spring 1982
'Primary Schools' (Digest)	*Education*	5 March 1982
'Society, Education and the State'	*British Journal of Sociology of Education*, Vol 3, No 2	June 1982

'The History of Education in the 1980s'	*British Journal of Educational Studies,* Vol XXX, No 1	February 1982
'Popular, Local and Democratic – Karl Marx's Formula' (Centenary Article)	*Education*	11 March 1983
Obituary: Lawrence Stenhouse	*Forum,* Vol 25, No 2	Spring 1983
'The Study of Education as a University Subject in Britain'	*Studies in Higher Education,* Vol 8, No 1	1983
'Twentieth-Century Education'	*History of Education Quarterly* (USA)	Spring 1983
'The Rise of Science and the Science of Education'	*International Standing Conference for the History of Education*	1983
'Secondary Education for All in the 1980s: The Challenge to the Comprehensive School' (The Raymond King Memorial Lecture)	*The New Era,* Vol 65, No 1	1984
'Brian Jackson: An Appreciation'	*Forum,* Vol 26, No 5	Summer 1984
'To Whom Do Schools Belong?'	*Forum,* Vol 27, No 1	Autumn 1984
'Breaking School Rules: An Analysis of the Tory Government's Educational Policy'	*Marxism Today,* Vol 28, No 9	September 1984
'Bringing Teachers to Heel'	*Education Today and Tomorrow,* Vol 37, No 1	Spring 1985
'Back to the Tripartite System'	*Education Today and Tomorrow,* Vol 37, No 2	1985
'Imposing Differentiation in Schools'	*Education Today and Tomorrow,* Vol 37, No 3	1985
'Comprehensive Ideals'	*Comprehensive Education,* No 50 (20th Anniversary)	October 1985
'The Tory Government and Education 1951-60: Background to Breakout'	*History of Education,* Vol 14, No 4	1985
'The 1944 Act: A Conservative Measure?'	*History of Education,* Vol 15, No 1	1986
'The Battle of the Blackboard'	*Marxism Today,* Vol 31, No 6	June 1986
'*L'Educacio i la classe treballadera; aspectes historics i metodologics*'	*Full Informativ,* No 4 (Catalonian History of Education Society)	1986
'The State of the Middle Temple – 100 Years Ago'	*Comparative Law Review,* Vol XIX, No 4 (Institute of Comparative Law, Chuo University, Tokyo)	1986
'The Legacy of Keith Joseph' (with Nanette Whitbread)	*Forum,* Vol 29, No 1	1986
'Lessons in Elitism'	*Marxism Today,* Vol 31, No 9	September 1987

'The Student Movement in England and Wales During the 1930s'	*History of Education*, Vol 18, No 3	September 1987
'Schooling Society: The Care of an Elite for the Masses in the Nineteenth and Twentieth Centuries'	*Pedagogisch Tijdschrift 12th Jahrgang* (Belgium)	July/Aug 1987
'The 1944 Education Act'	*Financial Times* (Centenary Number)	12 Feb 1988
'Has Mr Baker Lost his Constituency?'	*Education*	15 April 1988
Obituary: Robin Pedley	*The Independent*	23 Nov 1988
Obituary: Robin Pedley	*Forum*, Vol 31, No 2	Spring 1989
'Baker's Dangers'	*Seven Days*	2 April 1988
'The Fight Against the Bill'	*Education Today and Tomorrow*, Vol 40, No 2	Summer 1988
'Maintaining Progress Towards a Fully Comprehensive System'	*Comprehensive Education*, Vol 11, No 1	1989
'The Education Act, 1988: Origins and Implementation'	*The Welsh Journal of Education*, Vol 1, No 1	1989
'The Building of the Educational State'	*Journal of Historical Sociology*, Vol 2, No 1	March 1989
'Thatcher's Third Tier, or Bribery and Corruption'	*Forum*, Vol 32, No 3	1990
'10/65 and All That' (25th Anniversary of Circular 10/65)	*Times Educational Supplement*	13 July 1990
Obituary: Harry Rée	*The Independent*	21 May 1991
'*Forum*, the Past and the Future'	*Forum*, Vol 34, No 1 (100th edn)	1991

CONTRIBUTIONS TO BOOKS

Title of Chapter	Title of Book	Date
'The Present Predicament'	*The Challenge of Marxism*, Brian Simon (ed.)	London 1963
'The History of Education'	*The Study of Education*, J.W. Tibble (ed.)	London 1966
'Private Schools in Leicester and the County, 1780-1840' (with Zena Crook)	*Education in Leicestershire*, *1540-1940*, Brian Simon (ed.)	Leicester 1968
'Local Grammar Schools, 1780-1880'	*Education in Leicestershire*, *1540-1940*, Brian Simon (ed.)	Leicester 1968

'Streaming and Unstreaming in the Secondary School' — *Education for Democracy*, (Penguin Education Special), David Rubinstein and Colin Stoneman (eds) — Harmondsworth 1970

'Classification and Streaming: A Study of Grouping in English Schools, 1860-1960' — *History and Education*, Paul Nash (ed.) — New York 1970

'Education in Leicestershire' — *Leicester and its Regions*, Norman Pye (ed.) — British Association 1972

'Research in the History of Education' — *Research Perspectives in Education*, William Taylor (ed.) — London 1973

'*Intelligens, race, klasse og uddannelse*' — *Introduktion til Marxistik Psykologi*, Arne Sjolund (erd) — Gyldendalske Boghandel (Denmark) 1974

'Comprehensive Education: Internal Structure and Organisation' — *Equalities and Inequalities in Education*, P.R. Cox, H.B. Miles and J. Peel (eds) — London 1975

'Countesthorpe in the Context of Comprehensive Development' — *The Countesthorpe Experience*: *The First Five Years*, John Watts (ed.) — London 1977

'Back to the Basics?' — *Education and Equality* — Harmondsworth 1979

'Education: The New Perspective' — *The Study of Education: Inaugural Lectures, Vol II The Last Decade*, Peter Gordon (ed.) — London 1980

'The Primary School Revolution: Myth or Reality?' — *Education in the Sixties*, Brian Simon and Edward Fearns (eds) — History of Education Society 1980

'Problems in Contemporary Educational Theory' — *Standards, Schooling and Education*, Alex Finch and Peter Scrimshaw (eds), (Open University Reader) — London 1980

'Why No Pedagogy in England?' — *Education in the Eighties*, *The Central Issue*, Brian Simon and William Taylor (eds) — London 1981

'ORACLE: Its Implications for Teacher Training' (with Maurice Galton) — *Research and Practice in Primary Classroom*, Brian Simon and John Willcocks — London 1981

'Education in Theory, Schooling in Practice' (Fink Memorial Lecture, 1981) — *Melbourne Studies in Education*, Stephen Murray-Smith (ed.) — Melbourne 1983

'History of Education' — *Educational Theory and its Foundation Disciplines*, Paul H. Hirst (ed.) — London 1983

'Can Education Change Society?'	*An Imperfect Past: Education and Society in Canadian History*, J. Donald Wilson (ed.)	Vancouver 1984
'The Explosion of Higher Education in Great Britain, 1960-1970/80'	*Higher Education and Society*: *Historical Perspectives* (7th International Standing Conference for the History of Education, Vol I.)	Salamanca 1985
'Systematisation and Segmentation in Education: The Case of England'	*The Rise of the Modern Educational System: Social Change and Cultural Reproduction, 1870-1920*, Detlef K. Müller, Fritz Ringer and Brian Simon (eds)	Cambridge 1987
'Secondary Education in the Nineteenth Century'	*Onderwijs, opvoeding en maatsch appij in de 19de en 20ste eeuw*, *Liber amicorum* Prof. Dr Mauritz de Vroede, M. Depaepe and M. D'Hoker (eds)	Leuven/ Amersfoort Acco 1987
'The Curriculum and the 'Reform' Bill'	*The National Curriculum* (British Educational Research Association)	London 1988
'Why No Pedagogy in England?'	*Frameworks for Teaching*, Roger Dale, Ross Ferguson and Alison Robinson (eds), (Open University Reader)	London 1988
'Education and the Social Order: The Contemporary Scene	*Education Policies: Controversies and Critiques*, Andy Hargreaves and David Reynolds (eds)	London 1989
'The History of Education' (from J.W. Tibble (ed.), *The Study of Education*, 1966)	*History of Education: The Making of a Discipline*, Peter Gordon and Richard Szreter (eds)	London 1989
'The Study of Education as a University Subject'	*British Universities and Teacher Education*, John B. Thomas (ed.)	London 1990
'How to Achieve Effective Learning in Spite of the Education Reform Act'	*Effective Learning: Into a New ERA*, Tim Everton, Peter Mayne and Steve White (eds), (1989 Curriculum Association Conference)	London 1990

PAMPHLETS AND OTHER PUBLICATIONS

Title	Publisher	Date
'Inequalities in Education'	Confederation for the Advancement of State Education (Annual Conference, 1965)	1965
'The Nature and Objectives of Professional Education'	Association of Social Work Teachers	1967
'Education: The New Perspective' (Inaugural Lecture, 1966)	University of Leicester	1967
'To Whom do Schools Belong?' (Lady Simon of Wythenshawe Memorial Lecture, 1978)	City of Manchester Education Committee	1979
'Defend Comprehensive Schools'	Communist Party	1986
'The National Curriculum, School Organisation and the Teacher' (The Lawrence Stenhouse Memorial Lecture, 1990)	University of East Anglia	1991
'The Future of Education: Which Way?' (Centenary Lecture, School of Education, University of Newcastle-Upon-Tyne)	University of Newcastle-Upon-Tyne	1991
'The Universities and Social Change' (The Charles Carter Lecture, 1990)	University of Lancaster	1991

NOTES ON CONTRIBUTORS

Caroline Benn was a member of ILEA and the education section of UK UNESCO Commission. She now teaches in adult education in London. Founder member of the campaign for comprehensive education and editor of *Comprehensive Education*, her publications include: (with Brian Simon), *Half-way There: A Report on the Comprehensive School Reform in Britain* (1970) and (with John Fairley), *Challenging the MSC on Jobs, Training and Education* (1986).

Kevin J. Brehony is a lecturer in Education at the University of Reading. After teaching in a number of primary schools, he commenced research on the history of child-centred education. He is currently engaged in research on school governors with Rosemary Deem.

Clyde Chitty is a lecturer in the School of Education at the University of Birmingham and a member of the University's Centre for Education Management and Policy Studies. A member of the Editorial Board of *Forum* since 1974 and co-editor since 1989, he has written extensively about the politics of educational policy making. His recent books include *Towards a New Educational System: The Victory of the New Right?* (1989) and *Post-16 Education: Studies in Access and Achievement* (1991).

Ian Davey is Dean of Graduate Studies at the University of Adelaide, South Australia. In his spare time he lectures on the social history of education, does research on class, gender and 19th-century school systems and is currently writing a book, *Assembling the School*, on the origins of mass schooling with Pavla Miller of the Phillip Institute of Technology, Melbourne.

Rosemary Deem is Professor of Educational Research at the University of Lancaster. She has published extensively in the fields of women and education, and gender and leisure, is an experienced school governor, and from 1981-89 was a Labour county councillor in Buckinghamshire. Currently undertaking research on school governing bodies with Kevin Brehony.

Richard Johnson was Director of the Centre for Contemporary Cultural Studies at the University of Birmingham and has written extensively on cultural history and the politics of education. He now teaches part-time in the Department of Cultural Studies in the hope of gaining more time for writing, politics and research.

June Purvis is Reader in Sociology and Women's History at Portsmouth Polytechnic. She is founding editor of two journals – *Gender and Education* and *Women's History Review* – and the author of *Hard Lessons: The Lives and Education of Working-class Women in Nineteenth-Century England* (1989) and *A History of Women's Education in England* (1991).

Ali Rattansi lectures in Sociology at City University, London. He formerly taught at the University of Leicester and the Open University and is the author of *Marx and the Division of Labour* (1982), the editor of *Ideology, Method and Marx* (1989) and co-editor of three recent collections (all published in 1991): *Postmodernism and Society*, *'Race', Culture and Difference* and *Racism and Antiracism*.

David Reeder was formerly Senior Lecturer in the School of Education and Victorian Studies Centre and Deputy Director of the Centre for Urban History at the University of Leicester. He is now a part-time teacher and consultant to two research projects, one of them on the change to comprehensive education in Britain. As an urban historian and educationalist, he has edited books and journals and written on various aspects of the Victorian city, including education.

Sallie Westwood is Senior Lecturer in Sociology and Adult Education at the University of Leicester. She has worked in Ghana, India and the USA. Publications include, *All Day Every Day: Factory and Family in the Making of Women's Lives* (1984) and, with Parminder Bachu, *Enterprising Women* (1988) plus the recent volume with Teddy Thomas for the NIACE, *Radical Agendas? The Politics of Adult Education* (1991).

Geoff Whitty is the Karl Mannheim Professor of the Sociology of Education at the Institute of Education, University of London. After teaching humanities in two comprehensive schools, he taught at the University of Bath, King's College London, Bristol Polytechnic and Goldsmiths' College. He has published widely on the sociology of education, curriculum studies and education policy studies. Among his books are *Sociology and School Knowledge* (1985) and (with Tony Edwards and John Fitz) *The State and Private Education* (1989).

INDEX